Reinventing Romantic Poetry

Studies of the Harriman Institute

Reinventing Romantic Poetry

Russian Women Poets of the
Mid-Nineteenth Century

Diana Greene

THE UNIVERSITY OF WISCONSIN PRESS

The University of Wisconsin Press
1930 Monroe Street
Madison, Wisconsin 53711

www.wisc.edu/wisconsinpress/

3 Henrietta Street
London WC2E 8LU, England

5   4   3   2   1

Printed in the United States of America

Library of Congress Cataloging-in-Publication Data
Greene, Diana.
   Reinventing romantic poetry : Russian women poets of the mid-nineteenth century /
   Greene, Diana.
   p. cm.—(Studies of the Harriman Institute)
   Includes bibliographical references and index.
   ISBN 0-299-19104-4 (alk. paper)
   1. Russian poetry—19th century—History and criticism.   2. Romanticism—Russia.
3. Russian poetry—Women authors—History and criticism.   4. Women and literature—Russia—History—19th century.   5. Rostopchina, Evdokiia, 1812–1858—Criticism and interpretation.   6. Krestovskii, V., 1824–1889—Criticism and interpretation.
7. Pavlova, Karolina, 1807–1893—Criticism and interpretation.   I. Title: Russian
women poets of the mid-nineteenth century.   II. Title.   III. Series.
PG3051. G74   2003
891.71'309145'082—dc21   2003006491

Contents

Acknowledgments   ix

Introduction   3

1. Social Conditions   21

2. Literary Conventions   38

3. Gender and Genre   57

4. Evdokiia Rostopchina   88

5. Nadezhda Khvoshchinskaia   112

6. Karolina Pavlova   137

7. In Conclusion: Noncanonical Men Poets   167

Appendix   177
Notes   219
Bibliography   281
Index   297

Acknowledgments

This book could not have been written without the generous help of many people, groups, and institutions. I am delighted to have this opportunity to thank them.

Responses that I received to early versions of this work greatly influenced its eventual scope and depth. My thanks to the Women in Slavic Culture and Literature group at the Summer Research Lab in Champaign-Urbana, to the participants in the Columbia University Seminar on Slavic History and Culture, to Katharina Brett, and Carol Ueland. Several people kindly took the time to read various chapters, providing many valuable insights and ideas: Barbara Heldt, Eliot Borenstein, Charlotte Rosenthal, Natalie Dehn, Nancy Burstein, Randall Spinks, Ann Kleimola, Romy Taylor, and members of the New York University Scholarly Writing Group. I am particularly grateful to those who read the entire manuscript, offering structural, bibliographic, and other expertise: Ron Meyer, Catriona Kelly, Sally Pratt, and especially Helena Goscilo for her transformative and exuberant comments on style as well as content. None of these people, of course, are responsible for the use I made of their suggestions.

Jehanne Gheith and Karen Rosneck generously shared Khvoshchinskaia materials with me. Elena Ermilovna Glafner at Rossiiskii gosudarstvennyi arkhiv literatury i iskusstva (RGALI) provided invaluable help with Khvoshchinskaia's notebooks. I consider myself very fortunate to know Antonina Strizhenko, who helped me unstintingly and repeatedly at Pushkinskii dom. Mikhail Fainshtein graciously opened doors for me in Saint Petersburg and Moscow on several occasions.

Lina Bernstein kindly sent me material on Elagina. Irina Gordon gave generous, meticulous, and expert help with Russian. I am also very grateful to Karina Melnikov and Irina Reyfman for advice on Russian, Claudine Verheggen on French, Ron Meyer on translation, and Masha Lykhina on Russian and Russian computers. Any mistakes that remain are my own.

Thanks to Mary Zirin for inspiration and to Gloria Rohmann, a friend in need. Ann Kleimola, Clara Evans, Shirley Glade, Ann Kaslow, Lucy Morganstern, and Randall Spinks supplied steady and much appreciated encouragement while I wrote and revised.

My work was greatly facilitated by two New York University Libraries Goddard Faculty Support Grants and an International Research and Exchanges Board Short Term Travel Grant. Harvard University Press kindly gave permission to reprint part of "I'm Nobody! Who Are You?" which appears in *The Poems of Emily Dickinson*. I wish to express appreciation to the University Seminars at Columbia University for their help in publication. Thanks to those most knowledgeable reference librarians of the Slavic Reading Room at the University of Illinois at Champaign-Urbana for research help over several summers. Also to my supportive colleagues at NYU's Bobst Library, who so effectively helped me with my reference questions, interlibrary loan requests, and computer problems, and to Chris Holden and the Bates College Library for making it possible for me to work there in very pleasant conditions.

And, of course, my thanks to my parents, who made everything possible.

A Note on Transliteration, Punctuation, and Abbreviations

I use modified Library of Congress transliteration of Russian—in modern orthography—with one exception: men's names ending in -ii are written as such in the notes (Belinskii) but changed to the more familiar -y (Belinsky) in the text. The reader will notice that many of the poems cited include the Romantic device of suspension points—three unspaced dots intimating the ineffable—which in the translations appear as three spaced dots without brackets. Suspension points should not be confused with ellipses—the three or four spaced dots in brackets indicating that I have left out part of the text.

The following abbreviations are used for archival sources:

PD   Institut russkoi literatury RAN (Pushkinskii dom)
RGALI   Rossiiskii gosudarstvennyi arkhiv literatury i iskusstva
RNB(OR)   Rossiiskaia natsional'naia biblioteka (Otdel rukopisei)

Reinventing Romantic Poetry

Romantic poets androcentric or even misogynist myths. For example, in Pushkin we find men engaged in oedipal struggles over the women who "belong" to powerful statues or generals ("Kamennyi gost'" [The stone guest], *Evgenii Onegin* [*Eugene Onegin*]). In Byron we find sexually available harem girls ("The Giaour," "The Corsair").

I suggest that mid-nineteenth-century Russian women poets had to find different ways to relate to the imagination, to nature and to myth and symbol. They had to transform male-defined traditions, genres, and themes in order to be able to address women's experiences or even to represent themselves as poets. That is, they had to reinvent Romantic poetry. Ironically, men critics, rather than recognizing these women's tremendous inventiveness in reworking literary forms, dismissed them as not "real" (that is, men) poets.[5]

This study, then, examines the poetic practices and achievements of mid-nineteenth-century women poets in relation to the gender-based issues they shared and their various responses to them.[6] I base my generalizations on the poetic practices of fourteen significant but generally unknown Russian women poets born between 1799 and 1824: Praskov'ia Bakunina (1810–80), Aleksandra Fuks (1805–53), Liubov' Garelina (1824–85), Anna Gotovtseva (1799–1871), Nadezhda Khvoshchinskaia (1824–89), Elisaveta Kul'man (1808–25), Mariia Lisitsyna (d. 1842), Anna Mordovtseva (1823–85), Karolina Pavlova (1807–93), Evdokiia Rostopchina (1811–58), Elisaveta Shakhova (1822–99), Ekaterina Shakhovskaia (1814–36), Nadezhda Teplova (1814–48), and Iuliia Zhadovskaia (1824–83).[7] I will focus on the work of three of these poets—Rostopchina, Khvoshchinskaia, and Pavlova—in greater detail.

For comparison I refer to the poetic practices of seven prominent Russian men poets born between 1798 and 1820: Evgenii Baratynsky (1800–1844), Anton Del'vig (1798–1831), Afanasii Fet (1820–92), Nikolai Iazykov (1803–46), Mikhail Lermontov (1814–41), Aleksandr Pushkin (1799–1837), and Fedor Tiutchev (1803–73). However, since not every man poet of this generation became canonical, we also must consider the poetic practices of contemporary noncanonical men poets. I have chosen Pavel Fedotov (1815–52), Eduard Guber (1814–47), Aleksei Khomiakov (1804–60), Aleksei Kol'tsov (1809–42), Apollon Maikov (1821–97), Evgenii Mil'keev (1815–46?), and Fedor Miller (1818–81), poets whose works have been anthologized but whom literary historians refer to as *vtorostepenii* (second rank or minor).[8] A full discussion of the poetical practices of canonical and noncanonical men poets, however, lies outside my scope. This study is not intended to be a general survey of Russian Romantic poetry. Rather, it is a corrective to scholars' tendency in the past to neglect issues of gender—and gender as a category of analysis—when looking at this period.

The women poets—all members of the generation that produced Pushkin and the Golden Age of Russian literature—came from a wide variety of social classes and circumstances. Mariia Lisitsyna was the daughter of an actor; Elisaveta Kul'man, whose civil-servant father died when she was young, lived and died in extreme poverty; Nadezhda Teplova was the daughter of a merchant. Liubov' Garelina, Anna Gotovtseva, Karolina Pavlova, Evdokiia Rostopchina, Elisaveta Shakhova, Ekaterina Shakhovskaia, Iuliia Zhadovskaia, and Aleksandra Fuks belonged to various levels of the aristocracy. Praskov'ia Bakunina and Nadezhda Khvoshchinskaia were both déclassé: their fathers were dismissed from government positions for embezzlement. The life span of these poets ranged from seventeen years (Kul'man) to eighty-six (Pavlova); some lived in Saint Petersburg (Kul'man, Rostopchina, Shakhova), some in Moscow (Bakunina, Lisitsyna, Pavlova, Shakhovskaia, Teplova), and others in the provinces (Fuks, Gotovtseva, Khvoshchinskaia, Mordovtseva, Zhadovskaia).

Their writings were equally varied. Many of them wrote prose works and plays, as well as poetry. Almost all of them wrote verse epistles, nature poetry, love lyrics, and folk poetry. In addition, their poetic genres included religious lyrics, visions, verse prologues for domestic theater, lullabies, anacreontic and other classical verse forms, fables, elegies, narrative poems (*poemy*), and verse tales (*povesti v stikhakh*), as well as *otryvki iz poemy* (excerpts or fragments from narrative poems, a genre in itself), ballads, epigrams, metaphysical poetry, civic poetry, and a novel in verse (*roman v stikhakh*).[9]

Yet despite their diversity, these women poets all faced common social and literary-historical issues as women writers. Perhaps the most obvious and fundamental was their difficulty in getting their works published. A major part of the poetry of Bakunina, Gotovtseva, Khvoshchinskaia, Mordovtseva, and Teplova—in quality as well as quantity—still remains entombed in archives. Much of the poetry of the others has been lost entirely: most of Pavlova's work after 1864, most of Kul'man's original poetry (as opposed to her translations), much of Teplova's early poetry and late prose, and all but three works by Shakhovskaia, one of which is a fragment of a larger work.[10]

Even when these poets managed to get their work published in journals or—against all odds—as books, the published versions often did not reflect their wishes. Pavlova's only poetry collection to appear during her lifetime, published in Russia in 1863, after she was already living abroad, was badly edited by two Russian friends. Khvoshchinskaia strongly objected to having her poetry "edited" for publication by Vladimir Zotov (then editor of *Literaturnaia gazeta*), to Zotov's amusement. Similarly, Nadezhda Teplova, who was forced to work through editor and Moscow University professor Mikhail Maksimovich, expressed annoyance at his attempts to improve her poetry.[11] These difficulties, I suggest, are the effects of social conditions for women, discussed in the next chapter.

This is not to deny that men writers also had trouble getting published and controlling their work. For example, Pushkin's first poetry collection did not appear until 1825 because the friend to whom he entrusted the manuscript in 1820 did not keep his promise to publish it. Guber's first book of poetry, although passed by the censor, never appeared in print, and the badly edited posthumous edition of his works (1859), according to the Soviet scholar E. M. Shneiderman, cannot be considered a reliable text. As for problems with artistic control, Osip Senkovsky, the editor of *Biblioteka dlia chteniia* (Library for reading), was notorious for reworking all authors' texts without their permission.[12] Nonetheless, most of the canonical and noncanonical men poets, as we shall see, not only enjoyed the help of powerful mentors at the beginning of their careers but also might themselves become publishers or editors of journals and *al'manakhi* (annual literary collections), thus gaining control of literary "means of production." I do not intend to suggest that the literary careers of the canonical men poets were typical for all men poets of their generation, but rather that social constraints made such achievements impossible for any woman.

A related issue for these women poets consists in the long interruptions we find in their careers, what Tillie Olsen calls "silences." Olsen observes that while men writers also fall silent for external reasons, women additionally have had to contend with social and family demands that make sustained writing especially difficult (*Silences*, 17, 23, 38–39). In her enumeration of silences, Olsen mentions writers "never coming to book form at all" (6), a term that describes Khvoshchinskaia, Bakunina, and Gotovtseva. Khvoshchinskaia published a great deal of poetry in *tolstye zhurnaly* ("thick" journals) and newspapers but never collected it in book form (although she did publish books of her prose). Bakunina and Gotovtseva may have "chosen" not to publish the notebooks of their poetry that still remain in archives, but that choice was probably conditioned by their society's images of the woman writer.[13] Olsen also mentions "one-book silences" (9), a term that describes Lisitsyna, Shakhovskaia, Garelina, and Mordovtseva.[14] (Here, as elsewhere, I am referring to books of poetry, not of prose.) Lisitsyna and Shakhovskaia each published a book early and then fell silent. Garelina and Mordovtseva, on the other hand, are examples of what Olsen calls "foreground silence *before* the achievement" (10, italics hers), having published their one book at the age of forty-three and fifty, respectively. In the context of such interrupted careers the accomplishments of Fuks, Pavlova, Rostopchina, and Shakhova, who each published several books of poetry, are all the more impressive.

Canons

Historically, these women poets have been excluded from the canon of Russian literature—that collection of authors and works generally considered central to the understanding of literature, as reflected in teaching and scholarship.[15] In the nineteenth century, men canon builders and gatekeepers—critics, book reviewers, editors, book and journal publishers—dismissed women's poetry because of prejudices against women writers (see chapter 1), but also because these men defined poetry in terms of male voice, viewpoint, values, experiences, and tastes, as well as male themes and use of genres.[16] Twentieth-century Russian literary scholars similarly underrepresented or omitted women from anthologies and studies of Russian Romantic poetry.[17]

Another factor that may have contributed to the exclusion of all women and some contemporary men poets from the canon is their lack of "literary social capital."[18] For the majority of Russian women of this generation expected to attract a husband and then run a household—that is, women of all classes except the peasantry—social capital primarily consisted of the size of their dowries, their fathers' social standing, and their physical attractiveness to men. In the male realm of literature, however, I would suggest that, along with wealth and social standing, social capital also included education, mentors, location—whether one lived in the provinces or the capitals—and personal connections with literary gatekeepers and opinion makers: in John Guillory's terms, "access to the means of literary production and consumption" (*Cultural Capital*, 17). I further suggest that such access often played a large part in a writer's literary reception and subsequent reputation. In the last chapter we shall see the importance of literary social capital in the lives of canonical and noncanonical men poets. Gender, however, also appears to have been an important component of a poet's literary social capital. Thus, for reasons that will be discussed in chapters 1 and 2, even well-to-do women poets who lived in Moscow or Saint Petersburg commanded less literary social capital than their men contemporaries.

But what constitutes canonicity in Russian Romanticism and what accounts for the absence of women poets? Pushkin, Russia's national poet, occupies what can be thought of as the first circle or the top of a hierarchy. Just below him we find his poet associates (Baratynsky), poet friends (Del'vig), and those whose work appeared in his journal, *Sovremennik* (The contemporary). The poets whom Pushkin mentored (for example, Iazykov) and Pushkin's "self-appointed successor," Lermontov, who suffered political consequences for his outraged elegy on Pushkin's death, also occupy ranks near the top.[19] Women poets who had personal contact with Pushkin (Rostopchina, Pavlova, Fuks), however, did not thereby enter the canon since Pushkin did not mentor—or respect—women poets and generally thought very little of women's intellectual and aesthetic capabilities.[20] Nor did critical attitudes toward Pushkin's women contemporaries improve during the rest of the nineteenth and the beginning of the twentieth century, with the exception of a short-lived Pavlova revival among the Symbolists (see chapter 6).

The Soviet era perpetuated negative attitudes toward women and women poets on a political and nationalistic basis. While, according to a Soviet slogan, the Revolution had "resolved the woman question," women's actual needs and concerns remained a low priority for the Soviet government, which fostered a paramilitary atmosphere in order to industrialize the country with all possible speed. Writers were expected to help build socialism by promoting and celebrating in literature these heroic goals—a literary climate unpropitious not only to the depiction of women characters but also to the reputations of women writers.[21]

So, for example, K. D. Muratova's 1962 index, *Istoriia russkoi literatury XIX veka: Bibliograficheskii ukazatel'* (History of Russian literature of the nineteenth century: A bibliographic index) lists only two post-1917 articles about Rostopchina, one published in Irkutsk. In 1965 V. S. Kiselev pronounced her a forgotten poet. In the case of Karolina Pavlova, now the best-known woman poet of her generation, we find shorter articles about her in the 1955 and 1975 *Bol'shaia sovetskaia entsiklopediia* (The great Soviet encyclopedia) than about her husband, Nikolai Pavlov, a littérateur whose entire literary output consisted of six *povesti* (tales). Pavlova is described in these encyclopedias as "Pavlov's wife" and an "authoress" (*pisatel'nitsa*). As late as 1991 a Soviet publication identified Pavlova as a "poetess"—although one of "surprisingly varied themes and genres"—to whom several well-known men poets dedicated poems.[22]

Soviet ideology appears to have promoted and even encouraged a condescending attitude toward women's writing. Collections appeared with such titles as *Serdtsa chutkogo prozren'em. . . : Povesti i rasskazy russkikh pisatel'nits XIX v.* (With the insight of a sensitive heart. . . : Tales and stories by Russian authoresses of the nineteenth century, 1991), *Moskovskaia muza* (The Moscow muse, 1998), and *Tsaritsy muz: Russkie poetessy XIX veka* (Queens of the muses: Russian poetesses of the nineteenth century, 1989). No collection of Russian men's poetry bore the title "The Moscow Muse" or "Kings of the Muses." Several Soviet scholars in studies of nineteenth-century women poets referred to them by their first names, something one cannot imagine them doing to male literary figures.[23] Nor were women poets even included in the minor canon known to literary specialists. In the scholarly Biblioteka poeta (Poet's library) series of the Soviet period only one nineteenth-century woman poet, Pavlova, had a volume entirely devoted to her work.

Methodological and Theoretical Considerations

Some methodological and theoretical issues should be clarified before we proceed. First, I have included women poets in this study on the basis of the quality and quantity of their poetry. Most published at least one book of poetry, a feat in itself for a Russian woman at this time; a few left notebooks of unpublished poems.[24]

Second, I have chosen to consider the work of these women poets in relation to that of their male contemporaries. Gynocritical studies that look at women writers in their own terms have been essential for recovering forgotten women writers, defining women's literary traditions, and developing "interpretive strategies" appropriate to their work.[25] However, many critics have realized the importance of eventually treating men and women writers together. Indeed, such a comparative approach is necessary in order to answer fully the question that Elaine Showalter calls central to feminist criticism: "What is the difference of women's writing?"[26]

Although, as I intend to show, the women poets of this generation approached poetry differently from the men, they also responded to and polemicized with men's poetry. A comparative approach, then, will have the additional advantage of illuminating specific poems throughout this study. For example, Iuliia Zhadovskaia's poem "P[erevleskomu] (Naprasno ty sulish', tak zharko slavu mne)" (To Perevlesky [In vain do you so warmly promise me glory], 1847) appears at first glance to be a typical example of what Anne Mellor calls the "modesty topos" (*Romanticism and Gender*, 8), in which women denigrated their own work, hoping to forestall attacks by men critics.[27] Readers, Zhadovskaia writes, do not respond to her *bednyi, grustnyi stikh* (poor, sad verse) and, she concludes,

> Я в мире промелькну падучею звездой,
> Которую, поверь, немногие заметят.
>
> ⸙
>
> (I will flash in the world like a falling star
> Which, believe me, not many will notice).[28]

Zhadovskaia's poem, however, seems a great deal less self-effacing if read against Baratynsky's well-known classical ode "Osen'" (Autumn, 1837), in which the following lines appear:

> Пускай [. . .]
> [. . . . . .]
> Звезда небес в бездонный мрак падет;
> Пусть загорится в них другая:
> Не явствует земле ущерб одной,
> Не поражает ухо мира
> Далекого ее паденья вой.
>
> ⸙
>
> (Let [. . .]
> [. . . . .]
> A star of the heavens fall into bottomless darkness;
> Let another begin to blaze in its place:
> The loss of the first will not be apparent to the earth,
> Its falling cry
> Will not strike the ear of the distant world.)

Baratynsky's image of the falling star refers to Pushkin, an allusion that readers would have understood, as the poem appeared in *Sovremennik*, the journal he had edited, just a few months after his death.[29] I suggest that Zhadovskaia knew Baratynsky's poem and consciously or unconsciously appropriated Baratynsky's reference to Pushkin for herself, an indication that she took herself more seriously as a poet than the language of her poem might at first suggest.

Similarly, our understanding of Nadezhda Khvoshchinskaia's poem "Kladbishche" (The cemetery, 1859) is enriched if we see it in relation to another Baratynsky poem, his album verse "V al'bom" (For an album, 1829), dedicated to Karolina Pavlova. In this poem Baratynsky jokingly compares albums to cemeteries, in which writers hope for immortality and dread judgment. Khvoshchinskaia's five-part poem "Kladbishche" uses Baratynsky's comparison as the basis for an extended meditation on life and death. Khvoshchinskaia's poem also responds to Lermontov's "Kladbishche" (1830) by echoing his syntax, but not his meaning. Likewise, Pushkin's "K moriu" (To the sea, 1824), in which the speaker regrets that he was not free to travel abroad, provides a counterpoint to Shakhova's "Progulka u vzmor'ia," (A walk by the seashore, 1839; see appendix), in which the speaker and her friend confront the far greater lack of freedom they experience as women. Pavlova's narrative poem *Kadril'* (Quadrille, 1859), which she dedicated to Baratynsky, should be read against Baratynsky's narrative poems *Bal* (The ball, 1828) and *Nalozhnitsa* (The concubine, 1831, later retitled *Tsyganka* [The gypsy]). Both of Baratynsky's poems have climactic scenes at a ball. Pavlova's work, consisting of a conversation among four society women just before going to a ball, implicitly criticizes Baratynsky's stereotyping of women characters as angels (Vera in *Nalozhnitsa*, Ol'ga in *Bal*) or as demonic, needy destroyers of the men they love and of themselves (Sara in *Nalozhnitsa*, Nina in *Bal*). Rather, Pavlova's four very ordinary women in *Kadril'* more realistically recount how much self-control, courage, and self-knowledge is required of women to perform successfully in society.

As for theoretical issues, this study raises three in particular. The first and most basic, which I shall save for last, concerns how we are to evaluate these unknown poets. The other two are interrelated: Are these mostly unknown women poets worth considering at all? And, if so, what are the advantages of viewing their work through the lens of gender? In fact, questions of gender can explain why these poets are unknown or have been unknown until very recently.

Only over the last twenty-five years have scholars in many literatures begun to challenge literary canons, questioning the bases on which writers are included in them and who decides what those bases are. Partly as a result of these challenges—and of the work accomplished in such disciplines as women's studies, African American studies, gay studies, and postcolonial studies—many previously unknown women writers have become "known," appearing on course reading lists, in anthologies, and as the subjects of journal articles, dissertations, and panel discussions. In the West, starting in the 1970s, Slavic scholars, inspired by the recovery of women writers in other literatures, began to recover Russian women writers. In the Soviet Union, from the mid-1980s, and perhaps in response to the Western women's movement, Russian literary scholars began to publish anthologies of Russian women's writing (see end of note 17), as well as separate editions of individual women writers' works and scholarship about them—although, as we have seen, without a feminist critical context. As a result of this work Pavlova, Rostopchina, and to a lesser degree, Zhadovskaia and Teplova are now "known."[30] Such expansions of literary canons suggest that we need not dismiss writers out of hand simply because no one until now has examined their work.

It is worth considering the bases on which literary scholars have challenged the canon of known writers. Some have questioned the assumption that literary canons embody universal, ahistoric values that are passed down intact from generation to generation. Rather, these scholars argue that standards of literary excellence are like gender—not essential, but "socially constructed" and political in the sense that they are used as instruments of power. Thus canons constantly evolve, reflecting cultural biases and ongoing literary political struggles. Indeed, some believe canons to be the means by which people in aesthetic power— the above-mentioned literary gatekeepers—keep out differing interests, values, and views of the world.[31] So, in regard to nineteenth-century American literature, Nina Baym writes of "the biases . . . in favor, say, of whaling ships rather than the sewing circle as a symbol of the human community" (*Women's Fiction*, 4). Certainly, the canon of nineteenth-century Russian literature generally reflected the views of upper-class men.

Other scholars have gone even further in deconstructing the assumptions behind literary canons, raising very provocative questions. Paul Lauter writes that canonized works and the standards of literary excellence that we extrapolate from them validate the experience of men rather than of women, the experience of whites rather than those of people of color. He reminds us that the "formalist virtues: economy, irony, well-articulated structure . . . complexity . . . emotional restraint, and verbal sophistication" were only promulgated in this century. One must ask, he writes, "where standards come from, whose values they embody, and whose interests they serve" (*Canons and Contexts,* 102–5). While, as we shall see, the "formalist virtues" may be found in the work of several of these women poets, Lauter's ideas encourage us to be open to other "virtues" in their work as well. Similarly, Patrocinio Schweickart, citing Annette Kolodny, writes that we all unconsciously have learned to look at literature in a way that supports and perpetuates the male canon. It is equally important, Schweickart feels, to develop new ways of reading, new "interpretive strategies" that will help us appreciate the achievements of women's writing ("Reading Ourselves," 29). Such new interpretive strategies will be discussed later in this chapter. Tania Modleski suggests that critics "enhance the superiority of the male hero and male text . . . at the expense of the feminine" because of a Western tendency to "elevate what men do simply because men do it" (*Loving with a Vengeance,* 12). Narrative pleasure, she believes, is constituted differently for men and women, but, rather than investigating these differences, critics have disparaged women's narratives (32). Might Modleski's ideas apply to nineteenth-century poetry as well?

Judith Fetterley attributes much of writers' canonical status to the scholarly resources allocated to them. We know canonized American writers are great before we read them—or even if we never read them—she states, because of the "context" they have been given: "critical books and articles, scholarly biographies, exhaustive bibliographies, special and regular [conference] sessions, hundreds of discussions in hundreds of classrooms . . . government-funded standard text editions," critical contexts that women writers until very recently rarely enjoyed (*Provisions,* 34). Fetterley's remarks are both controversial and intriguing in relation to the Russian men and women poets under discussion and their sharply contrasting reputations and critical "contexts." Pushkin and his pleiad (among them Anton Del'vig, Evgenii Baratynsky, and Nikolai Iazykov) are considered to represent the Golden Age of Russian literature. Fedor Tiutchev and Afanasii Fet received a great deal of Soviet scholarly attention (Fet despite his "unprogressive" political views), and Mikhail Lermontov is the subject of his own encyclopedia. In contrast, until the last few decades virtually no one had heard of the women writers of this generation.[32]

Ultimately, the thinking of those who challenge literary canons leads us beyond the idea of expanding those canons to questioning their meaning altogether, along with definitions of the history of literature, literary periods, literary standards, the hierarchy of genres, and the very definition of literature itself.[33] Although I will not attempt to address

such issues, and although, I hasten to add, I do not question the importance of men writers of the Golden Age, this study to a large degree
grows out of the questions that such canon studies raise. They make it
possible to read with an open mind the work of writers who as yet have
no critical "context"; they keep us from labeling the poetry of these
women as substandard and inept simply because it differs from that of
their male contemporaries. Rather, such questions encourage us to consider whether this poetry's formal and aesthetic differences (discussed
in chapters 2 and 3) might not also have meaning and value.

Looking at these women's poetry through the lens of gender not only
helps to explain why these poets are unknown but also offers a new perspective on the Golden Age and Romanticism in Russia. How might
women poets have experienced the social and literary environments of
early nineteenth-century Russia? What effects might these environments have had on their writing? Did these women use poetic devices
and genres differently from men, and can we define those differences?
What functions might those differences have served? Did these women
in fact subscribe to a different and definable aesthetic? Such questions
form a necessary basis for evaluating the work of these women poets.

My purpose in this study, then, is neither to establish a new literary
canon nor to add writers to the one that presently exists; as we shall see,
a great deal of theoretical and recovery work will have to be done before
the canon can be reevaluated.[34] Rather, I explore the poetry and poetic
practices of several Russian women writers, both in their own terms and
also in comparison with those of their male contemporaries. Another
purpose is to show the need for critical tools ("interpretive strategies")
that will allow us objectively to evaluate women's poetry in comparison
to men's. I would add that on a personal level I consider these particular unknown writers well worth investigating and recovering because
much of their poetry moves and excites me, and I imagine that others
may find it meaningful as well.

Let us return to our first and most difficult theoretical question, one
that is central to this study of unknown women's writing: How are we
to evaluate these poets' work in order to determine whether they have
been justly or unjustly forgotten? What criteria can we use in the absence of the "context" of critical and interpretive essays, book-length
studies, biographies, reference work entries, conference sections, a place
on the syllabus, and annotated critical editions of their work? Or, to put
it another way, what does it mean to say that a poet is "good"?

Some critics, as mentioned in the preceding discussion, have argued that literary standards are not class, race, or gender neutral, but rather validate the experiences and tastes—defined as "universal"—of people in cultural power. It is worth considering how the experiences and tastes (aesthetics) of nineteenth-century women influenced their poetic practices—and their reception by men critics.

In the next chapter we shall see what these poets shared as Russian women of their generation. Here I would like to suggest some of the more general physical, social, and metaphysical conditions they shared as nineteenth-century Western women, conditions that influenced the form and content of their work. I am not suggesting that these poets wrote differently from their male contemporaries because of some essential female difference, but rather because their raw materials—the realities and experiences of their lives—were not the same.[35] Any evaluation of their work must take these differences into account.

On the physical plane, one scholar (Donovan, 102–3) has suggested that in the nineteenth century menstruation and the lack of birth control may have caused women to experience their projects as more interruptible than did men. Certainly, women were expected to put aside their own activities when called upon by parents, children, spouses, brothers, and others. The interruptibility of women's lives may be reflected in the many short forms, such as lyrics and ballads, that these poets used, or, even as Elaine Showalter has suggested, some women's use of small, self-contained units to structure extended forms. Showalter compares the structure of *Uncle Tom's Cabin*, for example, to a quilt made of many small pieces sewn together ("Piecing and Writing," 234–37).

It also seems likely that the high infant mortality rate in the nineteenth century affected women more immediately than it did men, leading them to view and depict death differently. Tania Modleski (*Loving with a Vengeance,* 189) argues that while for men, as Walter Benjamin writes, death reveals meaning, for women at that time death and especially the death of a child represented the end of meaning. We shall discuss in chapter 3 these Russian women's poems about the death of children or young women, a theme that is not common in the poetry of their canonical male contemporaries.[36]

Also on the physical plane, Tania Modleski has made the intriguing suggestion that there might be a relationship between narrative pleasure and sexual response. She suggests that the plots of twentieth-century popular genres such as soap operas and television serials appeal to women because they are "open-ended, slow paced, and multi-climactic" (*Loving with a Vengeance,* 98). In contrast, the plots of hardboiled detective stories, Westerns, or "action" movies appeal to men because they have a more focused, forward thrust. It might be interesting to apply this idea to "high art" as well—to contrast, for example, the plots of Virginia Woolf's novels with the well-made play as codified by Aristotle (exposition, complication, turning point, climax, and resolution).[37] Or to contrast the structure of Rostopchina's novel in verse, *Dnevnik devushki* (A girl's diary, 1845), with that of Pushkin's novel in verse, *Evgenii Onegin.*

On the social plane, all nineteenth-century women were trained to be caretakers, the overseers of a nonprogressive, repetitive, and cyclical domestic sphere defined as the complement to the male-dominated public sphere of action and accomplishment. Nineteenth-century women spent more time waiting than men, waiting for marriage, for family members to come home or leave, for pregnancies to end. And, indeed, as we shall see in chapter 3, the themes of boredom, futility, and isolation are very common in these women's poetry. On the other hand, women's isolation may have had artistic advantages. As Josephine Donovan points out, the products of women's domestic work traditionally have had use value rather than exchange value. The domestic sphere therefore remains the site of "relatively unalienated labor," with women retaining "creative control over [their] time and over the design and execution of [their] products"—principles that women could apply to their poetry as well ("Toward a Women's Poetics," 102). Or as Shari Benstock writes, women's marginal status also granted them "freedom and dispossession of existence outside the law."[38] Because Russian women poets tended not to be part of groups or schools, their poetry is often unconventional or even experimental. One thinks, for example, of Iuliia Zhadovskaia's sophisticated meters and rhymes or Nadezhda Khvoshchinskaia's atypically long, powerful lines.

On the metaphysical plane, women were defined as the Other, the complement of men, and the object of the male gaze in art and in life. Modleski writes of women "continually forced to look at themselves being looked at" and of the self-consciousness and desire for transcendence this engendered (*Loving with a Vengeance*, 111–12)—themes particularly strong in the poetry of Teplova, for example ("Vysota" [Height, 1831], "Pererozhdenie" [Rebirth, 1835], "Kogda vo vpadine okna" [When in the curve of the window, 1842], "Verbnoe voskresenie" [Palm Sunday, 1847]).[39] In all Western religions women were associated with the body and temptation, a linkage that led several of these women poets to express a more complex and uncomfortable relation with God and nature than did their male contemporaries (see chapter 2).

As for women's tastes, the scholar Anne Mellor argues that women's different experiences in the nineteenth century resulted in different artistic concerns and a different aesthetic, at least among British Romantic women writers. In contrast to Romantic male concerns with the "creative imagination . . . the achievements of genius . . . the spontaneous overflow of powerful feelings," she writes, British women writers were interested in "right feeling" ("Criticism of Their Own," 30), "the workings of the rational mind" (31), joining sensibility with "correct perception" (39), and an "ethic of care" (32). Instead of celebrating "the transcendental ego standing alone," British women writers represented "a self that is fluid . . . with permeable ego boundaries," one that "locates its identity in its connections with a larger human group" (31). That is, British women writers placed women's concerns (nonviolence, gender equality, education of the young) in the foreground, opposing both the patriarchal values of neoclassicism, and those of the alienated Romantic artist. Several of the Russian women poets we are considering likewise appear to have subscribed to this aesthetic. Aleksandra Fuks in her "Grecheskaia skazka" (A Greek tale, 1834) warns against the dangers to women of romantic love untempered by the rational mind. Karolina Pavlova in *Dvoinaia zhizn'* (*A Double Life*) and "Za chainym stolom" ("At the Tea Table") emphasizes the importance of educating women in rationality and accurate perception. The many poems these poets addressed to groups of friends and to family members, discussed in chapter 3, indicate a self that locates its identity in connection with larger groups.

I suspect that contemporary men critics, unfamiliar with the experiences underlying these women's poetry, found it alien and incomprehensible and therefore dismissed it as substandard.[40] For example, as we shall see in chapter 3, Vissarion Belinsky, Russia's best-known critic, denigrated as *rebiacheskii* (puerile) a poem by Teplova in which the speaker dreads her inevitable separation from her sister in death and promises, should she die first, to return to tell her sister of her experiences. Teplova's poem, addressed to a family member and treating death as an extension of life, was typical of women's, but not men's, poetry.

Another factor in men critics' reception of these women poets was the gendering of "genius," a favorite Romantic concept, as male. The scholar Christine Battersby defines the genius as "a superior type of being who walked a sublime path . . . described in terms of male sexual energies" (*Gender and Genius*, 103). "To be . . . a 'genius,'" Battersby writes, "the artist must be positioned by the critics at a point within that tradition that is viewed as the boundary between the old and the new ways . . . located within the (patrilineal) chains of influence and inheritance out of which 'culture' is constructed" (142)—a position never granted to women. One thinks of Belinsky's statement: "We know many women poets but not one woman genius; . . . Nature sometimes spares them a spark of talent but never gives them genius."[41]

Can we develop interpretive strategies for these Russian women poets based on their different, but not necessarily less important, experiences and aesthetic concerns? Scholars have begun to develop several such strategies for reading nineteenth-century British and American women's poetry that also may apply to nineteenth-century Russian women's poetry. It should be emphasized, however, that these interpretative strategies are preliminary, fragmentary, and even speculative. Alice Ostriker identifies the device of "duplicity," in which a poet "driven by something forbidden to express but impossible to repress" produces a poem that "means both what it says and its opposite" (*Stealing the Language*, 40). For example, Emily Dickinson's poem "I'm Nobody!" (1861) simultaneously rejects and expresses a longing for fame and power. Ostriker maintains that duplicity—doubleness of meaning—should be appreciated on aesthetic grounds, since "the highest art is that which presses most matter and spirit into least space" (41). Among the Russian poets we have mentioned, we can see an example of duplicity in Bakunina's "Siialo utro obnovlen'em" (The morning shone with a renewal, 1840), in which the speaker struggles to reconcile her mourning for a dead child with the religious duty to accept God's will. Similarly, in "A. S. P." (1829) Gotovtseva simultaneously expresses her awe of Pushkin's high artistic status and her anger at his depiction of women. And Khvoshchinskaia's *Dzhulio* (Julio, 1850) depicts an artist's drive to separate from his family in order to succeed, along with the guilt that the separation arouses.

Cheryl Walker similarly employs as an interpretive strategy nineteenth-century American women poets' ambivalence "toward the desire for power, toward their ambitions, toward their need to say, 'I am' boldly and effectively" (*Nightingale's Burden*, 9–10). We see such ambivalence in Kul'man's "K Anakreonu" (To Anacreon, see chapter 2), in Pavlova's introduction to *Kadril'* (see chapter 6), in Rostopchina's "Kak dolzhny pisat' zhenshchiny" (How women should write, see chapter 4), and many others.

Still another interpretive strategy is Sandra Gilbert's discussion of Edna St. Vincent Millay as a "female female impersonator . . . looking at herself being looked at" ("Female Female Impersonator," 298). Millay, writes Gilbert, used "the fetishized private life of the woman to comment on the public state of the world," an affirmation that "the personal is poetic" (309). This is an approach that fruitfully could be applied to the poetry of Garelina, Zhadovskaia, and Rostopchina.

In addition, literary scholars could explore the use of irony by many nineteenth-century women poets, not exuberant "Romantic irony," but, rather, irony in the dictionary sense: the use of words to express the opposite of the literal meaning.[42] As men writers of the time used Aesopian (metaphorical) language to smuggle forbidden ideas past the censorship, women writers used irony to criticize the constraining circumstances of their lives. I suggest that critics, both nineteenth-century and contemporary, have remained oblivious to much of this irony because it never occurred to them not to take literally everything in women's poems, just as it did not occur to them that women might create personae (see chapter 2). We find irony in poems that warn women of the dangers of writing poetry (for example, in Teplova's "Sovet" [Advice, 1837]), throughout Pavlova's *Dvoinaia zhizn'*, especially in the descriptions of Cecilia's upbringing and surroundings, and in much of Rostopchina's poetry (see chapter 4). These and other interpretive strategies can enrich our appreciation not only of nineteenth-century women's writing but also of men's writing. For example, Ostriker describes Milton's ambivalent depiction of Satan in *Paradise Lost* as an example of duplicity.

Men critics often ignored women's poetry even if it did not address women's experience. Beyond creating new ways of reading women's—and men's—poetry, is it possible to find gender-neutral, inclusive standards to evaluate men's and women's poetry together? Only in this way, to return to our third question, can we determine if these and other forgotten poets are "good." Although developing such standards will require a great deal of rethinking by aestheticians, historians, literary historians, and literary critics, the possibility of doing so is suggested by the work of one aesthetician. Tomas Kulka describes a tradition of aesthetic evaluation, based on theories of Plato and Aristotle, which analyzes art on the basis of three nongendered principles: unity, complexity, and intensity. Kulka defines unity, which he considers the most important, as the balance and harmony of a work's elements, the inner logic of its structure and style. "A perfectly unified work of art . . . can only be spoiled but not improved by alterations of its constitutive features" (*Kitsch and Art*, 65). He identifies complexity as concern for detail, richness, contrast, and variety. Intensity he describes as expressiveness, vitality, and vividness of presentation. "The more intensive the work, the more complex and diverse elements have been unified within its bounds, the better it is. . . . The degree of intensity can be thus conceived of as the degree of specificity or the degree of aesthetic functioning of the work's constitutive features" (46, 70–71).[43] Although one can imagine many other aesthetic standards—Kulka's echo Paul Lauter's "formalist virtues" mentioned earlier in this discussion—these at least do not exclude women's art by definition. As we shall see in chapter 3, it is possible to define a major Romantic genre, the lyric, in gender-neutral terms as well. Having discussed the methodological, theoretical, and common European bases of this study, let us now turn to the specific conditions these women poets experienced in Russia.

1

Social Conditions

The social conditions that these poets shared included Russian women's educational, economic, legal, and literary-historical status.[1] As we shall see, these poets responded to those conditions in a great variety of ways.

During the first half of the nineteenth century the only education available for nonserf women—all the poets in this group—was provided by home tutors, *instituty* (government-run boarding schools for girls of the nobility), or private *pensions* of varying quality.[2] The first *gimnaziia* (secondary schools) for women would not be established until 1858.

Economically, such women could only survive outside of marriage by remaining dependent on relatives or by entering a convent.[3] Few if any opportunities existed for them to earn money, and they inherited considerably less than their male siblings.[4] Within this group of fourteen poets, all of them married except for Kul'man, who died at age seventeen, Shakhova, who became a nun, and Bakunina, who inherited an estate from an aunt, where she was able to live with her two unmarried sisters. Lisitsyna's biography remains unknown.

But although marriage represented the only option for most Russian women, it also put women at a disadvantage. The law not only required a woman to live "in absolute obedience" (*v neogranichennom poslushanii*) to her husband—whose permission she needed to work, go to school, or travel—but also condoned a husband's corporal punishment of his wife "short of severe bodily injury." Even if a severely assaulted woman managed to get her husband convicted of the crime, the law still required her to live with him when he returned from prison or exile; Russian Orthodox canon law, which regulated marriage law, did not recognize legal separations. Nor did abuse, no matter how severe, constitute grounds for a divorce or annulment, which, in any case, were virtually impossible to obtain (Freeze, 743). In cases of life-threatening abuse the government occasionally stepped in "on special directives from the emperor" and granted a woman a separate residence permit. Russian women were thought to have an advantage over women in the West because they could own property and, in theory, legally possessed their dowries. In fact, however, neither women's upbringing, nor marriage law, nor custom, nor the church gave women the resources they needed to enforce those rights.[5]

While I do not wish to imply that every Russian wife was a victim of abuse, the experiences of several of these women poets illustrate the lack of physical and financial protection for married women. Pavlova's husband, Nikolai Pavlov, who married her for her money, managed her fortune and dissipated it in compulsive gambling and in establishing a second household with Pavlova's cousin, Evgeniia Tanneberg, with whom he had three children. Mordovtseva fled from her first husband, Nikandr Paskhalov, because of his physical abusiveness. Her second husband, the writer Daniil Mordovtsev, impoverished and abandoned her. Khvoshchinskaia's husband, Ivan Zaionchkovsky, whom she married late in life, reportedly also was abusive.[6]

At the very least, marriage and children made it more difficult for these women to concentrate on their writing, not to mention their careers. Although Rostopchina and Pavlova were able to continue writing after their marriages, the uncondensed, improvisatory quality in much of Rostopchina's work may indicate her inability to make art her first priority. Pavlova had only one child but expressed guilt on at least one occasion for writing at all. Teplova, who had three children, virtually stopped writing after her marriage. Although previously she had managed to publish two books of poetry, two years after her marriage she wrote to professor and editor M. A. Maksimovich, "Existence and household cares have largely swallowed me up, and it often occurs to me that I am not a poet at all" (Vatsuro, "Zhizn' i poeziia Nadezhdy Teplovoi," 33). Zhadovskaia, who lived until 1883, stopped writing poetry around the year of her marriage in 1862, when she reportedly told her niece and secretary, Nastas'ia Fedorova, "Love has disappeared from my heart and poetry has abandoned me." Gotovtseva, we are told, stopped writing after her marriage because of "unfavorable [*neblagopriiatnye*] family circumstances" (*Russkie pisateli*, 2: 659). Mordovtseva, who had six children by two husbands, wrote poetry from the

1840s, but published her first and only book of poetry in 1877, after her second husband abandoned her. Only the unmarried poets—Shakhova (a nun) and Kul'man (recognized as a child prodigy)—enjoyed the luxury of being able to concentrate on their art.[7]

For most of the men poets of this generation, however, marriage not only did not interfere with their writing but indeed advanced their careers. Tiutchev successively married two widowed German baronesses. The first, Emilia-Eleonor Botmer, helped establish him in diplomatic and literary circles in Munich through her wealth and connections. The second, Ernestine Pfeffel, edited a posthumous edition of Tiutchev's poetry. She also, in D. S. Mirsky's words, showed "wonderful tact and forbearance" (*History of Russian Literature*, 133) in Tiutchev's fourteen-year affair with Elena Denis'eva, the governess whose reputation he felt guilty about destroying. Fet married Mariia Botkina, the wealthy sister of Vasilii Botkin, the critic who promoted Fet's career. Baratynsky's wife, the very intelligent Anastasiia Engel'gardt, we are told, devoted herself to creating a peaceful domestic atmosphere for her husband. Baratynsky discussed his work with her and generally followed her suggestions for revision. Del'vig's wife, Sof'ia Saltykova, a student of Pushkin's friend the Moscow university professor P. A. Pletnev, established a successful literary salon attended by Pushkin, Pletnev, Odoevsky, Mickiewicz, and other literary figures. And while Pushkin's wife did not express a great deal of interest in his poetry, there is no evidence that he felt he should curtail his writing to care for their three children.[8]

Domestic Ideology

The doctrine that justified the educational, economic, and marital constraints experienced by these poets was domestic ideology. Arising in Europe and the United States between 1790 and 1830 and coming to Russia in the 1820s, domestic ideology held that "ladies" belonged in the home, where they were to exhibit the qualities of "piety, purity, submissiveness and domesticity" (Welter, *Dimity Convictions*, 21; see also Cott, *Bonds of Womanhood*, 8). The princesses from Denmark, Germany, or Prussia who married Paul I, Alexander I, Nicholas I, and Alexander II appear to have brought domestic ideology to Russia with them, promulgating it through the prestigious *instituty* they administered. By 1827 the rigorous academic program that Catherine II had originally mandated for Smolny, the first *institut*, had been reduced to "the law of

God, essential learning [*neobkhodimye nauki*], useful handiwork and
home economics [*domashnee khoziaistvo*]" (Likhacheva, *Materialy dlia istorii zhenskogo obrazovaniia v Rossii*, 3: 7).[9]

Domestic ideology entered Russia through the periodic press as well.
"Thick" journals (*tolstye zhurnaly*) reviewed Russian translations of
French, English, and German conduct books, beauty guides, and marriage manuals that spread the ideology, to the general praise of reviewers, with the notable exception of Vissarion Belinsky.

Along with the rise of domestic ideology came attacks on intellectual
women. By the 1820s, writes the scholar Marlon Ross, the once positive
term "bluestocking"—a woman (originally also a man) with intellectual or literary interests—had become exclusively a term of derision.[10]
Byron, for example, in his satire "The Blues: A Literary Eclogue" (1821)
implied that women cannot understand, much less write, poetry. In Russia, Pushkin, too, in *Evgenii Onegin* attacked intellectual women:

> Не дай мне бог сойтись на бале
> Иль при разъезде на крыльце
> С семинаристом в желтой шали
> Иль с академиком в чепце!

> *~≫~*

> (God forbid that at a ball
> Or on the porch as I am leaving
> I should meet a seminarian in a yellow shawl
> Or an academician in a woman's cap!)
>
> (3: xxviii)

Critics subjected women writers to even fiercer scorn than bluestockings; it was no longer considered acceptable or even normal for
women to write. The woman writer was seen as usurping male prerogatives, an unrespectable "crossdresser . . . wearing the ill-fitting literary
apparel intended for men," a woman "prone to scandal"—epitomized
for many at this time by George Sand.[11] In Russia, too, attacks on literary women began in the 1820s. Baratynsky in his poem "Sovet" (Advice, published in *Moskovskii telegraf*, 1826, later retitled "Epigramma"
[Epigram]), warned women that if they tried to write poetry not only
would they be ridiculed as unfeminine but also their work would be
pronounced incompetent and promptly forgotten:

> Не трогайте парнасского пера,
> Не трогайте, пригожие вострушки!
> Красавицам не много в нем добра,
> И им Амур другие дал игрушки,

Любовь ли вам оставить в забытьи
Для жалких рифм? Над рифмами смеются,
Уносят их летийские струи—
На пальчиках чернила остаются.

～

(Don't touch the Parnassian pen
Don't touch it, my comely, sprightly ones!
There is little good in it for beauties
And Cupid has given them other toys
Will you really consign love to oblivion
For pitiful rhymes? They will laugh at rhymes
The currents of Lethe [the river of forgetfulness] will carry them away
And ink will remain on your little fingers.)[12]

Such disparagement escalated during the 1830s and 1840s in the Russian periodic press. Now women writers were depicted not only as ludicrously incompetent but also as destroyers of their families, murderers of their children, women "asking" to be raped, unattractive bores, or sexual objects, as can be seen from three literary works with nearly the same title.[13]

In "Zhenshchina pisatel'nitsa" (The woman writer or The authoress, 1837), a *povest'* (tale) by Rakhmannyi (pseud. N. N. Verevkin), a woman writer carelessly drops her child, causing it irreparable injury. During the child's long decline, only his father cares for him while the mother pursues her writing career. When the child finally dies, the mother is too busy at a performance of her play to go home to kiss him farewell. Her play, of course, is a failure.

A second depiction of a woman playwright destroying her family may be found in a play, similarly titled *Zhenshchina-pisatel'nitsa* (1848), apparently based on Rakhmannyi's story. Ironically the author was a woman, Mar'ia Korsini (1815–59). In Korsini's work the protagonist, Glafira Platonovna, not only fails as a playwright and almost demolishes her family but also barely escapes being raped by a man writer before being saved by her husband. Korsini, however, provides a happy ending: Glafira Platonovna renounces her foolish desire to be a writer to return to her proper role as wife and mother.

A third work, a story, again called "Zhenshchina-pisatel'nitsa," presents two women writers. The first, an unattractive bore, literally puts the male narrator to sleep when she reads from her work. The second woman writer, in contrast, embodies the narrator's ideal. She is brilliant, beautiful, dislikes other women, and although surrounded by admiring men, responds only to the narrator. Unfortunately, at this point the narrator awakens as the first woman writer's reading ends, and he realizes he has been dreaming. The story is by Aleksandr Druzhinin, author of *Polinka Saks,* who in Russian literary history is depicted as a champion of women's rights.[14]

Little girls also received warnings about the evils of literary women. In a children's story, "Perepiski sestry s bratom" (Correspondence between a sister and brother), thirteen-year-old Masha makes the mistake of telling her older brother that she would like to be a writer.[15] He replies with shock, outrage, and threats: "A writer! . . . Do you understand the importance of this word, little girl? Of course not! It must be that you [. . .] only [want] people to talk about you [. . .] friends and strangers to praise you, perhaps even to publish some of your works" (43). "Yes, believe me, my dear Masha, any little girl who already wants to see her little trivialities in print deserves to be punished" (44). Masha is suitably chastened, as is their mother for having let Masha get so out of hand. In her last letter Masha tells her brother that she has renounced her *"brazen literary schemes [derzkie literaturnye zatei]"* (102) "and I am even afraid of the name *woman writer [pisatel'nitsa]"* (103). In the final letter, her brother congratulates her upon her reformation. Here, as in the other stories about women writers, women's (or girls') writing is implicitly equated with "sexual display."[16]

At the same time that women playwrights and prose writers were being attacked, the cultural definition of woman poets gradually shifted to accommodate the idea of "woman's sphere." In England a new consensus arose between 1790 and 1830 that divided "the terrain of poetry . . . into two complementary spheres, masculine and feminine" (Ross, *Contours of Masculine Desire,* 189). Women could now be "poetesses" (as opposed to poets) and still remain respectable ladies as long as they were content to "nurture culture as a sociomoral handmaiden" (192) rather than assume the "visionary" "prophetic stance" (91) that was the prerogative of men poets.

This new consensus soon spread to Russia as well. But even those critics who praised Russian poetesses did not create an encouraging environment for women's writing. The very term poetess (*poetessa*) both described women poets and implied the inferiority of their poetry to that of men. Critics routinely referred to women's poetry with condescension, as *milaia* (sweet), *skromnaia* (modest), and *iskrennaia* (sincere, signaling artless). One article that appeared in a Russian journal in 1851 praised North American poetesses for treating poetry as an "accomplishment" rather than an art while complacently noting that their "pure and irre-proachable" morality resulted in monotonous poetry.[17] In effect, women poets had to choose between being women and being poets.[18]

The Poetess

The poetess, a nineteenth-century figure that has survived into the twenty-first century, is worth considering in more detail. She repre-sented the feminine "Other" of the poet, whose masculinity was per-ceived as the universal norm. The twentieth-century scholar Alicia Os-triker notes that "some of our most compelling terms of critical discourse imply that serious poetry is more or less identical with potent masculinity" (*Stealing the Language*, 3). She mentions Harold Bloom's im-age of the oedipal struggle between "strong" poets, and such terms of critical approbation as size, greatness, stature, and hardness. Similarly, Gilbert and Gubar discuss the literary tradition that identifies the pen with the penis and the author with the "authority" of a patriarchal God (*Madwoman in the Attic*, 6, 8).

But, the scholar Svetlana Boym argues, while the poet's masculine gender is perceived as neutral, the poetess's "exposed genderedness" (*Death in Quotation Marks*, 197) (in Russian represented by "marked" feminine adjectives and past-tense verbs) renders her an "an aesthetic obscenity" (203), "a grotesque conglomeration of *lack* and *excess*" (194, italics in text). The poetess lacks objectivity, taste, genius (inventiveness, originality), and social responsibility—the cultural authority of mas-culinity—while suffering from an excess of subjectivity, of feelings, manifested as hysteria (194). Boym gives Marina Tsvetaeva as an ex-ample of a poet caught between the images of the tasteless, vulgar, trans-gressive "poetess" and the high culture "woman poet," a conflict men poets do not routinely face.[19]

Several other scholars have written of the "exposed genderedness" not only of poetesses but also of women writers in general. In the twen-tieth century Susan Gilbert wrote that the woman poet's body of work is treated like the body of the poetess ("Female Female Impersonator," 299). Similarly, the scholar Mary Ellmann observed that "books by women are treated as though they themselves are women and criticism embarks at its happiest upon an intellectual measuring of busts and hips" (*Thinking about Women*, 29). One thinks of Aleksandr Ska-bichevsky's review of Zhadovskaia's poetry, which verges on a sado-masochistic fantasy: "On all of [her poetry] lies the seal of trampled happiness and of long years of heavy bondage. It is the groans of female slavery with all its tortures, its feelings of helplessness, loneliness, bitter humiliation, shame before its own impotence, and vain efforts to console itself and forget, now in religious paroxysms, now in contemplation of nature's beauty" ("Pesni o zhenskoi nevole," in *Sochineniia*, 2: 551).

Or of Vil'gel'm Kiukhel'beker's sexualizing of Kul'man's work and life: "She herself is immeasurably better than her verses. . . . There is no doubt that I would have fallen in love with her, but that love would have been as beneficial to me as are harmful my little passions for petty, vain creatures" ("Dnevnik Vil'g.," 351–52). Ellmann in *Thinking about Women* shows how "phallic criticism" describes both women and women writers in stereotypes of excess and inadequacy: "formlessness, passivity, instability, confinement, piety, materiality, spirituality, irrationality, and compliancy." "Femaleness," Ellmann wryly concludes, "is a congenital fault, rather like eczema or Original Sin" (34).

The women poets we are considering responded to these literary limitations as women traditionally have responded to social limitations placed on them—with a combination of "accommodation" (conformity) and "resistance."[20] Some writers ostensibly accommodated to the patriarchal order by presenting themselves either as frivolous poetesses, sociomoral handmaidens, or both. One thinks of Rostopchina, who in several of her poems depicted women as superficial, capricious, amoral, governed by feelings, and living only for men, depictions that can extend to her poetic personae as well.[21]

> А я, я женщина во всем значеньи слова,
> [.   .   .   .   .]
> Я только женщина . . . гордиться тем готова, . . .
> Я бал люблю! . . отдайте балы мне! . .
>
> ⤳
>
> (But I, I am a woman in the full meaning of the word,
> [.   .   .   .   .]
> I am only a woman . . . and am prepared to be proud of it . . .
> I love a party! . . . Give me parties! . . .
>   "Iskushenie" [Temptation, 1839])[22]

Zhadovskaia assumed the stance of a sociomoral handmaiden in poems chiding society women (but not men) for their worldliness and urging children to pray for the brave soldiers dying for the tsar ("T. Go-i," [To T. G., 1858], "Ne sviatotatstva, ne grekhi," [Not a sacrilege, not a sin, 1858], "Polnochnaia molitva" [Midnight prayer, 1858]). Bakunina, too, in her published religious poetry depicted women and women poets (but not men) as fallen and sinful creatures (for example, "Rozhdenie nezabudki" [The birth of the forget-me-not, 1841] and "Groza" [The thunderstorm, 1840]). As English poetesses "positioned themselves against bluestockings to delineate their own 'normality'" (Ross, *Contours of Masculine Desire*, 190), so Bakunina in a literary epistle dissociated herself from A. V. Zrazhevskaia, who expressed anger at men critics' prejudice against women writers.[23]

Other writers in the group, however, resisted various aspects of the poetess role, implicitly demanding that they be taken seriously as poets. They often suffered attacks from men critics: Kul'man for her erudition and knowledge of Greek and Latin poetics and classical allusions; Gotovtseva for daring to allude to Pushkin's condescending attitude toward women; Shakhovskaia for writing a "pretentious" visionary poem, *Snovidenie* (A dream, 1833); Pavlova for caring about art and technique in her work; and Khvoshchinskaia for having intellectual content. One critic complained that he sometimes had to read her poems twice to understand them.[24]

This is not to suggest, however, that accommodation and resistance are mutually exclusive qualities; most of these poets showed some combination of the two. For example, if we consider Rostopchina's great success and popularity as a poet during the 1830s and 1840s, the attention and praise she received from Pushkin, Viazemsky, Zhukovsky, Lermontov, and others, we begin to understand that her "accommodation" to her society's gender stereotypes allowed her to satisfy a powerful and very "unfeminine" ambition for literary recognition. In effect, Rostopchina accommodated to her society's gender stereotypes in order to resist the social pressure that would have excluded her from the realm of literature. Similarly, Zhadovskaia, who was born with no left arm and only a few fingers on her right hand, managed to have an astonishingly successful career by accommodating to her society's ideas about women's love poetry. Bakunina, too, who in her published poetry accommodated completely to patriarchal religious views of women, in her unpublished poetry expressed pride in herself as a poet and even dabbled in a Russian folk paganism dominated by witches and *rusalki* (water spirits).[25] (See her "Ballada" and "Prolog" in the Appendix.)

Nor did the "poets" always resist the poetess role. Pavlova, as we have seen, on occasion denigrated her poetry writing. In one poem ("My sovremennitsy, grafinia" [We are contemporaries, countess, 1847]), she even positioned herself against Rostopchina, whom she depicts as a scandalous "George Sandist," in order to delineate herself as a virtuous supporter of Slavophile patriarchy. The poem ends:

> Не требую эмансипаций
> И самовольного житья;
> Люблю Москвы я мир и стужу
> [. . . . .]
> И отдаю я просто мужу
> Свои стихи на строгий суд.
>
> ⤙
>
> (I don't demand emancipation
> And a self-willed existence;
> I love the peace and the hard frost of Moscow,
> [. . . . .]
> And I simply give my husband
> My verses for his stern judgment.)
>   (*Polnoe sobranie stikhotvorenii*, 134–35)

From what we know about Pavlova's disintegrating relationship with her husband at this time, it is difficult to read these verses as expressing anything other than an ideological stance.[26]

Perhaps the ultimate accommodation was to fall silent, as did Ekaterina Shakhovskaia, after publishing her visionary epic, *Snovidenie* (1833).[27] Mariia Lisitsyna, who resisted both literary and social expectations for women, disappeared from literature after the early 1830s, perishing, according to a poem written in her memory by her friend Nadezhda Teplova, "a victim of passions and delusions" ("pogibla zhertvoiu strastei i zabluzhdenii") (Vatsuro, "Zhizn' i poeziia Nadezhdy Teplovoi," 21).

Exclusions

Besides legal, social, and literary constraints, this generation of women poets shared a less obvious but equally significant limitation: their tangential relationship to the world of their male contemporaries, a world that included the Napoleonic wars and the invasion of Russia, the Decembrist uprising and its aftermath, the Polish uprising, the 1848 European revolutions, the censorship terror, and the professionalization of Russian literature as it moved from aristocratic salons and *kruzhki* (literary circles) to "plebian" journals. These events grew out of male political, social, and literary institutions, from which women were excluded: the military and its pastimes, dueling and gambling, the civil service, lyceums and the classical education provided there, universities, university student groups, literary circles and their *al'manakhi* (annual literary collections), extended travel, and residence abroad. These institutions formed the men poets of this generation as men and as poets, providing both the subject matter and the genres of their poetry.[28]

To understand the effect on women poets of exclusion from these male institutions, one need only consider their centrality to men's lives and works. Military life, dueling, and gambling played a vital role in both the lives and the works of Davydov, Kiukhel'beker, Pushkin, and Lermontov. The civil service experience of Pushkin, Viazemsky, and Tiutchev, however irritating and confining, showed them very concretely how their government operated, inevitably affecting their attitude toward it. The lack of such experience may account for Shakhovskaia's naive and unrealistic patriotism in *Snovidenie*. The lyceums that Pushkin, Del'vig, Kiukhel'beker, and Tiutchev attended gave them lifelong friendships with fellow poets, as well as a classical education, including a knowledge of Latin.

The importance of Latin as a male institution in the first half of the nineteenth century should not be underestimated. Latin has been described as "a sexually specialized language used almost exclusively for communicating between male and male," a code in which boys learned "a body of relatively abstract tribal lore inaccessible to those outside the group," that is, to all women and lower-class men.[29] As we have seen, women like Elisaveta Kul'man, who knew Latin and Greek, were considered unnatural.

Most of the Russian men poets of this generation studied Latin. The works of Pushkin, Baratynsky, Del'vig, Iazykov, Fet, and Batiushkov, as well as Maikov, Khomiakov, and Guber, not only contain allusions to classical poets but make use of Latin poetic genres, such as the elegy, the ode, and the epigram. Several scholars have argued that the Romantic movements of all countries reworked rather than rejected the literature of Greece and Rome.[30]

The fact that Latin was a male language led to the canonization of androcentric or even misogynist genres and themes. For example, the anacreontic ode, named for the Greek writer Anacreon, enjoyed great European and Russian popularity during the first third of the nineteenth century. Its subject was male drinking parties and the sexual use of women or boys. Pushkin, Baratynsky, and Iazykov as well as virtually

all the poets in the generation preceding them, including Goethe and
Schiller, wrote or translated anacreontic odes. So much a part of the
canon were they that Karl Grossheinrich unselfconsciously used them
to teach Greek grammar to the thirteen-year-old Elisaveta Kul'man and
then had her translate them into eight languages. Kul'man's introduction to her translations, in which she uncomfortably asks Anacreon for
his blessing, expresses some of the awkwardness she apparently felt
with the subject matter.[31]

Another "traditional" and widespread genre of the time were Bacchic
songs (*vakkhicheskie pesni*), which describe men's encounters in the
woods with bacchantes, understood to be sexually available women—
although the man was often depicted as forcing himself on the bacchante. In his third Pushkin article, Belinsky, who despised etiquette
books as oppressive to women, approvingly quoted in full Batiushkov's
"Vakkhanka" (The bacchante, 1814–15)—a poem that eroticizes violence and celebrates rape:

> [. . .] она бежала
> Легче серны молодой.
> Эвры волосы взвевали,
> Перевитые плющом;
> Нагло ризы поднимали
> И свивали их клубком.
> Стройный стан, кругом обвитый
> Хмеля желтого венцом,
> И пылающи ланиты
> Розы ярким багрецом,
> И уста, в которых тает
> Пурпуровый виноград,—
> Все в неистовой прельщает!
> В сердце льет огонь и яд!
> Я за ней . . . она бежала
> Легче серны молодой;
> Я настиг—она упала!
> И тимпан под головой!
> Жрицы Вакховы промчались
> С громким воплем мимо нас . . .

> ([. . .] She ran
> More lightly than a young antelope
> Zephyrs lifted her hair
> Interwoven with moss
> Impudently her garments rose
> And they twisted into a tangle
> Her graceful figure wound round

With a wreath of yellow hops
And her glowing cheeks
Like the rose's bright crimson
And her mouth in which melts
Purple grapes—
Everything entices me to fury
Pours fire and poison into my heart
I run after her. She ran
More lightly than a young antelope
I overtook her. She fell!
And the timbrel under her head!
The priestesses flashed past us
with a loud wail.)
(Belinskii, *Polnoe sobranie
sochinenii*, 7: 227–28)

Batiushkov's poem reworks an original by Parny. One scholar has noted that while Parny's bacchante is an incarnation of Venus who chooses the speaker, Batiushkov's is a mortal woman whom the speaker pursues and violates (Brown, *History of Russian Literature of the Romantic Period*, 1: 251). In addition, Batiushkov's speaker implies that not he, but the woman's provocative appearance is responsible for his actions.

Access to Latin would have enabled the women poets of this generation to challenge the misogynist classical themes and genres extolled as art, to modify androcentric classical forms, and to look for gynocentric traditions within the classics—as did Elisaveta Kul'man, who knew both Latin and Greek. Kul'man, however, exerted little influence in Russia because of her early death and her orientation to German classicism rather than to contemporary Russian literature.[32]

The university, another male institution, played a central role in the development of such poets as Iazykov, Lermontov, Tiutchev, Fet, Khomiakov, and Maikov. Several Moscow and Saint Petersburg University professors used their editorial positions to help their men students publish their works. For example, Aleksandr Nikitenko (1803–87) and Petr Pletnev, both professors of Russian literature at the University of Saint Petersburg, also at various times worked as editors of *Sovremennik* (The contemporary). Osip Senkovsky, professor of Near Eastern languages at Saint Petersburg University, edited *Biblioteka dlia chteniia* (Library for reading). Mikhail Pogodin, professor of history at Moscow University, edited *Moskovskii vestnik* (Moscow messenger) and *Moskvitianin* (The Muscovite). N. I. Nadezhdin, professor of arts and archeology at Moscow University, edited *Teleskop* (Telescope). Semen Raich, who taught at the Moscow University Gentry Pension, published *Novye aonidy* (New muses), *Severnaia lira* (Northern lyre), and *Galatea*. M. A. Maksimov, professor of botany at Moscow University, published the *al'-manakh Dennitsa* (Morning star). Many men poets of this generation benefited as well from the all-male student groups, literary circles, and the annual literary collections and journals that grew out of them such as Del'vig's *Severnye tsvety* (Northern flowers), Maksimovich's *Dennitsa*, Kiukhel'beker's *Mnemozina* (Mnemosyne), and Pushkin's *Sovremennik*. Although women occasionally contributed to such journals—for example, Teplova and Gotovtseva both appeared in *Severnye tsvety*—they never acted as editors or publishers.[33]

These men's institutions allowed interactions that made it comparatively easy for young men poets to find mentors and get published. For example, Vasilii Zhukovsky, "the acknowledged patriarch of the Golden Age" (Mirsky, *History of Russian Literature*, 75), who met Pushkin in literary circles, presented him in 1820 with a portrait inscribed "to a victorious pupil from a defeated master," later editing (with Petr Pletnev) the first collection of Pushkin's poetry (1825). Zhukovsky, who also arranged with Petr Viazemsky for the first significant publications of Tiutchev's and Lermontov's poetry in Pushkin's *Sovremennik*, used his court influence on behalf of Pushkin, Lermontov, and Baratynsky when they experienced problems with the authorities. He also tried to help Khomiakov publish his Slavophile poems abroad when they could not be published in Russia. Zhukovsky himself—who was the illegitimate son of a landowner—had been given entrée into Russian literature by the prose writer and journalist Nikolai Karamzin. Pushkin acted as literary sponsor for his schoolmate Del'vig, who in turn sponsored his friend Baratynsky. Pushkin and Baratynsky sponsored Iazykov. Fet received help from his university friend, the literary critic Apollon Grigor'ev, who edited Fet's first poetry collection and then gave it an enthusiastic review; Fet also received editing help for his other collections from Ivan Turgenev, the critic Nikolai Strakhov, and the poet and philosopher Vladimir Solov'ev. Other critics played important roles in making the critical reputations of men poets. Belinsky helped build the reputations of Pushkin, the other members of his pleiad, and Lermontov. He also arranged publication for Kol'tsov's first collection of poetry (1835) and wrote a long introduction for the second (1846). Nikolai Nekrasov renewed Tiutchev's career in 1850 by reprinting Tiutchev's early poetry together with a laudatory essay in *Sovremennik*. Among the noncanonical men poets, Apollon Maikov received encouragement to turn from painting to poetry from his professors at Saint Petersburg Uni-

functioned very differently for men than they did for women. For up-per-class men poets, salons offered the opportunity to receive friendly criticism from an audience of peers who shared their experience and values. For nonaristocratic men writers—for example, Pogodin, Raich, Kol'tsov, Nikitenko, Pavlov, and even Belinsky—salons offered an op-portunity for social advancement and acceptance into an aristocracy of merit. But aristocratic women as a rule were excluded from men's literary gatherings. Even women who hosted their own salons did not often read their work there, with the exceptions of Pavlova, Rostopchina, and Fuks, who, as we shall see, incurred ridicule for doing so.[38] Unlike nonaristocratic men, nonaristocratic woman poets never found men-toring in a salon. Nor are there any examples of a salon hostess organ-izing a journal or an annual literary collection. In any case, it seems that the role Russian women played as salon hostesses has been exagger-ated. One collection of memoirs about Russian salons of the first half of the nineteenth century described six hosted by women and forty-three hosted by men.[39] In the list of over two hundred Russian literary asso-ciations (*literaturnye ob"edineniia*) from the eighteenth century to the 1860s, compiled by M. Aronson and S. Reiser, women appear as host-esses of only eleven salons, three evenings, and one musical morning. No women appear in connection with the more serious, although gen-erally shorter-lived, literary circles (*kruzhki*), in which writers discussed literary issues (*Literaturnye kruzhki i salony*, 301–5). Aronson and Reiser emphasize the difference between the two kinds of groups: "The circle is more connected with the writer, the salon with the reader. . . . If the circle helps us illuminate questions of literary production, then the sa-lon illuminates for us questions of literary consumption" (37).

Another formative factor for men largely unavailable to women was travel, whether through the army or civil service, living abroad, or in-ternal exile. Such travel, although often involuntary, enriched the men's poetry; exotic places constituted an important theme in the Romantic Age. Iazykov lived in Dorpat from 1822 to 1829, Tiutchev in Germany for twenty-two years, Baratynsky in Finland for six years. Pushkin trav-eled to Kishinev, the Caucasus, and the south of Russia, Lermontov to Georgia, and Kiukhel'beker to France, the Caucasus, and Siberia. Among the noncanonical men writers Mil'keev and Kol'tsov traveled several times to the two Russian capitals from Siberia and Voronezh, re-spectively, and both Khomiakov and Maikov spent extended periods of time in Europe. In contrast, none of the women poets traveled within the Russian Empire or abroad, except Mordovtseva and Khvoshchinskaia (who traveled to Saint Petersburg from Saratov and Riazan', respectively), Bakunina, Rostopchina, and Pavlova (and only after she left Russia). Fuks, a lifelong inhabitant of Kazan', was able to create exotic settings, thanks to her ethnographic studies.

But perhaps the most important male institution for the poets of this generation as discussed in the previous chapter, was the Romantic Movement itself. All of these women poets—along with their contemporaries in the West—faced common problems: the conflict between the modesty required of women and the self-assertion required by a poetic vocation in the Romantic period; the issue of who their audience was; the question of how to respond to the male Romantic personification of poetic inspiration (the muse) as female sexual partner and nature as idealized mother; the dilemma of how to get published in a literary establishment consisting almost entirely of men gatekeepers (editors, publishers, reviewers), who often did not take them seriously as poets. Most basically, they had to find a way to relate to a poetic institution that conflated male experience with human experience, the male poetic tradition with the poetic tradition, and the male voice and viewpoint with poetry making. Not only did these women lack literary social capital—access to the education, mentors, literary gatekeepers and opinion-makers, and often the social connections they needed to make a successful poetic career. They also did not enjoy the credibility—the right to the title of "poet" along with its prestige—automatically accorded to men. In such circumstances these women had to resolve the questions of how to find their voice, write about their experience, and claim a professional identity as a poet.

2

Literary Conventions

Several literary critics have argued that Romanticism was a male-gendered institution. Certainly we find in the Russian poetry of the first half of the nineteenth century such blatantly male-centered Romantic conventions as the friendly epistle (*druzheskoe poslanie*) celebrating the cult of male friendship, anacreontic odes, and Bacchic poetry.[1] Here I would like to consider some of the ways that women poets of this period dealt with two less obvious but more basic androcentric Romantic conventions: poetic representations of the self and of nature.

Romantic Self-Representation

Both Western and Russian Romantic men poets commonly represented themselves as priests, prophets, and "unacknowledged legislators of the world," all occupations barred to women. In Russia we find many men poets appropriating God's voice and authority to chastise men and even rulers.[2] For example, in Pushkin's "Prorok" (The prophet, 1826) the prophet-poet becomes God's surrogate, able to burn people's hearts "with the word." In Baratynsky's "Poslednii poet" (The last poet, 1834) the poet's death expresses the ultimate condemnation of a civilization that has rejected both nature and poetry. Other examples of the poet as priest and prophet can be found in Del'vig's "Vdokhnovenie" (Inspiration, 1822), Lermontov's "Poèt" (1838) and "Poet i tolpa" (The poet and the crowd, 1828), Khomiakov's "Poèt" (1827), "Rossii" (To Russia, 1839), "Sud bozhii" (God's judgment, 1854), and Maikov's "Sny" (Dreams, 1885).

Russian men poets also represented themselves with the trope of the warrior-bard.[3] While poetic self-representation as glorifiers of war can be traced back at least as far as Homer, in late eighteenth-century Russia and Europe the bardic tradition gained new life from the ballad revival, with its focus on minstrels, as well as from James Macpherson's very popular Ossian poems.[4] As late as 1919 one literary historian of Russia's Golden Age hypothesized that all "professional epic-lyric poetry" originates in battle songs and stories (Verkhovskii, "Poety pushkinskoi pory," in *Poety pushkinskoi pory*, 16–17). In addition, men poets represented themselves in explicitly sexual terms—as seducers of women or in sexual relationships with desirable female muses or muse surrogates.[5]

Women poets, in contrast, had few mythic or historical models from which to create female images of the poet. The two most eminent women poets known at this time were the classical Greeks Sappho and Corinna, whose work only survives in fragments.[6] Women poets avoided using Sappho as a model, not only because they lacked a male classical education and thus had no direct access to her poetry but also, it seems likely, because men poets and critics used the term *russkaia Safo* (the Russian Sappho) in sexualizing epigrams and *ad feminam* attacks. One Russian scholar cites a series of epigrams directed at women poets from the beginning of the nineteenth century that implied they suffered from unrequited love for a particular man poet, as Sappho is supposed to have done for Phaon. Other epigrams encouraged women poets to follow Sappho's example by jumping from the promontory of Leucas or expressed the epigrammatist's desire to do so rather than listen to their poetry.[7] Such demeaning allusions to Sappho and women poets continued at least into the middle of the century. In 1847, when V. R. Zotov, editor of *Literaturnaia gazeta*, started publishing Nadezhda Khvoshchinskaia's poetry, he placed the first two selections below a serialized article about Sappho's career as a courtesan ("Safo i Lezbosskie getery" [Sappho and the courtesans of Lesbos]). In the article, the author, M. Mikhailov, refers to Sappho as "this lamentable mixture of such depravity and such genius" ("eto plachevoi smeshenie takoi isporchennosti i takogo geniia"), while describing in great detail Sappho's training as a courtesan, presumably for the delectation of men readers.[8]

How, then, could women poets represent themselves? As mentioned earlier, some enacted the culturally encouraged but unsatisfying stance of *poetessa* or "sociomoral handmaiden." Several wrote poems about the impossibility of being both a woman and a poet in their society or ironically advised women, in poetry, not to write poems at all, or counseled them to write only those appropriate to poetesses. For example, Shakhova's "K zhenshchinam poetam" (To women poets, 1845):

> Сестры! Жребий роковой!
> [. . . . .]
> Нам чело венец лавровый
> Давит, колет и теснит,
> Торжествует ум суровый,—
> Сердце женское грустит. [. . . .]

(Sisters! A fatal lot!
[. . . . .]
On our brow the laurel crown
Presses, pricks and constrains us,
The stern mind exults,
The woman's heart grieves. [. . .])

or Teplova's "Sovet" (Advice, 1860):

> Брось лиру, брось и больше не играй,
> И вдохновенные, прекрасные напевы
> Ты в глубине души заботливо скрывай;
> Поэзия—опасный дар для девы!

(Throw away your lyre, throw it away and don't play any more.
And your beautiful, inspired songs
Carefully hide in the depths of your soul;
Poetry is a dangerous gift for a maiden!)

or Rostopchina's "Kak dolzhny pisat' zhenshchiny" (How women should write, 1840):

> Но только я люблю, чтоб лучших снов своих
> Певица робкая вполне не выдавала
> [. . . . .]
> Чтоб повесть милую любви и сладких слез
> Она, стыдливая, таила и скрывала;
> [. . . . .]
> Да! женская душа должна в тени светиться, [. . . .]

(But I only like it when the shy woman singer
Hasn't entirely given away her best dreams,
[. . . . .]
When she has bashfully hidden and covered
The story of dear love and sweet tears;
[. . . . .]
Yes! A woman's soul must shine in the shadows. [. . .])

Many of these women, however, chose to represent themselves as poets, reworking elements of men's poetic self-representation. In so doing, they appropriated cultural prerogatives reserved for men: positions of "sacred authority"—the role of priest or prophet—as well as the power to "experience and narrate the sacred" (S. Friedman, "Craving Stories," 24), although they did so with ambivalence, with what Gilbert and Gubar call "anxiety of authorship" (*Madwoman in the Attic*, 49).

Interestingly, the only woman poet in this group to represent herself as prophet was Rostopchina, who, as we shall see, generally has been perceived as enacting the *poetessa* role.[9] However, if women could not be prophets, they could narrate the sacred as visionaries; seven out of the fourteen women poets we have been considering wrote poems describing religious visions, poems usually titled "Videnie" (Vision). Perhaps it is significant that while there are no instances in the Bible of God speaking directly to a woman, there are models for women having religious visions in the Annunciation and in the three Marys' vision of the resurrected Christ.[10] However, these Russian women poets express ambivalence about assuming even such limited religious authority. Zhadovskaia's two poems, "Videnie proroka Ieziekiila" (Vision of the prophet Ezekiel) and "Kto mne rodnia?" (Who is kin to me? both 1858), are "cross-gendered," that is, written in the masculine voice. Shakhovskaia's ambitious religious-patriotic vision significantly is called *Snovidenie* (A dream) rather than "Videnie" (Vision). Gotovtseva's and Teplova's poems, both called "Videnie," focus more on the female narrator's feelings for the angel than on the vision itself.[11]

As for the representation of poets as bards and part of a military-poetic complex, a number of women poets appropriated this role as well. It may be, as Paula Feldman and Theresa Kelley have suggested, that "nationalistic or patriotic convictions allowed some women writers to strengthen their claim to authorship."[12] In addition, these writers may have been encouraged to portray themselves as patriotic and even militaristic by the literary fashion for Joan of Arc—Robert Southey's epic *Joan of Arc* (1796), Schiller's *Die Jungfrau von Orleans* (1802), which Zhukovsky translated into Russian in 1820 and Karolina Pavlova translated into French in 1839—as well as by Pushkin's sponsorship of the memoirs of Nadezhda Durova, who fought for Russia in the Napoleonic Wars disguised as a man. The most exaggerated example of such patriotism is Shakhovskaia's vision *Snovidenie*, which describes a heaven occupied exclusively by Russian and Roman soldiers and the poets who glorify them and is dedicated to *moia otchizna* (my fatherland). Only

Mordovtseva, whose son died in the Russo-Turkish War, questioned militarism, and her work appeared at a much later date.[13]

Finally, as regards men poets' self-representation in terms of sexual prowess, it would have been impossible for women to appropriate this image at a time when society so strictly limited their sexual expression. Nonetheless, several created unconventional male muse figures with whom a sexual relationship is implied—although these relationships generally seem marital in contrast to men poets' pre- or extramarital muse relationships. Bakunina in one unpublished poem alludes to her *chertenok* (little demon), who distracts her from sewing by tempting her with his lyre. In an unpublished play he appears on stage as her constant companion. Khvoshchinskaia's muse is a more frightening *prizrak* (phantom), who seems to represent a past painful romance. Teplova, Zhadovskaia, and Bakunina all write about their *genii* (genius).[14]

The scholar Mary DeShazer has suggested that a male muse poses problems for a woman poet that a female muse does not present for a man. "While [the man poet] asserts his authority over the muse by naming and subordinating her," she writes, "the woman poet may feel overpowered and violated by her 'authoritative' masculine muse" (*Inspiring Women*, 28). "Will a patriarchal muse inspire or control, aid or appropriate her writing?" (3). The woman poet, DeShazer suggests, may have difficulty "separating the male muse from other intimidating and debilitating male forces, those that limit rather than expand her female identity" (30). These Russian women poets seem to have experienced similar problems with male muses. Kul'man, for example, evokes Anacreon as vengeful antimuse in "K Anakreonu" (To Anacreon, 1839), her introduction to her translations of his verse. The poem begins:

> Анакреон любезный!
> Ты сердишься! Сегодня
> Я видела со страхом
> Тебя во сне.

> (Dear Anacreon!
> You are angry! Today
> I had a terrifying dream
> About you.)

Kul'man then attempts to persuade Anacreon to approve her translation of his work. And as we shall see, Pavlova similarly evoked another dead man poet, Pushkin, as an oppressive antimuse.[15]

Indeed, some of these women poets chose a female or ambivalently

Kul'man in "Korinna" (1839, see appendix) implies that her heroine's muse is Diana—goddess of the moon but apparently more supportive of women poets than the god of the arts, her brother Apollo. We find no muse figures at all in the poetry of Garelina, Gotovtseva, Lisitsyna, or Rostopchina. In this literary period, I would suggest that the absence of muse figures—that is, of projected creativity—in women poets' work indicates their discomfort within the male-defined role of poet. Such absence also may have led men critics to question further women's credibility as poets; every one of the seven canonical men poets under consideration wrote several poems to a traditional muse.[16] It is not surprising, however, that so many women poets chose a nonsexual muse or decided to dispense with one altogether. For many heterosexual men poets of this period, muses represented an unproblematic fusion of their sexuality with their creativity. Women, on the other hand, were subject to even stronger prohibitions against expressing their sexuality than those against writing. Aside from the other problems that male muses presented, women poets may not have been able to conceive of a muse relationship that was both satisfying and socially acceptable.

Men poets represented themselves not only archetypally, as prophets, bards, or Don Juans, but also as individuals, through the literary devices of signatures and personae—devices that women poets modified as well. Signatures, as one scholar has shown, allow poets to represent themselves either in the "sincere" and "natural" pose of poets who always sign their own name (for example, Wordsworth) or in a "theatrical" pose, in which there is a "deliberate creation of multiple selves" (for example, Wordsworth's contemporary Mary Robinson).[17] During the first part of the nineteenth century most Russian poets used pseudonyms from time to time; Masanov (*Slovar' psevdonimov*, v. 3) lists sixteen for Baratynsky, for example, and thirty-three for Pushkin. For women poets, however, female pseudonyms carried the added significance of allowing them to disguise their identity in a society where their poetry writing was considered controversial. Further, if a woman poet chose a male-sounding pseudonym and avoided feminine past-tense verbs and adjectives, she could disguise her gender, thus gaining more favorable reactions from male literary gatekeepers.[18] Indeed, several of these fourteen women poets occasionally used "unmarked" pseudonyms.[19] None of the canonical or noncanonical men, on the other hand, ever signed their poetry with a feminine pseudonym.

Surprisingly, however, despite the benefits of an unmarked pseudonym, these women poets very rarely used them. Most of the time they either signed their poems with their full name—as did Gotovtseva, Lisitsyna, Pavlova, and Khvoshchinskaia, who, however, used a male pseudonym, V. Krestovsky, for her prose–or chose female-gendered pseudonyms.[20] Bakunina, for example, used P. B-na; Garelina used Nadezhda Libina, Neskazaeva, and L. G-a; Rostopchina used gr–ia, R-a, russkaia zhenshchina, S-va, D., and many others. Even Mordovtseva, who published her one book of poetry under the unmarked signature A. B-z, established herself as female in the first poem—which concerns her poetic vocation—by using marked female verbal endings. It would appear that these poets wanted to write as women, even if doing so adversely affected their reception.

A self-representational device related to signature is the persona or speaker in a poem. Poets may choose personae closely identified with themselves, for example, the speaker in Wordsworth's *Prelude,* or completely separate, for example, Alfonso II, Duke of Ferrara, the speaker in Browning's "My Last Duchess," or somewhere in between, for example, the speaker in Eliot's "Love Song of J. Alfred Prufrock."[21] Men critics have often assumed women poets to be too "artless" to use personae at all, taking for granted that anything a woman writes in a poem is completely autobiographical. Emily Dickinson found it necessary to explain to Thomas Higginson, poetry critic of the *Atlantic Monthly,* "When I state myself, as the representative of the verse, it does not mean me, but a supposed person" (Bianchi, *Life and Letters of Emily Dickinson,* 242). Even in the twentieth century at least one Russian critic in his discussion of the "lyric heroine" (*liricheskaia geroinia*) assumed that women poets use the same persona in every poem.[22]

Yet, while some men critics assumed women to be incapable of creating personae, others urged women not to use them. Belinsky in his review of Rostopchina's first poetry collection suggested that in the future she write "poetic revelations of the world of the feminine soul, melodies of the mysticism of the feminine heart. Then they would also be more interesting to the other half of the human race, which, God knows why, has appropriated the right of judgment and reward."[23] Similarly, Petr Viazemsky advised Gotovtseva in an open letter, "Don't write verses on general problems. . . . There is a special charm in women's confessions. . . . For God's sake, don't put on masks."[24] One wonders whether such critics were motivated by voyeurism, hoping to gaze upon women's naked souls in poetry as they gazed upon women's naked bodies in paintings and at the ballet. Certainly, men critics praised, if condescendingly, the "sincerity" of women poets like Rostopchina and

Zhadovskaia, who assumed confessional personae; such critics, however, often attacked or ignored women poets like Pavlova, Khvoshchinskaia, or Fuks, who did not pretend to be exposing their most intimate feelings.[25]

Despite men critics' views that women could not and should not create fictional personae, these fourteen women poets used a great number and variety of them, possibly more than did the men. Many of the women wrote at least one poem in which they combined a male persona with "unmarked" male grammatical endings and pseudonyms in order to disguise their gender. Men poets, it should be noted, wrote far fewer such "cross-gendered" poems; Pushkin for example, wrote none, except for a draft of "Dioneia" (1821) from which he subsequently eliminated the female-marked verb endings. Among the other men poets we are considering I found only two by Del'vig, five by Fet, one by Tiutchev, four by Kol'tsov, two by Miller, and one by Maikov. Perhaps the men felt uncomfortable in assuming the lower-status female role.[26]

Even among the women poets, however, cross-gendered poems represent an insignificant number of works. Most of their fictional personae are female, suggesting that they were less interested in disguising their gender than in exploring different personalities and perspectives. Gotovtseva, for example, juxtaposes poems with similar vocabulary but very different viewpoints. In the last stanza of one poem, "Odinochestvo," (Solitude, her translation of Lamartine's "L'Isolement," 1819) and in the first stanza of the next "K N. N." (To N. N.) the same word, *poblekshii* (withered), appears, first seriously and then mockingly: "Kogda poblekshii list na zemliu upadaet" (When the withered leaf falls to the earth), as opposed to

> Зачем поблекшие цветы
> Ты легкой кистью оттеняешь?

> (Why do you with a light brush
> Shade withered flowers?)[27]

Similarly, Zhadovskaia starts one poem "Ty skoro menia pozabudesh'" (You will soon forget me, 1858) and another "Ty menia pozabudesh' ne skoro" (You won't forget me soon, 1858). In Fuks's collection *Stikhotvoreniia* (Poems, 1834), "Zhenikh" (The bridegroom), a poem satirizing romantic love, is followed by "Aneta i Liubim" (Aneta and Liubim), which exemplifies it. Similarly, in this collection, which appeared under Fuks's name, "Schastlivye druz'ia!" (Lucky friends!), a poem with a female-voiced speaker about unhappy love, is followed by "Poslanie k drugu" (Epistle to a friend) and "Pavel i Virginiia" (Paul and Virginia), two unhappy love poems with male-voiced speakers.

Several poets wrote dramatic monologues in which they speak in a woman character's voice: Kul'man in "Safo" (Sappho, 1839); Pavlova in "Doch' zhida" (The Jew's daughter, 1840) and "Donna Inezil'ia" (1842); Rostopchina in "Kak liubiat zhenshchiny" (How women love, 1841), in which she speaks as Charlotte Stieglitz, wife of the German poet Heinrich Stieglitz (1801–49); and Khvoshchinskaia in "Solntse segodnia za tucheiu chernoi takoi zakatilosia" (Today the sun disappeared behind such a black cloud, 1852), in which she speaks as a nanny.[28] It is possible that men poets found the androcentric poetic modes of self-representation discussed earlier so comfortable, natural, and transparent that they were less concerned with persona as a poetic device. Women poets, on the other hand, had to expend a great deal of energy to modify the "conventional" male poetic persona, which fit them so badly, and as a result may have turned to exploring other fictional personae as well.

A final aspect of poetic self-representation is the audience that poets address—both the "you" of a poem and their implied reader. In the poetry of men poets, even when the addressee of the poem is a woman, the implied audience is almost always men.[29] In the poetry of these and other women poets, in contrast, both the addressee and the "implied reader" (the intended audience) are often female. Several Western scholars have suggested that there were two nineteenth-century literatures: a male, supposedly "universal" literature, written by, for, and to men, which women also read, and a female literature, written by, for, and to women, which, with few exceptions, men considered second-rate and ignored. We can see the split between the two literatures perhaps most clearly in the United States, where economic factors maintained it. At a time when middle-class women generally were entirely dependent upon men, American women could support themselves by writing for the many U.S. women's magazines. To do so, however, they had to conform to editors' expectations that they assume the poetess role and confine themselves to a "special feminine discourse" of "affect and domesticity," reflecting "woman's sphere."[30] Such strictures, of course, made for rather superficial poetry. The absence of a market for "women's poetry" in Russia may have decreased the number of women who wrote poetry, but also the number writing as poetesses.

Several of these fourteen Russian poets, however—and not only those who could be described as *poetessy*—addressed themselves primarily to women. Perhaps they assumed men would not be interested in the realities of their lives. Or perhaps they chose as their implied reader an audience that had also experienced those realities. Teplova, for example, in about twenty of her poems directly addresses women friends and relations. Pavlova dedicated *Dvoinaia zhizn'* (*A Double Life*) to society women:

> Рабыни шума и сует.
> [. . . . .]
> Вас всех, Психей, лишенных крылий
> Немых сестер моей души!

> (Slaves of noise and vanity.
> [. . . . .]
> All of you Psyches deprived of wings
> The mute sisters of my soul!)

In digressions throughout the work Pavlova's narrator addresses this audience. Several other women poets wrote poems to groups of women friends.[31]

The implied reader can affect a poet's attitude toward the poem's subject. Rachel Blau DuPlessis finds that many lyrics by men poets objectify and silence women. Such poems depict "masculine heterosexual desire looking at and framing a silent, beautiful, distant female; an overtly male 'I' speaking as if overheard in front of an unseen but loosely postulated male 'us' about a (beloved) 'she'" ("'Corpses of Poesy,'" 71). In women's poetry written to women friends, audience and addressee are the same and such objectification does not occur. Furthermore, in these Russian women's poems the male Other is often allowed to speak or even have the last word, if only to demonstrate his insensitivity to women. For example, in Garelina's "Bezumnaia" (The madwoman, 1870)—in which a count's son seduces and abandons a priest's daughter, who drowns herself—the poem closes with her seducer dismissing her as a madwoman. We do occasionally find poems by these women in which the male Other is framed and silenced, for example, Pavlova's two poems "10 noiabria 1840" (10 November 1840, 1840) and "Na 10 noiabria" (For 10 November, 1841) about Mickiewicz. We also find a very few poems by men in which a nonaristocratic male Other speaks. For example, in Pushkin's "Besy" the coachman speaks to tell his passenger, who narrates the poem, that they are lost in the snowstorm; in

Guber's "Ia po komnate khozhu" (I pace the room, 1845) an apparently poor speaker condemns a rich nobleman for seducing and abandoning a servant. In men's poetry, however, the silenced female Other appears to be the rule.[32]

Of course, Russian women poets also wrote many epistles and poems to men and participated in men's discourses—for example, Pavlova's engagement with Slavophilism in "Razgovor v Kremle" (A conversation in the Kremlin, 1854). These poets could not afford to ignore a male audience or men's concerns if they wished to publish their works. At the very least they needed to win the support of a man editor or influential family friend, and doing so often required conforming to men's ideas of what women's poetry should be. Nonetheless, women poets related differently from men poets to their male audience. Rather than taking a male audience for granted, the women poets, as Gitta Hammarberg describes writers of album verse, engaged in a "peculiar form of double address, with a sideward glance at potential other readers"—in this case, male ("Flirting with Words," 299).

Nature

Men poets, in addition to gendering the poet as male, also continued a long tradition of gendering nature as female, identifying women with nature, men with culture, and asserting the moral superiority of the male over the female.[33] Hélène Cixous discusses these equations as part of a system of binary "hierarchical [that is, unequal] oppositions" that she believes structure Western thought: activity/passivity, logos/pathos, high/low, culture/nature, form/matter, day/night, father/mother, and, most basically, man/woman. In each pair, the first term is presented as inherently superior to and ultimately victorious over the second, its negation or Other. As a result of such thinking, women are defined only in terms of how they differ from men, those differences being considered aberrations from the norm ("Sorties," 101–2). Romantic men poets expressed these ideas in a recurring image noted by several literary critics: the man poet's usurpation or colonization of the procreative powers of female nature.[34]

Certainly, the Russian men poets of this generation often depicted nature in terms of a woman—variously characterized as the dangerous, devouring, alluring, repulsive, attainable, or unattainable Other. In Pushkin's "Rusalka" (The rusalka, 1818), for example, a hermit living in the wilderness, who tries and fails to resist the seductive wiles of a female nature figure, drowns.[35] In "Tsygany" (The gypsies, 1824) the free-spirited gypsy heroine Zemfira is identified with nature, which is described as opposing man-made law (culture). Her fickle heart, we are told, is like the "free moon" (*vol'naia luna*), which men's laws cannot control. Aleko—the representative of Russian society or culture, despite his rebellion against it—unable to control Zemfira verbally with threats, murders her.[36] In "Kobylitsa molodaia" (Young little mare, 1828, originally subtitled "An imitation of Anacreon," a reference to Anacreon's "To a Little African Mare") (*Sobranie sochinenii*, 2: 571) the speaker identifies the female horse with a woman by describing how he will subjugate it, using language suggestive of rape:

> И тебе пришла пора;
> [. . . . . . .]
> Погоди; тебя заставлю
> Я смириться подо мной
>
> ⬥
>
> (Your time has come, as well
> [. . . . .]
> Just you wait;
> I will force you to submit to me [literally, "under me."])
>   (*Sobranie sochinenii*, 2: 142)

In "Osen' (otryvok)" (Autumn [a fragment], 1833), Pushkin describes autumn as *chakhotochnaia deva* (a consumptive maiden). "Mne ona mila . . . ulybka na ustakh uvianuvshikh vidna" (she is dear to me . . . a smile can be seen on her withered lips) (*Sobranie sochinenii*, 2: 309–10).

We find similar images of nature as woman and Other in the poetry of Del'vig, Tiutchev, Lermontov, Iazykov, and Fet. In "Dshcher' khladna l'da!" (Daughter of cold ice! 1812–13), Del'vig characterizes the Russian winter as "Boginia razrushen'ia . . . rossiian mat'" (Goddess of destruction . . . mother of Russians). His "Luna" (The moon, 1822) identifies the moon with the perfidious (*kovarnaia*) Lila.[37] Tiutchev anthropomorphizes both winter and spring as women: winter as a spiteful witch (*ved'ma zlaia*) ("Vesna" [Spring, 1836]), and spring as a beautiful and powerful queen ("Vesennie vody" [Spring waters, 1832] and "Vesna" [Spring, 1839]).

In Lermontov's "Morskaia tsarevna" (The sea princess, 1841), a prince struggles with and kills a sexually aggressive female nature figure, a mermaid. In "Vecher" (Evening, 1830–31) and "Noch'" (Night, 1830–31), the speaker identifies natural settings with a woman's inconstancy. Iazykov goes even further, merging nature and women into objects of male sexual fantasies. In "Bessonitsa" (Insomnia, 1831), spring breathes its sweet breath on the poet's face and breast and the moon kisses his eyes as he thinks about his lover. Nature provides a sexualized backdrop for even more explicitly described sexual encounters in "Vesenniaia noch'" (Spring night, 1831), "Pesnia (Ia zhdu tebia, kogda vechernei mgloiu)" (Song [I wait for you when like the evening darkness], 1829), and "Elegiia (Zdes' gory s dvukh storon stoiat)" (Elegy [Here mountains stand on both sides], 1839).

Fet, too, presented nature as the female object of male sexual fantasies. Spring is a sexually alluring peasant woman in "Eshche vesny dushistoi nega" (Still the voluptuousness of fragrant spring, 1854), and a sleeping beauty whose body is described in voyeuristic detail in "Glub' nebes opiat' iasna" (The depths of the heavens are clear once again, 1879). A May night is a trembling bride in "Eshche maiskaia noch'" (Another May night, 1857); morning on the steppe is like a "newly married queen before her powerful groom" ("Utro v stepi" [Morning on the steppe, 1865]); a woman is compared to a May breeze, and her sexual response to an Aeolian harp, which, despite its few strings, always finds new sounds ("Kak maiskii golubookii zefir" [Like a blue-eyed May zephyr], 1842). Like Iazykov, Fet often describes a sexualized, feminized nature as a backdrop for sexual encounters with women.[38]

It is not my intention to suggest that these poets represent nature only as female Other. They also use the nightingale (male gender, *solovei*) as a symbol for the man poet, Pan to represent the spirit of nature, and the masculine word for *moon* (*mesiats*) as well as the feminine (*luna*), although in different contexts worth examining.[39] But it seems significant that they preferred to exemplify nature with feminine nouns—for example, *zvezda, luna, vesna, zima, berezka, roza, noch', buria*—rather than masculine- or neuter-gendered nouns (*les, mesiats, veter, oblako, vecher, solntse, tsvetok*). At the very least, we can say that a strong literary tradition identified the poet as male, while identifying women with a feminized and sexualized nature.

This tradition left Romantic women poets of this generation in a quandary: should they identify with the figure of the man poet, or with nature as female Other, or try to invent some other way of relating to these two concepts? As we have seen, for a woman to identify herself as a man poet, as opposed to a poetess, was to transgress cultural norms. But, as Margaret Homans observes, it was equally dangerous for women poets to identify with nature: "Mother nature is . . . prolific biologically,

not linguistically, and she is as destructive as she is creative. . . . [E]nor-
mous as her powers are, they are not the ones that her daughters want
if they are to become poets" (*Women Writers and Poetic Identity*, 13–16).
Not surprisingly, we find a wide variety of attitudes toward nature in the
work of these fourteen women poets, as well as conflicting attitudes
within the work of some. These variations indicate how difficult they
found the female gendering of nature and also how inventive they were
in finding ways to address their dilemma.

Some of these Russian women poets accepted the prevailing paradigm with modifications or reservations. Lisitsyna, for example, represents women, nature, and especially the moon as inconstant, and herself as a fallen woman; but she often refers to the moon as *mesiats*
(masculine gender) rather than as *luna* (feminine) and describes men's
inconstancy as well as women's ("Golubok," [The dove]; "K S[erafime]
S[ergeevna] T[eplov]-oi" [To S[erafima] S[ergeevna] T[eplova]]; "K nevernoi" [To an unfaithful woman]; "K mesiatsu" [To the moon]; "Zavet-
naia gora" [The cherished mountain]). Bakunina avoids romantic
themes altogether, but in her published poetry also seems to identify
with nature as the fallen female principle, spiritually inferior to the god-
like male (see "Rozhdenie nezabudki" [The birth of the forget-me-not,
1841], "Groza" [The storm, 1840], and "Nad Koreizom nebo iasno" [The
sky is clear over Koreiz, 1851]).

Teplova identifies herself with the beauty of the natural surroundings
of her childhood in "K rodnoi storone" (To native parts [1827]) and with
nature's gloominess in "Osen'" (Autumn, 1837). Gotovtseva in two unpublished poems, "Derevnia" (The country) and "Sad" (The garden), depicts nature as a close friend and safe haven. Similarly, the heroine of Rostopchina's *Dnevnik devushki* (A girl's diary, 219–20) apostrophizes the
moon as a friend. Khvoshchinskaia, while depicting nature as feminine,
expressed a wide range of attitudes toward it, from longing ("O daite
mne pole, shirokoe, gladkoe pole!" [Oh, give me a field, a wide, smooth
field! 1847]); to finding nature more meaningful than her writing ("U
okna" [At the window, 1853]); to rejecting nature as less important than
the struggle for social justice ("Zhila-b v tebe moia dusha, o mat'
priroda" [If only my soul lived in you, O, Mother Nature, 1858]).[40]

At the same time these women poets often used a variety of devices
to avoid identifying nature with the feminine. Bakunina, who in her published poetry identifies herself with fallen nature, in her unpublished poetry creates a pagan world in which nature is represented by gods, god-
desses, and Slavic folk figures of both genders (for example, "Prolog

igrannyi v Uiutnom 8 iul' 1835 v den' rozhdeniia M. M. Bakunina" [Prologue performed at Uiutnyi on July 8, 1835 on M. M. Bakunin's (her father's) birthday], see appendix).[41] Although Teplova identifies herself with nature in the two poems mentioned in this discussion, in "K charodeiu" (To the magician, 1832) she characterizes nature as Other and male. Pavlova for the most part appears to have ignored or suppressed the dilemma, or perhaps she was indifferent to it. Nature does not figure prominently in most of her poetry. While she uses such metaphors as crossing deserts or climbing mountains to describe life's difficulties, the mountains and deserts are abstract, almost cardboard ("Strannik" [The wanderer, 1843], "Zovet nas zhizn'" [Life calls us, 1846], "Kogda odin" [When alone, 1854], "Ne pora!" [It is not time! 1858]). In *Dvoinaia zhizn'* she implies that for those of her class, nature, like the life of peasants, is completely unknowable (*Polnoe sobranie stikhotvorenii*, 260, 262).

The most startling depiction of nature in these women's poetry, however, is not as feminine, masculine, or irrelevant, but as alien and indifferent to humanity. In Pavlova's "Nebo bleshchet biriuzoiu" (The heavens sparkle turquoise, 1840), flowers bloom indifferently on graves. In Mordovtseva's "Vzglianula na sad ia, v sadu opustelom" (I cast a glance at the garden, in the deserted garden, 1877), the sun and the sky cheerfully but indifferently regard the earth. In Zhadovskaia's "Rusalka" (The rusalka), an equally indifferent *rusalka* steals a young woman's flower wreath. Woman and *rusalka* seem to inhabit reflecting worlds that do not touch; the young woman's eyes, glittering with tears and sadness, are reflected by the *rusalka*'s eerily glittering eyes and spiteful laughter at the end of the poem. Zhadovskaia's "Sovet" (Advice, 1846) suggests that there is no communication at all between people and nature, that the only meaning we find in it is what we project onto it.

Such representations of nature, anticipating twentieth-century existentialism, do not appear in the work of the men poets we have been considering. Even Tiutchev—who depicts nature as mysterious and having a separate life from humanity—implies that a relationship is possible or necessary, that the basic harmony between humanity and nature may be apprehended, if only fleetingly, that humanity is part of nature, although that unity may only become clear at death ("Ne to, chto mnite vy, priroda" [Nature is not what you think, 1831–36], "Priroda—sfinks" [Nature is a sphinx, 1869], "I grob opushchen uzh v mogilu" [And the coffin already lowered into the grave, 1831–36], "Ot zhizni toi, chto bushevala zdes'—" [From this life, which raged here, 1871]). Interestingly, however, we do find a similar representation of nature in a poem by a

Others tried to avoid confronting male religious authority by separating God (male-gendered *Bog*) from fate (female-gendered *sud'ba*), attributing all their sufferings to the latter. Garelina, for example, writes in "Molisia obo mne" (Pray for me, 1870): [45]

> Молися обо мне, чтоб тяжкий крест терпенья
> Ниспосланный судьбой, я с кротостью несла;
>
> ⤳
>
> (Pray for me that I carry with humility the heavy cross of suffering
> Sent down by fate;)

Similarly, in Zhadovskaia's "Nikto ne vinovat" (No one is to blame, 1847), the speaker blames fate (rather than God) for her unhappiness. In several poems Rostopchina depicts fate as responsible for romantic disappointments and God as benevolently supporting all the speakers' desires and actions, including adultery. In *Dnevnik devushki* (1850), the speaker complains about the cruel fate that took her lover away:

> Судьба тебя умчала
> Далеко, может быть, навеки от меня!
> Жестокая!
>
> ⤳
>
> (Fate hurtled you away from me
> Far away, perhaps forever!
> Cruel!)
>
> (*Dnevnik devushki*, 241)

while in *Neizvestnyi roman*, "Pri svidan'i" (An unknown romance, At the rendezvous, 1857) the married speaker, who is about to meet her lover, says:

> Бог милостив!.. Меня он не забудет...
> Будь он за нас, я не боюсь людей!..
>
> ⤳
>
> (God is merciful!... He will not forget me...
> If he is for us, I will not be afraid of people!...)

Such a compartmentalization seems unconvincing to the contemporary reader. Nonetheless, I would suggest that these women poets' discomfort with a cosmology that cast them as Other also spurred them to find ways to transform that cosmology, adding a level of philosophical complexity and depth to their poetry absent from the men's.

The women of this generation faced a daunting array of male-defined

Romantic conventions that offered them no useful models for representing themselves as poets—or in relation to their creativity, their audience, or nature. Their refusal to be limited by androcentric images and their varied responses to them is a tribute to their courage, imagination, and originality. As we shall see, they were equally fearless and original in their reworkings of Romantic genres, themes, and myths.

3

Gender and Genre

The previous two chapters outlined the social conditions that the poets we have been considering faced as women, as well as their varying responses to male-defined literary conventions. In this chapter I would like to consider their distinctive use of genre and themes, which, as we shall see, are interrelated.

Recently some scholars have dismissed genre as arbitrary, if not meaningless: "Genre is any group of works selected on the basis of some shared feature" (Reichert, "More Than Kin," 57). Most, however, still consider it an essential literary concept: "There can be no meaning without genre" (E. O. Hirsch quoted in Gerhart, *Genre Choices, Gender Questions*, 16); "genres underlie, motivate and organize all literary discourse" (Curran, *Poetic Form and British Romanticism*, 5). Because literary genre is such an ambiguous and multifaceted concept—with a history extending back at least to Aristotle's *Poetics*—in any such discussion it is essential to define one's terms and approach.[1]

For our purposes I find most useful Alastair Fowler's functional description of genre as "a communication system for the use of writers in writing and readers and critics in reading and interpreting" (*Kinds of Literature*, 256). So, for example, if we know we are watching farce, we might laugh at something that we would not laugh at in a tragedy. Fowler sensibly points out that genres change, combine, and divide over time. The epic, for example, encompasses works as diverse as the *Iliad* and *Paradise Lost*. Rather, Fowler prefers to discuss "kinds" of literature—genres of a specific period, such as the romance, picaresque novel, revenge play, ode, or dystopia—further subdividing "kinds" into "subgenres" on the basis of their subject matter or motif. For example, within the eighteenth-century ode there are birthday odes and marriage odes;

within the twentieth-century novel, the factory novel, school novel, war novel, crime novel, and so on. For Fowler, then, genre and theme are interrelated.[2]

Fowler's concept of genre as a communication system has been extended in recent scholarship that analyzes the ideology implicit in various genres, along with its effect on writers and readers.[3] Some scholars claim that genres as "literary institutions" (Fredric Jameson quoted in Cranny-Francis, *Feminist Fiction*, 18) "encode [ideological discourses]" (Cranny-Francis, 18), that is, inscribe power relationships, "fram[ing] readers as well as texts"—indeed, that "genres are built on premises about gender" (Gerhart, *Genre Choices, Gender Questions*, 189–90) and about class and race. One thinks, for example, of the eighteenth-century neoclassical comedies such as Molière's *Le bourgeois gentilhomme* or Mozart's *The Magic Flute,* in which the lower-class "comic" lovers act as foils for the upper-class "serious" lovers. Or of the "comic" African American maid, who appeared in so many American film comedies of the 1930s and 1940s, or of the inevitably terrorized or murdered young white woman in slasher films.

But beyond communicating ideology, genres, according to literary critic and author Joanna Russ, are actually structured by assumptions about gender ("gender norms"), which can be seen more clearly when they are reversed. She asks us to imagine, for example, a story about two strong women battling for supremacy in the early West, or a young woman finding her womanhood by killing a bear, or a stupid but seductive heterosexual young man who represents "the essence of sex, the 'soul' of our corrupt culture, a dramatization of the split between the degrading necessities of the flesh and the transcendence of world-cleaving Will" ("What Can a Heroine Do?" 7). Russ concludes that a writer who does not accept the gender norms of a genre either will be reduced to silence or forced to reinvent the genre. But, she continues, writers who reinvent male-centered genres generally do not receive praise for their originality; rather, critics find such work "formless" and "inexperienced" in comparison to the "traditional" male-centered literary conventions and myths that have been "distilled, dramatized, stylized, and above all clarified" through centuries of use (11).[4]

In this critical context I propose, first, to define the most important Russian poetic genres of the 1820s to 1850s, along with their gender norms; next, to consider the different ways men and women poets used these genres; and finally, to examine the implications of such differences for the critical reception of women poets.[5] What were the most important Russian Romantic poetic genres? Scholars of both European and Russian literature have shown that throughout the period neoclassical genres remained central for Romantic poets, despite their challenges to neoclassical values. In Europe as early as 1674, Nicholas Boileau had codified neoclassical practice in his *Art poétique* by distinguishing the major genres—comedy, tragedy, and epic—from the minor ones—elegy, ode, sonnet, epigram, and ballad. In Russia, Lomonosov in his "Predislovie o pol'ze knig tserkovnykh v Rossiiskom iazyke" (Preface concerning the use of church books in the Russian language, 1757) modified Boileau's hierarchy by designating as high genres odes and epics, as middle genres tragedy, epistles, and elegies, and as low genres comedies, epigrams, and songs. It is true that beginning in the mid-eighteenth century writers began to defy these rules of "decorum"; previously disdained folk forms became prominent, as the ballad revival in Germany and England and Macpherson's Ossian poems extended the concept of epic to folk material. Poets began to mix genres, as can be seen in the titles of Wordsworth's "lyrical ballads" (1798) or Lamartine's *Méditations poétiques* (1820). Victor Hugo in his *Préface de Cromwell* (1827) even rejected the neoclassical injunction against mixing the comic and the tragic, the grotesque and the beautiful. Nonetheless, the genres named by Boileau and Lomonosov remained vital and very prestigious, even when combined with folk elements or with one another. For example, one recent study considers the "principle fixed forms and genres" of British Romanticism to be the sonnet, the hymn, the ode, the pastoral, the romance, and the epic, all, except the romance and the sonnet, classical genres.

The persistence of classical genres is not surprising. Romantic poets, mostly upper-class men, continued to receive classical educations that included the Greek and Latin canons on which neoclassical genres were based.[6] So, for example, Byron wrote not only Romantic fragments, songs, and ballads, but also neoclassical odes, mock epics, and epistles. Shelley wrote odes, elegies, and epithalamia, as well as ballads and fragments.

Neither classicism nor the medieval popular forms that modified it, however, were indigenous to Russia. Nonetheless, in the late eighteenth and early nineteenth century Russian writers enthusiastically and almost simultaneously imported both trends from Europe, as the poet and critic Petr Viazemsky (1792–1878) ironically recounts: "We never had

Middle Ages or knights or Gothic buildings, with their gloom and peculiar impressions; the Greeks and Romans, sad to say, have not weighed
upon us. . . . But the Romantic Movement, of course, has attracted us
too. . . . Immediately there were formed among us two armies, two
camps: classicists and romanticists have come into inky combat."[7]

Like their European counterparts, classically educated Russian men poets also combined neoclassical and folk genres. Zhukovsky wrote odes,
elegies, and idylls, as well as translating and adapting thirty-nine German and English ballads. Pushkin's *Ruslan i Liudmila* combined a mock
epic with folk motifs. We can surmise the importance of classical and folk
genres—and of genre itself—from Russian Romantic poets' frequent
use of generic titles for poems. Pushkin, for example, subtitled four
works published during his lifetime "Poemy" (verse epics), and titled
four poems "Elegiia" (elegy), one "Ballada" (ballad), ten "Romans" (romance), and several "Pesnia" (song) and "Epigramma."[8] Iazykov, Lermontov, Del'vig, Fet, Baratynsky, Maikov, Khomiakov, and Guber also
gave many poems generic titles such as "Elegiia," "Sonet," "Duma,"
"Oda," "Idiliia," "Pesnia," or "Russkaia pesnia."

For the period of 1820 to 1850, three literary genres, or "kinds," to use
Fowler's terminology, stand out as the most characteristic and significant:
the epic, with its offspring the Romantic *poema* and ballad; the elegy;
and the lyric.[9]

Epic, *Poema, Ballada*

The epic was the most prestigious of all neoclassical kinds of literature;
many critics also consider it the source of both the *poema* (verse epic)
and the *ballada* (ballad).[10] For these reasons the gender norms of the
epic, which applied to both authors and characters, exerted particular
influence.

Various definitions of the epic describe it as a male-gendered genre,
written by men, about men, and for men. One scholar writes that the epic
gives voice to "the commonly shared values and aspirations of a large
group of men in a certain place and age. . . . [T]he action concerns some
crucial episode in the history of a nation or other homogenous group"
(Wilkie, *Romantic Poets and Epic Tradition,* 7–9). Ezra Pound called it "the
speech of a nation through the mouth of one man" (quoted in S. Friedman, "Gender and Genre Anxiety," 204). Mikhail Kheraskov (1733–
1807), who wrote the first Russian *poema Rossiada* (The Russiad, 1779),

similarly described the genre as containing "some important memorable, famous event . . . or . . . an event [that] . . . serves the whole nation's glory" (quoted in Terras, *Handbook of Russian Literature*, 344). The scholar Susan Friedman argues that because epic norms, like norms of masculinity, are "public, objective, universal, heroic," women find it particularly difficult to write epics: "For male poets, writing within the epic tradition has been an extension of a culturally granted masculine authority to generate philosophical, universal, cosmic, and heroic discourse. For women, no such cultural authority has existed. . . . Their very marginality as women writing has made it impossible to narrate 'the tale of the tribe'" ("Gender and Genre Anxiety," 205). The few women who have attempted epics, she demonstrates, do so with "anxiety of poetic genre" (203).[11] In the nineteenth century such anxiety would have been increased by men writers' tendency to cast themselves as epic heroes—something women could not do because of the gender norms governing characters in epics.[12]

The protagonist, the epic hero, has virtually always been male. One critic describes these heroes as "champions of man's ambitions" who seek to "win as far as possible a self-sufficient manhood" (S. Friedman, "Gender and Genre Anxiety," quoting C. M. Bowra, 204). Another describes the archetypal epic hero as "not merely a representative man but a national leader. . . . He epitomizes his culture as warrior, as imperialist, and as explorer of the unknown" (Curran, *Poetic Form*, 173). A third critic writes, "No poem can be an epic unless it presents a portrait, either composite or individual, express or implied, of the perfect man" (Wilkie, *Romantic Poets*, 20). The same critic mentions women characters only as part of what he calls the Dido-and-Aeneas convention, which "sees woman as an obstacle to duty" (13). This is a device, he adds complacently, "that appears with varying emphases in all the great literary epics from Virgil on [and] is part of the pattern of heroic renunciation recognized by any culture whose values have risen above purely martial ones. . . . One of the most interesting things about the Romantic epics is their obsession with the Dido-and-Aeneas convention" (22). Friedman observes, "In the epic women have mainly existed at the symbolic peripheries as static rewards or temptations, as allies or antagonists, as inspirations or nemeses" ("Gender and Genre Anxiety," 205).[13]

In England the national epic remained a vital genre throughout the Romantic period. In Russia, however, the *poema* evolved through three more or less successive stages: first, the *klassicheskaia poema* or *geroicheskaia epopeia* (classical or heroic verse epic)—for example, Kheraskov's

Rossiada—along with its mock-epic parodies, for example, Vasilii Maikov's *Elisei ili razdrazhennyi Vakkh* (Elisei or Bacchus Furioso, 1771), and Pushkin's *Ruslan i Liudmila* (1817–20). Next appeared *poemy* inspired by the Decembrist movement that culminated in the abortive uprising of 1825; these *poemy*, which, like the classical kind, focused on national destiny, also served as covert calls to overthrow Russian autocracy—for example, Kondraty Ryleev's *Voinarovsky* (1823–25) and *Nalivaiko* (1823–25). Finally, the Romantic *poema*, the kind that concerns us here, was introduced by Pushkin—for example, *Bakhchisaraiskii fontan* (The fountain of Bakhchisarai, 1822) and *Tsygany* (The gypsies, 1824). Pushkin's first Romantic *poemy* showed the strong influence of Byron's *Eastern Tales* ("The Giaour" [1813], "The Bride of Abydos" [1813], "The Corsair" [1814]), which, as the Soviet scholar V. A. Zhirmunsky has shown, included elements of the ballad and the lyric, as well as the epic. The Romantic *poema*, however, despite significant generic differences from the classical epic—and these include a rejection of "public, objective, universal and heroic" norms—nonetheless inherited from the epic several of its central characteristics.[14]

First, the Romantic *poema* continued the epic's focus on national destiny, but with a very different ideology. Poets replaced the epic's glorification of empire building or the founding of a nation with an implied approval of revolutionary politics. Byron's literary influence on the *poema* cannot be separated from his political influence as a well-known supporter of revolutionary causes. Contemporary readers thus understood in a broader political context one of the central conventions of the Romantic *poema*—the hero's seemingly personal quest for freedom expressed in his rebellion against authority. Another source for the revolutionary ideology of the Romantic *poema* may have been the Decembrist *poema*. In any case, Pushkin's open return to the theme of national destiny in his last *poema*, *Mednyi vsadnik* (*The Bronze Horseman*, 1833), suggests that this theme was always potentially present in the genre.

Second, like the epic, the Romantic *poema* remained a very prestigious form. V. A. Zhirmunsky maintains that the new genre of Romantic *poema* had the same significance that the heroic epic did for the neoclassical eighteenth century. One scholar writes that in Pushkin's time, "It became almost obligatory for a poet of the new tendency [Romanticism] to write a Romantic *poema*. It was, in its way, the final exam of poetic maturity."[15]

Finally, the Romantic *poema* inherited from the epic its gender norms, both for authors and for characters. Russian women poets appear to have experienced as much "genre anxiety" in relation to the Romantic *poema* as did their Western counterparts in relation to the epic. While four out of the seven canonical men poets we have been considering (Pushkin, Baratynsky, Lermontov, Iazykov) and four of the noncanonical ones (Maikov, Khomiakov, Guber, Miller) wrote at least one work that they titled or referred to as *poema*, not one of the fourteen women did so.[16] At a time when writing a *poema* was considered essential to be taken seriously as a poet, the gender norms of the genre made it almost impossible for women write one.

Some clarifications are necessary. V. M. Zhirmunsky notes that the term *romanticheskaia poema* was not used consistently by poets and that only at the end of the 1820s did the term begin to be used in its present-day meaning. Perhaps for this reason, Zhirmunsky, in his study of Byron's influence on Pushkin and Pushkin's imitators, treats the subtitle *poema* as interchangeable with *povest'* (tale), *turetskaia povest'* (Turkish tale), *finliandskaia povest'* (Finnish tale), and so on. He considers *Kavkazskii plennik*—which Pushkin subtitled *povest'*, corresponding to Byron's subtitle of "a tale" for "The Corsair"—to be the first *romanticheskaia poema* (*Bairon i Pushkin*, 238–39, 28). Nonetheless, it does seem significant that none of these women poets used the term *poema* as a generic subtitle, whereas several of the men did. Even Pushkin, whose *Kavkazskii plennik: povest'* introduced the genre of Byron's *Eastern Tales* to Russia, apparently liked the prestige of the term *poema*. In 1827, he referred to selections from *Bakhchisaraiskii fontan*—certainly as much an Eastern tale as *Kavkazskii plennik*—as "Otryvki iz poemy, *Bakhchisaraiskii fontan*" (Excerpts from the *poema* The fountain at Bakhchisaray). And although Pushkin originally published chapter 1 of *Evgenii Onegin* in 1825 with the generic subtitle *roman v stikhakh* (novel in verse), in 1824 and 1826 parts of chapter 2 appeared as "Otryvki iz *Evgeniia Onegina*: Poema" before Pushkin changed it back to *roman v stikhakh* in 1827. Excerpts from *Tsygany* also appeared with the generic subtitle *poema* in 1826, although as *stikhotvorenie* in 1827 and as part of *Poemy i povesti Aleksandra Pushkina* in 1835.[17]

Baratynsky used the generic subtitle *poema* for *Tsena iz poemy Vera i neverie* (1835) (Scene from the *poema* Faith and lack of faith), *Nalozhnitsa* (The concubine, 1831), and *Piry: Opisatel'naia poema* (Feasts: A descriptive *poema*, 1820), although the last is not a *poema* in the sense discussed earlier. It would appear that for Baratynsky such generic subtitles as *povest' v stikhakh* (verse tale) were matters of style rather than declarations of genre—such subtitles did not keep him from thinking of these works as *poemy*. For example, Baratynsky wrote to N. V. Putiate of *Bal* (The ball, 1828), which he published as *povest' v stikhakh*, that he was writing "novuiu poemu" (a new *poema*). In addition, extracts from *Bal* appeared in *Moskovskii telegraf* under the title "Otryvok iz poemy," and in *Severnye Tsvety* under the title "Otryvok iz poemy *Bal'nyi vecher*" (Excerpt from the *poema* Evening of the ball). Extracts from *Eda* (1826), subtitled *finliandskaia povest'*, appeared in *Mnemosiia* in 1825 under the title "Otryvki iz poemy: *Eda*" (Excerpts from the *poema* Eda).[18]

   I should add that it is important to distinguish between the way poets themselves titled or referred to their works (my focus here) and the way critics or scholars later labeled them. For example, the *Lermontovskaia entsiklopediia* states that Lermontov wrote thirty *poemy* (Manuilov, 438), while B. M. Eikhenbaum in the 1948 edition of Lermontov's *Polnoe sobranie sochinenii* describes twenty-one of Lermontov's works as *poemy* and *iunosheskie poemy*. In fact, according to Eikhenbaum's excellent notes for that same edition, Lermontov himself only used the term *poema* for five works. Similarly, Karolina Pavlova's *Dvoinaia zhizn'*, which is half prose, half poetry, was referred to as a *poema* during her lifetime and appeared in a section headed *poemy* in the 1964 *Polnoe sobranie stikhotvorenii* (Complete poetic works). Pavlova herself, however, subtitled the work *ocherk* (sketch).[19] Fowler writes that in the nineteenth century in particular, generic subtitles constituted an important literary convention, which authors "used rather exquisitely or disingenuously to suggest unobvious generic ingredients" (*Kinds of Literature*, 98). The generic subtitle that an author chooses, along with that author's other references to the genre of the work, therefore, must be considered a significant part of the work.

Among the women poets we are considering, only Aleksandra Fuks wrote anything resembling *romanticheskie poemy*, and those, not surprisingly, differ significantly from Zhirmunsky's prototype. Within the genre as Zhirmunsky discusses it—works variously subtitled *poema*, *povest'*, *turetskaia povest'*, and so on—gender norms for women characters were as circumscribed as in the epic. Zhirmunsky, hardly a feminist critic, describes the narrowness of those norms, basing his conclusions on 120 Romantic *poemy* and eighty "excerpts from *poemy*," a kind in itself, that appeared in Russia between 1821 and 1842. The *romanticheskaia poema*, according to Zhirmunsky, invariably features a male, disillusioned (*razocharovannyi*), and complicated protagonist and his female love object, the *krasavitsa geroinia* (heroine-beauty), whose essential trait, as her name implies, is her appearance. Like her Byronic prototype, she is either a dark-eyed, dark-haired, "passionate harem beauty"—a *vostochnaia zhenshchina* (Eastern woman)—or a blue-eyed, golden-curled, "ideally chaste Christian"—a *severianka* (Northern woman). In either case, Zhirmunsky notes, unlike the hero, her "psychological life is never described, even in those cases when the story's tragic outcome is motivated by [her] action" (304–7).

Monika Greenleaf further analyzes the Eastern woman in the Romantic *poema* as an example of the "literary orientalism" that Pushkin inherited from Byron and Enlightenment Europe. Literary orientalism contrasted the supposedly "rational, active, dynamically male" West to an "irrational, passive, decadent" East, a binary opposition similar to the more general male and female dichotomy (*Pushkin and Romantic Fashion*, 104). Writers depicted all Eastern people as the Other, and Eastern women—"oriental" and female—as doubly so. Greenleaf notes that in the Romantic *poema* "it appears to be of utmost importance that the object of love be a non-native speaker of the (male) erotic discourse" (113). This principle, she concludes, even extends to Pushkin's Tatiana, who writes her love letter to Onegin in French, rather than in Russian (254).[20]

But if these women poets generally did not write *romanticheskie poemy,* several told women's stories in narrative poems and fragments or wrote *povesti v stikhakh* (verse tales).[21] In 1828 Baratynsky and Pushkin first used the term when they jointly published Baratynsky's *Bal* and Pushkin's *Graf Nulin* under the title "Dve povesti v stikhakh." Russian literary historians subsequently have distinguished this genre from the *romanticheskaia poema* as more realistic, contemporary, and ironic. Women poets may have found the *povest' v stikhakh* less intimidating and more hospitable to their stories and experiences because of its lack of classical resonances—for example, Pushkin's allusions to Ovid in his *romanticheskaia povest' Tsygany.* Furthermore, in contrast to the obligatory "exotic" settings of the *romanticheskaia poema,* the *povest' v stikhakh* was generally set in Russia, an advantage to women poets, who had fewer opportunities to travel.[22]

I suggest that several of these women poets, despite genre anxiety in relation to the *poema* and even the *povest' v stikhakh,* attempted to redesign these male-centered genres to accommodate women's stories, that is, stories with women protagonists. In the process they rejected the "distilled" and "clarified" male-centered myths and conventions of the *poema,* producing works that ranged from the "formless," "inexperienced," and ambivalent, to works of great originality and freshness. Even the formless and inexperienced works, however, are worth considering because of what they tell us about the aesthetic problems women faced.[23]

Aleksandra Fuks, in her two *povesti v stikhakh, Osnovanie goroda Kazani* (The founding of the city of Kazan', 1837) and *Kniazhna Khabiba* (Princess Khabiba, 1841), struggled with the gender norms of the *romanticheskaia poema*. Both works have women-centered plots and strong women protagonists whose motives are clearly described. Princess Khabiba rebels against the femininity and domesticity her clothes-conscious mother would force on her, eventually disguising herself as a man to run away to her lover. Fatima, the wise and brave heroine of *Osnovanie goroda Kazani*, urges the tsar to move the city because its distance from the river creates a hardship for the women who have to carry the water. Like Joan of Arc, she refuses to renounce her convictions, even when threatened with death, declaring her willingness to die for her people (although, unlike Joan of Arc, in the end she marries the tsar's son, who is in love with her). In contrast to the usual disposable, generally abandoned or murdered heroines we find in men's works, both of Fuks's heroines completely dominate the emotions of their men. This female power fantasy may have appealed to Fuks's women readers as much as the "love them and leave them" fantasy apparently did to men readers. However, in these works Fuks continues to privilege the male-centered literary conventions of the genre. Khabiba, an "Eastern" woman in Greenleaf's terms, is punished for assuming male privileges of dress and sexual choice. Fatima, a virtuous "Northern"-type woman, is domesticated by marrying the khan's son.[24] Thanks to Fuks's detailed knowledge of Tatar culture and history, the result of her ethnographic research, she is able to create the required "exotic" settings. She depicts much less convincingly, however, the conversations between men characters, battles, and army life scenes that she seems to feel obliged to include. These *povesti v stikhakh* remain awkward and unbalanced amalgams of male- and female-based conventions.

Perhaps the clearest example of genre anxiety in relation to the *povest' v stikhakh* is Pavlova's *Kadril'* (*Quadrille*), a narrative poem consisting of a frame and four stories told by women. It was first published in full in 1858, although sections of it appeared in 1844 and 1851. Despite her considerable poetic powers and great artistic sophistication, Pavlova was unable to define for her readers or even apparently for herself the genre of this work. An excerpt appeared in 1844 in the journal *Moskvitianin* under the title "Otryvok iz romana" (Excerpt of a novel), a possible allusion to Pushkin's novel in verse, although Pavlova's work consists of four stories. In 1851 another section, "Rasskaz Lizy," appeared in the literary collection (*al'manakh*) *Raut*, under a confusing note that described it successively as *otryvok, povest' v stikhakh, poema,* and *rasskaz*: "This excerpt (*otryvok*) from a tale in verse (*povest' v stikhakh*) is not an excerpt, but an entire *poema* written in trochaic pentameter, something one rarely meets among us, especially in an entire piece. In this tale (*povest'*), four ladies meeting at a masquerade recount to one another some events from their lives. Each story (*rasskaz*) is written in a different meter."[25] Although the publisher of *Raut,* N. V. Sushkov, signed the note, one suspects that it reflects Pavlova's own indecision. In 1859 *Kadril'* appeared in full in the journal *Russkii vestnik* without any generic subtitle.

Pavlova further expresses nervousness about her undertaking in her invocation to the dead Pushkin, whom she describes as the "specter of the *bogatyr'* (epic hero) of singers" (*prizrak pevtsa-bogatyria*). She depicts Pushkin as a kind of antimuse who, instead of helping her, sternly condemns her for daring to enter with her "childish verse" the "cherished world" of his Tatiana, that is, for daring to compete with his poetic skill and to dispute his depiction of women.

> Зачем, качая головою,
> Так строго на меня смотря,
> Зачем стоишь передо мною
> Призрак Певца-богатыря?
> Ужели дум моих обманы
> Увлечь дерзнут мой детский стих
> В заветный мир твоей Татьяны?

⚜

> (Why, shaking your head,
> Looking at me so sternly,
> Why do you stand before me,
> Specter of the *bogatyr'* of singers?
> Can it be that my thoughts' deceptions
> Dare entice my childish verse
> Into the cherished world of your Tatiana?)[26]

Pavlova's genre anxiety in *Kadril'* may have been heightened further by her polemics with Evgenii Baratynsky, whom she considered her mentor. In 1842 she had written to him in "E. A. Baratynskomu" (To E. A. Baratynsky)

Меня вы назвали поэтом,
[.   .   .   .   .]
И я [. . .]
Тогда поверила в себя.

⸎

(You called me a poet
[.   .   .   .   .]
And I [. . .]
Then believed in myself.)

Pavlova dedicated *Kadril'* to Baratynsky, who died in 1844, the year the first excerpt from the work appeared in print. It seems likely that Pavlova intended it to be a response to Baratynsky's *povest' v stikhakh,* *Bal,* which rather dramatically recounts the suicide of the femme fatale Nina after she meets her lover and his new love at a ball. *Kadril'*, set just before a ball, tells of more realistic and sympathetic women who suffer at the hands of unsympathetic men. I shall discuss *Kadril'* at greater length in chapter 6.

In contrast to Pavlova, Khvoshchinskaia does not seem to have suffered from generic subtitle anxiety—she clearly subtitled her seven-chapter narrative poem, *Derevenskii sluchai* (A country incident, 1853), "povest' v stikhakh." But this work, too, represents an uncomfortable compromise between androcentric form and gynocentric content, in this case the result of Khvoshchinskaia's ambivalence about telling women's stories. Supposedly, the protagonist is Nikolai, a young Saint Petersburg civil servant. However, the story often threatens to veer off toward his far more interesting sister, Liza. Another site of tension is Khvoshchinskaia's unexplained female-voiced digressions, which, in contrast to Pushkin's in *Evgenii Onegin,* speculate about parents' unconscious cruelty to children or directly address women readers on the subject of their experiences in pensions. Khvoshchinskaia is far more successful in her shorter, untitled narrative poem in which a woman tells a stranger about the forced marriage of a relative that took place in the 1730s ("'Vy ulybaetes'? . . . Razdum'e ne meshaet'" [You are smiling? . . . My pensiveness doesn't prevent me, 1852]). This work (discussed in chapter 5), while more fragmentary, powerfully focuses on a woman's story.[27]

Elisaveta Shakhova also chose the term *povesti v stikhakh* for three works that focus more directly on women than does Khvoshchinskaia's *Derevenskii sluchai.* Shakhova solved the problem of how to tell women's stories in a genre that defined women as Other by combining the *povest' v stikhakh* with a second genre in which women's stories could be told—

the Gothic tale. The result, however, is an awkward combination of stylistic effects, plot, and characters seemingly from Pushkin, Lermontov, and Ann Radcliffe. Lidiia, in *Perst Bozhii* (The finger of God), dies on her wedding day as the result of a family curse. Elena in *Strashnyi krasavets* (The frightening handsome man) is pursued by a diabolical Greek. In *Izgnannik* (The exile), a story with incestuous overtones, Ida falls in love with her sister's fiancé. She sacrifices herself for him by marrying his evil old miserly uncle, who would otherwise forbid the match. Although Shakhova's experiments were not successful—and she was not nearly as good a poet as Pavlova and Khvoshchinskaia—she recognized the importance of combining the androcentric *povest' v stikhakh* with a gynocentric genre.[28]

Iuliia Zhadovskaia, while working on a much smaller scale than either Pavlova or Khvoshchinskaia, wrote two successful women-centered narrative poems. Like Shakhova, Zhadovskaia combined her *povest' v stikhakh* with other narrative genres more open to women's stories: the green world fantasy—which Annis Pratt (*Archetypal Patterns in Women's Fiction*) describes as an archetype in narratives of women's development—and also the *svetskaia povest'* (society tale). In the green-world fantasy the female protagonist lives in an ideal natural world until she becomes "marriageable," at which point she is forced into the constraints of society. This archetype appears in Zhadovskaia's "Otryvki iz neokonchennogo rasskaza" (Excerpts from an unfinished story, 1859). Nadezhda, the protagonist, enjoys an idyllic life in the country, reading good books with her adoring widowed mother, listening to her nanny's fairy tales, taking long walks alone at night, and swimming in the moonlight. This idyll is shattered when a neighbor insists on taking Nadezhda to a ball. On the way, the neighbor berates Nadezhda for her reluctance to go into society and makes fun of her pensiveness. The excerpt breaks off here.[29]

The second work, "Poseshchenie" (The visit, 1849), has no generic subtitle but resembles the *povest' v stikhakh* in its contemporary Russian setting and ironic narration. Zhadovskaia tells of a young woman who is not at home to receive a visit from the man she loves. He, upon learning she is to be married, leaves town before he can receive her note begging him to save her from the marriage being forced on her by her family. Here, as Pavlova would in *Kadril'*, Zhadovskaia makes use of the *svetskaia povest'*, or society tale, a prose genre of the 1830s and 1840s in which upper-class writers often called attention to women's disadvantaged position in society. While, unlike the *svetskaia povest'*, Zhadovskaia's story takes place in the country, like the *svetskaia povest'* it depicts the world as hostile to true feelings, presents marriage as a calculated economic transaction, revolves around an unhappy love triangle, and protests "woman's lot."[30]

The most successful recasting of the *povest' v stikhakh* to accommodate women's stories is Mordovtseva's *Staraia skazka* (An old fairy tale, see appendix), a thinly-veiled autobiographical work that bears comparison to Wordsworth's "personal epic," *The Prelude*. Judging from internal biographical evidence, *Staraia skazka* probably dates from the late 1840s or early 1850s. Mordovtseva probably wrote it around 1848, when she left her first husband, or shortly thereafter. Nina, the protagonist, is married off by her family to a much older man, who abuses her. He takes Nina from the country to Saint Petersburg, where she has a one-sided romance with a younger man. When her husband also begins to abuse their five children, Nina escapes with them back to the country. The works ends with Nina's journal, which is composed of philosophical poems—a device that anticipates Pasternak's *Dr. Zhivago*. *Staraia skazka*, despite the genre anxiety indicated in its self-deprecating or ironic title (An old fairy tale), is a very powerful work, particularly in its subtle descriptions of Nina's intellectual development and moods. This work deserves further study.[31]

Ballada

The ballad has been described as a narrative poem of twenty to eighty lines, characterized by compressed, objective narration, with an emphasis on action rather than character. Both motivation and denouement are often described enigmatically. Other characteristics include an abrupt opening question, violent plots with supernatural elements, revelation through dialogue, lack of moralizing, and fragmentariness. Although the ballad—an oral folk genre of medieval origin—would not seem to be an obvious descendent of the classical epic, during the late eighteenth and the nineteenth century it was accepted as such because of the polemics surrounding the European ballad revival.[32]

In the early eighteenth century English and German collectors began to publish ballads supposedly transcribed from folk sources, but, in fact, significantly reworked: Thomas Percy's *Reliques of Ancient English Poetry* (1765); Scott's *Minstrelsy of the Scottish Border* (1802); collections by J. G. Herder, and others.[33] By the middle of the eighteenth century these ballads were being compared to the works of Homer as part of the on-going "Homeric question," the debate over whether Homer was one or many authors. European poets who wrote literary imitations of the genre represented themselves as Homeric bards (as discussed in chapter 2). As recently as 1978 a Russian scholar described the ballad as a "lyrico-epic genre" (Iezuitova, "Ballada v epokhu romantizma," 138).

European literary ballads differed significantly from their folk models. From the beginning ballad collectors and imitators mixed the originally stark ballad genre with the richer, metrical romance—stories of knights and medieval pageantry, told in more flexible octosyllabic couplets. In England, for example, writes Albert Friedman, poets not only intermingled "bardism, primitive poetry, minstrelsy and balladry" (*Ballad Revival*, 175), but also added psychological descriptions, a variety of meters, a greater emphasis on the narrator, and many elements from urban folk forms, such as broadsides and street calls (257, 260).

If European literary ballads differed appreciably from their folk models, Russian literary ballads differed from them even further. At the end of the eighteenth century no collections of Russian folk ballads existed, nor did even the concept of such a genre. European models, therefore, provided Russian writers with their knowledge of both folk ballads and literary imitations of them.[34]

Vasilii Zhukovsky popularized the European literary ballad in Russia by translating or writing thirty-nine ballads based on European models. His ballads both reflected and established gender norms for writers and characters. Like other ballad writers, Zhukovsky represented himself as a bard, a tribal poet-singer, and a declaimer of verses about heroes and their deeds—for example, in "Pesn' barda nad grobom slavian- pobeditelei" (Song of the bard at the grave of the Slavic victors, 1806) and "Pevets vo stane russkikh voinov" (The singer in the camp of Russian warriors, 1812)—a literary stance not possible for women, as we have seen in chapter 2. As for gender norms for characters, one of Zhukovsky's most pervasive themes is men's violence against women; many of his ballads depict men as representatives of evil or death who victimize young women. In "Liudmila" (1808), for example, the heroine's beloved, who comes for her at midnight, turns out to be a corpse. After their ride together Liudmila dies as well. The heroine of "Adel'stan" (1813) marries a knight who nearly succeeds in sacrificing their child to evil forces. Other such examples can be found in "Eolova arfa" (The Aeolian harp, 1814) and "Dvenadtsat' spiashchikh dev" (The twelve sleeping maidens, 1810). Zhukovsky's one depiction of an old woman ("Ballada, v kotoroi opisyvaetsia, kak odna starushka ekhala na chernom kone vdvoem, i kto sidel vperedi," 1814)—a translation of Robert Southey's "Old Woman of Berkeley: A Ballad: Shewing how an old woman rode double and who rode before her" (1799)—tells of an evil witch whom the devil drags down to hell. The next generation of men poets in their ballad/romances not only, like Zhukovsky, depicted women as victims of male violence but also as gratuitously false and evil. Neither image was very useful for those women poets who wished to tell women's stories.[35]

Nonetheless, Russian women poets seem to have experienced somewhat less genre anxiety in relation to the ballad than to the *poema*, perhaps because they had greater access to the sources of the ballad. While few of these women writers knew Greek and Latin, many of them knew German, French, and even English, which allowed them to read European folk and literary ballads in the original.[36] In any case, Russian women poets seem to have felt freer to experiment with the genre, in order to make it fit their needs.

Interestingly, it was a woman, Anna Turchaninova, who wrote the first ballads published in Russia, "Pesenka ob Leonarde i Blondine" (see appendix) and "Villiam i Margarita" (both 1799–1800). "Leonard i Blondina," an original ballad set in Spain, tells of a woman whose beloved dies in the bullring. While the story seems conventional enough, we note that Blondina serves neither as the primary victim of the story nor as the capricious cause of the hero's death. It is Leonard's father who demands that Leonard fight the bull to prove his manhood to Blondina. When Blondina protests that she does not want her fiancé to risk his life in such a demonstration, Leonard's father tells her she is not fit to be the mother of his future grandsons. Leonard fights the bull, which fatally gores him and Blondina, who runs to his aid. The lovers are reunited as ghosts. The ballad could be seen as a comment on the cult of machismo in Spain and elsewhere.

The second ballad, "Villiam i Margarita," is a Russian translation of the German translation of an English reworking of two ballads from Percy's *Reliques*. It tells of a man who sees the ghost of the woman he has betrayed and the next day dies on her grave. This theme of a woman taking postmortem revenge on a faithless lover also appears in Lisitsyna's "Byl'" (True story, 1829), her "Romans" ("Sir Artur byl khrabroi voin" [Sir Arthur was a brave warrior], 1829), and Rostopchina's "Revnost' za grobom" (Jealousy beyond the grave, 1852). This recurring theme may reflect the anger and powerlessness upper-class women felt in the face of such betrayals.[37]

Five of the women poets we have been considering wrote ballads or poems with strong balladic elements. Some of these follow male norms in depicting faithless, evil, or victimized women. For example, in Garelina's "Za reshetkoiu v temnitse" (Behind the grille in the dungeon, 1870), a prisoner sees in a prophetic dream his beloved being unfaithful to him. In Khvoshchinskaia's "Blednaia deva: Videnie: Ballada" (The pale maiden: A vision: A ballad, f. 541, no.1, ed. kh. 3, 33, 1842, RGALI), a knight meets a *belle dame sans merci.* Other ballads by women, like those by men, narrate men's stories, for example, Pavlova's "Ballada," (1841). Several, however, tell very different stories. Mordovtseva follows Turchaninova in questioning the military ethic. Her "Ballada" (1870) tells of a young man who leaves his fiancée to go to war, where he is killed. The fiancée is left with only a medal and some poems. Many of Pavlova's ballads tell even less conventional stories. Her "Doch' zhida" (The Jew's daughter, 1840), for example, depicts a recently captured woman in a harem about to murder the emir with a knife she has hidden. Byron's Gulnare in "The Corsair" also kills the sultan who has held her captive, but only after many years, when she has met another man (Conrad) whom she prefers. Pavlova's captive also contrasts with another harem captive, Pushkin's Mariia in *Bakhchisaraiskii fontan* (The fountain at Bakhchisarai, 1822). Although, like Mariia, Pavlova's heroine remains pure, unlike Mariia, whom the khan's jealous favorite murders, Pavlova's heroine is not victimized by another woman. In "Starukha" (The old woman, 1840) Pavlova presents an old woman who, in contrast to Zhukovsky's repulsive *starushka,* captivates a beautiful young man through her ability to tell him stories, that is, her power as an artist. In "Ogon'" (Fire, 1841) a male, rather than a female, succumbs to the temptation of an evil serpent—here in the guise of a fire—destroying an Eden-like idyll.

Garelina also presents an unusual ballad subject: a woman in an unhappy marriage. In "Mama! Chto ty vse vzdykhaesh'?" (Mama, why are you always sighing? 1870) a woman is anxiously asked by her child why she is sighing over a man's portrait. The woman comforts and asks the child to pray for her. Shakhova appears to comment on men's and women's ideas of altruism in "Dva sna, Ballada" (Two Dreams, a Ballad, 1849). A husband says he would let his children drown to save his wife. She says she would sacrifice herself and their children for her husband.[38]

As with *povesti v stikhakh*, women poets used the ballad to tell very different stories from men.

The Elegy

In Russia the elegy may be considered a central—or even the central—Romantic poetic genre. At the dawn of Romanticism, the writer and historian Nikolai Karamzin wrote, "The first poetry was elegiac" ("Pervaia Poeziia byla Elegicheskaia"), referring to the genre's combination of natural surroundings and laments over the loss of love (Grigor'ian, "'Ul'traromanticheskii rod poezii,'" 95, capitalization is Karamzin's). The Russian poet and critic Vil'gel'm Kiukhel'beker (1797–1846) identified the elegy with Romanticism in "O napravelenii nashei poezii, osobenno liricheskoi, v poslednee desiatiletie" (On the direction of our poetry, especially the lyric, in the last decades, 1824), an article that criticized Russian poets for slavishly following European models and writing poems full of clichés (Grigor'ian, "'Ul'traromanticheskii rod poezii,'" 108). Belinsky described the elegy as "ul'traromanticheskii rod poezii" (the ultraromantic "kind" of poetry) (97).

Elegy, which comes from the Greek word for *lament,* confusingly describes two kinds of poem. The first, a poem of mourning and consolation, is based on the classical pastoral elegy expressing "ceremonial mourning for an exemplary figure." This tradition extends from Theocritus and Bion, through Tasso, Ronsard, Spenser, Milton, and Shelley, and continues in England and America into the twentieth century. It also continues as elegiac verses or "poems in the elegiac mode," dealing with loss, grieving, and consolation, for example, Gray's "Elegy Written in a Country Churchyard" (1751), which was very influential in Russia. The second "kind" of elegy, based on the Latin love elegy, is a "meditation on love or death."[39] This tradition, which Boris Tomashevsky traces to Pushkin through Ovid, Propertius, Catullus, Horace, and Parny, also includes Boileau, Chenier, and Schiller.[40] In the interests of clarity and coherence, I shall focus on those elegies and elegiac poems of both kinds that treat loss—whether of love, happiness, or a beloved person—and consolation.

Like the ballad, both kinds of elegy were imported to Russia in the late eighteenth century. Early examples include poems by Aleksandr Sumarokov (1718–77), Aleksei Rzhevsky (1737–1804), and Mikhail Murav'ev (1757–1807). It was Zhukovsky, however, who popularized the elegy, as he had the ballad, with his translation of a European model:

Gray's "Elegy Written in a Country Churchyard" ("Sel'skoe kladbishche: Elegiia," 1802).

As with the *poema*, the implied gender norms of the elegy led women poets to write them differently from men. Boris Tomashevsky observes that the elegist made himself the hero of poems that described his feelings of unrequited love, jealousy, grieving, sadness, and loneliness and his thoughts about the end of youth or the approach of an untimely death. The poet, Tomashevsky continues, by his use of the pathetic fallacy, made nature a character that sympathizes with those feelings (*Pushkin*, 1: 120). That is, a male poet/protagonist grieves his lost love, youth, or friend in the midst of a female-gendered nature. Since women poets did not always feel comfortable with a female-gendered nature (see chapter 2), we would expect their elegies to tell different stories.

We can infer other gender norms of the elegy from the work of the twentieth-century American scholar Peter Sacks, whose influential study of the English elegy may be applied to many nineteenth-century Russian elegies.[41] Sacks's discussion of the elegy is particularly male-centered because he relies on the theories of Freud and Lacan, which often conflate the male with the human. For Sacks the elegy concerns the "renunciatory experience of loss and the acceptance, not just of a substitute but of the very means and practice of substitution" (*English Elegy*, 8). Sacks identifies the "means and practice of substitution" with the capacity for symbolic behavior, and more specifically with the Oedipus complex, thereby implicitly excluding women from art:

> There is a significant similarity between the process of mourning and the oedipal resolution. . . . In the elegy, the poet's preceding relation with the deceased (often assimilated with the mother or Nature or a naively regarded Muse) is conventionally disrupted and forced into a triadic structure, including the third term, death (frequently associated with the father, or Time). The dead, like the forbidden object of primary desire, must be separated from the poet, partly by a veil of words. . . . [This] castrative aspect should not be slighted, for it lies at the core of the work of mourning.[42]

Sacks claims that the Freudian model of mourning applies equally to men and women, that both mourn in the same way their necessary "renunciation of primary [sexual] desire," "separation from [the] mother," and the "internalization and identification with the idealized parental figure" (that is, the father) (*English Elegy*, 12, 11, 15). Whether or not this is a true, other twentieth-century writers have suggested that women additionally mourn their induction into second-class citizenship, their loss of agency, freedom, and power in the world. For example, Annis Pratt maintains that in the nineteenth century women, unlike men, experienced puberty as "enclosure" and "atrophy" (*Archetypal Patterns in Women's Fiction*, 30). Carol Gilligan sarcastically quotes Freud, who wrote that a girl's puberty is marked by a "wave of repression" necessary to transform her "masculine sexuality" into the specifically feminine sexuality of her adulthood (*In a Different Voice*, 11). Karen Horney wrote in 1926, "In actual fact a girl is exposed from birth onward to the suggestion—inevitable, whether conveyed brutally or delicately—of her inferiority" (*Feminine Psychology*, 69). Horney felt that women's resulting low self-esteem along with discrimination against them made it extremely difficult for them to find any meaningful life's work aside from child rearing (69–70, 185–86). Sacks himself acknowledges, if somewhat obscurely, this difference in women's experience. He writes of twentieth-century women poets: "Whereas the male figure's castrative loss of actual force is compensated by its subsequent wielding of symbolic power, the female figure has been robbed by its cultural occlusion, of even this latter compensation" (*English Elegy*, 324). We have seen in chapter 1 just how little symbolic power nineteenth-century Russian women poets could wield.

On the other hand, as Gilligan, Horney, Modleski, and Simone de Beauvoir have suggested, women receive other consolations: the ability to bear children; closeness and community with their mothers, sisters, and friends; a period of sexual power over some men; and social approval if they do not violate the rules of decorum.[43] These differences between men and women's experiences, I submit, are reflected in their elegies.

As with the *poema*, fewer women poets than men titled works "Elegiia," possibly because they found the classical origins of the genre intimidating. Among the men poets we have been considering, Pushkin titled four poems "Elegiia," Baratynsky six, Del'vig two, Lermontov two, Fet four, Iazykov thirty-four, Khomiakov two, Maikov two—and he also used the word as a section heading for several poems—Guber two, Kol'tsov one. Among the women poets only three—Shakhova, Lisitsyna, and Teplova—wrote poems they titled "Elegiia," but virtually all of them—as did all the men poets—wrote poems elegiac in tone and content.[44]

And, as in the case of *romanticheskye poemy* and ballads, the elegies written by these women poets differ from those of their men contemporaries in focusing on women's experiences. Some losses described in men's elegies—for example, of the ability to love, or of graphically described sexual pleasure—appear infrequently in the women's, as does the consolation that there will be other lovers.[45] Nor did these women, like Pushkin and Del'vig, write parodies of elegies.[46] Such themes would have violated women's gender role at the time and probably were unthinkable. In addition, while several of the canonical and noncanonical men wrote funerary elegies on the death of poets and other famous men—never women—only two women did so: Teplova on Pushkin ("Na smert' A. S. Pushkina" [On the death of A. S. Pushkin, 1837]) and on Lisitsyna ("V pamiat' M. A. L-oi" [In memory of M. A. L-oi, 1842]), and Rostopchina on Lermontov ("Pustoi al'bom" [The empty album, 1841]).[47] The women poets may have suffered from genre anxiety in regard to funerary elegies, a genre traditionally concerned with "initiation and continuity, inheritance and vocation," rewards difficult or impossible for women of the era to attain.[48]

Conversely, some losses mourned in women's elegies rarely or never appear in those of their men contemporaries, for example, the death of a child or a young woman: in Bakunina's "Siialo utro obnovleniem" (The morning shone with a renewal, 1840); Mordovtseva's entire book of poetry dedicated to her son, who died in the Turkish war (*Otzvuki zhizni* [Echoes of life, 1877]), as well as her "Pri smerti bol'nomu rebenku" (To a mortally ill child, 1877); Lisitsyna's "Smert' iunosti" (Death of youth, 1829); Teplova's "Na smert' devy" (On the death of a girl, 1831), "Na smert' docheri" (On the death of my daughter, 1846); and Gotovtseva's "Na smert' A. N. Zh-oi" (On the death of A. N. Zh-oi, 1825).[49] In contrast to funerary elegies, in which death allows the poet to sum up the meaning of the subject's life, these elegies mourn lost potential. Interestingly, the theme of lost potential finds its way into Teplova's funerary elegy on Pushkin. And, conversely, Fet's elegy to his young nephew ("Na smert' Miti Botkina" [On the death of Mitia Botkin, 1886]) focuses on the meaning of his life. It would appear that Tania Modleski's remark about twentieth-century U.S. popular culture also applies to nineteenth-century Russian poetry: for men death reveals the meaning of life, whereas for women it represents the end of all meaning and hope (*Loving with a Vengeance*, 88–89).

A second group of elegiac themes that appear more often in the work of these women poets is depression, unbearable emotional suffering, isolation, and constraint: for example, Garelina's "Vse pogiblo, vse poteriano" (Everything has perished, everything is lost, 1870), Mordovtseva's "Byvaiut strashny, tiazhely mgnoveniia" (There are terrible, painful moments, 1877), Zhadovskaia's "Uvy i ia kak Prometei" (Alas, I, too, like Prometheus, 1858), Pavlova's "Proshlo spolna, vse to, chto bylo" (Everything that was, has completely passed, 1855), and Lisitsyna's elegy "Akh! Zhizn', moia zhizn'!" (Ah! Life, my life! 1829). Although we also find such poems of extreme emotional suffering among men poets—for example, Pushkin's "Ne dai mne Bog soiti s uma" (Please God, don't let me lose my mind, 1833), Kol'tsov, "Vopl' stradaniia" (A cry of suffering, 1840), and the first part of Mil'keev's "Den' rasseiannyi, den' nestroinyi" (A scattered day, a discordant day, 1842)—the greater number of such poems among women poets most likely reflects their greater experience of social limitations and lack of agency, freedom, and power.

Not only do the women's elegies mourn different losses from men's but also they portray different consolations. Many elegies are addressed to a woman friend or a circle of friends who appear to provide some comfort in a time of sorrow and despair. The speaker in Garelina's "Druz'ia moi! Ne smeites' nado mnoi" (My friends! Do not laugh at me, 1870) asks her friends to help her in her love sickness. Conversely, in Fuks's "Poslanie k drugu" (Epistle to a friend, 1834) the speaker offers comfort to a woman who is suffering. Other such poems that evoke a female community include Garelina's "Molisia obo mne" (Pray for me, 1870); Pavlova's "Da, mnogo bylo nas" (Yes, we were many, 1839), Zhadovskaia's "Ty sprosila otchego ia" (You asked why I, 1858), and Gotovtseva's "K druz'iam" (To my friends, 1840). This theme, too, occasionally appears in men's elegies—for example, Pushkin's "Elegiia," "Opiat' ia vash, o iunye druz'ia!" (Again I am yours, O young friends, 1817), but much less often than the *druzheskoe poslanie* (friendly epistle) or anacreontic male "cult of friendship, of good company and wine" discussed in chapter 1.[50]

A second consolation found almost exclusively in women's elegies is religion: imagined meetings with the spirits of loved ones, a professed faith in God, and belief in heaven or acceptance of the will of God. In Bakunina's "Siialo utro obnovleniem" the speaker is grieving the death of an infant when its spirit returns to her as an angel to tell her not to mourn. Teplova in "Son" (A dream, 1860) imagines catching a glimpse of her dead husband on Judgment Day and in "Vospominanie" (Memory, 1860) is comforted by the shade of her dead friend. In "V pamiat' M. A. L-oi" the speaker asks her dead friend, who is in heaven, to forgive her grieving. Similarly, Gotovtseva in "Osen'" (Autumn) finds consolation in heaven's eternal spring. Perhaps, as in the case of the ballad, women poets projected their earthly longings onto the next life, as they saw little possibility for consolation in this one. Or perhaps closer emotional ties among women made the final separation of death especially hard to bear, inspiring fantasized reunions beyond death. Paradoxically, however, these women poets gain from religion what men elegists, according to Sacks, gain from the funerary elegy, a "consoling identification with symbolic even immortal figures of power."[51]

One final factor specific to Russian culture must be considered in relation to the gender norms of the elegy: the lament, or *prichitanie*. This is a Russian folk genre that peasant women traditionally improvised and performed at funerals, when army recruits left their village (for as long as twenty-five years), and as part of the wedding ritual, in which the bride mourned leaving her family and her loss of freedom (*volia*). The lament differs significantly from the elegy in function and form. In contrast to the classical, male-centered, literary elegy, the *prichitanie* is oral, improvised, public, and performed by women. Rather than a private act of mourning, it voices the grief of a community around life-cycle events. The *prichitanie* differs from the elegy in poetic form as well; it is composed in two- or three-stress accentual verse, with varying intervals between the stresses, as opposed to the more regular metrical verse of the elegy. In addition, the *prichitanie* features repeated questions, exclamations, parallelisms, and, in the case of funeral laments, reproaches to the dead for leaving or injunctions to them to come back to life. The word *prichitanie* comes from the word meaning "to list or enumerate"; the performer enumerates all that can be remembered in connection with the tragic event, in contrast with the elegist's attempts at synthesis.[52] Whereas the consolation in the lament comes from having one's grief witnessed by the community, the elegy works through literary tradition to "reintegrate [the poet's] destructive solitary experience into the community" (Greenleaf, *Pushkin and Romantic Fashion*, 90).

Nonetheless, the genres are related in that both address grief, mourning, and consolation, and both are repetitive in form. Monika Greenleaf describes the elegy as a genre of "repetition compulsion," which uses such repetitive conventions as echoing and refrain (*Pushkin and Romantic Fashion*, 88). It is also likely that the lament directly influenced the Russian elegy. Certainly, Russian writers knew about the lament. Although the first serious ethnological transcriptions took place in Russia in the 1860s, laments or references to them can be found in Russia's epic *Slovo o polku Igoreve* (The lay of Igor's host) and in such works of eighteenth- and nineteenth-century men writers as Radishchev's *Puteshestvie iz*

Peterburga v Moskvu (Journey from Saint Petersburg to Moscow, 1790) and in Pushkin's *Kapitanskaia dochka* (The captain's daughter, 1836) and *Boris Godunov* (1825). We can see the influence of the *prichitanie* on the elegies of the Russian men poets we have been discussing—for example, in Fet's "Na smert' Brazhnikova" (On the death of Brazhnikov, 1845)— but more markedly on those of Russian women.

Perhaps because, to paraphrase Susan Friedman, the *prichitanie* granted Russian women cultural authority to express grief, these women poets appear to have felt free to write elegiac poems even if they avoided the classical title "Elegiia" ("Gender and Genre Anxiety," 205). Interestingly, two of the poems titled "Elegiia," those of Lisitsyna (1829) and Shakhova (1849), are written in the three-stress line of the lament. The influence of the lament can also be seen in Teplova's poem "Na smert' docheri," in which the speaker asks her dead daughter to tell what angered her enough to leave.

The *prichitanie* may have influenced women's elegiac verse on a deeper level as well. All elegies offer the poet (and the reader) consolation by translating grief into art. But while the elegies that Sacks discusses, and that many of the men poets write, describe the direct consolations of inheritance and symbolic power, many of those written by these women resemble the *prichitanie* in simply expressing grief. For example, in Garelina's "Gde ty, schast'e, skhoronilos'" (Where have you hidden yourself, Happiness, 1870), the speaker acknowledges that joy, hope, and love no longer exist in her life. The speaker in Mordovtseva's "Vzglianula na sad ia" (I cast a glance at the garden, 1870) compares her heart, which is bereft of hope and dreams, to a desolate garden in winter. Nor does she find any comfort in the heavens. Unconsolable sorrow also appears in Khvoshchinskaia's "Net, ia ne nazovu obmanom" (No, I will not call a deception, 1851) and "Shumit osennii dozhd', noch' temnaia niskhodit'" (The autumn rain pounds, dark night falls, 1854); Pavlova's "Da, mnogo bylo nas" (Yes, we were many, 1839) and "Byla ty s nami nerazluchnoi" (We were inseparable, 1842); Zhadovskaia's "Teper' ne to" (Now it's not the same, 1858), "Ia plachu" (I weep, 1858), and "Uvy i ia kak Prometei" (Alas, I, too, like Prometheus, 1858); and in Rostopchina's "Ne skuchno, a grustno" (It is not tedious, but sad, 1862) and "Osennie listy" (Autumn leaves, 1834). I do not wish to suggest that only women wrote such lamentlike elegies. We also find them among their male contemporaries: Pushkin's "Elegiia" "Bezumnykh let ugasshee vesel'e" (The extinguished gaiety of mad years" 1830); Lermontov's "Elegiia" "O! Esli b dni moi tekli" (Oh, if my days flowed, 1829);

Iazykov's "Elegiia" "Mechty liubvi—mechty pustye!" (Dreams of love are empty dreams, 1826). Such elegies, however, are far more characteristic of the women writers.

How have such differences between men's and women's elegies affected the literary reception and reputations of these women poets? In a study of English-language elegies, Melissa Zeiger writes that, traditionally, the elegy has been considered a male genre. Male mourning was "accredited" and privileged, she writes, while women's mourning was dismissed as hysteria or depression, "doomed to remain speechless, incoherent or excessive" (*Beyond Consolation*, 6). While Zeiger may appear to overstate the case, we find some support for her views in a review of Garelina's *Stikhotvorenie Nadezhdy Libinoi* (1870). The reviewer sarcastically writes of Garelina: "[A]nd so the situation of the poor woman went from exhaustion and despair to the loss of self-control to the desire, finally, for death" ("Stikhotvorenie Nadezhdy Libinoi," *Deiatel'nost* 178 [Sept. 16, 1870]: 2). And "No matter how great the suffering, there still remained enough endurance and pride to hide from people the pain and tears. . . . If there was such a strong desire to hide her pain from people, then why proclaim it in print, and even in a separate edition of verse? . . . It is better to amuse oneself and be amusing than to bore everyone with constant complaints about everything, about fate, people and oneself ("Stikhotvorenie Nadezhdy Libinoi," *Deiatel'nost* 179 [Sept. 17, 1870]: 1).

It is hard to imagine a reviewer similarly chiding a man poet for boring everyone with his complaints, or reducing a man poet's book of poetry first to autobiography and then to psychopathology. We also see here a man reviewer's inability to conceive that a woman poet might use one or several poetic personae (as discussed in chapter 2). It would appear that in the elegy, as in other genres, definitions and assumptions need to be expanded to embrace women's writing as well as men's.

The Lyric

The final and most encompassing poetic genre, or "kind," to be discussed is the Romantic lyric. *Lyric* originally referred to one of three modes of literature—a musical mode, sung to the lyre, as opposed to the epic and drama. In this sense the ballad and the elegy are genres of lyric. However, since the Renaissance the lyric itself has come to be considered a genre—a poem with such characteristics as "brevity, metrical coherence, subjectivity, passion"(*New Princeton Encyclopedia of Poetry and*

Poetics, 714). During the Romantic period the lyric was a central poetic genre; one scholar notes that the Romantics equated the lyric with poetry in general (Fowler, *Kinds of Literature*, 235).

The Russian scholar Lidiia Ginzburg attributes the development of the nineteenth-century Russian lyric to the breakdown of the neoclassical poetic "genre system." In the eighteenth and the early nineteenth century, she writes, poets did not create the subject of their poems but rather chose a poetic genre: ode, elegy, epistle, satire (*O lirike*, 53). The subject and mood of a poem were implicit in its genre.[53] By Lermontov's time, however, the poet himself had become the lyric subject. The distinguishing feature of the lyric, Ginzburg maintains, is that the poet, besides being author and subject, also is "included in the aesthetic structure of the work as its active element" ("v kachestve deistvennogo ee elementa") (*O lirike*, 7). In Fet's poetry, for example, the poet does not appear as the lyric subject, yet is nonetheless present. The early nineteenth century also saw the lyric of thought—the ode—merge with the lyric of feeling—the elegy.[54] After 1820, Ginzburg continues, a demand for a "poetry of thought" arose among the Decembrist poets, the "Liubomudry" (Lovers of wisdom, a group of Moscow writers who studied and discussed Schelling's philosophy), as well as Belinsky and his circle. At this time the central issues of the Romantic lyric became the image of the poet, poetic inspiration, genius, and "the crowd" (91–92).

M. H. Abrams, writing during the 1970s, as did Ginzburg, also described thought as central to English and German Romantic poetry. For Abrams the defining characteristic of Romantic poetry is its close relation to the philosophy of the time: the concern of both Romantic poets and Romantic philosophers (Schelling, Fichte, Hegel) with polarities, antitheses, unity lost and regained, "the fall from primal unity to self-division, self-contradiction, and self-conflict," and a circular or spiral quest that ended in a "loving union with the feminine other."[55]

More recent scholarship, however, has begun to question these and other assumptions about Romanticism and the Romantic lyric. One scholar points out that *Romanticism* as a general term for European poetry of the first part of the nineteenth century was first introduced only in the 1860s; the poets we now call Romantics did not refer to themselves in this way. He further suggests that the meaning of Romanticism changes with each generation's shifting "Romantic" canons.[56] As noted in the introduction, during the "Romantic" period men and women poets occupied themselves with different issues. Recent scholars have shown that while men poets wrote about subjective idealism (the archetype of the poet, egoism, escapism), literary primitivism (bards, minstrels, ballads, and romances), and a return to nature—and, one could add, the search for nation—women poets more typically concerned themselves with female heroism; female desire; domestic affections; home, family, and community; female childhood; education; motherhood; and careers (Wolfson, "Romanticism and Gender," 385–96). If Romanticism describes only the concerns of men, it may not make sense to speak of women Romantic poets—unless we expand our definition of Romanticism.

This is not to suggest that these women poets did not write lyrics on the Romantic themes of the poet, nature, and nation, as well as love lyrics. We have seen in chapter 2 that they did, although usually from their own point of view. I would suggest, however, that because the work of women poets does not conform to the gender norms of Romantic poetry—for example, the male's quest to be reunited with the female Other—their work has been marginalized or considered insufficiently intellectual, philosophical, or "universal." Of course, middle- and upper-class women—whose lives were characterized by physical, legal, and often psychological limitations, financial dependency, and expected subservience to men—would not have found relevant the metaphor of a quest, even for a male Other. Nor could the German philosophical striving for an idealized yet sexualized "eternal feminine" serve as a tenable basis for their poetry. In addition, the mythology available to men poets could not help them depict women's experiences. A recent study of Romanticism includes chapters on the male archetypes of Werther, Faust, Prometheus, Napoleon, the dandy, and Don Juan.[57] The only female Romantic archetype discussed is La Belle Dame Sans Merci, a soulless man-destroying character, who has much in common with the archetype that Dolores Barracano Schmidt calls the "Great American Bitch" ("The Great American Bitch," 900–905).

Like their European counterparts, these Russian women poets in their lyrics not only reinterpreted male Romantic themes but also treated the "women's themes" just mentioned. Images of female heroism, for example, appear in Kul'man's poems about Korinna and Sappho, Pavlova's "Jeanne d'Arc" (1839), Rostopchina's "Kak liubiat zhenshchiny: predsmertnaia duma Sharloty Stiglits" (How women love: The dying thoughts of Charlotte Stieglitz, 1841), Bakunina's "legend in verse" about the early Christian martyr Iulianiia Nikomidiiskaia (1849), and in Fuks's *Osnovanie goroda Kazani* (1837). The theme of female desire appears in the lyrics of almost all these women poets, but without the pornographic overtones that often accompany descriptions of male de-

Будто всё напрасно,
Что мы просим страстно

(As if everything for which we passionately ask
Were in vain.)

("Duma," 1840)

The word "naprasno" occurs less frequently in men's poetry.[62] Some poems depict death as a desired goal or a means of transcendence.[63] Such themes occur rarely, if at all, in the poetry of their male contemporaries.

Reception

We have looked at some differences in the way these women poets approached the most characteristic Romantic poetic genres: the *poema*, the ballad, the elegy, and the lyric. How did such differences affect the reception of their work? As mentioned in the introduction, it seems likely that men literary gatekeepers—publishers, critics, editors—ignored women's poetry or found it irrelevant or meaningless because they had no knowledge of the experience it evoked. For example, as mentioned in the introduction, Belinsky pronounced Teplova's poem "Sestre" (To my sister) *rebiacheskii* (puerile), one suspects because canonical men poets generally did not write poems to family members, although all fourteen of the women poets did.[64] In addition, the debate about women's writing (discussed in chapter 1) appears to have fostered a condescending or hostile attitude among men reviewers toward women poets.

Contemporary reviewers, as I have shown elsewhere, reduced several of these women poets to then-current female stereotypes: Kul'man to a virgin martyr, Zhadovskaia to an object of pornographic fantasy, Teplova to a wallflower, Pavlova to a masculine woman, and Rostopchina to a whore.[65] And, as discussed in chapter 1, it would appear that at least some negative nineteenth-century attitudes toward women writers persisted into the twentieth century, continuing to affect the critical evaluation of these poets.

Is it possible to expand the definition of Romanticism—which, as we saw in chapter 1, has been considered a male institution—to include the work of women writers? Romanticism has been described as encouraging "revolutionary political ideas" (Harmon and Holman, *Handbook to Literature*, 452), expressing "an extreme assertion of the self" (Drabble,

Oxford Companion to English Literature, 842), championing "absolute creative freedom" (Preminger, *Princeton Encyclopedia of Poetry and Poetics,* 718), and as having for its fundamental tenets liberty and individualism. Although many women found Romantic ideology inspiring, their relationship to it was necessarily more ambivalent than men's, since it was never intended for them. In revolutionary France, Olympe de Gouges, who answered the Declaration of the Rights of Man with her "Declaration des droits de la femme et de la citoyenne" (1791), was guillotined in 1793 for "having forgotten the virtues which belong to her sex."[66] Also in 1793, the same year that the French revolutionary government granted universal male suffrage, it denied women the right of public assembly and of citizenship—along with the demented, minors, and criminals. In the United States, John Adams found it amusing when his wife, Abigail, asked him during the Second Continental Congress of 1776 to "remember the ladies" in the future U.S. law code.[67] Jean-Jacques Rousseau, whose name in Russia was synonymous with revolutionary thought up to the second half of the nineteenth century, wrote in *Emile* (1763), his highly influential treatise on education: "Woman is made to please and to be subjugated. . . . Thus the whole education of women ought to relate to men. To please men, to be useful to them, to make herself loved and honored by them, to raise them when young, to care for them when grown, to counsel them, to console them, to make their lives agreeable and sweet—these are the duties of women at all times and they ought to be taught from childhood" (*Emile or on Education,* 358, 365).[68] In Russia, the "men of the forties" (Nikolai Stankevich, Vissarion Belinsky, Mikhail Bakunin, and others), who immersed themselves in German philosophy, imposed the "hierarchical binary oppositions" of German Romantic gender ideology on real women, producing, in Ginzburg's words, "inevitable emotional catastrophes" (*O lirike,* 141).[69] It is not surprising, then, that both European and Russian women's poetry differs from that of their male contemporaries by focusing on women's often restricted experience, as well as by referring less frequently to the philosophical concepts in vogue with men.

If we wish to expand the concept of Romanticism to include women, we must focus on the elements that women's and men's poetry shared. For example, one gender-neutral definition of the Romantic lyric describes it as expressing sensuality, feelings, and mysticism.[70] While these women poets did not write poems of overt sensuality, they wrote many poems that verbalized feeling and mysticism, poems that could be compared fruitfully with those of their male contemporaries. Such comparisons might give us a more complete and three-dimensional view of Romanticism.

These first chapters have analyzed the commonalties among these women poets: historical and social circumstances, literary conventions, practices, and genres. In the next three chapters we shall change our focus to consider the individual achievements of three of the most significant of these women poets—Rostopchina, Khvoshchinskaia, and Pavlova—and shall examine the varied and pervasive effects of gender ideology on their lives, work, and literary reputations.

4

Evdokiia Rostopchina

Evdokiia Rostopchina (1811–58), one of the few recognized women poets of her generation, has been the subject of numerous biographical accounts by memoirists and literary critics. One finds, however, a surprising uniformity among these biographies.[1] The same episodes repeatedly reappear in the same way, almost in the same words, like scenes from a saint's life. This "official biography" has in turn shaped ideas about Rostopchina's work, influencing her literary reputation. It is worth examining the standard version of Rostopchina's life—the choice and interpretation of events, as well as the assumptions about gender inherent in them. Could these episodes be interpreted in other ways? Are there excluded or underemphasized circumstances that might give us a different understanding of her life and work? I suggest that in addressing these questions we may gain a richer, more complex, and truer appreciation of Rostopchina as a poet.

One often-repeated scene from Rostopchina's life concerns her initiation into literature. Petr Viazemsky, the well-known poet and critic, while visiting the family of the eighteen-year-old Rostopchina (née Sushkova) came upon her poem "Talisman." He secretly copied it, then without Rostopchina's knowledge or permission published it in Anton Del'vig's al'manakh, *Severnye tsvety* (Northern flowers) for 1831.[2] This story differs from accounts of how contemporary men poets entered literature, in its suggestions of a virgin birth.[3] As a powerful male spiritual force impregnates Mary without her knowledge or permission, so a powerful male literary force sweeps the equally innocent Rostopchina into literature. As Mary therefore cannot be accused of the sin of lust, so Rostopchina cannot be accused of the sin, for a woman, of literary ambition.

This connection between lust and literary ambition—for women—

emerges even more clearly from another frequently recounted episode: the scandal that erupted when "Talisman" appeared, and Rostopchina's relatives discovered that she, an unmarried woman, was the author of a published poem.[4] Rostopchina's brother Sergei writes, "Everyone found that for a well-born young unmarried woman (*blagorodnaia baryshnia*) to occupy herself with composition was indecent and to print her works was absolutely shameful!" (S. Sushkov, "Biograficheskii ocherk," 1: vi). Although Rostopchina had been "seduced" into literature without her knowledge, her family treated her as a fallen woman— as if the published poem, the evidence of her fall, signified an illegitimate child. The poet's grandmother demanded that she swear on an icon that she would never again write poetry. Instead, Rostopchina agreed not to publish any more poetry until after she was married, when presumably poetry writing, like sex, was considered permissible for women. It is hard to imagine such a scene greeting a man poet on his literary debut. Although we invariably find this episode recounted with amusement, as an indication of the quaintness of old-fashioned Russian high society, no one has speculated on the effect it may have had on Rostopchina's feelings about herself as a woman poet.

A third, often-recounted story suggests that, just as Viazemsky can be credited for Rostopchina's literary debut, so another powerful male literary figure, Nikolai Gogol, can be credited for her most politically courageous act as a writer. This was the publication of "Nasil'nyi brak" (The forced marriage, 1845), in which Rostopchina used the allegory of a forced marriage to protest Russia's forced annexation and oppression of Poland.[5] It was Gogol, we are told, who encouraged Rostopchina to submit the poem to Faddei Bulgarin and Nikolai Grech's conservative literary daily, *Severnaia pchela* (The northern bee), assuring her that no one would understand the allegory. Rostopchina did so, and the poem passed the censorship, appearing in the December 17, 1846, issue of the paper.[6] Within a few weeks, however, people became aware of the poem's allegorical meaning. According to Rostopchina's daughter, Lidiia, the police destroyed all the copies of the offending issue they could find, using subscription lists to retrieve those held by subscribers. Nicholas I threatened to close down the newspaper, and one of its two editors, Nikolai Ivanovich Grech (1787–1867), was asked by the Third Section (Nicholas I's secret police) to explain in writing how he could have accepted such a poem for publication. The other editor, Faddei Venediktovich Bulgarin (1789–1859), without being asked, also wrote an explanation, no doubt feeling vulnerable because he was Polish.

Although the poet Nikolai Vasil'evich Berg (1823–84) claims in a memoir to have heard about Gogol's involvement from Rostopchina herself, the more closely one looks at this story, the more unlikely it appears. By October 1845—when Gogol supposedly encouraged Rostopchina to smuggle into print a poem critical of the Russian government—he had become increasingly reactionary. In July of 1846 he would send to Saint Petersburg the first six chapters of his *Vybrannye mesta iz perepiski s druz'iami* (*Selected Passages from Correspondence with Friends*), a book that would shock Russia's liberal camp when it appeared in 1847. Nor is there any evidence that Gogol sympathized with the plight of Poland under Russian domination. A third problem is that although Rostopchina wrote the poem in September 1845, and according to the story met with Gogol in Rome shortly thereafter, she did not send the poem to Bulgarin until August of 1846, almost a year later. Gogol, then, was not the immediate cause of her sending Bulgarin the poem, even if the story of their meeting is true. The effect of this story, however, is to give credit to Gogol and depict him as a liberal, while decreasing Rostopchina's responsibility for her own political act.[7]

Biographers rarely mention that Rostopchina sent Bulgarin along with "Nasil'nyi brak" nine other poetical works, as well as the drama *Donna Maria Kolonna Manchini*. She requested in her cover letter that three of the poems, "Liubovnik i moriak" (The lover and the sailor), "Nasil'nyi brak" (The forced marriage), and "Sosna na Kornishe" (The pine at Cornish), be printed in that order, supposedly because they would not reveal her gender.[8] No one has ever asked whether Rostopchina might have had artistic reasons for grouping these poems together or has bothered to analyze "Nasil'nyi brak" in relation to the accompanying poems. Critics, in focusing on the "scandal" of "the forced marriage" have ignored Rostopchina not only as agent but also as poet.

Many other episodes repeated in these Rostopchina biographies similarly inscribe nineteenth-century gender ideology: Rostopchina Meets and Pleases Pushkin at a Ball, Rostopchina Perhaps Has an Affair with Lermontov, Rostopchina Is Seduced and Abandoned and Spends the Rest of Her Life Pining for Her Former lover, Rostopchina as Salon Hostess Bores Her Guests When She Forces Them to Listen to Her Own Works.[9] That is, while Rostopchina was able, very temporarily, to please men, including great poets, with her body, she always bored men with her writing.

In conjunction with these accounts of Rostopchina's life, we find prominent and often detailed descriptions of Rostopchina's body as the

object of the male gaze—even in the biographical sketch her brother
Sergei published thirty years after her death:

> She had straight, delicate features and a swarthy color to her
> face. Beautiful and expressive black eyes edged with long lashes,
> black hair shiny, fine and not thick. . . . She was of medium
> height, her figure was not distinguished by a graceful form;
> beautiful hands; she was not strikingly beautiful, but she was at-
> tractive. (S. Sushkov, "Biograficheskii ocherk," 1: xxxiv)

> Not of great height, unusually shapely for her thirty-five years
> with a well-developed bust, a healthy flush that our female gen-
> eration would envy, with big, protuberant [*pochti na vykate*] ex-
> tremely intelligent eyes.[10]

> At that time (1849) she was rather young, rather shapely, and
> could please [men]. . . . [When Rostopchina attended a reading
> of Ostrovsky's *Bankrot* (The bankrupt) in 1849] all eyes looked
> only at her and it seems that everyone found her pleasing.[11]

Biographies of men poets' lives generally do not contain such sexualized descriptions of their bodies.

These stories of Rostopchina's life have affected Rostopchina's literary reputation directly, as their common effect is to trivialize her as a *poetessa* whose sexuality defines the significance of her work. No biographers have similarly looked for the meaning of Lermontov's life and art
in his love affairs, or highlighted the scandal of Pushkin's ménage à trois
with his wife and his sister-in-law, or read Tiutchev's poetry through his
fourteen-year extramarital affair with Elena Denis'eva, a woman
twenty-three years his junior, with whom he had three children.[12] Interestingly, the biographers who trivialize Rostopchina range from nineteenth-century radical critics, to modernists, to Soviet critics, to post-
Soviet critics. It would appear that despite dramatic changes in Russian
literary politics in the course of the nineteenth and twentieth centuries,
the tendency to denigrate women poets remained constant.

In addition to reiterating the same episodes and focusing on Rostopchina's physical appearance, these biographies also share the same
lacunae. For example, while many of the biographies state that in some
way Rostopchina's husband, Andrei Rostopchin, made her unhappy,
none specify how he did so, surely relevant biographical information.
Perhaps the critics' reticence results from their respect for Andrei Rostopchin's father, Fedor Vasilevich Rostopchin, the governor general of
Moscow during the Napoleonic invasion and a hero of the War of 1812.

We are left, however, with intriguing half-hints. While all memoirists describe relations between Andrei Rostopchin and Rostopchina as antagonistic and characterize him as a spendthrift, Rostopchina's daughter, Lidiia, implies that he also was physically abusive. Rostopchina's brother Sergei Sushkov, Vladislav Khodasevich, and V. S. Kiselev suggest that Rostopchin was homosexual or, in any case, not interested in sexual relations with Rostopchina. It is true that she did not have any children for the first three years of her marriage while she and her husband were living on his estate, Selo Anna, outside of Voronezh. When she returned to Saint Petersburg in the fall of 1836, she appears to have had several affairs and at least two children by another man.[13]

Another strange gap in Rostopchina's biography is the period between 1841—the year her first book of poetry appeared to very enthusiastic reviews—and the fall of 1845 when she, her husband, and their three children left for a trip to Europe, which lasted until September 1847. V. S. Kiselev-Sergenin in a recent article is the first to discuss this period, when Rostopchina was at the height of her popularity, but he does so exclusively in relation to her affair with Andrei Karamzin, the son of the Russian historian.[14] It would be interesting to know more about Rostopchina's literary activities during this time. Addressing these and other neglected aspects of Rostopchina's biography (such as her relationships with women) might reveal a more complex and compelling picture of her life.[15] More generally, a fresh look at all the facts of Rostopchina's life would allow new and possibly truer stories to be told about her, stories that also might affect the evaluation of her work.

One obvious but underemphasized fact about Rostopchina's life is that she surmounted childhood abandonment and almost total neglect to become a celebrated poet. On the death of Rostopchina's mother when Rostopchina was five, her father left her and her two brothers with their maternal grandparents in Moscow while he worked first in Orenburg, then in Saint Petersburg. According to accounts by both of Rostopchina's brothers, their grandparents hired inadequate and dishonest tutors, otherwise ignoring the children, while the two maiden aunts who lived in the household treated them with active malice.[16] In 1826, when Rostopchina was fourteen, her father returned to Orenburg, taking his two sons, but not his daughter, to live with him. One need not be a Freudian to imagine that Rostopchina felt rejected by her father and abandoned by her brothers in an unpleasant living situation, as she had already been abandoned by her mother's death, her father's absence, and her tutors', grandparents', and aunts' indifference or hostility.

Many of Rostopchina's male contemporaries—Pushkin, Iazykov, Lermontov, Fet, Tiutchev, Del'vig, and Baratynsky—received excellent formal educations, encouragement in their poetic vocation, and mentoring. Rostopchina, however, with the exception of one governess during her tenth and eleventh years, appears to have been given very little guidance in her development as either a person or a poet and no systematic education. Yet she taught herself to read French, German, Italian, and English literature in the original, while acting on her determination to become a woman poet—a career for which she had no models—in the face of horrified family reaction. She may have been helped to persevere by knowing of the many writers on her father's side of the family: her father's brother, Nikolai Sushkov, writer, critic, and editor of the *al'manakh Raut;* her father, who wrote and translated plays; her grandmother, Mariia Vasil'evna Sushkova (née Khrapovitskaia, 1752–1831), a poet, essayist, and translator of works into Russian from Italian, French, and English, including Milton's *Paradise Lost.*[17]

An overemphasized but underanalyzed factor in Rostopchina's biography—and, indeed, in the biographies of all aristocratic women writers of this generation—is the significance for them of high society (*svet*, literally, "the world"). Vissarion Belinsky, echoed by the radical critics, contemptuously described Rostopchina's poetry as "fettered to the ball," and all her thoughts and feelings leaping to the music of a fashionable galope.[18] Other biographers have charitably explained that for Rostopchina society was a way to forget her domestic unhappiness or uncharitably called it her drug.[19] One could more accurately say that for aristocratic women of Rostopchina's time and social class, society was, indeed, the world. As discussed in chapter 1, upper-class women had no access to the public places available to many men: universities, university discussion groups, literary circles, editorial offices of journals and newspapers, and so on. For such women, society represented their only public forum, as important for a sense of self, association, competition, and achievement as is the workplace today. Rostopchina in her poem, "Tsirk 19-ogo veka" (The circus of the nineteenth century, 1850) expresses how high the stakes seem to guests at a Russian ball by comparing social encounters and their emotional undercurrents with gladiatorial combat in ancient Rome. Similarly, Pavlova in *Kadril'* has Ol'ga compare herself at her first ball to a raw recruit facing his first battle.[20] Although men poets of this generation may not have written as extensively as Rostopchina did about society, certainly many of them also frequented balls, dinners, salons, and receptions, despite their access to other public venues, without being accused of superficiality by their biographers.[21]

For Rostopchina, one can imagine, success and popularity in Moscow society as a young woman seemed a solace and a recompense for an unhappy childhood. In a society where the only "career" open to women was an advantageous marriage, a proposal from Andrei Rostopchin, a rich count, represented a social triumph over spiteful relatives as well as a way to leave an unpleasant home. Rostopchina enjoyed even more social success in Saint Petersburg, where she lived from 1836–38 and from 1840–45. Here, according to her brother Sergei, she hosted dinners for Zhukovsky, Pushkin, Viazemsky, Pletnev, Lizst, and Glinka, received the attentions of Nicholas I at balls, and attended the Empress Aleksandra Fedorovna's intimate social gatherings. Rostopchina gave a copy of her first poetry collection (1841) to the empress with a long personal dedication.[22]

In this context we may surmise that Rostopchina experienced the publication of her protest poem, "Nasil'nyi brak," and its consequences as a fatal watershed in her life. By all accounts Nicholas I never forgave her for it. When, almost a year after the poem appeared, the Rostopchins returned from Europe to Saint Petersburg in the fall of 1846, not only did Nicholas not receive Rostopchina at court, but he also made it clear that she was no longer welcome to live in Saint Petersburg. Rostopchina was forced to return to Moscow, where she had spent her unhappy childhood. She wrote to Viazemsky in 1848 "Moscow is hell for me. . . . [M]ore and more, more sincerely, more often, more keenly do I regret the sweet past, the enlightened lands and country, and my friends on the shores of the Neva" (Ranchin, editor's introduction, 6). She wrote to Odoevsky the same year, "[I]f I am not completely deceased, I am definitely interred in the filth, arguing, and desolation of what they dare to call 'Moscow life.' A fine life! It is the same as death, but it does not have its advantages—solitude and silence!"[23]

Rostopchina experienced additional public humiliation in being turned away from a ball to honor Nicholas's visit to Moscow. Even after Nicholas's death, Alexander II refused Rostopchina's request to have her daughters presented to him at his coronation on the grounds that he could not receive the daughters of an individual who had displeased his father. Although Rostopchina tried to make the best of her life in Moscow by establishing a literary salon, her letters suggest that she felt exiled there.[24]

Taking these and other factors into account would allow critics to cre-

ate other depictions of Rostopchina's life. One could envision Rostopchina, for example, as a woman who longed equally for social acceptance and for self-expression, but whose society forced her into the
role of sexual/political rebel. To be sure, Rostopchina longed for social
success and reveled in conducting salons, hosting dinners, and social-
izing with the emperor and empress. The inscription that she wrote for
Empress Alexandra Fedorovna in 1841 suggests that Rostopchina saw
her as the ideal woman, perhaps as the mother she had lost: "And to
whom, then, Madame, would one address [this book] if not to Your
Majesty, to Her, the most eminent Woman among all women, the sweet-
est, most tender, the most right-thinking and the most richly endowed
in feelings, imagination, and kindness?"[25]

Yet there appears to have been another equally strong side to Rostopchina that demanded freedom, self-determination, and self-
expression. That is, her rebellion against being sexually confined in an
unsatisfactory marriage may have been of a piece with the works of social protest she wrote throughout her life. Her support of the Decembrists, for example, expressed in such poems as "Mechta" (A dream,
1830) and "K stradatel'tsam" (To the sufferers, 1827) did not end with her
youth. In the 1840s and 1850s she sent copies of "K stradatel'tsam" with
a warm inscription to two Decembrists, Z. G. Chernyshov and Sergei
Bolkonsky. On her deathbed she translated Pushkin's Decembrist poem
"Vo glubine sibirskikh rud" (In the depths of Siberian ore, 1827) into
French for Alexandre Dumas.[26] She wrote other works of social protest
as well, as shall be discussed later. One could argue that in "Nasil'nyi
brak" Rostopchina made the forbidden connections between the oppression of women, the oppression of Russians, and the oppression of
Poles (patriarchy, autocracy, and imperialism) and paid dearly for it.

Rostopchina faced an additional problem: the social requirement that
she pretend to conform to social standards for women. So in "Vmesto
predisloviia" (Instead of an introduction), the foreword to her 1856 collected works, she wrote:

> Горжусь я тем, что в чистых сих страницах
> Нет слова грешного, виновной думы нет,—
> Что в песнях ли своих, в рассказах, в небылицах,
> Я тихой скромности не презрела завет!
> Что женщиной смиренно я осталась,
> И мыслию, и словом, и душой!..
> [. . . . .]

Горжусь я тем, что в этой книге новой
Намека вредного никто не подчеркнет
[. . . . .]
Горжусь я тем, что дочери невинной
Ее без страха даст заботливая мать,—
Что девушке, с душою голубиной,
Над ней дозволится и плакать и мечтать! . .

(I am proud that in these pure pages
There is not a sinful word or a guilty thought,
That neither in my songs, nor stories or fables
Have I scorned the command of quiet modesty!
That I have remained a meek woman
In thought, word, and soul! . . .
[. . . . .]
I am proud that in this new book
No one will underline a harmful hint
[. . . . .]
I am proud that a solicitous mother
Will give it without fear to her innocent daughter,
That the girl with a dovelike soul,
Will allow herself to cry and dream over it! . . .)[27]

Rostopchina protested her "purity" too much, providing a target for radical critics; they could safely invoke the patriarchal double standard to attack Rostopchina as an immoral woman in order to attack her covertly as an aristocrat of increasingly conservative views. Those critics who fought against the inequities of class politics—the autocratic control over men's civil rights—did not choose to extend their analysis to sexual politics, the patriarchal control over women's sexuality.[28] Conservative biographers, on the other hand, have "defended" Rostopchina, also on patriarchal grounds, as a "one-man," that is, pure and loyal woman, even if that one man—variously identified as Platon Meshchersky; his brother, Petr Meshchersky; or Andrei Karamzin—was not her husband.[29] Whether viewed by enemies or apologists, however, Rostopchina remains the titillating object of the male gaze. It is worth repeating that biographers generally do not consider the sexual behavior of men poets central to the evaluation of their work.

Literary Reputation

As suggested in the preceding discussion, the gender ideology that shaped accounts of Rostopchina's life also played a large role in her reception and literary reputation. Viewed chronologically, the criticism of Rostopchina's work reveals some surprising changes—and continuities.

To those who have read only twentieth-century Rostopchina criticism, the high praise she received in the 1830s and 1840s comes as a surprise. Vissarion Belinsky and Petr Viazemsky compared Rostopchina's work with Pushkin's, while after Pushkin's death Petr Pletnev called her "without doubt the first poet now in Russia."[30]

Although Belinsky revised his opinion of Rostopchina's work downward starting in the 1840s, her literary reputation, according to her brother Sergei, started to fall to its present low level around 1852, as a result of her increasingly religious, patriotic, and antirevolutionary beliefs. As mentioned previously, these attitudes led radical critics such as Dobroliubov, Chernyshevsky, and others who increasingly controlled the periodical press to launch *ad feminam* attacks on Rostopchina, whom they disparaged as an immoral, boring writer.[31] By the end of the nineteenth and beginning of the twentieth century modernist critics such as Petr Bykov, Vladislav Khodasevich, and Sergei Ernst found Rostopchina's work banal and trivial. They ignored or noted with embarrassed incomprehension the praise she had received from prominent male contemporaries.[32]

During the Soviet period literary scholars treated Rostopchina ambivalently. Up to the 1960s they published nothing by her and almost nothing about her, presumably because of her social background and high-society themes. Starting in the 1970s and 1980s, however, Rostopchina's work began to appear in anthologies and in several separate collections. In introductions and notes Soviet scholars, following the radical critics, dismissed Rostopchina as a second-rate poet, denounced her as a privileged aristocrat, and cringed at the references to sexuality in her work. But while condemning her later political conservatism, they applauded the revolutionary sentiments of her Decembrist poems and of "Nasil'nyi brak." They also attempted to save her for socialist realism by depicting her as a Russian patriot and as one who protested against the inequities of high society—albeit in a limited and ineffectual way.[33]

Perhaps reacting against the Western women's movement, these Soviet critics anthologized and highlighted Rostopchina's most "feminine" poems. So, for example, the introductory essay to a 1987 collection of Rostopchina's poetry is tellingly entitled "Da, zhenskaia dusha dolzhna v teni svetit'sia'" (Yes, the feminine soul must shine in the shadow), a citation from Rostopchina's poem "Kak dolzhny pisat' zhenshchiny" (How women should write, 1840). Rostopchina's poem, which encourages women to be "shy singers" who "with shame hide and conceal the dear story of their love and sweet tears," was reprinted in no less than six Soviet collections of the 1970s and 1980s.

Also frequently cited and reprinted was Rostopchina's poem "Iskushenie" (Temptation, 1839), especially its final lines, which at first glance appear to define the feminine as mindless, superficial, and proud of it:

> А я, я женщина во всем значеньи слова,
> Всем женским склонностям покорна я вполне;
> Я только женщина, . . гордиться тем готова . . .
> Я бал люблю! . . отдайте балы мне! . .

> (But I, I am a woman in the full meaning of the word,
> To all feminine inclinations I am fully obedient;
> I am only a woman, . . . prepared to be proud of this, . . .
> I love a party! Give me parties!")

I will return to "Iskushenie" later in this chapter.

Other such often-cited poems are "Kogda-by on znal" (If only he knew, 1830), "Nadevaia albanskii kostium" (Putting on an Albanian costume, 1838), "Russkim zhenshchinam" (To Russian women, 1856), and "Chernovaia kniga Pushkina" (Pushkin's notebook, 1838). We very seldom find reprinted in these collections, however, Rostopchina's most intense works about art and social injustice: "Moia Igrushka" (My toy, 1847), which Khodasevich compared to Sologub's poetry, "Poslednii tsvetok" (The last flower, 1835), "Baiu-baiu" (Rockabye, 1836), and "Negodovanie" (Indignation, 1840). Nor did Soviet scholars provide any critical context to help readers appreciate Rostopchina's poetry as art.

Western critics, influenced by Barbara Heldt's work on Karolina Pavlova, have reexamined the writings of Pavlova and other women poets in a feminist context but have not done the same for Rostopchina.[34] They may have been dissuaded by Rostopchina's often-republished "feminine" poems, which appeared to constitute most of her work. Perhaps, too, the endless stream of criticism that has sexualized and trivialized Rostopchina's life and work has had a numbing effect, discouraging even feminist critics from taking Rostopchina seriously as a poet. An examination of repeated themes in Rostopchina criticism may help clear the way for Rostopchina's recovery as a more complicated and "modern" poet than previously suspected.

Sexualization

Not only Rostopchina's life but also her work have been sexualized by both positive and negative criticism. The "positive" earlier reviews condescendingly but dismissively praised her work for its "femininity" or leeringly pointed to its revelations of feminine secrets. The negative reviews condemned Rostopchina for being banal and boring (too feminine) and/or immoral or indecently sexual (not feminine enough):

> Definitely the best verse that has ever fluttered down to paper from sweet, ladylike little fingers. (critic Aleksandr Nikitenko, reviewing her 1841 collection, cited in Romanov, editor's introduction, 17)

> Here are ten years of a woman in full bloom, here is the story of a most beautiful creature in its most beautiful period [Rostopchina's poems were dated 1829–39, that is, from her seventeenth to twenty-seventh year]. (Konstantin Aksakov, 1841 review)[35]

> A woman of high society, in whom all the best gifts of nature and fate are crowned by the star of a poetic gift, gives us her secrets, her intimate thoughts. (Stepan Shevyrev, 1841 review, "Kritika," 171)

> A coquette, generally speaking, can only be a woman with a dry, evil heart and an empty head. And if a woman can become a coquette, she will remain a coquette to the end of her life. . . . Now judge whether the persona that Countess Rostopchina favors [in her poetry] belongs to the usual woman of society. . . . She has found all her happiness only at balls . . . in the course of the last twelve years. (Nikolai Chernyshevsky, "Stikhotvoreniia grafini Rostopchinoi" [1856], 6–7)

> A girl from the gentry, a lady—these are the images that first and foremost arise before us in the biography of the poetess. . . . Rostopchina's life, so ordinary and so touching in its banality, is all the same, somehow more prominent than her poetry. (Vladislav Khodasevich, "Grafinia E. P. Rostopchina" [1916], 35)

> Her collected poetry is a woman's motley diary. (Boris Romanov, editor's introduction [1986], 24)

> Of course, the author of such a lyrical novel [*Neizvestnyi roman*] could only be a woman—"a woman in the full meaning of the word" (as she herself recommended herself). (V. Kiselev-Sergenin, "Taina grafini E. P. Rostopchinoi" [1994], 284)

Some critics, abandoning any pretense of evaluation, simply use Rostopchina's work to titillate or shock readers by suggesting that it provided the details of her sex life. Chernyshevsky claims that Rostopchina wrote poetry in order to seduce men.[36] Another, citing a passage from *Neizvestnyi roman* (An unknown romance, 1857), writes, "Here is how the secret meetings went between Andrei Karamzin and his beloved [i.e., Rostopchina] according to *Neizvestnyi roman*" (Kiselev-Sergenin, "Taina grafini E. P. Rostopchinoi," 277). Other critics sexualize Rostopchina's work by suggesting that she became a poet only because of her sexually unfulfilling marriage:

> By nature she was created chiefly for happy connubial love and a peaceful family life, but fate refused her just this happiness. (Sergei Sushkov, "Biograficheskii ocherk" [1890], 1: xlv)

> The subject of much of Dodo's later poetry and prose is the life of a neglected and misunderstood wife. (Louis Pedrotti, "Scandal of Countess Rostopčina's Polish-Russian Allegory" [1985], 197)

> The marriage turned out to be unsuccessful. Evdokiia's unrealized expectations and dreams and undissipated feelings found release in poetry. (V. V. Uchenova, *Tsaritsy muz* [1989], 418)

No one has ever suggested that Pushkin (or any other man poet) only became a writer because of his inability to find a woman who could sexually satisfy him.

Trivialization

Critics have trivialized Rostopchina's poetry by denying it the status of art. As women poets have frequently been considered incapable of creating personae (see chapter 2), so Rostopchina's critics often describe her poetry as a "diary," assuming that every time she uses the first person or even the third person in a work she refers directly to herself. Thus the introductory essay to a 1986 collection of Rostopchina's work is titled "Evdokiia Rostopchina's Lyric Diary."[37] Critics do not similarly deny the status of artist to men poets and writers who use autobiography in their works or who dramatize their lives in poetry (Pushkin, Lermontov, Blok, Thomas Wolfe, James Joyce).[38]

Several critics triumphantly quote Rostopchina's own words to prove that her writing should not be considered art. Four of them cite Rostopchina's 1841 dedication to the empress: "This is not a book—it is a completely sincere and feminine revelation of the impressions, memories, and enthusiasms of the heart of a young girl and a woman."[39] One critic quotes her letter to Viazemsky concerning the 1856 edition of her works: "These are leaves from the secret diary of my heart, which up to this time were hidden and not shown to anyone" (Ranchin, editor's introduction, 9). Still another also "proves" Rostopchina's novel in verse, *Dnevnik devushki*, to be in fact an autobiography, citing her brother's assertion that some episodes are based on her experiences as a girl (Romanov, editor's introduction, 22–23). It is doubtful that any of these critics would discuss Lermontov's *Geroi nashego vremeni* (*A Hero of Our Time*) purely as autobiography. Or consider that Byron's work should not be taken seriously because he self-deprecatingly titled one of his poetry collections *Hours of Idleness*. Or that *Evgenii Onegin* should be disregarded because Pushkin referred to it in his dedication as

> Небрежный плод моих забав,
> Бессонниц, легких вдохновений [. . .]

> ✑

> (The careless fruit of my amusements
> The light inspiration of my insomnia).

Or, indeed, that they would take literally anything men poets modestly wrote about their work. Rostopchina, however, has been considered incapable of metaphor or topos.[40]

Critics have further trivialized Rostopchina's work by going to great lengths not to describe it as original or influential, despite evidence to the contrary. Belinsky, for example, criticized Rostopchina for making up the word *oblistannyi* (unleafed, that is, with fallen leaves) in "Poslednii tsvetok." One critic described her startlingly modern-sounding poem, "Moia Igrushka," as a "reverse anachronism." Another described her poem "Kholod serdtsa" (The heart's coldness, 1829), which Lermontov probably read and which is echoed in a later poem, as an "anticipation" of the Lermontov poem rather than an influence on it.[41]

In several cases critics have simultaneously sexualized and trivialized Rostopchina's work by attributing her success in the 1830s and 1840s only to her looks, connections, and social position. This variation on "she slept her way to the top" does not appear in relation to such well-connected men poets as Pushkin, Del'vig, Baratynsky, Zhukovsky, Fet, and others, whom a male network of mentors, editors, and critics helped to achieve literary success:

> The verses of a beautiful woman, not to mention one who is well
> known in high circles for her beauty, magnificence, and con-

quests, were read and are read without any special compulsion, because there is something in it, *ils avaient quelque chose là*, undoubtedly there is talent in them. (N. V. Berg, "Grafinia Rostopchina v Moskve" [1893], 693)

Her talent, beauty, affability, and hospitality drew and won everyone over to her side [*podkupali v eia pol'zu vsekh*]. (Dmitrii Pogodin, "Grafinia E. N. Rostopchina i ee vechera" [1893], 401)

She was young, attractive in appearance and mind, belonged to high society, her circle included many relatives and intimate relations, and she succeeded while still young in making the acquaintance through the Pashkovs with several of our literary luminaries who gave sympathetic attention to the works that were born of her poetic gifts. (Sergei Sushkov, "Biograficheskii ocherk" [1890], 1: vii)

Her immediate success as a writer was due in part to her vivacious personality, because it was at social functions that she met many of the literary lights of the day, Pushkin and Lermontov among them. (Louis Pedrotti, "Scandal of Countess Rostopchina's Polish-Russian Allegory" [1986], 197)

Still other critics have suggested that Rostopchina's work was widely published only because she accepted little or no money for it.[42]

Rostopchina as *Poetessa*

But she never even thought of renouncing the feminine quality of her poetry, to try to become a Poet, and not a Poetess. (Afanas'ev, "'Da, zhenskaia dusha,'" 9)

Critics have also trivialized Rostopchina's work by invoking the *poetessa* archetype to describe it. In chapter 1 we discussed the contrast between the terms *poèt*, which, as one scholar has remarked, in Russia "is honorific as much as descriptive," and "*poetessa*," which connotes both excess and lack.[43] Except for a brief period in the 1830s and 1840s, critics have invariably referred to Rostopchina as a *poetessa* rather than a *poèt*, and virtually all of them have characterized, and trivialized, her work as excessive and lacking.[44] So, for example, Ivan Aksakov in a review of Rostopchina's first poetry collection, referred to her as *poèt* but engaged in what could be described as "botanical" or "taxonomical" criticism. His review, rather than addressing the content of individual poems, tallies them by year and place of composition, supplying number counts for each.[45] That is, he treats the poems as if they were an endless and excessive proliferation of insects or plants to be dealt with generically.

Sergei Ernst similarly lists the sources of Rostopchina's epigraphs and the subjects of what he calls her "souvenir" poems, without discussing their content ("Karolina Pavlova i gr. Evdokiia Rastopchina [*sic*]," 23, 29).

Other critics more directly disparage Rostopchina's work as excessive by stating that she wrote "too much": "It is impossible not to be amazed at the unusual fecundity of Countess Rostopchina" (Bykov, "Russkie zhenshchiny-pisatel'nitsy," 240). Several stated that her works were too "drawn out" (*rastianutyi* or *zastianuty*).[46]

Critics also described Rostopchina's work as lacking. Several attributed Rostopchina's success to the popularity of her poetry with women, by implication an undereducated and undiscriminating audience. Others criticized her work as too personal, specific, and lacking in universality. One wonders if perhaps women readers found Rostopchina's poetry more "universal" than did men because it described their experience. How "universal," one might ask, is Pushkin's poem "Net, ia ne dorozhu miatezhnym naslazhden'em" (No, I do not value stormy pleasure, 1831), in which a man speaker describes his enjoyment in having sex with a reluctant woman? Or Baratynsky's *Bal*, in which women are depicted as angels or devils?[47]

Irrelevance

The most pervasive theme in Rostopchina criticism, however, is the depiction of her work as time- and space-bound, therefore as irrelevant to the present:

> An evaluation of this first volume [of Rostopchina's collected works] will show you what social importance the poetry must have had in its own time. . . . Let's give full due . . . to this talent that was respected by our teachers and our predecessors. (Druzhinin, "Stikhotvoreniia grafini E. P. Rostopchinoi," [1856], 7: 157, 159, 160)

> It is not surprising that in former days Rostopchina's verses created something of a furor—those were other times. (Bykov, "Russkie zhenshchiny-pisatel'nitsy" [1878], 242)

> Rostopchina outlived herself, outlived her glory as a (woman) writer. . . . Her works are forgotten by posterity and will not be read. (Nekrasova, "Grafinia E. P. Rostopchina" [1885], 42, 81)

> On the whole, the work of Countess Rostopchina is for us a rich monument to its time, and its creator one of the best representa-

tives of the *vieux regime*. (Ernst, "Karolina Pavlova i gr. Evdokiia Rastopchina" [1876], 34)

Once famous, now forgotten. (Khodasevich, "Grafiniia E. P. Rostopchina" [1916], 35)

It's understandable that she could not avoid all the conditions of the society in which she was brought up. . . . to our current taste Rostopchina's verses . . . sometimes are somewhat mannered . . . full of conventions, even prejudices. . . . Rostopchina occupies perhaps a modest, but special place in the poetry of the 1830s and 1840s. (Romanov, introduction [1986], 13, 26)

Circumstances facilitate or constrain, but every *oeuvre* has its own internal limits. In her lyric productions of the '30s and '40s . . . Rostopchina attained it. Her attainments, when repeated, threaten to turn into clichés. (Ranchin, editor's introduction [1991], 6)

Criticism of canonical writers, in contrast, always asserts the timelessness of their work, and its inevitable, eternal relevance to the present:

The consciousness of Pushkin's supremacy and centralness in Russian literature and civilization grew apace, unostentatiously, but irrevocably. The twentieth century received it full grown. (D. S. Mirsky, *History of Russian Literature* [1926], 102)

[Baratynsky's] poetry is, as it were, a short cut from the wit of the eighteenth-century poets to the metaphysical ambitions of the twentieth (in terms of English poetry from Pope to T. S. Eliot). (D. S. Mirsky, *History of Russian Literature* [1926], 106)

A modern reader is involuntarily struck by the immediate importance of this poetry. . . . He [Baratynsky] posed questions that will never cease to occupy thinking and feeling people. . . . "It is high time that Baratynsky finally get the place on the Russian Parnassus that has long belonged to him." Today this wish of Pushkin has come true. (George Kline, 1985)[48]

Lermontov managed to create a fictional person whose romantic dash . . . [is] of lasting appeal to readers of all countries and centuries. (Vladimir Nabokov, translator's foreword to *A Hero of Our Time* [1958], xvii)

The creative spirit of a person revealing the world and its beauty, the subtlety of the perception of the word and the exactness of its reproduction, these qualities of the poet [Fet] have become more and more noticeable. Now this lyric poetry is our intellectual heritage, rightly considered the wealth and pride of our national literature. (L. A. Ozerov, introduction to *Stikhotvoreniia* [1970], 24–25)

Frank Kermode's interesting study, *Forms of Attention*, illuminates this contrast between the irrelevance that critics attribute to Rostopchina and the eternal relevance they bestow on canonical writers. Kermode writes that in literary, as in religious, canons "permanent modernity is conferred on chosen works," while "others are allowed to become merely historical." "To be inside the canon," he continues, "is to be protected from wear and tear, to be credited with indefinitely large numbers of internal relations and secrets, to be treated as a heterocosm, a miniature Torah." Kermode observes that works can only become and remain canonical through "continuity of attention and interpretation."[49]

In considering the history of Rostopchina criticism, one is struck by the continuity of negative attention and disparaging interpretations of her work—the sustained effort over time to show that Rostopchina does not belong in the canon. But if she is truly irrelevant and merely historical, one might ask, why do these critics pay her so much attention?

Other Approaches

It is natural for readers to accept such repeated denigration of Rostopchina's poetry over time as proof of its inferior quality. These negative opinions, however, could also be explained by the factors of class politics and cultural misogyny described in the preceding discussion. Rostopchina's work, like her biography, is worth reconsidering with an open mind.[50]

We have noted critics' use of the term *poetessa* to disparage Rostopchina.[51] However, in reconsidering Rostopchina's significance, we must ask if she is a "poetess" in the well-defined European and American sense of the word.[52] Nineteenth-century American and European literary scholars describe the poetess as a "sociomoral handmaiden" (Ross, *Contours of Masculine Desire*, 192) who did not "demonstrate ambition, . . . [was] not to lecture on public issues or speculate on philosophic or religious ones" (Ostriker, *Stealing the Language*, 31) or "[challenge] the status quo" (Walker, introduction to *American Women Poets of the Nineteenth Century*, xxvi); who embodied the feminine "sphere of the domestic affections, religious piety, and patriotic passions, and of the female (more particularly maternal) responsibility for binding these sensibilities together."[53] Such a poetic stance, if maintained consistently, would indeed be unlikely to produce deep or meaningful or even interesting poetry. But do these characteristics of the poetess describe Rostopchina's work?

It is true that Rostopchina did not speculate on philosophic or religious questions. Also, as we have seen, at the end of her life she wrote many poems that embodied "religious piety and patriotic passions" (see note 31), as did Iazykov, and Pushkin in "Klevetnikam Rossii" (To the slanderers of Russia, 1831). Even then, however, Rostopchina did not unconditionally support the status quo. She welcomed home the Decembrists, freed after Nicholas I's death, defended poets against autocracy ("Ot poeta k tsariam" [From a poet to the tsars, 1856]), and expressed rage at men's treatment of women:

> [W]omen are always better, that is, kinder, more loving, less selfish, more truthful than men; . . . but she [woman] is perverted and corrupted by shortcomings, insults, dissuasions, ordeals—and from whom, dare I ask, does she suffer and endure them if not from you men? . . . Who leads, seduces, and abandons her? Who takes her from the pedestal . . . to bend her, break her pride, and throw her to her knees like a mute and defenseless slave? Who, if not your vanity, your lust, your pettiness, your emptiness, in a word, your debauchery? *Messieurs, vous savez ce que vous faites.*
> . . . As a result of such convictions I hold the pen in my hand like a weapon, the only one given to us against you.[54]

The other characteristics that literary scholars attribute to the poetess mentioned previously apply even less to Rostopchina. Far from expressing no ambition, she published six books during her lifetime, including two editions of her collected works, a remarkable feat for a woman of that time.[55] Rostopchina also expressed ambition by polemicizing with Russia's most famous men authors. She wrote *Vozvrashchenie Chatskogo* (Chatsky's return, 1856), a sequel to Griboedov's *Gore ot uma,* as well as *Dnevnik devushki* (A girl's diary, 1845), the only other nineteenth-century Russian novel in verse besides Pushkin's *Evgenii Onegin.*

Nor did Rostopchina hesitate to write on public issues. We have already mentioned her support of the Decembrist uprising in "Mechta" (A dream, 1830) and "K stradatel'tsam-izgnannikam" (To the suffering exiles, 1831) and her criticism of Russia's oppression of Poland in "Nasil'nyi brak" (The forced marriage, 1845). In addition, in "Negodovan'e" (Indignation, 1840) she criticized U.S. treatment of the Seminole Indians, and in "Moim kritikam" (To my critics, 1856) and "Oda poezii" (Ode to poetry, 1852) she polemicized with Russian literary critics.

Finally, Rostopchina's poetry can in no way be said to embody the sphere of domestic and maternal affection. Rather than describing the joys of marriage and motherhood, she depicted the joys and pains of extramarital love (for example, her cycle, *Neizvestnyi roman*, which was first published in its entirety in 1856). In the only lullaby she wrote ("Baiu-baiu," 1836) the speaker tells her own heart, soul, and imagination to go to sleep since life is meaningless.

Indeed, Rostopchina's challenges to contemporary understandings of woman's role may be the reason that she incurred so much hostility from her critics. In "Iskushenie" (Temptation, 1839) a young mother watching her two children sleeping wishes she could be at a ball. Here Rostopchina depicts a mother with feelings and desires independent of her children, a challenge to cultural assumptions about instinctive maternal self-sacrifice and the insignificance for women of mere pleasure compared to the sacred joys of motherhood. Many critics have commented on, and been scandalized by, this poem. They routinely identify the speaker with Rostopchina, berating her for frivolity and immorality.[56]

These critics, however, ignore the poem's moral sophistication. The title "Iskushenie" serves to name the speaker's feelings and to frame them for the reader. Rostopchina establishes the speaker as a moral agent who can choose whether or not to act on temptation. Perhaps that in itself frightened critics who preferred that a mother's submersion in her children be complete, unquestionable, and mandatory.

However, a more objective reading of the poem shows that these critics missed its point. The poem does not concern the speaker's temptation to reject motherhood in order to glitter in high society. At the beginning of the poem she says:

> Теперь находишь ты меня
>   За книгой, за работой, . .
> Двух люлек шорох слышу я
>   С улыбкой и заботой.
> И светел, сладок мой покой,
>   И дома мне не тесно, . .

⟶

> (Now, you [Midnight] find me
>   At a book, at work, . . .
> I listen to the rustle of two cradles
>   With a smile and with concern
> And my feeling of peace is bright and sweet
>   And home doesn't constrain me, . . .)

Rather, the speaker struggles with the polarization that her society creates in her between two of her roles: the poet ("at a book, at work") and the woman:

> [. . .] гонители невинной суеты! . .
> Неумолимые, вы женщине-поэту
> Велите мыслию и вдохновеньем жить,
> Живую молодость лишь песням посвятить,
> От всех блистательных игрушек отказаться,
> Все нам врожденное надменно истребить
> [. . . . .]
> Вам, судьи строгие, вам недоступен он,
> Ребяческий восторг на праздниках веселых!

> (Implacable persecutors of innocent vanity
> You command the woman-poet
> To live by thought and inspiration.
> To dedicate her lively youth only to songs [i.e., poetry]
> To renounce all glittering toys
> To extirpate everything innate in us
> [. . . . .]
> To you, harsh judges, to you
> Childish ecstasy at happy celebrations is inaccessible!)

The speaker feels she must choose between the male image of the poet, which she perceives as dry, harsh, joyless, and disembodied, and her own "feminine" desire to enjoy herself. Yet although the speaker's last words are a demand for pleasure, affirming that she is a "woman," not a "poet" ("I love a party, give me parties!"), she has chosen to express herself in a poem. None of the critics have commented on, or perhaps even noticed, this deliberate irony.

This is not to suggest that Rostopchina never took the poetess stance, never promoted or even exploited the idea of the "essential feminine" in her poetry, but rather to suggest that her work deserves a different kind of reading. Like "Iskushenie," other poems by Rostopchina—lines of which are often quoted out of context—might better be understood as her struggle to deal with the tensions inherent in her "society's concepts of being a writer and a woman" (Feldman, introduction to *British Women Poets of the Romantic Era*, xxviii).

In "Chernovaia kniga Pushkina," for example, Rostopchina describes her feelings when Vasilii Zhukovsky, Pushkin's longtime mentor and friend, presented her with a notebook he found among Pushkin's effects after Pushkin's death. Zhukovsky had written a few poems in the blank notebook before sending it to Rostopchina with a letter requesting that she fill it with her poetry. In the 1856–57 edition of her works Rostopchina included the letter before her poem that concludes:

И мне, и мне сей дар! мне, слабой, недостойной,
Мой сердца духовник пришел его вручить,
Мне песнью робкою, неопытной, нестройной
Стих чудный Пушкина велел он заменить!..
Но не исполнить мне такого назначенья,
Но не достигнуть мне желанной вышины!
Не все источники живого песнопенья,
Не все предметы мне доступны и даны:
Я женщина!.. во мне и мысль и вдохновенье
Смиренной скромностью быть скованы должны.

⌇

(And this gift is for me, for me!
My heart's confessor arrived to entrust it to me, weak and unworthy.
He commanded me with my shy, inexperienced, ungraceful song
To replace the marvelous verse of Pushkin!
But it is not for me to fulfill such an assignment,
It is not for me to attain the desired heights!
Not all the sources of living poetry
Not all subjects are accessible and given to me:
I am a woman! . . . in me both thought and inspiration
Must be constrained by humble modesty.)

While critics often cite the last two lines of this poem as an example of Rostopchina's "femininity," one notes the tension between their apparent humility and the repetition of "mne" (to me) eight times in the last ten lines of the poem.[57] And perhaps Rostopchina in these last two lines does not so much humbly prescribe and glorify her lesser role as a woman poet as simply note the limitations to which she is subject. One thinks of similar lines by the American poet Frances Sargent Osgood (1811–50), born the same year as Rostopchina:

Ah! Woman still
Must veil the shrine,
Where feeling feeds the fire divine,
Nor sing at will,
Untaught by art
The music prison'd in her heart![58]

"Art" here, one suspects, means artifice. Other poems by Rostopchina yield richer, denser, and more complex meanings in the light of the "interpretative strategies consonant with the concerns, experiences and formal devices of women writers" discussed in the introduction (Schwe-ickart, "Reading Ourselves," 29). For example, as suggested in the comments on "Iskushenie," one profitably might look for irony in Ros-topchina's work.[59] Or one might apply to "Kak dolzhny pisat' zhen-shchiny"(How women should write, 1840), "Na lavrovyi venets" (On a laurel wreath," 1846), and *Dnevnik devushki* (A girl's diary, 1845, 6: iii) Ali-cia Ostriker's concept of "the duplicitous," in which contrary meanings coexist with equal force; in these works Rostopchina both denies and as-serts the autonomy of the woman writer. These poems might also be read in relation to Cheryl Walker's discussion of women writers' "am-bivalence" toward power, ambition, and creativity. Similarly, one might reexamine the often-republished "feminine" poems about balls men-tioned earlier in the light of Sandra Gilbert's concept of "female female impersonation" or "womanly masquerade," in which the poet looks at herself being looked at.

Such interpretative strategies would help us better appreciate Ros-topchina's novel in verse, *Dnevnik devushki,* a very original work both in form (metrics) and content. In the nineteenth century Dobroliubov sar-castically remarked on its abundance of epigraphs, but the work re-ceived no other notice. In the twentieth century it has been charac-terized only as "unsuccessful," and "drawn out."[60] Except for brief excerpts, it has not been republished since 1866.

Rostopchina's extensive use of epigraphs in this work should be con-sidered in relation to Catriona Kelly's remarks on the "difference, in-deed 'otherness,' of intertextuality in poetry by women." Kelly writes that in contrast to men writers, who observe "a respectful cult of cultural artifacts," women writers are "anticanonical"; their subtexts are not "carefully integrated," but rather "assembled by accretion, bricolage" ("Reluctant Sibyls," 132). In *Dnevnik devushki* Rostopchina assembles an alternative European literary tradition. Citations from now-forgotten gynocentric works by women writers (for example, Delphine Gay's "Napoline" [1833], Mme. de Krudener's *Valerie* [1803], Lady Morgan's *Woman, or, Ida of Athens* [1809], Mme. Roland's *Memoirs* [1795]) and from appropriated works by men (Byron, Zhukovsky, Goethe, Pushkin, and others) create a background against which a woman's story may be told. It is a work that deserves further study, both in relation to Elizabeth Bar-rett Browning's contemporaneous but "canonically" intertextual novel in verse, *Aurora Leigh* (1856), and also in relation to *Evgenii Onegin.*

All this is not to argue that Rostopchina's poetry belongs in the canon of Russian literature, but, rather, to point out that much of what has passed for the "reception" of her work more accurately may be characterized as sexual harassment.[61] Rostopchina's poetry deserves a fresh consideration on its own terms, and this includes reading it with the same respect for Rostopchina's "concerns, experiences, and formal devices" that scholars automatically accord her male contemporaries.

5

Nadezhda Khvoshchinskaia

While Nadezhda Khvoshchinskaia (1824–89) has been recognized for the novels and stories she wrote under the pseudonym V. Krestovsky, the wonderful poetry that she wrote under her own name has been forgotten.[1] There are many reasons for the disappearance of these works from literary history. First, in the course of her life Khvoshchinskaia herself seemed to lose interest in her poetry: she neither published nor apparently wrote any poems after 1859, nor did she collect her more than eighty published poems, although she published a six-volume edition of her prose works. Second, much of her poetry still remains unpublished in notebooks, which are now in archives. Third, the poems that were published during her lifetime appeared in distorted form and, moreover, did so not in "thick" (*tolstye*) literary journals, but chiefly in newspapers. Such works are less likely to become part of the literary canon since, like newspapers themselves, they tend to be considered ephemeral. In addition, recovery of such works is not easy, as newspapers are less likely than journals to be preserved. Other more basic factors, however, contributed to the disappearance of Khvoschinskaia's poetry from Russian literary history.

These factors, I suggest, had nothing to do with the quality of Khvoshchinskaia's poetry—which is well worth recovering—but rather with the gender issues discussed in previous chapters. As we shall see, despite her ability to ignore or overcome the constraints of gender norms in her career, they ultimately affected her reception and reputation as a poet.

Khvoshchinskaia was born in Riazan' in 1824.[2] Her father, Dmitrii Kesarevich Khvoshchinsky, was a civil servant, first working in the department of horse breeding, then as a surveyor. Her half-Russian, half-Polish mother, Iuliia Vikent'eva, born Drobysheva-Rubets, was well educated and fluent in French, which she taught her children. Khvoshchinskaia had three younger sisters and a brother. One sister died in childhood; the other two, like Khvoshchinskaia, became writers: Sof'ia, under the pseudonym Iv. Vesen'ev, and Praskov'ia, under the pseudonym of S. Zimarov.

Khvoshchinskaia did not have a typical childhood because her family was déclassé. Her sister Praskov'ia recounts that in 1831 their father, falsely accused of embezzling money from the government, lost his position, and to settle the judgment against him was forced to sell all his property. For fourteen years the family lived in poverty—with occasional help from wealthy relatives[3]—until 1845, when Dmitrii Kesarevich finally proved his innocence and was reinstated. These events made Khvoshchinskaia aware of social, political, and economic realities from an early age.[4]

Another factor that made Khvoshchinskaia's childhood atypical for a girl was the encouragement she received from her father to develop her intellectual and artistic powers. Although as a result of her family's financial difficulties, Khvoshchinskaia at about age seven had to leave the *pension* where she was studying, this did not end her education. She spent more than a year with a Moscow uncle studying Italian, music, and drawing. In addition, she studied Latin with her brother and enjoyed unlimited use of her father's library. Most significantly, in working as her father's secretary—from age nine until his death, according to one biography —Khvoshchinskaia acquired an education in aspects of provincial life, politics, economics, government, and the civil service, unavailable to most women of the time. Within her family Khvoshchinskaia appears to have enjoyed prerogatives usually reserved for men. Her sister Praskov'ia writes, "N. D. always had the right to express herself [*pravo golosa*] in our house; she had heated arguments with Father, and she boldly maintained her opinions and views, something we could not allow ourselves."[5]

In addition, Dmitrii Kesarevich encouraged Khvoshchinskaia to write poetry. On the inside front cover of a notebook of Khvoshchinskaia's poems dating from her twelfth year (1836), now in RGALI, we find his verse inscription:

> Черная книга светлых идей
> Черной головки дщери моей;
> Талант самобытный признан уж в ней.
> Пиши, не ленись, чернил не жалей,
> В ряды вдохновенных втеснися скорей.

(A black book of bright ideas
From the dark little head of my daughter;
With her original talent already acknowledged,
Write, don't be lazy, don't spare the ink,
Thrust yourself quickly into the ranks of the inspired.)[6]

After Khvoshchinskaia earned her first money as a writer—for the *povest'* (tale) *Anna Mikhailovna* (1850)—Praskov'ia Khvoshchinskaia recounts that their father gave Khvoshchinskaia a desk, their mother gave her an inkwell, and they both always provided a corner where she could write undisturbed. In addition, Dmitrii Kesarevich, at the urging of Vladimir Zotov, the editor of *Literaturnaia gazeta,* in 1852 took Khvoshchinskaia to Saint Petersburg for several weeks to make the literary contacts necessary to advance her career. In the 1850s Khvoshchinskaia stopped publishing poetry, for reasons that will be discussed below, to concentrate only on prose. She eventually became a highly respected novelist, critic, and translator who, after the deaths of her father and sister Sof'ia, managed with her writing to support her mother, sister, two aunts, two nephews, and husband.

But if Khvoshchinskaia's unusual childhood promoted intellectual self-confidence and the ability to have a successful literary career, it produced less positive social and psychological effects. One suspects that social life for Khvoshchinskaia in Riazan' would have been uncomfortable in any case because of the legal judgment against her father as well as the family's severe financial problems. In addition, one biographer states that Khvoshchinskaia's writing cut her off from conventional female society (Tsebrikova, "Ocherk zhizni," 7), although, as we shall see, she always had many close relationships with women relatives and friends. Khvoshchinskaia herself wrote that her neighbors thought her crazy, while *diady generaly, kuziny freiliny* (her uncles the generals, and her cousins the ladies-in-waiting) considered her writing, especially the prose, a disgrace to the family.[7] Furthermore, Khvoshchinskaia throughout her life struggled with severe depression, at least at one point, after her sister Sof'ia's death, becoming suicidal.[8] Some biographies suggest that Khvoshchinskaia often became involved with people who abused her emotionally and/or financially.[9]

Despite Khvoshchinskaia's unconventional upbringing and its social and psychological costs, however, in at least one respect her life remained typical for a woman of her time: she lived and wrote in a gynosocial world. The scholar Ol'ga Demidova compares the Khvoshchinsky household with that of the Brontës, because in both cases three sisters, living in provincial isolation, wrote and shared their work with one another.[10] The most intense relationship in Khvoshchinskaia's life appears to have been with her sister Sof'ia, her closest friend. Several biographers also mention Khvoshchinskaia's many aunts and women friends—N. E. Fon Vinkler, M. Andreevna, A. G. Karrik, her goddaughter Sonia, and Vera Aleksandrovna Moskaleva, with whom she lived for the last eight years of her life.[11] Even Khvoshchinskaia's marriage could be considered an extension of her relationship with a woman: she told an acquaintance that she had married Sof'ia's doctor, Ivan Zaionchkovsky, two months after her sister's death (in 1865) "because I was afraid of loneliness" (Vinitskaia, "Vospominaniia o N.D. Khvoshchinskoi," 152). The marriage was unsuccessful; the couple lived together for only two years, and Zaionchkovsky died abroad in 1872.

It was the atypical and unconventional aspects of Khvoshchinskaia's life, however, that preoccupied her biographers. I suggest that Khvoshchinskaia's achievements as poet, author, and critic—an implicit challenge to gender assumptions about women—made her contemporaries very uncomfortable. We see this discomfort both in accounts of her life and in the critical reception that led her to abandon poetry and be forgotten as a poet.

Biographers dealt with the "unfeminine" anomaly of Khvoshchinskaia's success in various ways. The writer A. A. Vinitskaia (1847–1914) concludes an envy-tinged memoir by suggesting that Khvoshchinskaia was a moral monster, that is, not a woman at all: "And [her] heart reflected neither warmth, nor light, nor any joys at all; nothing animated it except her own work and literary successes." In contrast, as we shall see, Mar'ia Tsebrikova (1835–1917), the feminist social critic and publicist, vigorously defended Khvoshchinskaia's femininity. Tsebrikova may well have believed that only in this way could she secure Khvoshchinskaia a serious hearing as a writer.[12] Other biographers (V. Semevsky, Vladimir Zotov) expressed their ambivalence by simultaneously defending Khvoshchinskaia's femininity and suggesting that she was an unnatural woman. These discussions of Khvoshchinskaia's femininity repay attention because they determined both her literary reception and reputation and also show the difficulties she confronted as a woman writer. In addition, the aspects of Khvoshchinskaia's life that interested her biographers—her appearance, personal habits, courting and marriage behavior, modesty, and relationship to money—indicate how femininity was constructed at the time. As we shall see, that construction has changed somewhat, indicating, as some scholars have argued, that femininity is at least in part culturally defined and prescribed.[13] It should not be surprising, however, that contemporary expectations affected and influenced Khvoshchinskaia.

As in the case of Rostopchina, most biographers and memoirists minutely describe and evaluate Khvoshchinskaia's physical appearance in terms of its attractiveness to men. Unlike Rostopchina, however, Khvoshchinskaia is portrayed as unappealing, possessing only one or two good features:

> A girl, not in her first youth, simply dressed, short, dark-complexioned, with crooked features but with large expressive black eyes. (Zotov, "Nadezhda Dmitrievna Khvoshchinskaia," 99)

> Her appearance was not effective for balls, although she had an original appeal, especially in her big, intelligent, and kind, black, brilliant eyes. (Tsebrikova, "Ocherk zhizni," 4)

> Very swarthy features, beautiful black hair and expressive black eyes. In general, her appearance was very original, sympathetic and piquant, despite her overly big lower lip. . . . In the years that she first attended balls, her appearance did not produce a favorable impression. (Semevskii, "N. D. Khvoshchinskaia-Zaionchkovskaia," 10: 55)

> As a woman, she produced a very unfavorable impression: short, stooped, with sharp features. . . [H]er sister [Sof'ia] was an ugly woman with an unfeminine, intelligent face, but more shapely and taller, [who] looked like what she was, a middle-aged old maid. N. D. looked more married.[14]

In regard to the last citation it should be noted that at this time Khvoshchinskaia, who was four years older than Sof'ia and would not marry until after Sof'ia's death, was also a "middle-aged old maid." Her later marriage appears to have retroactively lent her the appearance of a married woman. I have cited these descriptions at length because men's evaluations of the physical attributes of successful women were so pervasive that one can easily stop noticing them. We therefore fail to recognize, much less question, the assumptions implicit in these usually unflattering descriptions: that a woman's achievements are less important than her attractiveness to men; that a woman only becomes an artist because she has failed to attract a man; that it is unnatural for a woman to be an artist.[15] Such beliefs may account for the fact that

Khvoshchinskaia's most often republished poem, appearing at least seven times, is "Net, ia ne nazovu obmanom" (No, I will not call it an illusion, 1851), which critics interpret as her humble acceptance of the fact that she will never find happiness because she is unattractive.[16]

Biographers rarely scrutinize and judge the personal habits of men writers, although no doubt much could be written about those of Gogol, Lermontov, and others. However, virtually all Khvoshchinskaia's biographers noted disapprovingly that she smoked cigars, a violation of gender norms. (*Russkii biograficheskii slovar'* [1900–1918] more circumspectly referred to Khvoshchinskaia's "masculine habits, acquired from her father.") Those defending Khvoshchinskaia's femininity pointed out that she also loved "women's work."[17] The biographer V. Semevsky writes: "Having become tired of working, N. D. would take up the crochet hook and begin to crochet: she loved all kinds of women's work very much" ("N. D. Khvoshchinskaia-Zaionchkovskaia," 142). Semevsky both defends Khvoshchinskaia as feminine and trivializes her writing by redefining her "female" pen as a metaphorical crochet hook. This comparison contrasts with the traditional equation of the "male" pen with a penis, explicated by Sandra Gilbert and Susan Gubar: "In patriarchal Western culture, therefore, the text's author is a father, a progenitor, a procreator, an aesthetic patriarch whose pen is an instrument of generative power like his penis. . . . The pen has been defined as not just accidentally, but essentially a male "tool" and therefore not only inappropriate but actually alien to women" (*Madwoman in the Attic*, 6–8). Such metaphors as Semevsky's maintain the double standard that valorizes men's writing as art while dismissing women's writing as amateur craft, not to be taken seriously. One thinks of Vissarion Belinsky's similar dismissal of eighteenth-century Russian women poets' work as "the poetic knitting of stockings, rhymed sewing."[18]

As for gender norms in the realm of courtship and marriage, Khvoshchinskaia's contemporaries apparently disregarded what we would call sexual/emotional orientation. That is, they did not question Khvoshchinskaia's femininity on the grounds that she had a series of intense relationships with women and lived with a woman for the last eight years of her life. Indeed, Semevsky, one of Khvoshchinskaia's most judgmental critics, approvingly described that relationship with Vera Aleksandrovna Moskaleva as "a most tender friendship" (*samaia nezhnaia druzhba*).[19] We find an explanation for these biographers' apparent inability to imagine a lesbian relationship in the work of Michel Foucault

and queer theorists, who argue that homosexuality as a "new specifi-
cation of individuals" (Foucault, *History of Sexuality*, 1: 42–43) or "category of identification" (Jagose, *Queer Theory*, 10) only appeared at the end
of the nineteenth century, and lesbianism in the first decades of the
twentieth.[20] Until then, male homosexual acts "were not understood to
constitute a certain kind of individual" (Jagose, *Queer Theory*, 11). As for
nineteenth-century women's romantic friendships, they were considered "unremarkable or even praiseworthy" because men's belief that
"normal women are blessed by sexual anesthesia" made it impossible
for them to perceive such friendships as sexual (Greenberg, *Construction
of Homosexuality*, 379, 378).[21] Khvoshchinskaia's short-lived marriage appears to have satisfied patriarchal norms. In any case, compilers of two
reference works, D. D. Iazykov and I. F. Masanov, listed Khvoshchinskaia
under her husband's name, Zaionchkovskaia, while four biographers
and bibliographers, Karrik, Semevsky, Tsebrikova, and Chizhkov, referred to her as Khvoshchinskaia-Zaionchkovskaia, although Khvoshchinskaia never wrote under any variant of her husband's name.[22]

Rather, biographers debated the "femininity" of Khvoshchinskaia's
sexual behavior either by defending her as submissive to men or by attacking her for appropriating male prerogatives. Tsebrikova, the champion of Khvoshchinskaia's femininity, depicts her as a self-sacrificing,
compliant wife, describing at great length the emotional, physical, and
financial abuse Khvoshchinskaia endured from Zaionchkovsky. Those
attacking Khvoshchinskaia depicted her as a sex-crazed spinster, point-
ing derisively to the fact that she first married at age forty a man thirteen years her junior, a circumstance that would have gone unnoted had
Khvoshchinskaia and Zaionchkovsky's genders been reversed. One
clearly uncomfortable memoirist—"the bride had already passed the
age allotted for marriage and was much older than the groom"—
claimed that Khvoshchinskaia only married Zaionchkovsky at her dying sister Sofia's request (Zotov, "Nadezhda Dmitrievna Khvoshchinskaia," 102). Praskov'ia Khvoshchinskaia specifically denied this story
("Nadezhda Khvoshchinskaia," xiii).

Khvoshchinskaia's contemporaries appeared to consider an even
more serious violation of gender norms the fact that Khvoshchinskaia
appropriated male prerogatives of language and behavior by verbally
cross-dressing and by "leading a woman on." Two memoirists describe
Khvoshchinskaia's correspondence with a provincial woman who, mis-
led by Khvoshchinskaia's male pseudonym (V. Krestovsky), started a
romantic correspondence with her.[23] Khvoshchinskaia at first did not

disabuse the woman, but when it eventually became necessary to do so, the woman refused to believe she had not been writing to a man.

In the interrelated realms of writing, money, and modesty / ambition, Khvoshchinskaia violated female gender norms by supporting not only herself but also a large family—including her husband. As noted in chapter 1, women who wrote for publication in the mid-nineteenth century were considered to be engaging in sexual display or prostitution. In addition, mid-nineteenth-century domestic ideology consigned "ladies" to the home, where, financially supported by their husbands, they were supposed to establish a haven from the crass commercial world. Ladies were not supposed to support their husbands.[24] Several biographers focused obsessively and almost pruriently on how much money Khvoshchinskaia earned from her writing—one calculated her income for each decade of her life.[25] We do not find such a preoccupation, for example, among the biographers of Dostoevsky, who also struggled to support many family members with his writing.

Domestic ideology required women to be "modest," that is, to renounce recognition or fame, certainly the fame of publication under their own names.[26] Khvoshchinskaia along with her sisters appear to have embraced this aspect of femininity, for which contemporary men biographers praised her.[27] All three sisters used male pseudonyms for their prose, separating their feminine "selves" from their masculine-defined activities and careers. Similarly, all three fiercely objected to having their biographies published. Khvoshchinskaia wrote to a would-be biographer: "Pseudonyms have no biographies at all. What is a pseudonym? No one. Then what is there to say about it? Nothing" (Bykov, *Siluety dalekogo proshlogo,* 187). One is reminded of the Emily Dickinson poem, mentioned in the introduction, which starts:

> I'm Nobody! Who are you?
> Are you-Nobody-Too?
> Then there's a pair of us!
> Don't tell! they'd advertise-you know!
> ("I'm Nobody!" in *Poems of Emily Dickinson,* ed. T. H. Johnson, 206)

One feels a similar ambivalence in Khvoshchinskaia's and Dickinson's renunciation of public identity.[28] In the same letter Khvoshchinskaia wrote admonishingly, "The inviolability of a pseudonym is one of the most elementary concepts of good (decent) respectable literary society. It is completely natural in view of the varied causes that can lead a writer to sign

an article with an invented name" (Bykov, *Siluety dalekogo proshlogo*, 186).
Khvoshchinskaia tried to prevent articles about her sister Sof'ia from being published after her death, and one surmises from one memoir, she
finally broke with her "mentor," Vladimir Zotov, when he published an
obituary of Sof'ia against Khvoshchinskaia's expressed wishes.[29] In this
context, it is significant that Khvoshchinskaia always signed her poetry
with her full name and freely used feminine grammatical endings in her
poems. Perhaps she felt more identification with her poetry than with her
prose, or perhaps she felt it was more acceptable for a woman to write
poetry.[30] Yet, if the latter is the case, why has her poetry disappeared? I
suggest it is because her poetry, too, violated gender norms.

Gatekeepers, Reception, Reputation

Khvoshchinskaia's career as a poet, according to Praskov'ia Khvoshchinskaia, began in 1847, when she was twenty-three. A friend of the family arranged to have a notebook of Khvoshchinskaia's poetry delivered
to Vladimir Zotov (1821–96), then editor of *Literaturnaia gazeta*. As discussed in chapter 1, women writers, lacking the entrée into literature that
men enjoyed through salons and universities, found it difficult to make
the contacts with men necessary to get published. Those women writers who, like Khvoshchinskaia, lived far from Moscow and Saint Petersburg, where the periodic press was concentrated, experienced even
more difficulty. A few months later, Praskov'ia Khvoshchinskaia continues, Zotov, looking for something to put in the poetry column of the
newspaper, read the notebook. He published six of Khvoshchinskaia's
poems in *Literaturnaia gazeta*, no. 38 (Sept. 18, 1847) under an effusive
note in which the twice italicized "lady" marked his astonishment (or
perhaps his doubt) that a woman could have written this poetry:

> Buried under bad poetry sent to us from all corners of verse-
> loving Russia we were very pleasantly and unexpectedly sur-
> prised by the verse delivered to us by a Miss N. D. Khvoshchin-
> skaia. We found in it much true poetry and warmth of feeling,
> heated by thought and originality. It is even more pleasant to ac-
> quaint the readers of our newspaper with a new poet because this
> poet is a *lady*. We have not read such wonderful and sonorous
> verses in Russian for a long time. We sincerely thank their author
> in particular on behalf of ourselves and the entire reading public,
> which no doubt will justly appreciate the new poetic gift of a *lady*
> who commands verse with more ease than many contemporary
> men poets have attained.

Between 1847 and 1859 Zotov published more than eighty of Khvoshchinskaia's poems.

Interestingly, Praskov'ia Khvoshchinskaia does not mention
Khvoshchinskaia's true poetic debut five years earlier, in 1842, when her
poem, "Zavetnye chuvstva" (Secret feelings) appeared in *Syn otechestva*
(no. 2). (The poem appears as "Na bale" [At the ball, no. 21] in her notebook, which is discussed later in this chapter). That same year "Materi"
(To my mother), Khvoshchinskaia's dedicatory poem to her translation
of Victor Hugo's "La prière pour tous" (1831), also appeared in *Syn otechestva* (no. 5).[31] How these poems came to be published remains unknown.

Vladimir Zotov, who arranged for all subsequent publications of
Khvoshchinskaia's poetry, has been described as her "mentor" and "in
the liberal camp."[32] Both terms require qualification. In regard to Zotov's
politics, it is true that in the 1840s he was friendly with the antigovern-
ment Petrashevsky circle, which included Dostoevsky and A. N. Pleshcheev, was arrested with them, but was then released.[33] And in the late
1850s and 1860s he helped Aleksandr Herzen collect censored Russian
literature to be published abroad. However, in 1861 Zotov praised the
reforms under which the serfs were nominally freed, but which more
radical social critics, for example, the Sovremennik group led by N. A.
Nekrasov, N. G. Chernyshevsky, and N. A. Dobroliubov, considered inadequate. And in 1858 he wrote an article described as "openly anti-
Semitic" in *Illiustratsiia*, which he edited from 1858 to1861, "protesting
against the idea of extending civil rights to Jews."[34]

Zotov's treatment of Khvoshchinskaia was equally equivocal. From
one point of view, it could be argued that Zotov did indeed act as
Khvoshchinskaia's mentor: he published her poetry in a wide variety of
newspapers and thick journals, making her known as a poet. He introduced her to Saint Petersburg literary circles and prevailed on her to
turn from poetry to prose, in which she experienced a great deal of
success. From another point of view, however, it could be argued that
Zotov exploited and abused Khvoshchinskaia, while appropriating
her work. Several sources observe that he did not pay her for her poetry.
As mentioned in chapter 2, he published the first two groups of her
poems below an article suggestively titled "Safo i lesbosskie getery"
(Sappho and the courtesans of Lesbos). As women poets generally
did not appear in *Literaturnaia gazeta*, it seems a strange choice to have
placed Khvoshchinskaia's work below an article that sexualized the
most famous classical woman poet. The poems of Khvoshchinskaia's

that Zotov did publish (fewer than half the poems she sent him) he re-wrote without her permission, continuing to do so over her protests. He never honored her wish that he help her publish a book of her poetry.[35] However, he did publish biographical articles about Khvoshchinskaia and her sister against Khvoshchinskaia's express request and at the end of his life published self-glorifying memoirs about having discovered her. He was not her mentor as Zhukovsky was Pushkin's mentor, and Pushkin, Del'vig's. While the latter helped their "mentees" advance to a position of professional independence, Zotov could more accurately be described as Khvoshchinskaia's literary guardian, and she as his permanent ward until she turned to prose.

Zotov somewhat condescendingly described his first impressions of Khvoshchinskaia's poetry, which he deemed "far from irreproachable" in form, "not entirely finished," but the work of a "naturally gifted" writer (*samorodok*) "that only required smoothing the rough edges" ("Nadezhda Dmitrievna Khvoshchinskaia," 94).This he proceeded to do, dismissing with amusement Khvoshchinskaia's requests, which he considered ungrateful and disrespectful, that her poetry be published as written. In one memoir he wrote:

> I received a letter without any respectful salutation and without closing assurances of "complete respect and devotion" and with the simple signature "N. Khvoshchinskaia." In the letter, thanking me for printing the poetry, she said "I am sending you a few other poems, but I ask only one thing: that you print them without changes. . . . Thank you for your condescension and attention [in changing my poems], but again I earnestly ask you not to do this. . . . If you find that something in my poetry is weak and requires reworking, don't print it at all." (94)

Zotov writes that Khvoshchinskaia continued to object to his editing even when he pointed out to her that he was "more experienced in literature" and had a "more mature point of view" (95).[36]

Khvoshchinskaia's irritation is easily understood when we compare her original poems to Zotov's "edited" versions. Zotov may have honestly thought he was improving the poems, but, as we shall see, his editing, especially of those poems protesting women's treatment in society, more accurately could be described as censorship—or mutilation. Certainly, he was unqualified to deal with Khvoshchinskaia's intellectual power and unconventional poetic genius.

At least two autograph notebooks (notebooks in Khvoshchinskaia's handwriting) still exist, one comprising 197 poetic works, the other 9, both located in RGALI, the Russian State Archive of Literature and Art. The larger notebook bears the inscription from her father on the inside front cover, quoted earlier in this chapter.[37] The second, in which Khvoshchinskaia wrote nine later poems, comes from France and has "Album buvard." (Blotter-album) stamped on the cover.[38] It has pockets in the back for correspondence, printed French poems in the front, and blank blotting pages in the middle, on which Khvoshchinskaia wrote her own poetry.

The larger notebook has a table of contents in which 72 of the 197 poem titles are underlined, apparently to indicate publication. Under the text of each of these poems a different hand identifies the issue and year of the newspaper or journal in which it appeared. Most, but not all, of this information is correct. By my count, 85 poems from both notebooks appeared in print. Also in the larger notebook a few vertical strokes in the left-hand margin indicate lines of poetry that did not appear in the printed versions. In a few cases lines are crossed out and rewritten in the same second hand. While it is tempting to see this second hand as Zotov's, that would not appear to be the case. Zotov did write in a memoir that he had received "an entire notebook from Riazan'" but describes it as having "more than half a hundred poems," not 197. And at the end of his life he wrote of having 120 of Khvoshchinskaia's poems.[39]

A comparison of the poems in these notebooks with the published versions shows many of Zotov's editorial changes to be gratuitous and others to spoil the poems. For example, it is difficult to see how Zotov improved the poem, "Dolzhna b ia vchera poplakat'" (I should have cried yesterday, no.121 in the notebook, published in *Literaturnaia gazeta*, no. 35 [Sept. 2, 1848]) by changing in line 8 Khvoshchinskaia's "i chto zhe?" to the synonymous "a chto zhe?" Equally arbitrary appears to be his change of Khvoshchinskaia's "sozdan'ia" (creation) to the synonymous "tvoren'ia" in lines 23 and 30 of "Melodiia (O daite mne pole, shirokoe, gladkoe pole!)" (Melody [O give me a field, a wide, smooth field!], no. 49 in the notebook, published in *Literaturnaia gazeta*, no. 39 [Sept., 25 1847]). Nor is it clear for what reason he added the word "ves'" (all) to the last line of "Segodnia vsiu noch'" (Today all night, no. 124 in the notebook, published in *Panteon*, no. 1 [Jan. 1854]), changing Khvoshchinskaia's "Chtob s pesneiu mir obletet'" (So as to fly around the world with a song) to "Chtob s pesn'iu ves' mir obletet'" (So as to fly around the whole world with a song). Or how he improved "V gostinoi ubrannoi roskoshno" (In a luxuriously decorated drawing room, no. 120 in the notebook, published in *Panteon*, no. 2 [Feb. 1855]) by changing in line 3 "Mezhdu kartinami, statuiami" (Between the pictures and statues) to "Mezhdu statuiami, kartinimi."

In several cases Zotov's editing marred Khvoshchinskaia's artistry. For example, in "Ia ne tebe otdam poslednie chasy" (I will not give you the last hours, no. 88 in the notebook, published in *Literaturnaia gazeta*, no. 38 [Sept. 18, 1847]), he destroyed Khvoshchinskaia's alliteration in line 8 by changing "Bezvestnyi, beznachal'nyi" (unknown, eternal [without a beginning]) to "Bezvestnii i dalekii" (unknown, far off). And in lines 11–12 of "Uzhasno skorbnykh dnei kholodnosti dozhdat'sia!" (It is terrible to wait for mournful days of coldness! no. 66 in the notebook, published in *Literaturnaia gazeta*, no. 39 [Sept. 25, 1847]) he destroyed Khvoshchinskaia's carefully crafted emphasis on "ko grobu" (to the grave) when he changed "i trepetno idti / Stopoiu robkoiu ko grobu" (and, trembling, to go / with timid tread to the grave) to "i trepetno ko grobu / Stopoiu robkoiu idti" (and trembling to the grave / with a timid tread to go).

Zotov also routinely changed Khvoshchinskaia's punctuation—adding exclamation points (four, for example, in "Druz'ia, vam istinno, vam shchedro zhizn' dana" [Friends, to you truly, to you generously life has been given, no. 76 in the notebook, published in *Literaturnaia gazeta*, no. 39 (Sept. 25, 1847)], discussed later in this chapter), or changing semi-colons to commas. A poet's punctuation, as Emily Dickinson scholars have long argued, must be seen as an important part of its meaning, providing clues about how we are to read and understand it.[40] This is certainly true of Khvoshchinskaia's clear and intelligent punctuation in the manuscript versions of her poems. Furthermore, Zotov printed all of Khvoshchinskaia's poems flush left, ignoring her line indentations, that is, her visual arrangement of the poem on the page. This, too, I would argue, is part of the poem's meaning. In many cases Zotov removed lines or virtually rewrote poems. For example, in addition to other changes, he removed eighteen lines from the five poems he published under the title "Otryvki iz dnevnika" (Fragments from a diary, in the notebook poems nos. 121, 122, 123, 125, and 119, published in *Literaturnaia gazeta*, no. 35 [Sept. 12, 1848]), rendering the second and the fifth unintelligible.[41] In another instance he changed twenty-three lines of the thirty-line poem "Melodiia (O daite mne pole, shirokoe, gladkoe pole!)," mentioned previously, and in yet another changed fifteen out of twenty-six lines of "Byvalo, s sestrami veseloi i shumnoi tolpoi" (My sisters and I in a cheerful and noisy crowd used to), discussed later in this chapter, never, I would argue, to these poems' advantage.

Examples of many such changes may be seen in the published version of "Druz'ia, vam istinno, vam shchedro zhizn' dana" (no. 76 in the notebook, published in *Literaturnaia gazeta,* no. 39 [Sept. 25, 1847])—one of Khvoshchinskaia's most powerful poems. (See the appendix for both the manuscript and the published version.)

In line 1 Zotov broke up Khvoshchinskaia's passionate oratory into lumpy iambs.

Khvoshchinskaia: Друзья, вам истинно, вам щедро жизнь дана

⤳

(Friends, to you truly, to you generously life has been given.)

Published version: Друзья мои! Вам всем так щедро жизнь дана

⤳

(My friends! To you all so generously life has been given.)

In line 3 he weakened Khvoshchinskaia's "strast'mi moguchimi" (with mighty passions) by changing it to "strast'mi sil'nymi" (with strong passions), and flattened Khvoshchinskaia's "liubvi sviatoi toskoiu" (the sacred anguish of love) to "liubov'iu i toskoiu." (love and anguish). In line 4, which sums up the first three lines, he changed the strong adjective "roskoshnaia" (luxurious, splendid) to the weaker "prekrasnaia" (beautiful, fine), moving "roskoshnaia" to the less emphasized second line.

While it would be tedious to discuss all of Zotov's changes, I would draw the reader's attention to line 25, in which he destroyed Khvoshchinskaia's parallel syntax:

Khvoshchinskaia: Где тут деятельность, где тут разгул для сил?

⤳

(Where here is activity, where here is the revelry for one's energies?)

Published version: Где деятельность тут, где тут разгул для сил?

⤳

(Where is the activity here, where here is the revelry for one's energies?)

and to the censored (and unintelligible) lines 35 and 36.

Khvoshchinskaia: Что, есть ли он иль нет? Он божье ль творенье
Или мечта людей!.. и прочь идет.

⤳

(What? Does it [the world] exist or not? Is it a god's creation
Or peoples' dream? . . . and he goes away.)

Published version: Что, есть ли он, иль нет? . . .
. . . И далее плывет.

✽

(What is it, or not? . . .
. . . And he sails on.)

Zotov made line 36 even less intelligible by removing Khvoshchinskaia's comma after "chto."

It might be argued that in the last case Zotov censored the lines that question whether the Christian God created the world and whether that world is real because he feared government or religious censorship. However, this poem appeared in September 1847, six months before Nicholas I launched the "censorship terror" in reaction to the European revolutions of 1848. One historian characterizes the decade before 1848 as "a time of reasonably benign censorship controls." I would argue that Zotov censored the lines, just as he rewrote the poem, for himself.[42]

Zotov also succeeded in obscuring the meaning of "Byvalo, s sestrami veseloi i shumnoi tolpoi" (My sisters and I in a cheerful and noisy crowd used to, no. 75 in the notebook, published in *Literaturnaia gazeta*, no. 38 [1847], see appendix), a poem that describes the withering effects of poverty. The speaker and her sisters are walking along a small-town lane, loudly talking and laughing, when the speaker notices a young woman in the window of a rundown house, enviously observing them. The young married woman, a poor seamstress, already feels there is no joy or hope for joy in her life.

Молодая, но бледная, [. . .]
[. . . . .]
Колечко на бледной руке [. . .]
[. . . . .]
Перед ней на окне и работа . . . [. . .]
Глядит, будто хочет сказать: "Верно праздник у них!"
И может быть труд своих долгих бессонных ночей
Узнает на беспечной подруге моей,
И столько печали в том взоре, и жалости столько немой
О грустно утраченной юности, светлой, роскошной, живой,
О жизни, что дал ей Господь, чтоб смеяться, и петь, и любить. . .
Что этого взора мне долго, вовек не забыть. . .

✽

(Young but pale [. . .]
[. . . . .]
A little ring on her pale hand [. . .]

[. . . . .]
Her work in front of her on the window . . . [. . .]
She looks as if she would say, "They're having a real holiday!"
And perhaps the labor of her long, sleepless nights [i.e., her sewing]
She recognized on my carefree friend,
And there was so much sadness in her gaze, and so much unspoken
   regret
For bright, splendid, lively youth sadly lost,
For the life which the Lord gave her to laugh and sing and love
That this gaze I will not forget, for a long time—for all time.)

Zotov's changes in the printed version of the poem all served to mute Khvoshchinskaia's contrast between the sisters' gaiety and the young woman's unhappiness. He removed "bezzabotno" (carefree) from line 10 and in line 11 changed "chasto sluchalos' [gromkoe slovo]" (there was often [loud speech]) to "neredko sluchalos'" (not infrequently there was [loud speech]). Clearly, young ladies should not be so boisterous. Zotov also removed Khvoshchinskaia's reference to the woman's youth, which underlines the sapping effects of poverty.

Khvoshchinskaia, Line 14: "Молодая, но бледная"

(Young but pale)

Published version: "Печальная, бледная"

(Sad, pale)

Rather, Zotov implied, by rewriting another line, the woman's sadness was attributable to disease, perhaps tuberculosis, which, nevertheless, made her beautiful:

Khvoshchinskaia, Line 16:   Яркий взор, томный лик среди мрачной
   кругом темноты

(A bright gaze, a languid face amidst the surrounding gloomy darkness)

Published version: Взор яркий и томный, болезненный вид красоты

(A bright gaze and a languid, sickly kind of beauty)

Zotov also eliminated Khvoshchinskaia's reference to the woman's sewing in line 19, making lines 21–22 difficult to understand. He added a tear on the young woman's eyelash, changing a picture of common domestic drudgery and misery to one of emotional crisis:

Khvoshchinskaia, lines 18–19:   И пыльный луч солнца на них, и
герcaний что грустно поблек
Перед ней на окне, и работа... [...]

(And the dusty ray of sun on [her braids], and the geranium which sadly
withered
Before her on the window and the work... [...])

Published version, lines 18–19: Слезу на реснице ... Гераний так
грустно поблек
У ней на окошке ... [...]

(A tear on her eyelash ... A geranium so sadly withered
Near her on the little window... [...])

Zotov also changed Khvoshchinskaia's understated last line from a relative clause to an effusion, complete with exclamation point:

Khvoshchinskaia, lines 23 and 26:   И столько печали в том взоре, [...]
[. . . . .]
Что этого взора мне долго, вовек не забыть ...

(And so much sadness in that gaze, [...]
[. . . . .]
That I will not forget that gaze for a long time, for all time ...)

Published version: О, этого взора мне долго, вовек не забыть! ...

(O, I cannot forget that gaze for a long time, for all time! ...)

Five years later, in 1852, Zotov took the opportunity to mutilate the
poem still further. In an article reprinting some of Khvoshchinskaia's
poetry, Zotov wrote:

> The *Literary Gazette*, in which these poems for the most part ap-
> peared in 1848 and 1849, has now become a bibliographic rarity
> and does not enjoy a great deal of prestige with the reading
> public. Therefore we are convinced that our readers will read
> with pleasure several excerpts from that newspaper to be fully
> convinced of the varied and brilliant talent of Miss Kvoshchin-
> skaia.[43]

Zotov reprinted the poem, which now started with the words "Byvalo, s podrugami" (My girlfriends and I used to) instead of "Byvalo,

s sestrami" (My sisters and I used to). Among other changes, he removed the last six lines of the poem without any indication to readers
that he had done so. It now ended: "Gliadit' budto khochet skazat':
'Verno prazdnik u nikh!'" (She looks as if she wanted to say, "They are
really having a holiday"). In this way Zotov eliminated the only remaining reference to the fact that the young woman was a seamstress—thus
making the poem incomprehensible—along with the speaker's suggestion that God did not intend this woman to be ground down by
poverty. I have not found this poem subsequently reprinted in any form.

In some cases Zotov went beyond obscuring a poem's meaning to re-
versing it, a fate that befell "'Vy ulybaetes'? . . .'" ("You're smiling? . . ,"
no. 152 in the notebook, first published in *Otechestvennyi zapiski*, no. 8
[1852], see appendix), an elegant, restrained, but effective critique of the
treatment of young women in society. Like "Byvalo, s sestrami," the
poem consists of a frame narrative and story.[44] In the frame narrative, a
woman, abstractedly playing with a wedding ring, notices a man smil-
ingly observing her. She shows him the ring, inscribed 1730, and tells
him its history. It belonged to a young woman whose parents married
her off to an unpleasant, elderly fool, despite the fact that she loved
another man. The young woman, too constrained from birth even to
protest, died soon after, mourned only by the man who loved her. We
return to the frame narrative, in which the narrator's interlocutor merely
responds, "No sto-vos'mnadtsat' let! . . . Ona b stara byla" (But 118
years! . . . She would be old!).

The man's response to the narrator's story indicates that only young,
attractive women interest him, not discussions about their freedom—
or survival. His response also allows the reader to realize that the poem
is set in 1848—118 years after 1730, the date inscribed on the ring.
Khvoshchinskaia, by having the poem take place in the year of European
revolutions, underlines women's lack of freedom in society and the need
for change.[45] She further emphasizes that need by suggesting that the
narrator shares the fate of the ring's original owner. Not only does the
narrator often pensively play with the ring, which she says is dear to
her, but also when she shows it to the man she says, "Vzglianite: mozhet
byt' ono i vas zaimet / Napomnit vam samim den' svetlyi il' pechal'nyi
. . ." (Have a look: Perhaps it will interest you as well / Remind you of a
bright or sad day . . .). The narrator's emphatic use of "i vas and vam
samim" in two successive lines, the placement of "pechal'nyi" in the
strong position at the end of the line, and the suspension points at the
end of the line, suggesting that there is something she cannot say, all

create the impression that the ring interests her by reminding her of the sad day of her wedding.

Perhaps Zotov felt uncomfortable with the poem's critique of the treatment of women. In any case, the poem appeared in print with most of Khvoshchinskaia's irony softened or removed. For example, the original line describing the ring's owner, "Kak ptichka chto rodom privykla k kletke tesnoi" (Like a little bird accustomed from birth to a narrow cage), appeared as "Kak ptichka grustnaia, privykshi k kletke tesnoi" (Like a sad little bird, accustomed to a narrow cage), blunting Khvoshchinskaia's point that the woman was doomed from birth. Zotov also removed Khvoshchinskaia's emphatic "samim" in line 7, which suggests a link between the narrator and the woman in the story. Her ironic "naznachennyi suprug" (assigned spouse) was changed to the more neutral "budushchii suprug" (future spouse). In the original poem, after an unflattering description of the assigned spouse, the incomplete line "Ona . . ." (She . . .) appeared, suggesting both the young woman's horrified reaction to him and also the impossibility of expressing that reaction or of protesting against the marriage. Zotov removed that line. When, on the night of the engagement party, the woman says good-bye to the man she loves, he weeps "O tom, chtob ne vinil on, pylkii i trevozhnyi / Pokornost' detskuiu chtoby prostil on ei" (About the fact that he, ardent and troubled, wouldn't blame her / Would pardon her childish obedience). The central words of those lines, and of the entire poem, "pokornost' detskuiu" (childish obedience), were changed to "V nevernosti ee" (her unfaithfulness). Instead of being a victim of her family and society, the woman is now depicted as responsible both for her own and—seemingly more importantly—also for a man's unhappiness. Zotov also changed the line "To byli slezy o blazhenstve nevozmozhnom" (And there were those tears over impossible bliss) to "o schast'i nevozmozhnom" (impossible happiness). Clearly, the sexual implications of the original version were too explicit—especially to have been written by a woman poet. The information enabling the reader to deduce that the poem takes place in 1848 remains, however; perhaps Zotov missed the reference.

Yet even in this bowdlerized form, the poem still retained enough power to cause one man editor to criticize it and bowdlerize it further. Nikolai Gerbel' included part of the poem in his 1873 anthology, *Khrestomatiia dlia vsekh: Russkie poety v biografiiakh i obraztsakh* (An anthology for everyone: Russian poets in biographies and examples). Strangely, in this anthology supposedly devoted to Russia's best poets,

Gerbel' praised Khvoshchinskaia as a prose writer, while disparaging her as a poet, specifically taking her to task for "'Vy ulybaetes'? . . .'": "Nevertheless, one does not note in her those qualities that make a person a poet. ["'Vy ulybaetes'? . . .'"] can serve as proof of our words. This wonderful poem is spoiled by the eleven introductory and two concluding lines [that is, the frame narrative], which are completely unnecessary and which a *poet* [author's italics] never would have introduced, especially the last two lines, which pour a spoonful of tar into the honey barrel."[46]

Gerbel''s version of "'Vy ulybaetes'? . . ,'" which appears after his introductory note under the title "Otryvok" (Excerpt), consists of Zotov's version of the poem, minus the objectionable frame narrative, which makes the parallel between women's position in 1730 and 1848. Gerbel' also removed, without comment, the two lines of the poem that recount the young woman's death and her lover's grief. In Gerbel''s version the poem ends

> [Чтоб] не винил он, пылкий и тревожный,
> В неверности ее, чтобы простил он ей.
>
> ⤿
>
> (That he, ardent and troubled wouldn't blame her
> For her unfaithfulness and would forgive her for it.)

Thus Gerbel' successfully finished transforming Khvoshchinskaia's poem about society's oppression and destruction of women into one about a man victimized by a woman's inconstancy. Gerbel' also made the poem virtually untraceable, since he removed its identifying first line (the poem has no title), while not clearly indicating that "Otryvok" was his version of "'Vy ulybaetes'? . . ,'" the poem he criticized in his introduction.

In the final stage of the poem's annihilation by men critics and editors, "'Vy ulybaetes'? . . .'" did not appear at all in B. Ia. Bukhshtab's anthology *Poety 1840–1850-kh godov* (1972), although he reprinted twelve of Khvoshchinskaia's poems, including two ("Svoi razum iskusiv ne raz" and "Solntse segodnia za tucheiu chernoi takoi zakatilosia"), which appeared with "'Vy ulybaetes'? . . .'" under the title "Piat' stikhotvorenii" (Five poems) in *Otechestvennye zapiski*, no. 8 (1852). "'Vy ulybaetes'? . .'" was the first, and for this reader at least, the most striking of the five.

Khvoshchinskaia's literary reputation as a poet suffered even more than Rostopchina's from biased critical opinion. One hesitates to use the word "reception" in relation to the *ad feminam* attacks, blatant distor-

tions, excisions, and suppression of her poetry that Khvoshchinskaia
suffered at the hands of men critics, editors, and publishers. It might be
more accurate to call this sexual-political censorship. I would suggest
that not only Khvoshchinskaia but also every woman poet of this generation who questioned women's subordinate position in society experienced such censorship. Sexual-political censorship was far more destructive than the purely political censorship that both men and women
poets endured. Political censors may have removed passages, but they
generally did not rewrite them to reverse their meaning. Political censors may have had the power to forbid publication, but unlike the sexual-political censors, who were editors, publishers, and anthologizers,
they did not decide what got published, or, like those who were reviewers, determine how works would be received. Most significantly, the
political censor reviewed a work just once, but sexual-political censors
reviewed women's works continually, resulting, as we have seen, in cu-
mulative depredations.

We need only compare the mutilation of the poems examined in
the preceding discussion with the purely political censorship of Khvoshchinskaia's poem "Kladbishche" (The cemetery, no. 9 in "Album
buvard," published in *Illiustratsiia*, no. 52 [Jan. 8, 1859], and which Zotov does not appear to have touched at all). Except for a very few punctuation changes, one censored line ("Sud'ba tsarei reshaetsia perom,"
II: 4 [The fate of tsars is decided by the pen]), and one substitution of
"kniazei" (of princes) for "tsarei" (of tsars, III: 20), the printed version
of the poem is exactly the same as the autograph. This appears to
be Khvoshchinskaia's last published poem. It may be that by 1859
Khvoshchinskaia could better control the form in which her work appeared; after the death of Nicholas I in 1855 the censorship eased as
well. Strangely, this poem, which even Gerbel' praised but did not include in his anthology, has never been reprinted.

Evaluation of Khvoshchinskaia's Poetry

There can be no meaningful evaluation of Khvoshchinskaia's poetry
without reliable versions of her work. Although over the years several
scholars have painstakingly compiled increasingly complete bibliographies of Khvoshchinskaia's published poetry, these 85 poems, even
when located and collected, cannot be used to draw any valid conclusions about Khvoshchinskaia's art.[47] Not only did Zotov rewrite most of
them to varying degrees, but also they represent much less than half of

Khvoshchinskaia's poetic corpus—and there is no reason to believe that Zotov chose her best or most representative work to rewrite and publish. We need a scholarly edition of the 205 poems contained in Khvoshchinskaia's two notebooks, as well as whatever other notebooks can be found.

A comparison of twenty-five of the published poems with their autograph versions shows that only two ("Uzh vecher" and "Ne mogu ia priniat'sia za delo") were published as Khvoshchinskaia wrote them, and one ("Kladbishche") with relatively trivial changes. For the rest Zotov changed anything from a final line to twenty-three out of the thirty lines of "O daite mne pole." Although these twenty-five poems may not be typical of Khvoshchinskaia's work as a whole, even a preliminary look at their themes—and most contain more than one—shows Khvoshchinskaia's range, originality, and power. Eight poems have social themes: "Byvalo, s sestrami" describes the effects of poverty on a young woman; "Vy ulybaetes'? . . ." forced marriages; "Bal detskii" the corrupting effect of balls; "Tri slova," "Mezh tem," and "Svoi razum" the failure of the political revolutions and movements of the 1840s to change society; "Uzhasno skorbnyi den'" and "Mezh tem" the conflict between generations. Seven are love poems, though often with unusual subjects. For example, "Uzh vecher" describes a muse/lover with vampirish overtones; "Ia ne tebe otdam poslednie chasy" the speaker's refusal to think of a lost love at midnight on New Year's Eve; "Dolzhna by ia vchera poplakat'" indifference to the final loss of a lover. Three of them directly address women's lack of freedom in society ("Druz'ia," "Dva-tri doma" ["Dva tri doma" in Zotov's version], "'Vy ulybaetes'? . . .'"). Three are metaphysical ("I dlia menia," "Uzhasno skorbnykh dnei," "Kladbishche"); three invoke diabolical forces ("Dva-tri doma," "Uzh vecher," "Solntse segodnia").

Of course, we cannot use twenty-five poems to establish how Khvoshchinskaia dealt with the issues, discussed in chapters 2 and 3, that faced the women poets of her generation—poetic self-representation; gender and genre; the poet's relationship with audience, nature, creativity, and cosmology. However, the way Khvoshchinskaia treats some of those issues in these poems does shed light on her subsequent career.

It may be significant that Khvoshchinskaia never represents herself with the word *poèt* in these poems, nor does she often describe writing poetry. In "Shumit osennii dozhd', noch' temnaia niskhodit" (The autumn rain sounds, the dark night falls), the speaker refers to "getting

down to insipid, dull work" ("Priniat'sia . . . za blednyi, vialyi trud"). Another poem begins, "Ne mogu ia priniat'sia za delo" (I can't get down to
the matter [business] at hand, no. 161 in the notebook, published in *Za-
zdravnyi fial: Al'manakh na 1852 god*, 7). Only in "Uzh vecher"—a poem
suffused with a sense of guilt and evil—does the speaker actually seem
to be engaged in writing poetry. Similar feelings pervade the "dra-
maticheskiaia fantaziia" (dramatic fantasy) *Dzhulio* (Julio, no. 70 in the
notebook, published in *Panteon* 3, no. 5 [May 1850]), which concerns an
artist. (As I did not compare the published version with the autograph,
I cannot consider this a reliable text.) In this work, written in iambic pentameter, a shepherd who wants to be an artist leaves his fiancée and aged
mother—who accuse him of selfishness and insanity—to go to the city
and study painting. After five years he returns to his village, a failure as
a painter, to find his fiancée married to another and his mother dead.

But while Khvoshchinskaia does not depict herself positively as
a poet in any of this material, in several of the twenty-five poems
("Uzhasno," "Mezh tem," "Bal destskii," "Svoi razum," "O esli by iz
slov," "Tri slova," "Kladbishche") she assumes the role of social critic.
In the largest group of these poems Khvoshchinskaia's implied audience as society in general. Fewer poems appear to be addressed primarily to women ("Byvalo, s sestrami," "Bal detskii," "Solntse segodnia")
or to men ("Druz'ia, vam istinno," "'Vy ulybaetes'? . . .'"). As for cosmology, all these poems express a tension between apathy/hopeless-
ness, on the one hand, and the knowledge that work can and must
be done in the world, on the other. Depression and even despair pre-
dominate in many of these poems: "Bal," "I dlia menia," "Uzhasno,"
"Druz'ia," "Est' dni," "Net, ia ne navozu," "Dva-tri doma," and "Solntse
segodnia." However, implicit in others ("O daite mne pole," "Byvalo,
sestrami," and "Kladbishche") is the belief that nature is good and heal-
ing, that God intends people to enjoy life, and that one must work to improve society. This poetic orientation, I suggest, explains in part how
Khvoshchinskaia was able to make the transition to socially engaged
novels and stories.

Let us return, then, to our original questions: Why did Khvoshchinskaia give up writing poetry for prose, and why has her poetry been lost
to literary history? From an economic standpoint, it might seem obvious that Khvoshchinskaia stopped writing poetry because she received
no money for it, and because after her father's death in 1856 her family
depended for its survival on the money she could earn writing prose.
While Khvoshchinskaia experienced a great deal of physical and emo-

tional stress from her responsibilities as breadwinner under difficult circumstances, she also appears to have enjoyed the freedom and respect her position gave her within her family. In addition, writing prose allowed Khvoshchinskaia to free herself from Zotov's literary guardianship and to deal directly with other editors.[48]

However, Khvoshchinskaia did not give up poetry willingly or easily. Zotov writes that it took him a long time to persuade her to try writing prose, which she felt neither the desire nor the ability to do.[49] Along with economic necessity, several literary-historical factors also may have pushed Khvoshchinskaia from poetry to prose. First, poetry had been going out of fashion since the 1830s, making it increasingly difficult to gain recognition as a poet.[50] In any case, Khvoshchinskaia's poetry was not widely praised. In 1852 the influential poet and critic Nikolai Nekrasov wrote that in Khvoshchinskaia's poetry "some kind of fogginess and vagueness is noticeable both in the expressions and thoughts. In addition, Miss Khvoshchinskaia does not have a completely free command of verse and perhaps too regards rhyme too freely." He gave several rhymes from "'Vy ulybaetes'? . . .'" as examples.[51] A year later he concluded a review of Khvoshchinskaia's verse tales *Derevenskii sluchai* (1853) by writing, "We would consider ourselves fortunate if our few remarks assisted the authoress of *Derevenskii sluchai* to bring herself to renounce verse tales (*povesti v stikhakh*). She has been given everything necessary to write successfully in prose."[52] It is hard to believe that Khvoshchinskaia would have been unaffected by these two reviews, which appeared in the prestigious *Sovremennik*.

Even her biographers appear to have been unenthusiastic about her poetry. In *Russkii biograficheskii slovar'* we read, "Several of [her poems], it is true, are somewhat vague and carelessly finished, but their originality and deep thought and feeling produce a deep impression on the reader" (21: 302). Another biographer wrote of Khvoshchinskaia's debut in *Literaturnaia gazeta*, "Six of these [poems] were printed with her full name in no. 38 of this publication with a kind, even too kind, note from the editor" (Semevskii, "N. D. Khvoshchinskaia-Zaionchkovskaia," 10: 54). A third opined, "In respect to artistry, N. D.'s first [published] poems were weak and distinguished themselves from the mass of published versified trash [*khlam*] only in their ideological content and genuine feeling" (Karrik, "Iz vospominanii," 12–13). I suspect that much of the vagueness that Khvoshchinskaia's contemporaries complained about can be attributed to Zotov's rewritings and deletions. I certainly found the autograph versions of Khvoshchinskaia's poems much clearer and more understandable than the published versions. Beyond not gaining recognition for her poetry, however, Khvoshchinskaia may have become discouraged by seeing her poems published in mutilated form. Perhaps, like Emily Dickinson, she eventually decided it was not worth publishing them at all.[53]

As to why Khvoshchinskaia's poetry disappeared from literary history, it seems likely that in addition to the factors already mentioned, her subject matter in several cases made Zotov and other men editors uncomfortable. These editors, in rewriting and repeatedly censoring such poems, eventually destroyed them by making them unintelligible. More generally, men publishers and anthologizers dismissed Khvoshchinskaia's poetry, as they did most of the women's poetry of her generation, because they could neither make sense of its different perspective nor identify with many of the experiences described. They assumed Khvoshchinskaia's poetry to be technically incompetent and her rhymes faulty. I suggest that a closer look will reveal, rather, creative and daring experiments with prosody, as is also the case with Zhadovskaia's poetry, which was similarly criticized.

It is useful to compare Khvoshchinskaia's poetic career with that of Emily Dickinson. These two near-contemporaries—Dickinson was born in 1830, six years after Khvoshchinskaia—faced several common problems but resolved them very differently because of different circumstances. Both women strongly felt their poetic vocation. Both sent their work to conventional, limited men editors who did not understand it and tried to improve it. Both had to make hard choices. Dickinson, despite her ambition and awareness of her poetic gifts, renounced publication and fame, although not easily or happily, to live an entirely domestic life.[54] In exchange she gained the freedom to continue writing poetry. She was able to make this choice because she did not have to support herself and her family, and because she was temperamentally and artistically suited to an isolated life; her poetry is inward and spiritual. Khvoshchinskaia, given her temperament and the circumstances of her life, had to choose otherwise. She was able and called upon to support her family, cared about social and political issues, and very much wanted to be in the world. She gladly left provincial Riazan' for Saint Petersburg, where she gained success as a prose writer and critic—but at the cost of her poetry. We can only speculate how high that cost was for Khvoshchinskaia personally and for Russian literature.

6

Karolina Pavlova

Over the past few decades Karolina Pavlova (born Jaenisch, 1807–93) has become the best-known Russian woman poet of her generation. This is not to suggest that she has received her due. As mentioned in the introduction, historically she has been considered less important than her husband, Nikolai Pavlov (1803–64), a littérateur who authored a total of six short stories. As recently as 1998 a five-hundred-page authorized Russian university textbook on mid-nineteenth-century Russian literature included seven index entries for Nikolai Pavlov, four for Pavlova, and no discussion of her poetry. Several anthologies of nineteenth-century Russian poetry do not include her work.[1]

Nonetheless, one is struck by the contrast between Pavlova's poetic reputation and that of Khvoshchinskaia. While Khvoshchinskaia never saw a book of her poetry in print—nor have any yet appeared—Pavlova during her lifetime published five books; four other editions of her work have been published since her death.[2] While no reliable printed versions of Khvoshchinskaia's poetry exist, much of Pavlova's work is available in the scholarly Biblioteka poeta series with notes and variant readings. While Khvoshchinskaia has been lost to literary history as a poet, Pavlova, especially since the 1970s, has been the subject of an increasing amount of scholarship and criticism. How can we account for such a contrast in the reputations of two excellent poets?

This chapter first considers those biographical factors that have made it possible for Pavlova to gain recognition as a poet, albeit sporadically and usually as a curiosity.[3] Such an examination may bring to light overlooked determinants of literary reputation. Next, since much of Pavlova's *oeuvre* up to the 1860s is available to us, we shall consider how in her poetry she responded to the literary issues facing the woman poets of her generation.[4] Finally, we shall look at a series of works Pavlova wrote over a twenty-year period about the position of women in society in order to trace the development of her views on this subject. As we shall see, gender issues played as important a role in Pavlova's life, poetic practices, reception, and literary reputation as they did for Khvoshchinskaia and the other poets of their generation.

One factor accounting for the contrasting literary reputations of Pavlova and Khvoshchinskaia may simply have been a difference in age. When Pavlova, who was seventeen years older than Khvoshchinskaia, started publishing her poetry in the early 1830s, no one would have urged her to write prose. By the 1840s, however, prose had begun to supplant poetry as the preeminent and more prestigious Russian genre.[5] I believe, however, that other factors played a significant role in these two poets' reputations—factors constituting "literary social capital" (see introduction).

Literary Social Capital

Although for reasons discussed in chapter 1 these women poets as a group enjoyed very little literary social capital—access to education, mentoring, social connections with literary gatekeepers and opinion makers, the opportunity to be a literary critic or journal editor—differences did exist among them. For example, in contrast with Khvoshchinskaia's impoverished, déclassé family living in the provinces, Pavlova's family was well-to-do, well connected, and lived in Moscow, one of the two publishing centers.

Of course, women poets, like other women, also could capitalize on their attractiveness to men, as did Rostopchina, but this generally did not help them professionally. Although, as we have seen, critics sexualized all women poets, they more often dismissed as a *poetessa* an attractive woman, for the very reason that she conformed to gender norms. Nor did capitalizing on the "feminine" characteristic of beauty protect women poets from *ad feminam* attacks. Beauty, like any source of female power, was seen as dangerous, even demonic. As the holy *Prekrasnaia dama* (beautiful lady) inevitably turns into the disreputable *neznakomka* (unknown woman) in the poetry of Aleksandr Blok, so the beautiful, refined poetess implies her binary opposite, the whore.[6]

Women poets as well as men poets could generate social capital by hosting salons, thus influencing literary production.[7] A salon not only allowed these women to earn the gratitude and good will of important men writers by offering them a forum to present their works. It also gave them a unique opportunity to interact on a more or less equal footing with men literary gatekeepers who could help them get published. In addition, such women commanded the power to present their own works to their men contemporaries, an opportunity they did not enjoy in the great majority of salons and literary circles, which as we saw in chapter 1, were run by men. Women with the temerity to present their own work, however, often provoked men's ire. We have mentioned Druzhinin's story, "Zhenshchina pisatel'nitsa" (The woman writer) in which the man narrator literally falls asleep when a woman reads her work. We have also noted the perceived connection between a woman presenting her writing and sexual display. In Pavlova's case, the poet Nikolai Vasil'evich Berg (1823–84) disapprovingly noted, "At Pavlova's literary evenings her works were read without fail," then sympathetically described what he perceived as Nikolai Pavlov's discomfort during these readings (cited in Briusov, "K. K. Pavlova," 282). The writers Dmitrii Grigorovich (1822–99), Aleksandr Nikitenko (1804–77), and Ivan Panaev (1812–62) in letters and memoirs ridiculed the manner in which Pavlova read her poetry or complained that she read it too much. Ivan Panaev, editor of the *Sovremennik,* wrote in an open letter to Pavlova, *"To spend an entire day in your company, listening to your verses is such a great pleasure* as cannot be quickly forgotten," his italics alerting readers to his sarcasm.[8] But even if men insulted those women who presented their work, they could not help noticing them. It is not a coincidence that the two best-known women writers of this generation, Pavlova and Rostopchina, both hosted salons.

In salons, too, we see the interplay of money, location, and connections. To conduct a salon anywhere required money. But those such as Pavlova's and Rostopchina's, located in Moscow and Saint Petersburg, enjoyed much more visibility, prestige, and renown than did those located in the provinces, for example, the salon of the poet Aleksandra Fuks in Kazan'. While the salons of the capitals became part of the Russian literary historical record, detailed in the published memoirs of numerous participants, Fuks's salon, which lasted twenty-five years, remains as unknown as her poetry.[9]

The final element essential to the success of a salon was literary connections. Literary historians often forget or ignore this factor, making it seem as if salons just "happened." Let us take, for example, the very successful salon that Avdot'ia Elagina (1789–1877) hosted in Moscow for over twenty years, from the mid-1820s until the end of the 1840s. The attendees, who included such luminaries as Zhukovsky, Karamzin, Pushkin, Gogol, Ivan and Petr Kireevsky, Chaadaev, Baratynsky, Viazemsky, Odoevsky, Venevitinov, Iazykov, Herzen, Samarin, Sergei and Konstantin Aksakov, Ogarev, Shevyrev, Pogodin, M. A. Maksimovich, and Vigel', were, in fact, a network of Elagina's relations and friends. Elagina grew up with Zhukovsky, who was her mother's half-brother and her tutor. She corresponded with him for many years, acting as confidant in his romance with her cousin Mar'ia Protasov and advising him on his poetry. According to one source, Zhukovsky, who acted as mentor to Pushkin, brought him to Elagina's salon. Iazykov lived with the Elagins. Several attendees were linked by marriage. Khomiakov married Iazykov's sister; Karamzin's second wife was Viazemsky's half sister. Elagina's sons by her first marriage, to Vasilii Ivanovich Kireevsky, were Ivan Kireevsky (1806–56), an architect of Slavophilism and editor of the *Evropeets* (1831–32), and Petr Kireevsky (1808–56), a prominent Slavophile and collector of Russian folk songs. Baratynsky was a good friend of Ivan Kireevsky and first read his poetry in Elagina's salon. Through these ties Elagina commanded a great deal of influence in literary circles, although her literary activity consisted of translating, editing journals, and writing familiar letters rather than writing poetry or prose fiction.[10]

What sources of literary social capital, then, did Pavlova enjoy, and how did they affect her literary reception? Her family background constituted an equivocal asset. Unlike most upper-class Muscovites, descended from old Russian families, Pavlova traced her roots to Western Europe. Her father, Karl Ivanovich Jaenisch, was a German-educated doctor of German descent. Her mother, a former singing teacher, was French and English on her father's side. Pavlova, who became an only child after the death of her seven-year-old sister in 1816, received an excellent European education at home. By the age of eighteen she not only spoke Russian, French, English, and German, as well as some Italian and Polish, but also knew these national literatures.[11] In some ways this unusual background—and perhaps the fact that Pavlova was a practicing Lutheran rather than Russian Orthodox—worked to her social disadvantage, alienating her from her contemporaries. The opening of Pavlova's *Dvoinaia zhizn'*, in which two men discuss the heroine, Cecilia, may reflect the attitudes Pavlova herself encountered: "'They say she isn't stupid, but who's stupid nowadays? . . . But she must have a dash of her father's German blood in her. I can't stand all these German and half-German women.'"[12] Indeed, Pavlova's linguistic abilities drew some envious ridicule from her contemporaries.[13] Yet her background also provided a prestigious connection to European culture at a time when it strongly influenced the Russian literary establishment and aristocracy. Throughout the 1830s and 1840s, for example, the thick journal *Biblioteka dlia chteniia* listed all books published in France, Germany, and England, in addition to running a column on literary life in these countries. Most thick journals regularly reviewed European books, and even *Zvezdochka* (1842–63), a journal for girls up to age fourteen, included many children's texts in French, German, and English, as well as Russian. Pavlova also turned her German background into Russian literary capital by sending her first translations to Goethe, whose letter praising her work she included in her album. As we shall see, Pavlova's cosmopolitan European background became an even greater asset posthumously, when it brought her work to the attention of Russian Symbolists and German Slavists.

Another equivocal social asset for Pavlova, as for every woman poet, consisted in her attractiveness to men. Although hostile male contemporaries focused on and disparaged Pavlova's appearance and manner,[14] the Pavlova scholar Munir Sendich quotes accounts indicating that Ivan Kireevsky and Nikolai Iazykov were in love with her, and that Mickiewicz's friend, Cyprian Daszkiewicz, killed himself because of his unrequited love for her. As mentioned previously, a woman's pleasing physical appearance could serve as an excuse for men critics to trivialize her work. And at least one literary historian—Valerii Briusov—seemed to assume that any critic who reviewed Pavlova's work favorably did so because he was sexually attracted to her.[15]

In any case, Pavlova's literary connections constituted an unambiguous source of literary capital. Thanks to her father's, Karl Jaenisch's, friendship with Avdot'ia Elagina, Pavlova in the mid-1820s received an invitation to read her poetry at Elagina's salon.[16] Pavlova not only became a constant attendee, meeting many important literary figures of her day, but also through Elagina's sons, Ivan and Petr Kireevsky, she gained entrée into the even more socially prominent salon of Zinaida Volkonskaia. Again the brilliance and success of Volkonskaia's salon can be attributed to her connections—specifically, her affair with Alexander I.[17] At Volkonskaia's salon Pavlova met Pushkin and Adam Mickiewicz, the exiled Polish national poet. It can only have increased Pavlova's social capital when Mickiewicz, with whom she was studying Polish, proposed to her. Although he subsequently broke their engagement, even this temporary connection with him has led to several articles that have helped keep Pavlova's name alive.[18]

Pavlova, however, did not find it easy to launch a literary career, despite these social advantages, all of which were outweighed by the primary social disadvantage of being female. I suggest that at the start of her career Pavlova attempted to create an additional form of social literary capital by translating the poetry of her male contemporaries into European languages. *Das Nordlicht,* which appeared in 1833, contained translations into German of poetry by Pushkin, Zhukovsky, Del'vig, Baratynsky, Iazykov, and Venivitinov. *Les préludes* (1839) included translations into French of Mickiewicz, Khomiakov, and Benediktov. Both volumes concluded with Pavlova's own poetry in German and French, respectively. It should be noted that while several of Pavlova's male contemporaries (Zhukovsky, Pushkin, Fet) also translated extensively, they translated foreign works into Russian rather than Russian works into foreign languages. Pavlova in the course of her career was to do both, as well as translating from German into French. But while the translations of Pavlova's male contemporaries did not detract from their reputations as poets—indeed, Zhukovsky's reputation as a poet rests primarily on his translations—Pavlova's seem to have reduced her to being only a translator of (men's) poetry, a handmaiden to the male poetic establishment. At the time of Pavlova's marriage in 1836, a friend of Pushkin wrote him, "N. F. Pavlov is getting married to Mademoiselle Jaenisch, known as an author, but more as a translator of your works." And Belinsky, who reviewed Pavlova's translations positively, did not similarly praise her poetry.[19]

Pavlova at the end of her life once again resorted to translating the work of a Russian male contemporary—this time to generate financial rather than literary capital. While living in poverty near Dresden, she translated into German, and by his account, improved the plays of A. K. Tolstoy, which were performed with great success in Germany. Tolstoy in return acted as Pavlova's literary agent in Russia, eventually arranging for her to receive a pension from Grand Duchess Elena Pavlovna.[20]

It was only after her marriage that Pavlova could produce the asset that most helped her poetic career—the very successful salon that she hosted from 1839 until the early 1850s. Here all the previously mentioned factors of literary social capital worked in Pavlova's favor—social standing, wealth, literary connections, location in Moscow, the gratitude of her male contemporaries for her translations of their works, as well as her husband's, Nikolai Pavlov's, journalistic connections. Attendees at the salon included such literary figures as the Aksakovs, Baratynsky, Belinsky, Berg, Fet, Gogol, Granovsky, Grigoriev, Herzen, Iazykov, Khomiakov, Kol'tsov, Lermontov, Nikitenko, the Panaevs, Pogodin, Shevyrev, and Viazemsky. The benefit of the salon to Pavlova's career becomes clear when we realize how many of her guests edited or published the periodicals in which her work appeared: Panaev and Nikitenko (*Sovremennik*), Grigorev, Ivan Kireevsky, Pogodin, Shevyrev (*Moskvitianin*), Ivan Aksakov (*Den'*), Herzen (*Russkaia potaennaia literatura XIX stoletii*). Pavlova's guests also appear to have helped place her poetry, along with their own, in several *al'manakhi* and collections: *Odesskii al'manakh na 1840 god, Literaturnyi vecher* (1844), *Moskovskii uchenyi i literaturnyi sbornik na 1847, Kievlianin* (1850), *Raut* (1851, 1854), and *Nezabudochka* (1853).[21]

In contrast to Khvoshchinskaia, who lacked all these sources of literary social capital, Pavlova was well known, influential, and widely published. Yet Pavlova, like Khvoshchinskaia, incurred criticism and ridicule from her contemporaries because she, too, violated gender norms by taking herself seriously as a poet. One memoirist wrote disapprovingly of her, "She imagined herself a genius in a skirt."[22] Here genius not only is gendered as male, as discussed in the introduction, but it also dresses in men's clothes. A woman genius thus constitutes an oxymoron, and Pavlova can be dismissed as both unnatural and presumptuous. In addition, as Barbara Heldt has shown, Pavlova's male contemporary poets never fully accepted her, considering her gender more significant than any poetic talent she possessed. In 1852, instead of supporting Pavlova's protests against her husband's behavior—Pavlov was squandering her estate in ruinous card games and had established a second household with a relative of Pavlova's, Evgeniia Tanneberg, by whom he eventually had three children—these poets closed ranks against her for daring to question male prerogatives. When, as a result of Pavlova's father's complaint to the governor of Moscow about Pavlov's financial dealings, Pavlov's papers were searched and he was arrested for having in his library books forbidden by the censorship. Pavlova's fellow poets attacked Pavlova and hailed Pavlov as a martyr. Driven from Moscow, Pavlova eventually settled near Dresden, where she died in poverty and obscurity in 1893.[23]

After Pavlova left Russia in the 1850s her social capital and literary reputation virtually disappeared as literary power shifted from the salons run by aristocrats to the "thick journals" edited by radical intellectuals of nonaristocratic origins (*raznochintsy*). When a collection of Pavlova's poetry appeared in 1863, radical critics ridiculed it as "frivolous" and out of date, while inaccurately characterizing her as uninterested in current social issues.[24]

Ten years after Pavlova's death the Russian Symbolists rediscovered her work. Valerii Briusov in a 1903 biographical sketch of Pavlova noted that while Baratynsky and many other well-known nineteenth-century writers had praised her work enthusiastically, no serious critical study of her poetry existed. In 1915 Briusov with his wife, I. M Briusova, published a two-volume edition of Pavlova's collected works, the first since 1863, which in turn produced a flurry of Pavlova scholarship.[25]

In the Symbolists' rediscovery of Pavlova, too, several factors of literary social capital played a part. Because of the Symbolists' interest in European literature (Ibsen, Nietzsche, Maetterlinck, Hauptmann, D'Annuzio, the French Symbolists), Pavlova's cosmopolitan European background worked in her favor.[26] The Symbolists' interest in the Pushkin pleiad made Pavlova, who had close connections with Baratynsky and Mickiewicz, a figure of importance to them, as did the fact that several well-known literary men contemporaries had published memoirs of her Moscow salon.[27] Perhaps because civic critics attacked the Symbolists for engaging in art for art's sake, the Symbolists championed Pavlova, who had suffered similar attacks at the hands of Mikhail Saltykov-Shchedrin and other radical critics. The Symbolists completely ignored, however, the poetry of Khvoshchinskaia and Mordovtseva, who lived in the provinces where they had no connections with the Pushkin pleiad or skirmishes with civic critics. This is not to suggest that Pavlova, who is a major poet, did not deserve to be rediscovered, but her case does illustrate the influence of social factors on literary reputation.

Unfortunately, the Symbolists in their recovery of Pavlova continued the same gender stereotyping and condescension that we find in earlier nineteenth-century criticism. Briusov, for example, after the first paragraph of his article, refers to Pavlova throughout by her first name, something one cannot imagine his doing to a man poet. Sergei Ernst depicts Pavlova as having fled into an artificial poetic life because of her unrequited love for Mickiewicz. He also characterizes her as having written a great deal of mediocre verse, all of it monotonously melancholy and depressing. Even Rapgof in his generally excellent biography of Pavlova expounds on her suffering after the break with her husband

and the significance of the break for her work (*Karolina Pavlova,* 41–44). One does not find similar discussions of how marital woes affected the work of unhappily married men writers such as Tolstoy, Del'vig, and Panaev.

In any case, all of Pavlova's assets turned into liabilities in the new critical atmosphere that followed the Russian Revolution. Once again Pavlova was relegated to oblivion, this time as an "unprogressive" poet with a suspicious upper-class, cosmopolitan background, who had been dismissed or satirized by the now canonized "revolutionary" critics. Pavlova's gender also continued to be a disadvantage, since, as mentioned earlier, Soviet literary ideologues tended to ignore or denigrate women writers. In Pavlova's case, for many years no criticism about her appeared in the Soviet Union. Although Soviet editions of Pavlova's works appeared in 1937 and 1964, one suspects this only came about because Briusov, who edited the last edition of her complete works in 1915, "accepted the Revolution" and therefore could be invoked to endorse Pavlova. Briusov's name appears at the beginning and the end of the introduction to the 1937 edition.[28]

In the West, however, Pavlova's cosmopolitan (German) background and gender contributed to the recovery of her work. Munir Sendich credits Dmitrij Tschiževskij with reviving Pavlova "from a protracted oblivion in Germany through his article in 1937" (63).[29] That article, however, like many during Pavlova's lifetime, discussed her, not as a poet, but as a translator—here of Pushkin, and probably in connection with the centennial of Pushkin's death. Almost thirty years later, however, in 1964 Tschiževskij did include a discussion of Pavlova's poetry in his *Russische Literaturgeschichte des 19. Jahrhunderts.* Since then additional German criticism has claimed Pavlova for German as well as Russian literature, based on the forty years she lived in Germany.[30] In the United States, Zoya Yurieff, who had attended Tschiževskij's lectures on comparative Slavic literature, suggested to her student Munir Sendich that he "resuscitate Pavlova's literary work."[31] Sendich's dissertation and series of articles on Pavlova—along with the 1964 Biblioteka poeta edition of Pavlova's poetry—laid the foundation for all subsequent Pavlova scholarship.

Sexual literary politics also played a role in the Pavlova revival. In the 1970s in the wake of a new wave of feminist literary scholarship, Barbara Heldt not only translated Pavlova's *Dvoinaia zhizn'* into English for the first time but also in her introduction placed Pavlova's life in a feminist literary context. Since then Pavlova has become a focus of feminist criticism and the subject of articles, translations, dissertations, a conference, and a book based on the proceedings. Perhaps as a result of Western interest, starting in the 1980s Russian criticism also witnessed a Pavlova revival.[32] Such a belated recovery has yet to come to other equally deserving poets of Pavlova's generation such as Khvoshchinskaia, Mordovtseva, and Fuks.

Pavlova and Literary Conventions

How did Pavlova respond to the literary issues facing the women poets of her generation? As regards self-representation, Pavlova never referred to herself as a *poetessa*. In "Sonet" (Sonnet, 1839, 76), she refers to herself as *poèt* only obliquely and in the third person: "Bespechnyi zhe poet vsegda dushoi ditia" (The carefree poet is always a child in soul). Three years later she more directly states in a poem to Evgenii Baratynsky:

> Меня вы назвали поэтом,
> И я [. . .]
> [. . . . .]
> Тогда поверила в себя.
>
> ❧
>
> (You called me a poet,
> And I . . .
> Then believed in myself.
>   ("E. A. Baratynskomu"
>   [To E. A. Baratynsky],
>   1842, 112)

By 1860 she describes herself with self-confident humor as the "crazy poet":

> Не дай забыть безумному поэту
> Мучительных уроков старины!
>
> ❧
>
> (Don't let the crazy poet forget
> The tormenting lessons of the past!)
>   ("Drezden," 1860, 218)

Perhaps because no images existed for women to represent themselves as poets (see chapter 2), Pavlova often wrote indirectly about her poetry making. Yet her best-known lines concern her feelings about her poetry:

Моя напасть! мое богатство!
Мое святое ремесло!

               ~

(My misfortune! My wealth!
My sacred craft!)
  ("Ty, utselevshii v serdtse
  nishchem" [You, who
  having remained whole in a
  destitute heart], 1854, 154)

As for poetic persona, from the beginning Pavlova used feminine endings when writing about herself as poet ("Sonet" [Sonnet], 1839, 76; "Da il' net" [Yes or no], 1839, 78; "Duma" [Meditation], 1840, 89; "Duma," 1843, 114), although she also wrote poems with unmarked endings (for example, "Est' liubimtsy vdokhnovenii" [There are inspiration's favorites], 1839, 79; "Motylek" [The butterfly], 1840, 83–84), and very occasionally verses in a male voice ("Vezde i vsegda" [Everywhere and always], 1846, 127; "Sputnitsa feia" [The fairy companion], 1858, 198). Pavlova's awareness of the issue of gender and poetic persona emerges clearly in "Fantasmagorii" (Phantasmagorias, 1856–58, 373–76). In the first section of this mixed-genre work she recounts the thoughts of a poet whose gender she carefully withholds. The poet plays with gendered metaphors to describe the act of writing: the writer is a rapist who attacks the "virgin" white page with a (phallic) pen, but also the princess Scheherazade, who must constantly find new ways to entertain a bored shah-public or face extinction. The section concludes, "It must be added that this was a woman" (376). Similarly, in *Dvoinaia zhizn'* Pavlova reveals the gender of the narrator only in the second stanza of the envoi when she uses a gender-marked verb:

И долго я в душе ее умела
Безмолвною сберечь себе одной

               ~

(And for a long time I was able
To keep [this thought] silently in my soul, only for myself)
                                 (306)

Such devices indicate that Pavlova, like other women writers discussed in chapter 2, while aware of the adverse judgments she would incur, chose to write as a woman.

As for audience, Pavlova addresses several of her poems to women: Iuliia Zhadovskaia, Evdokiia Rostopchina, A. V. Pletneva, Ol'ga

Novikova, A. D. Baratynskaia, and the unidentified N. P. B-a (132, 103, 134, 540–41, 208, 505, 203, 186). In addition, Pavlova dedicated *Dvoinaia zhizn'* to young women who, like her heroine, experience the constraints of women's role in society:

> Рабыни шума и сует.
> [. . . . .]
> Вас всех, Психей, лишенных крылий,
> Немых сестер моей души!
>
> ⤿
>
> (Slaves of noise and vanity.
> [. . . . .]
> All of you Psyches deprived of wings,
> The mute sisters of my soul!)
>   (231)

She also wrote about the friends of her youth, Joan of Arc, and the poets Lucretia Davidson and Delphine Gay (500–503, 80, 124–27). However, far more of Pavlova's poetry is addressed to men—Adam Mickiewicz (90, 93, 118, 136), Evgenii Mil'keev (75, 185), Evgenii Baratynsky (112), N. M. Iazykov (119, 133), I. S. Aksakov (131, 136), Nikolai Pavlov (149), the unidentified S. K. N. (137), Boris Utin (153, 154, 155, 157, 169), A. K. Tolstoi (221, 223)—or treats male historical figures. This is not surprising, as the dominant voices in the literary establishment of Pavlova's day as well as its gatekeepers were male.

Gender and Genre

Like other women poets of her generation, Pavlova confronted genres not designed to tell women's stories. And like many of her women contemporaries, she ingeniously adapted and transmuted these forms. Even her early ballads and narrative poems, influenced by German and Russian Romanticism, modify gender stereotypes to make women subjects, not objects. In "Doch' zhida" (The Jew's daughter, 82–83) Pavlova reworks the romantic motif made famous by Byron's *Eastern Tales* and Pushkin's *Bakhchisaraiskii fontan* (1822), the "pure" woman forced into a harem. Pavlova's Jewish captive, however, unlike her predecessors, does not passively allow herself to be raped or murdered. Rather, she plans to kill the emir with a concealed knife, calling on the memory of her mother to give her courage. Perhaps Pavlova was thinking of such Old Testament heroines as Judith and Jael.[33] In "Starukha" (The old woman, 85–88) an old and ugly woman casts a spell on a young and beautiful man through her ability to tell him stories, that is, her power as an artist. In "Ogon'" (Fire, 94–97) a male, rather than a female, succumbs to the temptation of an evil serpent—here in the guise of a fire—thus destroying an Edenic idyll. In *Dvoinaia zhizn'* Pavlova modified and combined several genres—the Bildungsroman, the physiological sketch, and the *svetskaia povest'* (society tale)—to tell her story. In "Za chainym stolom" she questions the very conventions used to narrate women's stories.[34]

Pavlova and *Polozhenie zhenshchiny*

While gender cannot be considered a major theme in Pavlova's oeuvre, over a twenty-year period she published five works that directly address *polozhenie zhenshchiny*, the position in society of ordinary and extraordinary women: "Jeanne d'Arc" (1839), "Tri dushi" (Three souls, 1845), *Dvoinaia zhizn'* (1847), *Kadril'* (1859), and "Za chainym stolom" ("At the Tea Table," 1859). A chronological examination of these works shows the evolution of Pavlova's ideas concerning women's position in society and literature. Since I have written elsewhere about "Tri dushi," *Dvoinaia zhizn'*, and "Za chainym stolom," here I focus principally on "Jeanne d'Arc" and *Kadril'*.[35]

Pavlova wrote her poem "Jeanne d'Arc" in French in connection with her translation (1839) into French of Schiller's very popular play *Die Jungfrau von Orleans* (1801). Zhukovsky had translated Schiller's play into Russian in 1821, the same year that Zinaida Volkonskaia used an Italian adaptation as the libretto for her opera *Giovanna d'Arco*, in which she performed the lead.[36] Pavlova in her "Jeanne d'Arc"—as well as in such works as *Kadril'*, "Doch' zhida," and "Za chainym stolom"—polemicized with men poets' images of woman-as-object by portraying women as subjects of their own experience.

To understand the significance of Pavlova's depiction of Joan of Arc, it is useful to look at those that preceded it. From the end of the eighteenth century several European authors had written literary works about Joan, who embodied Romantic values of national liberation and an unmediated, personal, visionary relationship with the sublime.[37] In addition, Joan of Arc's conflict with an authoritarian church over her religious experiences could be understood as the struggle of the individual against oppressive social institutions. Furthermore, she represented a woman warrior at a time when gender roles were beginning to be questioned.[38]

In contrast to earlier works, Robert Southey's ten-book epic *Joan of Arc* (1796), the first Romantic depiction of Joan, presented her in a heroic light. In Shakespeare's *The First Part of Henry VI* (1592), for example, the male characters variously refer to Joan as "witch," "strumpet," "vile fiend and shameless courtesan," "foul fiend of France and hag of all despite," "railing Hecate," "giglot [wanton] wench," ugly witch," "fell banning [cursing] hag," "sorceress," "wicked and vile," and "cursed drab." In one scene Pucelle, as she is called in the stage directions, conjures devils to help her defeat the English, and in a second she denies her father, who wishes to save her. Elsewhere she falsely claims to be a virgin and then just as falsely accuses three different men of having made her pregnant in an attempt to avoid being burned at the stake. That is, Shakespeare establishes a binary opposition between evil, the feminine, France, and the rejection of rightful male authority, on the one hand, and virtue, the masculine, England, and the acceptance of rightful male authority (Henry VI), on the other. Voltaire presents Joan no more heroically in his semipornographic mock epic *La Pucelle* (1730), an account of the sexual escapades of the French and the English during the Hundred Years War and especially the supposed fate of Joan's virginity.[39]

Although Southey in his preface to his epic virtuously declares that he never has "been guilty of looking into [the *Pucelle* of Voltaire]" (*Poetical Works*, 1: 18) and does not mention Shakespeare, he appears to be responding to both. In making Joan the subject of an epic, as opposed to a satiric mock epic, he could depict her as pure in heart and mind. And Southey deliberately reverses Shakespeare's binary oppositions: in his work female virtue, France, and nature oppose male corruption, England, and the organized church. Southey's epic was considered politically radical and even subversive when it appeared. In his preface Southey stated that the work was written in "a republican spirit" and in the belief that "a happier order of things had commenced with the independence of the United States and would be accelerated by the French Revolution" (*Poetical Works*, 1: 19). Discussing his modification of the epic form he wrote that he had "acted in direct opposition" to the rule "that the subject [of epics] should be national," choosing instead for his subject "the defeat of the English."[40] Southey further challenged epic conventions and the conservative politics of his times not only by creating a female epic hero—a rarity—but also by having her echo Rousseau's ideas about the goodness of nature. In book 3 a group of priests in Chinon examine Joan's religious beliefs before allowing her to take command of the Dauphin's army. She tells them she has outgrown a "God of Terrors" (bk. 3, line 425) because she saw

> The eternal energy pervade
> The boundless range of nature.
> (Bk. 3, lines 427–28)

When the priests tell her that Nature is sinful. Joan protests:

> It is not Nature that doth lead to sin:
> Nature is all benevolence, all love,
> All beauty! [. . .]
> [. . .]
> Nature teach sin!
> Oh blasphemy against the Holy One.
> (Bk. 3, lines 509–10)

Like Southey's epic, Schiller's play *Die Jungfrau von Orleans* also responds to Shakespeare and Voltaire. Schiller reverses Shakespeare's scene in which Joan denies her father by having Joan's father deny her. As early as the prologue he fears she may be in league with the powers of hell; he later denounces her as a witch before the crowd assembled for Charles VII's coronation. In contrast to Voltaire, whose work highlights sexual activity, Schiller focuses on sexual desire. Joan can be victorious only as long as she remains above desire. Her one lapse, emotional, not physical, leads to the loss of all her powers and to temporary rejection by the French.[41]

In each of these works Joan serves as a vehicle for the author's political/literary views, as evidenced in the denouement of each. At the end of Shakespeare's pro-English play Joan is led away to a rightful execution. In Voltaire's risqué mock epic Joan, after almost losing her virginity to a seductive donkey possessed by evil spirits, celebrates her victory over the English by bestowing it on her faithful captain, Dunois. Southey's anti-English, pro-France epic concludes with the coronation of Charles VII. Schiller ends his play (which he subtitled "Eine romantische Tragödie" [A romantic tragedy]) by defying both the natural world and the historical record. The English capture Joan and put her in chains, but once Joan conquers her weakness for the English Lionel, the bonds that hold her miraculously burst. She runs to the battlefield, where she dies gloriously in the arms of Charles VII. Interestingly, all the writers who followed Shakespeare avoided dealing with Joan's death at the stake, although the scene in Southey's epic in which the priests at Chinon question Joan and suggest she be subjected to trial by ordeal may be viewed as a displacement of her torture and death.

In comparison to these epics, mock epics, and plays, Pavlova's "Jeanne d'Arc" is much more modest in scope: a poem of seventeen stanzas with no nationalistic stance. It could be argued, however, that Pavlova's depiction of Joan is the most powerful and intense of all. The poem consists of three sections, each showing Joan at a decisive point of her career. In the first section of seven stanzas Pavlova portrays Joan listening to her voices. While in Southey's work the voices that Joan hears belong to Saint Agnes and in Schiller's to the Virgin Mary, in Pavlova's poem they belong to the Holy Spirit ("l'Esprit"), depicted as male, merciless, and even sadistic:

> Son implacable voix qui lui parle à l'oreille;
> [. . . . .]
> Malheur à toi! Malheur, ô jeune condamnée!
> [. . . . .]
> Le souffle du très-haut a rempli sa victime
>
> ⸎

> (His implacable voice, which speaks in her ear;
> [. . . . .]
> Misfortune to you! Misfortune young convict!
> [. . . . .]
> The breath from on high has filled its victim)

Pavlova's description of Joan's interaction with the spirit suggests repeated rape or forced marriage:

> Elle doit revenir demain, comme aujourd'hui,
> Subir en frissonnant son approche fatale,
> Durant toute la nuit rester, muette et pâle,
> Face à face avec lui.
>
> ⸎

> (She must return tomorrow, as she did today,
> To submit, trembling, to his inevitable approach,
> Throughout the entire night remain mute and pale,
> Face to face with him.)

In Pavlova's version the spirit takes away Joan's humanity:

> Elle doit [. . .]
> Ignorer toute joie et tout amour humain,
> [. . . . .]

Obéis! fais ton coeur impitoyable et sourd;
Brise tous tes bonheurs, ferme à jamais ton âme!

⁓

(She must [. . .]
Remain unaware of all joy and all human love,
[. . . . .]
Obey! Make your heart pitiless and deaf;
Crush all your joys, forever close your soul!)

Pavlova's depiction of the sublime in terms of horror and assault is comparable to Pushkin's in "Prorok" (The prophet, 1826).

И он к устам моим приник,
И вырвал грешный мой язык,
И празднословный и лукавый,
И жало мудрыя змеи
В уста замершие мои
Вложил десницею кровавой,
[. . . . .]
И Бога глас ко мне воззвал:
Восстань, пророк, и виждь, и внемли,
Исполнись волею моей.

⁓

(And he pressed himself to my mouth,
And tore out my sinful, idle, crafty tongue,
And put the sting of the wise serpent
Into my frozen mouth
With a bloody hand
[. . . . .]
And the voice of God called to me, "Arise, prophet, and behold and hear
And be filled with my will.")

Like Pushkin, Pavlova implicitly compares her prophet's experience of the sublime with that of the poet.

Car Dieu ceindra ton front d'ardentes auréoles,
Sur tes lèvres viendront de sublimes paroles,
Et tu devras frémir à tes propres accents:

⁓

(For God will encircle your forehead with blazing haloes,
Sublime words will come to your lips,
And you will have to shudder at your own voice:)

In the second section of "Jeanne d'Arc," which consists of three stanzas, Pavlova shows Joan in battle, a figure of horror as well as a victim.

Dans la profonde horreur des fumantes batailles
Elle marche en avant, sans coeur et sans entrailles,
[. . . . .]
Haletante, au pouvoir d'un force cruelle.

❧

(In the deep horror of the smoking battles
She marches forward, without heart and without feelings,
[. . . . .]
Gasping in the power of a cruel force.)

The final section, which like the first consists of seven stanzas, shows Joan just before her execution with no suggestion of Schiller's miraculous deliverance.

Eh bien, pâle martyre, achève ton calice!
Que l'épreuve terrible aujourd'hui s'accomplisse!

❧

(Well, pale martyr, drain your cup!
Let the terrible ordeal be carried out today!)

We see Joan discarded by an indifferent God, who no longer needs her:

Aujourd'hui l'oeuvre est faite, Il permet que l'on brise
L'inutile instrument.

❧

(Today the work is done, he allows
The useless tool to be broken.)

However, Pavlova implies that Joan has become a Christlike member of the Lutheran elect, predestined for salvation:

Car tous s'écarteront de la Prédestinée!
[. . . . .]
Oh! Tu le savais bien, en quittant la chaumière,
[. . . . .]
Que tu succomberais sous la croix des Elus!

❧

(For everyone will stand back from the predestined one!
[. . . . .]
Oh! You knew well when you left the thatched cottage,
[. . . . .]
That you would perish under the cross of the elect!)

In the last line, "Marche au bûcher ardent!" (March to the flaming stake!), Pavlova in her literal use of the word "ardent" (flaming) ironically echoes her previous metaphorical usage: *ardents aureoles* (blazing haloes) and *ardent archange* (ardent archangel). In a direct response to Schiller's "Romantic" and fantastic tragedy, Pavlova in her poem more realistically balances the glory of Joan's fate with its horror.

Unlike Shakespeare and Voltaire, who punish Joan for being effective and independent, Schiller, who punishes her for having desire, and Southey, who depicts her as a Kālī-like phallic woman for the delectation of his men readers, Pavlova presents Joan with empathy.[42] Pavlova attributes to Joan not so much national-political as sexual-political significance. Her portrait of Joan as an extraordinary woman—and a type of woman artist—challenges cultural assumptions that women could not experience and communicate the sublime. Rather, Pavlova shows that both Joan of Arc and the woman poet risk being destroyed—becoming both more and less than human—by the very power of the forces they contain. Nonetheless, neither Joan nor the woman poet receive recognition from "the crowd," that is, society:

> [C]e peuple insensé, qui maintenant te crie
> Sa malediction .
>
> ⤳
>
> (These foolish people who now scream
> their curse at you.)

Of course, Pavlova's male contemporary poets also describe society's rejection of them ("the poet and the crowd" motif). But Joan as an extraordinary woman suffers an additional curse, the accusation of witchcraft—of violating divine order—something the man poet does not face. Unlike extraordinary men, Joan as an extraordinary woman experiences no glory, only a lonely and reviled end—as did Pavlova herself. In "Jeanne d'Arc" Pavlova creates a complex but believable depiction of Joan in her own terms. Pavlova's is the least sentimental and sensational depiction of Joan's glory and the most frightening vision of the inhumanity of the divine.

Pavlova depicts the same pitiless cosmology in her "Tri dushi" (Three souls), a poem that also concerns extraordinary women with a divine mission. In contrast to Joan, however, these women, who are poets, are not even granted the satisfaction of accomplishing their mission before they perish. As I have suggested elsewhere, in "Tri dushi" Pavlova uses the Biblical parable of the sower and the seeds (Matthew 13) to describe the fates of three women poets—Delphine Gay (1804–55), Lucretia Maria Davidson (1808–25), and herself—all born around the same year.

At the beginning of the poem a harsh God decides to test their souls by
throwing them on unfallow ground, telling them not to blame him if
they become despondent:

> И если дух падет ленивый
>   В мирском бою,—
> Да не винит ваш ропот лживый
>   Любовь мою.

⤙

> (And if your lazy spirit becomes despondent
>   In the terrestrial battle
> Don't in your false grumbling
>   Blame my love.)

As in the Biblical parable, thorns, the thorns of society, "grew up and
choked" the first soul, Gay. The second soul, Davidson, like the seeds
thrown along the road, perishes in the American wilderness through
lack of nurture. Pavlova imagines that her own fate, like that of the seeds
thrown into shallow soil, will be to grow quickly at first, but then to die
without bearing fruit. This view of the extraordinary woman's fate is
even darker than the one she presents in "Jeanne d'Arc."

In *Dvoinaia zhizn'*, often considered her best work, Pavlova moves
from the fate of the extraordinary woman (the artist) in society, to that
of the "ordinary" woman—the artist manquée—whom Pavlova does
not depict as ordinary at all.[43] She dedicated the work "To you . . . slaves
of noise and vanity. . . . Psyches, deprived of wings, the mute sisters of
my soul" (231), that is, to upper-class women whom society has deprived of their creativity and voice. This theme of *polozhenie zhenshchiny,*
women's constrained position in society, had appeared in several society tales of the 1830s and 1840s (for example, those of Elena Gan, Mar'ia
Zhukova, Evdokiia Rostopchina, Avdotiia Panaeva, and Vladimir
Odoevsky), but Pavlova gives a more direct analysis of the causes and
implications of women's restricted lives. She shows that society, in order
to make young women "marriageable," condemns them to banal, empty,
soul-destroying lives strictly governed by propriety. As a result, women
lose their inherent creativity and even the so-called good matches they
manage to make—marriages to rich men—bring them nothing but unhappiness. On a verbal level, Pavlova evokes women's lack of physical
and mental freedom by creating what Tschižewskij calls a "semantic
field" consisting of such words as *rab* (slave), *uznitsa* (prisoner), *skovali*

(fettered), *umstvennyi korset* (mental corset), and *prigovor* (judicial sentence).[44]

> Та узница людского края,
> Та жертва жалкой суеты,
> Обычая раба слепая
> [. . . . .]
> Тебя они сковали с детства,

⤫

> (That prisoner of the human realm,
> That victim of pitiful vanity,
> Blind slave of custom,
> [. . . . .]
> They have fettered you from childhood.)
>
> (243)

> Так иди ж по приговору,
> Беззащитна и одна

⤫

> (So go, according to your sentence,
> Undefended and alone)
>
> (303)

И ныне она, осьмнадцатилетняя, так привыкла к своему умственному корсету, что не чувствовала его на себе более своего шелкового, который снимала только на ночь.

⤫

(And now at eighteen, she was so used to her mental corset that she didn't feel it any more than she did the silk one that she took off only at night.)

> (249)

In a series of dreams, Pavlova's heroine, Cecilia, a marriageable young woman in Moscow society, discovers a realm of poetry, truth, and spiritual values beyond the stifling world in which she lives. Although Cecilia seems very ordinary, the narrator shows us her thwarted poetic genius, which can only emerge in her sleep. Cecilia, however, cannot escape her lot, and having been given a glimpse of her "legacy: freedom of feelings and the kingdom of thought" (243), she must return to what the reader realizes will be an unhappy marriage and an early death. The presence of an ironic and passionate narrator commenting on the banality of Cecilia's daytime life, a narrator who at the end of the work reveals herself to be a woman poet, underlines Cecilia's wasted possibilities. Pavlova implies that there is no qualitative difference between the extraordinary woman, regarded as a freak by her society, and every other woman.

Another link between *Dvoinaia zhizn'* and the works discussed earlier can be found in the mysterious, "stern," reproachful but "loving" male figure who appears in Cecilia's dreams each night—a fitting representative of the sadistic but supposedly loving God we have already encountered:

> Стоит он, полон строгой мощи,
> Стоит недвижный и немой;
> Он ей глядит очами в очи
> Глядит он в душу ей душой.
> Какой вины, какой ошибки
> Упрек нахмурил эту бровь?
> На этом лике без улыбки
> Какая грустная любовь!

> (He stands, full of stern power,
> He stands motionless and unspeaking,
> He looks straight into her eyes,
> He look straight into her soul.
> Reproach for what guilt, what mistake
> Clouds his brow?
> On that unsmiling face
> What sad love!)

> (237)

As we shall see, this figure in various guises continues to appear in Pavlova's later works.[45]

Pavlova turned even further from cosmology to social issues in the last two works to be discussed, *Kadril'* (Quadrille) and her short story "Za chainym stolom." Pavlova first published both in 1859 in *Russkii vestnik* but wrote them over a period of about twenty years. Perhaps as a result, both combine the protests against women's lack of freedom in society (*polozhenie zhenshchiny*) typical of the 1840s with the more radical issues of self-determination surrounding the woman question (*zhenskii vopros*) of the late 1850s.[46] Like Cecilia in *Dvoiana zhizn'*, the heroines of both works are "ordinary" women in society. However, unlike her they are older and wiser survivors of their first painful encounters with love. We shall consider *Kadril'* first. Not only did it appear a few months earlier, but it introduces issues that Pavlova further develops in "Za chainym stolom," her most radical critique of women's position in society and literature.

Starting with *Kadril'*, Pavlova no longer focuses on women's relationships with an unsympathetic God, but rather on their struggle with an inimical society and with the literary models that limit and objectify them.[47] In *Kadril'* four women gather in a countess's house before going to a ball. The countess opines that women cause their own sufferings because their weak characters lead them to make bad choices. The other three protest that, unlike the rich and powerful countess, most women have little freedom to make choices. To illustrate the social forces that constrain them, each woman then tells of her first painful love experience. The scholar Susanne Fusso points out that each story deflates some aspect of the Romantic Russian hero ("Pavlova's *Quadrille*," 120, 121). As in "Jeanne d'Arc," "Tri dushi," and *Dvoinaia zhizn'*, these stories replace androcentric images of women with women-centered narratives.

In the first story Nadina recounts how her mother, despite Nadina's attraction to a "handsome Hungarian," pressured her into marriage with Andrei Il'ich, a "fat, stooped, bald and pockmarked" (316) but rich landowner. Until the last moment Nadina resists the wedding, but when a thief steals the costly jewels her fiancé has given her, she feels she has no choice but to go through with the ceremony. In an ironic twist, Nadina admits that five years later she finds herself very content with her husband and her life. Fusso writes that Nadina's story debunks the Karl Moor prototype ("Pavlova's *Quadrille*," 121); Pavlova's very Romantic-looking thief remains completely unmoved by Nadina's pleas that he not condemn her to an unwelcome marriage by stealing the jewels. The story also debunks Tat'iana's tragic fate at the end of *Evgenii Onegin:* married to a fat general, but still in love with Onegin, the Romantic hero. In contrast to Tat'iana, Nadina at the story's end has achieved peace of mind. She has realized that Romantic heroes will not save her and are not worth pining over; they are either indifferent to her, like the Hungarian, or thieves. On a still deeper level, Nadina realizes that the Romantic hero is not the antithesis of the undesired husband, but rather an extension of him. The thief who steals her jewels does Andrei Il'ich's work for him in forcing Nadina to consent to the marriage. Pavlova underlines the identity between Romantic hero and unromantic husband in the dream Nadina has just before the caballero-thief enters: Andrei Il'ich comes into her room dressed as a caballero complete with sword, sombrero, and guitar. He throws the guitar at Nadina, shattering a mirror, the mirror, one suspects, of her illusions.

In Liza's story, as Fusso remarks, Pavlova debunks Pushkin's *Pikovaia dama* (*The Queen of Spades*) ("Pavlova's Quadrille," 120–21). Pavlova's Liza, like her Pushkinian namesake, grows up as the ward of an evil-natured, reputedly rich aunt who enjoys tormenting her. As in *Pikovaia dama*, a young man who pretends to be in love with Liza sees her only as a means to the aunt's wealth. In contrast to Pushkin's Gothic tale of madness, secrets, and ghosts, however, in Pavlova's society tale Aleksei simply rejects Liza because he considers the legacy she receives from her aunt insufficient. While Pushkin depicts Liza's tragedy as Germann's rejection of her, Pavlova recenters the story on Liza's psychological coming of age. Liza has gained self-knowledge and the ability to see beyond the myth of romantic love. Looking back she says of Aleksei:

> [. . .] я нем нашла предлог
> Для любви, для счастия без меры.
> Все же мы, мечтая и любя,
> Дань свою кладем к ногам химеры,
> Все в другом мы ищем лишь себя.
>
> ⁓
>
> (In him I found a pretext
> For love, and for happiness beyond measure.
> We all, dreaming and loving,
> Place our gift at the feet of chimeras,
> We all are only searching for ourselves in the other.)
>
> (329)

More than the loss of her relationship with Aleksei, Pavlova's Liza grieves her loss of spiritual balance and self-respect. Her desire for Aleksei blocked any compassion for her unpleasant but suffering aunt, leading Liza simply to wish her dead. Standing over her aunt's body, Liza silently says a requiem for her aunt and for herself. By the time she recounts the story, however, Liza, like Nadina, has achieved some peace of mind.

Ol'ga's story concerns the humiliation she experienced at her first ball. Innocent, awkward, and defenseless, with no male relative to protect her, Ol'ga becomes a victim of the cruelty of several men: they ignore her, reject her, and finally make her the butt of a practical joke by introducing her to a madman who proposes to any woman on sight. Ol'ga takes his proposal seriously until she overhears the jokers congratulating themselves. Once again, romantic-appearing heroes—this one is not a thief but a madman—cannot help women. Ol'ga, like the other women, has learned to rely on herself and now commands respect in society.

Countess Polina, we learn, did have a male relative to protect her. However, she could never please her judgmental and dour cousin Vadim, who oppressed her with his disapproval. To spite him, Polina flirts with a guardsman at a party. When a count comments on her behavior, Vadim challenges him to a duel in which Vadim dies. Thirteen years later the countess still cannot forgive herself for having caused her cousin's death. The fact that Polina is now a countess suggests that she has married the count who killed Vadim, perhaps as a penance.

The countess in her story sums up the cause of women's unhappiness in society:

И бестолковость женской роли—
Смесь своеволья и неволи,
[. . . . .]
Где в лабиринте воспитанья
Руководительная нить? . .

⤳

(The senselessness of a woman's role—
A mixture of caprice and bondage
[. . . . .]
Where in the labyrinth of our upbringing
Is the guiding thread?—)

(366)

In fact, these women have had no guidance. Nadina has no father; her sick mother only worries about her daughter's material well-being. Liza is an orphan dependent on an aunt who resembles an evil stepmother. Ol'ga, too, has no father. Her mother can neither teach her what she needs to know nor protect her from being abused in society. The countess has no mother, only an over-indulgent father and an aunt. Nor can the harsh and judgmental Vadim give her the guidance she needs.

In structure *Kadril'* is a double-frame narrative.[48] Not only do the four women discuss one another's stories (the first frame), but, as in *Dvoinaia zhizn'*, a woman poet narrates the entire work, providing a second frame in a prologue. By connecting the various narrative levels of the work, Pavlova reduces even further than she did in *Dvoinaia zhizn'* the distinction between extraordinary women—the poet-narrator—and the "ordinary" woman in society. First, in contrast to the more aloof and impersonal narrator of *Dvoinaia zhizn'*, the narrator of *Kadril'* verges on being a character. She declares her gender immediately, at the beginning of the first digression:

Южной ночи
Не знаю я, России дочь

⁓

(I, a daughter of Russia, do not know
A southern night.)
                                                               (309)

She also provides personal information about herself, for example, that
she loves Moscow and has a small son.

Second, Pavlova flattens the distinction between ordinary women
and poets by having the women characters narrate their own stories,
thus emphasizing their similarity to the poet-narrator. Third, Pavlova
brings the narrative levels together syntactically by repeating in the four
women's stories motifs and "semantic fields" from the narrator's introduction. For example, the narrator tells us:

Прошли воображенья чары;
Давно не возмущают сна
Ни андалузские гитары . . .

⁓

(Imagination's spells have passed,
For a long time my dreams have not been perturbed
Either by Andalusian guitars . . .)
                                                               (310)

As we have seen, the Andalusian guitars reappear in Nadina's story.

The word "detskii" (childish), which the narrator self-deprecatingly
applies to her poetry ("detskii stikh" [childish verse]), also recurs with
variations throughout the four stories, culminating in that of the countess.
Nadina's tale:

Жила я жизнию простой и детской,

⁓

(I lived a simple and childish life.)
                                                               (314)

Что детская некстати тут причуда

⁓

(That my childish caprices were inappropriate here.)
                                                               (319)

Ol'ga's tale:

Ребенок ветреный исчез

(The fickle child disappeared.)
(319)

The countess's tale:

Что я бессмыссленно-упряма
И малодушна как дитя

(That I was senselessly stubborn
And faint-hearted, like a child.)
(358)

Как тешилась я в злобе детской

(How I amused myself in childish spite.)
(359)

Не будь упорнее дитяти

(Don't be more stubborn than a child.)
(361)

The repetition of the word "detskii" (childish) underlines Pavlova's theme: that women can only gain freedom by renouncing the social conditioning that encourages them to remain children.

Pavlova creates the most striking echo between narrative levels, however, in the similarity between the countess's description of Vadim in the culminating story and the narrator's depiction of Pushkin (noted by Fusso in "Pavlova's *Quadrille*," 125). We see in Vadim yet another incarnation of the disapproving, harsh, but loving God from the earlier works. Polina says,

[. . .] я хулы его нежданной
Всегда боялась как огня
[.   .   .   .   .]
Но дивно шло к бровям тем строгим
Противоречье кротких губ.

(I always feared his unexpected criticisms
Like fire

[. . . . .]
But the contradiction of those severe brows went wonderfully well
With his gentle lips.)[49]

(354–55)

The narrator in her introduction presents Pushkin as similarly judgmental: as the last and most unappealing incarnation of the stern, dis-
appointed, disapproving God (or male "muse" discussed in chapter 2),
inimical to women's achievements. Nor do we find in this depiction even
the redeeming glimpse of tenderness or love we have seen in previous
versions of this figure. As noted in chapter 3, the narrator imagines
Pushkin condemning her work in advance:

> Зачем, качая головою,
> Так строго на меня смотря,
> Зачем стоишь передо мною,
> Призрак Певца-богатыря?

⚘

> (Why, shaking your head,
> Looking at me so sternly,
> Why do you stand before me,
> Specter of the *bogatyr* of singers?)

(310)

She compares Pushkin with the armored body of the Cid, which, placed
on a horse at the head of the Spanish army, routed the Moors, who did
not realize he was dead. This death-in-life image is echoed by the countess's comparison of Vadim to Pushkin's Stone Guest.[50] In these menac-
ing and lifeless depictions the figure seems to have reached his culminating form. He does not appear in subsequent works.

Pavlora's *Kadril'*, in innovative, masterly verse, challenges and rede-
fines several literary traditions—the *svetskaia povest'*, the *povest' v
stikhakh,* and the *poema*—as well as the standard depiction of women
in Russian literature. Critics, however, have ignored this remarkable
achievement. The work deserves a great deal more attention.

In "Za chainym stolom," the last of these works, and Pavlova's only published short story, cosmology is completely absent. If *Kadril'* questioned
and rewrote specific plots by men (Baratynsky and Pushkin), "Za
chainym stolom" looks at the assumptions underlying such stories—the
androcentric social and narrative conventions that govern stories about
women—and how those stories are told.

"Za chainym stolom" develops further several themes from *Kadril'*. The discussion about women's nature now takes place between men and women at tea instead of exclusively among women before a ball. A countess again leads the conversation, but this countess expresses more self-confidence and less ambivalence about women. Her analysis of the inadequacies of women's upbringing seems like an expansion of her counterpart's terse diagnosis in *Kadril'*.

Kadril':

> The senselessness of a woman's role—
> A mixture of caprice and bondage. (366)

"Za chainym stolom":

> One would think that almost every woman is brought up by her worst enemy, so strangely do they care for her. She cannot earn money like a man, and by law is virtually deprived of paternal inheritance, so they instill in her a need for luxuries. She cannot propose to a man, so from childhood they frighten her with spin-sterhood as a shameful disaster, make her incapable of inde-pendence, and teach her to look upon it as indecent. A frivolous choice can make her unhappy for life, so they train her to be friv-olous and capricious. A momentary attraction is enough to ruin her irrevocably. Knowing this, they develop coquettishness in her and the inclination to play with danger, and they repress any-thing that could give her a serious direction.[51]

Unlike her counterpart in *Kadril'*, the countess in "Za chainym stolom" does not denigrate women. Here it is a man, Aleksei Petrovich, who argues that women are physically and morally inferior to men. To prove his point, Aleksei Petrovich tells of a princess who discovers that her fiancé, apparently sweet, humble, and simple, is in fact a poor, bril-liant, and ambitious man using this pose among aristocrats to support himself and his mother. The princess calls off the wedding, telling her fiancé that she cannot bring herself to become the wife of a man who dis-sembles so well. The countess responds to Aleksei Petrovich's story by suggesting that women do not differ from men at all. She asks him, "Do you think that if it were reversed, if [the man] were a woman and the princess a man, that the man would have acted differently?" Aleksei Petrovich is forced to admit he does not know.

Pavlova also further develops the motif of the coquettish woman who causes a duel in which a man dies. However, Princess Alina in "Za chainym stolom," unlike the countess in *Kadril'*, refuses to accept all the blame, telling the surviving duelist when he reproaches her that he must take responsibility for his own actions including his decision to duel with his friend.

As I have discussed elsewhere, in "Za chainym stolom" Pavlova has an audience of women question the biases and one-sidedness of men's stories about them. On a formal level the work questions the very narrative conventions that produce such stories, such as the death-or-marriage ending. In one of the story's epigraphs Pavlova writes, "I would like there to be not one finished story; it's the ending that spoils everything. . . . An ended story, after all, is a garden enclosed by a stone wall that doesn't allow you to see into the distance." Pavlova, in fact, dispenses with the death-or-marriage ending. In the story itself Aleksei Petrovich concludes, "I cannot report any kind of ending to you because neither Khozrevsky nor Wismer nor the princess died, and because she didn't marry either one."[52] In offering another ending for women, neither death nor marriage (the "destruction or territorialization of women"), the story challenges both literary and social conventions.[53]

Until the 1980s critics and scholars discussed Pavlova's work only in terms of its connections with the male literary tradition, at best granting Pavlova, as an "extraordinary woman," the status of honorary man. As I hope to have shown, however, in these works at least, Pavlova, who knew she was extraordinary, did not write as an honorary man but "as a woman." She emphatically rejected the idea of any essential gulf between extraordinary and ordinary women, depicting extraordinary women as very human and ordinary women as extraordinary. Pavlova's movement in these five works from cosmology to a sophisticated analysis of the cultural and literary assumptions that hamper women in society showed her growing interest in the conditions that all women shared. It seems likely that Pavlova read and was influenced by Russian and European women writers as well as men, and I suggest it would be worthwhile to examine her work in the context of women's literary traditions.

7

In Conclusion
Noncanonical Men Poets

In this study I have attempted to define the social and literary factors that led men literary gatekeepers and canon-makers of the Romantic period to dismiss the poetry of their women contemporaries. I have examined the social conditions under which these women poets lived, their re-working of male-centered literary conventions, and the critical assumptions that affected their reception and subsequent literary reputations. I also have indicated some literary approaches to these women's poetry that might deepen our understanding of it and allow us to evaluate it on its own terms. Most of the theoretical and recovery work, however—including the development of gender-neutral aesthetic standards to evaluate men and women's writing together—remains to be done.

But while none of the women poets of this generation has entered the canon of Russian literature, neither has every Russian man poet. In conclusion it will be useful to consider what factors beside gender—or in combination with gender—have affected poets' canonicity. We can do so by returning to the noncanonical men poets mentioned in the introduction and asking questions about them similar to those we have asked about their women contemporaries. What social conditions did they experience? What were their literary practices and how was their poetry received? Did they, too, rework poetical conventions? Have they been excluded from the canon because of social and literary-political factors? Or did they simply write inferior poetry? While a detailed consideration of the lives and works of noncanonical men poets lies outside the scope of this study, a brief discussion of these questions will allow us to draw more general conclusions.

In characterizing Pavel Fedotov, Eduard Guber, Aleksei Khomiakov, Aleksei Kol'tsov, Apollon Maikov, Evgenii Mil'keev, and Fedor Miller as noncanonical I have taken several indicators into account.[1] Like their women contemporaries, these poets generally are not found in course surveys of nineteenth-century Russian literature or as subjects of research. They appear only very briefly, when at all, in such Russian literature reference works as Victor Terras's *Handbook of Russian Literature*. Two major canon builders of Russian literature, Belinsky and Mirsky, generally ignored or dismissed them.[2] In addition, two of them are not identified primarily as poets: Fedotov is known as an artist, and Khomiakov as an architect of Slavophilism. All of these noncanonical poets, however, have some poetic status. Four of them appear in an anthology that is part of the prestigious Biblioteka poeta series, *Poety 1840–1850-kh godov*, while Khomiakov, Kol'tsov, and Maikov are the subjects of their own Biblioteka poeta editions.

Social Conditions for Canonical Poets

One conclusion we can draw from this admittedly miniscule sample of three groups of poets—canonical men, noncanonical men, and noncanonical women—is that some correlation exists between canonicity and literary social capital. As mentioned earlier, literary social capital for the poets we have been discussing included such factors as social position, education, location in Moscow or Saint Petersburg, mentors, and personal connections with literary gatekeepers and opinion-makers. The canonical poets of this generation whom we have considered (Pushkin, Del'vig, Baratynsky, Iazykov, Lermontov, Tiutchev, Fet) all came from privileged, aristocratic backgrounds and received excellent educations.[3] In addition to being tutored at home, Pushkin and Del'vig graduated from the prestigious Tsarskoe Selo Lyceum; Lermontov, Tiutchev, and Fet attended Moscow University; Baratynsky attended the Corps of Pages, an aristocratic military school, and Iazykov spent many years at the university at Dorpat (Tartu). They all lived in the center (Saint Petersburg and/or Moscow), as opposed to the periphery (the provinces), for significant periods of time, and as noted in chapter 1, they all benefited from close connections with the literary establishment. They also enjoyed male privilege, which included access to a classical/university education, study groups and literary circles, mentors as opposed to literary guardians, and the possibility of editing a journal or *al'manakh*. As we have seen, no women poets—not even aristocrats who lived in the capitals, for example, Rostopchina, Pavlova, and Bakunina—possessed these advantages.

Social Conditions for Noncanonical Men Poets

Like all the women poets, most of the noncanonical men poets enjoyed less literary social capital than the canonical men; this because they were some combination of lower class, poor, uneducated, non-Russian, and provincial. Pavel Fedotov, the son of a retired lieutenant, grew up in a large and poor Moscow family. Although he attended the élite Cadet Corps, from which he graduated as an ensign, he struggled with poverty for most of his life. Evgenii Mil'keev, also the son of a minor civil servant who died when Mil'keev was three, grew up in poverty in Tobol'sk (Siberia). After four years of education at a Tobol'sk school, he worked as a scribe. Aleksei Kol'tsov, whose father was a cattle dealer, grew up in Voronezh, where he had less than one and a half years of schooling. Fedor Miller was a charity student at a Lutheran school in Moscow but managed to become certified as an apothecary's assistant and then as a home tutor of German and Russian literature. Eduard Guber grew up in Saratov, spoke German as his first language, and graduated as a military engineer from the Saint Petersburg Institute of the Transportation Corps (Institut korpusa putei soobshcheniia).

For several of these noncanonical men poets, their lack of economic resources appears to have affected their physical and psychological resources. Many died early of causes reflecting the stresses of poverty. Fedotov died insane at thirty-seven. Mil'keev killed himself at age thirty-one. Guber, whose health was undermined by lifelong poverty, died of a heart attack at thirty-three. Kol'tstov also died at thirty-three of tuberculosis. The canonical men poets generally died much later (Zhukovsky at sixty-nine, Fet at seventy-two, Tiutchev at seventy) or of causes connected with their upper-class status: Pushkin at thirty-seven and Lermontov at twenty-seven in duels, Baratynsky at forty-four while traveling abroad, Iazykov at forty-four of syphilis contracted while at the European University of Dorpat.[4]

But while literary social capital appears to have been necessary, it certainly was not a sufficient condition for canonicity. Aleksei Khomiakov and Apollon Maikov, for example, graduated from Moscow and Saint Petersburg University, respectively, spent a great deal of time in the capitals, traveled abroad, and benefited from many literary connections; Khomiakov was married to Iazykov's sister, and Maikov was able to publish six editions of his complete works during his lifetime. Both Kho-miakov and Maikov have separate Biblioteka poeta editions of their works, perhaps another indication of literary social capital. However, Khomiakov is known primarily as a Slavophile philosopher and is considered to have subordinated his poetry to his Slavophilism. Maikov won many honors in the course of his life, but critics have called his poetry "flat," "weak," and "overworked."[5]

The noncanonical poets, however, did share male privilege with the canonical poets, which may account for the wider variety of social classes they occupied than the women poets. As discussed in chapter 1, men's literary social networks generally extended to men of all classes but excluded women. Belinsky helped Kol'tsov, the son of a Voronezh cattle dealer, publish his first book of poetry, but one cannot imagine him similarly helping the daughter of a Voronezh cattle dealer. Zhukovsky brought Mil'keev, the orphaned son of a Siberian petty civil servant, to Saint Petersburg to be educated as a poet, but one doubts he would have similarly sponsored Mil'keev's sister. Guber, whom Pushkin befriended and encouraged in his translation of Goethe's *Faust*, became a literary critic for the journal *Biblioteka dlia chteniia*. Miller founded his own journal, *Razvlechenie* (1859–81). Fedotov received encouragement to pursue his career as an artist from the fable writer I. A. Krylov and was embraced by the *Sovremennik* group (Druzhinin, Nekrasov, Panaev, etc.). Such opportunities were not available to women.

Poetical Practices

As we have noted in the course of this study, the poetical practices of non-canonical men and women poets resemble each other, while differing from those of the canonical men. Many women and men noncanonical poets avoided classical themes, presumably because they lacked a classical education. Both women and men noncanonical poets wrote many more prayers, poems to family members, and poems about children (lullabies, elegies on their deaths).[6] Noncanonical men poets less frequently personify nature as a female sex partner than do the canonical men and do not generally address poems to a sexualized female muse.[7] They also write more cross-gender poems than do their canonical men counterparts. In short, in some ways they could be said to write "like a woman."[8]

Such similarities in the poetic practices of noncanonical men and women poets bring to mind Julia Kristeva's definition of femininity, not as a quality, but as a "position." For Kristeva the feminine, along with the working class and some avant-garde writers, are defined by their marginalization from the "patriarchal symbolic order."[9] Similarly, in the case of Russian poets, some of the writing practices that women and noncanonical men poets share may be a function of their marginalization from Russian literature, of being perceived as Other.

We have seen that some women poets ambivalently exploited their feminine Otherness in the "poetess" stance. Nonaristocratic men poets similarly exploited their provincial or uneducated Otherness. For example, Kol'tsov appeals to presumably wealthy and aristocratic readers in the capitals to pity his unhappy, uncivilized youth in the following repeatedly cited lines:

> Скучно и нерадостно
> Я провел век юности:
> В суетных занятия
> Не видал я красных дней.
> Жил в степях с коровами

> (I spent my youth
> Bored and joyless:
> In empty occupations
> I saw no beautiful days.
> I lived on the steppe with the cows.)
> ("Povest' moei liubvi" [The tale of
> my love, 1829])[10]

Mil'keev similarly prefaced his one book of poetry with a twelve-page letter to Zhukovsky describing his unhappy, uncivilized youth: "[Priroda] naznachila rodit'sia i zhit' v takoi sfere, gde nichto ne moglo sposobstvovat' svoevremennomu probuzhdeniiu i obrazovaniiu etogo instinkta. . . . Ne garmonicheskii tot klass, iz kotorogo ia proiskhozhu." ([Nature] appointed me to be born and live in a sphere where nothing could assist the awakening and development of that instinct [for poetic sound]. . . . The class I come from is not harmonious).[11] While Kol'tsov had a well-to-do if despotic father, Mil'keev lived in poverty. This is reflected in the conclusion of his open letter to Zhukovsky, in which Mil'keev asks not only for sympathy and recognition but also for help finding a job in Saint Petersburg that would provide enough free time for him to continue writing poetry.

Fedotov, in addressing the aristocracy, took a more ambivalent, clowning attitude toward his lack of a university education and lower

social status. In "K moim chitateliam, stikhov moikh strogim razbirateliam" (To my readers, strict examiners of my verse, 1850), he argues
that because as a soldier he cannot afford Romantic preoccupations with
nature, glory, and love, he therefore cannot be a poet. His aristocratic
readers, he concludes, rather than criticize his poetry for these defi-
ciencies, should be indulgent, since at least he does not publish it. Like
Rostopchina in "Iskushenie" (discussed in chapter 4), Fedotov ironically
has written a poem arguing that he is not a poet. In all these examples
we see the mixture of accommodation and resistance to the role of Other
(discussed in chapter 1) that marks women's poetry as well.

I suspect that, as with women's poetry, an examination of noncanonical men's poetry would reveal original reworkings of traditional literary conventions and categories. For example, Fedotov wrote at least two
poems in connection with his painting "Svatovstvo maiora" (The major's wooing): "Popravka obstoiatel'stv, ili zhenit'ba maiora (predislovie
k kartine)" (An improvement in circumstances or the major's marriage
[foreword to the picture]), and "Ratseia (Ob"iasnenie kartiny 'Svatovstvo maiora')" (Lecture [explanation of the picture "The major's wooing"]). Although literary historians consider these poems curiosities—
minor historical commentaries on the painting—the fact that Fedotov
wrote them indicates that he viewed the painting by itself as incomplete.
It might make sense, then, to analyze the painting-poems as a separate
and original genre. Fedotov's fables à la Krylov also should be read in
the context of his paintings. Khomiakov's work might repay examination on its own terms as well, in the tradition of religious or philosophical poetry. That is, along with interpretive strategies for women's writings and gender-neutral aesthetic standards, we also need interpretive
strategies for the writings of nonaristocrats and class-neutral aesthetic
standards. Such speculations, however, which can only be verified by
close analyses of these poets' works, cannot be pursued in this study.

Reception of Noncanonical Men Poets

While none of these poets is considered "first rank," their reputations
range considerably. I would suggest that as sexual politics has influenced the reception of the women poets, so literary and class politics
have influenced the reception of the noncanonical men. Let us take, for
example, the contrasting literary receptions of two nonaristocratic poets from the provinces, Kol'tsov and Mil'keev.

Kol'tsov was discovered in Voronezh by the philosopher and poet

Nikolai Stankevich (1813–40) and mentored by Vissarion Belinsky. Belinsky read Kol'tsov's poems and made suggestions for revising them before they were submitted to journals, helped publish and favorably reviewed Kol'tsov's first book of poetry, and wrote a long introduction to the second, posthumous edition. According to one Soviet critic, Belinsky, as a Westernizer, saw in Kol'tsov's work a way to refute the Slavophiles' idealization of traditional Russian family life. Other radical critics such as Dobroliubov and Saltykov-Shchedrin followed Belinsky's lead in praising Kol'tsov, as did Soviet literary critics. Kol'tsov's works were reprinted in numerous Soviet scholarly and popular editions—no fewer than thirty-two between 1921 and 1989.[12]

Mil'keev, the second poet, was discovered when he brought some of his poems to Zhukovsky, who was visiting Tobol'sk in western Siberia. Zhukovsky was so impressed by the poems that he took Mil'keev back to Saint Petersburg. In Moscow a few months later Mil'keev gained the sponsorship of writers identified with Slavophilism and the journal *Moskvitianin:* Stepan Shevyrev (1806–64), who wrote literary criticism for *Moskvitianin*, A. S. Khomiakov, Karolina Pavlova, and her husband, Nikolai Pavlov. But while Belinsky warmly praised Kol'tsov's poetry in reviews, he harshly criticized Mil'keev's. Belinsky may have been affected by his ideological differences with Mil'keev's Slavophile sponsors as well as by his dislike of the poetry of Vladimir Benediktov (1807–73), a strong influence on Mil'keev.[13] No doubt, Belinsky's canonical position in Soviet literary scholarship affected Mil'keev's reputation. During the Soviet period only a few of Mil'keev's poems appeared in anthologies, while criticism about him was confined almost entirely to local Siberian publications. It might be concluded that Kol'tsov simply wrote better poetry than Mil'keev, but such is not necessarily the case. The prerevolutionary scholar Mark Azadovsky points out that Vasilii Zhukovsky, Karolina Pavlova, and Petr Pletnev (1702–1865, Saint Petersburg University professor and critic) all thought highly of Mil'keev's poetry and that surely their judgment must be given as much credence as Belinsky's.[14] More work on Mil'keev—as well as on the other noncanonical men and on the influence of literary politics on reputation—needs to be done.

What, if any, conclusions about canonicity may we draw from this study? I suggest that just as a national history can be seen as a story told about a people, so a literary canon may be seen as a story told about a literature—a story that keeps changing. However, until now, all stories about the Golden Age of Russian literature and Russian Romanticism

Appendix

Notes

Bibliography

Index

Appendix

Praskov'ia Bakunina (1810–80)

Notebook in f. 15 (Bakunin Archive), op. 10, n. 5, Pushkinskii dom.
"Moi chertenok" (1834? This poem, undated in Bakunina's notebook,
    appears between poems dated 1833 and 1835.)   179
"Ballada." From the play "Igrannoi v Uiutnom pred zakrytiem teatra
    19 avgusta 1835."   181
"Prolog igrannom v Uiutnom 8 iulia 1835 goda v den' rozhdeniia
    M. M. Bakunina."   182

Nadezhda Khvoshchenskaia (1824–89)

Archival versions in f. 541, op. 1, ed. kh. 3, RGALI
Published versions:
"Druz'ia . . ." *Literaturnaia gazeta,* no. 39 (Sept. 25, 1847).   188
"'Vy ulybaetes'? . . .'" *Otechestvennyi zapiski,* no. 8 (1852).   190
"Byvalo s sestrami." *Literaturnaia gazeta,* no. 38 (1847).   192

Elizaveta Kul'man (1808–25)

"Korinna." In *Piiticheskie opyty Elisavety Kul'man: V trekh chastakh,*
    66–70. 2nd. ed. Sankt-Peterburg: V tip. Imperatorskoi Rossiiskoi
    Akademii, 1839.   194

Anna Mordovtseva (1823–85)

"Staraia skazka." In *Otzvuki zhizni, 1842–187-,* 9–31. Saratov: Tip.
    P. S. Feokritova, 1877   203

Elisaveta Shakhova (1822–99)

"Progulka u vzmor'ia." In *Stikhotvoreniia Elizavety Shakhovoi,* 35–37.
    Sankt-Peterburg: R[oss.] A[kad.], 1839.   215

Anna Turchaninova (1774–1848)

"Pesenka ob Leonarde i Blondine." From the play *Nochekhodets,
    ili Lunatik. Ippokrena, ili utekhi liuboslaviia,* pt. 4 (1799): 273–85.   217

Прасковья БАКУНИНА
(1810–80)

Пушкинский Дом. f.15 (Бакунины), op. 10 n.5

МОЙ ЧЕРТЕНОК
(1834?)

Колдунью при моем рожденьи
Забыли на обед позвать.
Она сердилась и в отмщенье
Чертенка вздумала прислать.
Ее велению послушный
К упрекам, просьбам равнодушный
С тех пор он с лирой всякий день
За мною следует как тень;
Возьму ли я работу в руки,
Сегюра стану ли читать
Чертенок тут и ну мешать.
Его чертовской лиры звуки
Волнуют ум, душа моя
Полна каким-то исступленьем,
Все чудно, странно вкруг меня.
Поэты бред сей вдохновленьем
Привыкли звать в своих стихах.
С волшебной лирою в руках
Я часто к небесам взлетаю,
На землю опускаюсь вновь,
И с дел минувших я срываю
Веками брошенный покров.
Мечта умерших воскрешает
Волшебной силою своей,
Душа к ним в грудь перелетает,
Живу я жизнью не моей.
И тут все чувства, все желанья
Легко в стихах мне изъяснить
Печаль же, радость, и страданье
В размер гармонии вложить.
В душе восторженной сливаясь
По струнам сладкий звук летит,
В слова земные облекаясь,

Стихами миру говорит!
Тогда объята восхищеньем
Чертенка называю геньем!
Но сила прекратится чар,
К рассудку возвращаюсь снова,
Тоска еще томит больного,
Когда пройдет и бред, и жар;
Так мне на свете пусто, скушно,
И модой избранной наряд
Не привлекает грустный взгляд,
На бал я еду равнодушно;
Но счастья возвратятся дни,
И на стихи опять мои
Смотрю с довольною улыбкой.
Смеюсь над старой ведьмой я,
Над странною ее ошибкой;
Ужасным мщением меня,
Она не слишком наказала.
К чертенку привыкаться стала,
В большом ладу мы жили с ним.
Но вдруг родным, друзьям моим
Колдунья верно прошептала,
Что тайну дивную стихов
Еще ребенком я узнала,
Язык понятен мне богов,
Хорей и дактили знакомы,
И вдруг как град ко мне альбомы
Кузины все и все друзья,
Стихов желают от меня.
Поэту нет от них спасенья.
Сменяя просьбою укор,
Как фероньерку, как убор,
Они просили вдохновенья!
Тут я узнала в первый раз,
Что мщения ударил час.
Как буря вдруг забушевала
И под землей и на земле,
И шум и хохот: на метле
Колдунья в воздухе летала.

БАЛЛАДА

(Играна в Уютном пред закрытием театра 19 августа 1835)

В ночь светлую летом под Троицын день,
Собрались русалки в приютную тень.
Качались на ветке, плескались в реке,
И слышны их хохот и песнь вдалеке.

Приблизиться к лесу никто не хотел,
И путник, внимая шум дальний, робел.
Себя ограждая всесильным крестом,
Забывши усталость, шел дальним путем.

Но кто же, бесстрашный, в приют их спешит,
Их хохот внимая, молитв не творит?
То дева младая, но думы полна,
Их хохот, их песни не слышит она.

И вот уж русалки веселой толпой
Сбежались, свилися вкруг девы младой.
Хохочут, щекочут. В ответ им она:
"Спасибо, подруги, мне смерть не страшна.

Всех пыток тяжеле мученья мои,
Мучения страстной презренной любви.
И смерть мне отрада, противен мне свет."
"Тебе мы поможем",—русалки в ответ.

"Родных отрекися и веру забудь,
Тебя он полюбит, русалкою будь.
Но счастью помеха твой крест золотой:
Брось в волны, надменный пленится тобой."

И дева срывает спасенья залог,
Вдруг грудь наполняет безумный восторг.
И пламень чудесный в потухших очах,
И хохот, и песня на бледных устах.

И вот к ним приходит красавец младой,
Пленился русалки он дивной красой;
Но жжет его пламень чудесных очей,
Страдает, томится, бледней и бледней.

И дева постигла, страданья полна,
Что взорам чудесным власть ада дана,
Что смертный не в силах их власть перенесть,
Но взор смертоносный не может отвесть.

Его убивая, все дева следит,
И вот уж в объятьях он мертвый лежит.
Мучение в сердце, отчаянный страх.
И хохот, и песня на бледных устах.

ПРОЛОГ

(Игран в Уютном 8 июля 1835 года в день рождения М.М.Бакунина)

Действующие лица:

П.М.Бакунина,
А.И.Цветкова,
(?) Гедвих

Русалка	–	К.М.Бакунина,
Леший	–	П.И.Цветков,
Домовой	–	П.И.Степанов,
Ведьма	–	Л.С.Творогова,
Посвист	–	И.Т.Дурнов

Явление 1.

(П.Бакунина и А.Цветкова сидят у стола и пишут. Гедвих играет на фор тепиано.)

П.Бакунина:

Вот видишь, Сашенька, она счастливей нас
Ну, право, хоть куда сыграла в этот раз.
И в звуках выразить желание,
В рождение приятной быть
И робкую игру простят ей за старанье
А мы с тобой . . .

А.Цветкова:

Их право, я излить
Стараюсь в чувстве все, и в сердце—их так много!
Ты знаешь, что как дочь об нем молю я Бога?
Признательность к нему я чувствую вполне,
Да рифмы не даются мне.
Однако ж хоть с трудом, а все я написала.

П.Бакунина:

Прочти.

А.Цветкова (*читает*):

Нет, не могу перед собраньем
Стихи незвучные читать,
Хоть и желала б передать,
Души заветные желанья;

Тому, кто путь мне указал
В страну надзвездную, святую,
Кто в дочери любимой дал
Сыскать подругу мне земную.
О, как ему желала б я
Излить души благодаренье,
Но силы нет; ведь в день рожденья
Уж не одна его семья,
Услышит мой привет нестройный
И как бывало с неземной
Улыбкой в сердце, взор довольный
На стих незвучный бросит мой!
Но тут, как будто пред судьями
Предстать пред всеми должно мне
С моими робкими стихами,
С боязнью грустною в душе.
И так надеюсь, что молчанье
Не охладит любви его
Ему известны все желанья
Младого сердца моего.
Чтоб дни грядущие летели
К нему приветною чредой
И жизнью б радостной светлела
Она как утренней зарей.
С семьей своей души бесценной
Покой, отраду б он вкушал
Трудами жизни утомленной
Их в лоне счастья забывал.

    П.Бакунина:

Так я одна не сочиняю.
В тупик чертенок встал.
И что сказать совсем не знаю,
Не любит он похвал.
А что им наша жизнь счастлива,
То каждый день наш светлый взгляд,
Улыбка радости игривой
Без слов понятно говорят.

(*Садится и задумывается*).

Явление 2.

Те же.

Русалка (*вбегает, хохоча*):

Что ж, поэтка, так уныло
Ты сидишь с пером в руках
И теряешься в мечтах
Ни стишонка не сложила?
В Белокаменной Москве
Про тебя уж знают все.
Петь при людях уж не ново
Дмитриев, славный наш певец,
Одобрил приветным словом.
Что же вышло наконец?
Тщетно кличешь Аполлона
Он от старости оглох,
Не услышит с Геликона,
А к нему уж путь заглох.
Что же нас ты позабыла,
Иль в тебе догадки нет?
Мода всех нас оживила
И в большой пустила свет.
Если б к нам ты обратилась,
Не оставили б тебя,
Вся б ватага согласилась:
Леший, ведьма с нами, я,
Покидая лес и воду
К православному народу,
Мы направили б свой путь.
И по-русски, в то ж мгновенье,
На авось, без вдохновенья,
Помогли бы как-нибудь.

Явление 3.

Те же.

Леший. Домовой. Ведьма. Посвист.

Русалка:

Вот наши все, но ты не веселися,
Пойди и ролею займися,
Мы не поможем уж ни в чем.
Мы от себя пришли поздравить

Вы ж после можете забавить
Плохой игрой, чужим умом.
Без нетерпенья, без досады
Прослушайте вы наш привет
Искусства в нас большого нет,
Но чем богаты, тем и рады.

Леший:

Я оставил темный бор,
Перелез через забор
И в саду твоем зеленом
Я приют себе нашел.
В нем под тополем, под кленом
Жизнь веселую я вел.
Позабыл я о заботе
Ночью путника водить,
Здесь по собственной охоте
Буду до света бродить.
Я от бури и от вьюги
Сберегу твои цветы,
Но прошу я за услуги
Мне приют средь темноты.
По твоей всесильной воле
Не гулял бы в нем топор.
И в моей счастливой доле
Я забуду мрачный бор.

Ведьма:

Не пугать в трубу я вылезла
Не наслать вам долю тяжкую
Нет, услышала я в древнем Киеве,
Что сироточку бесталанную
Ты призвал к себе как родную дочь.
Все младенчество протекло ее ночью бурною
В те года как радость резвая
Украшает всем дни беспечные,
Она свыклася уж с кручинушкой
И изведала слезы горькие.
Но в дому твоем красно солнышко
Озарило ей юность счастием.
Как услышала я добру весточку
Как взыграло вдруг сердце русское,
Оседлала я метлу скорую,
Полетела я в Москву дальнюю,
Чтобы высказать все желания
И сказать тебе, что отныне я

Слугой верною буду век тебе.
И невзгодушки все бывалые
Размету тебе я метлой своей.
Не коснется тебя горе новое,
Под радушный кров тоска хищная
Не взлетит опять гостью страшною,
Но со дня твоего рождения
Дни считать ты будешь радостьми.

Домовой:

Мне в доме жить здесь тесно,
Я в городе живу.
Лихим, как всем известно,
Я ездоком слыву.
Но будьте без заботы—
Я пешего коня
Не трону: здесь работы
Довольно без меня.
От всех скажу желанья
Как житель городской,
И, верно, все собранье
Их повторит со мной.
Чтоб праздновать рожденье
Несметные года
Мы все без исключенья
Являлися сюда.

Русалка:

Навек оставляя днепровские волны,
Пленившись красою цветочных брегов,
Не буду на гибель заманивать челны
Я песнею звучной средь бурных валов.
Забуду русалок я хитрый обычай,
В ваш пруд поселившись, я буду добрей.
Мне рыбарь оплошной не будет добычей,
Но лодочку вашу рукою моей
Поддерживать стану, и вал беспокоить
Не будет мой хохот и песня моя,
Но хохотом, пеньем лишь буду я вторить
Веселостям вашим средь светлого дня.

Посвист:

Славянский Бог, я бог могучий
Вам красный день дарую я
Иль солнце засылаю тучей:

Подвластна мне погода вся.
В твоих трудах мое участье:
Не бойся холода, дождей,
С сих пор и ведра, и ненастье
Я с волей соглашу твоей.
Лучами солнца я раскрашу
Цветы взращенные тобой
Я прилечу на дачу вашу
Дождя с прохладною струей.
И никогда твои растенья
Не утомит палящий зной,
Но людям всем на загляденье
Я разукрашу садик твой.

Русалка, Леший (*поют*):

Русалка, Леший вам желают
Веселье, радость и покой.
И с ними вместе поздравляют
И леший вас, и домовой.
Актеры ждут, совсем готовы,
Они робеют. И за них
Замолвить вам хотим мы слово
Примите благосклонно их.

Конец.

Надежда ХВОЩИНСКАЯ

(1824–89)

Archival versions (РГАЛИ, f.541, op. 1, ed. kh. 3) vs. published versions.
To facilitate comparison I have italicized in the archival versions lines that were
changed or deleted in the published versions.

ДРУЗЬЯ ...
"Литературная газета," номер 39 (25 сентября, 1847)

Archival version:

*Друзья, вам истинно, вам щедро
жизнь дана,*
Со всею полной красотою;
*Страстьми могучими, любви святой
тоскою*
Кипит богатая, роскошная она.
5 Вам отданы ее тревоги и волненья,
Вам отданы ее заботы и труды,—
*Чтоб у судьбы стяжать борьбы
плоды,*
Вы бьетесь с ней до утомленья!
И в утомленьи том есть счастье! В
битве той
10 Великое сознанье воли скрыто,
И силы все тяжелою борьбой
Как у бойца могучего развиты;
Не жалуйтесь, что труден подвиг
тот—
Зато велик! Не говорите,
15 Что жизнь свою вы отдадите
За жизнь без слез и без забот—
Вот, за мою! ..
О разберем без спора,
*Достойна ль зависти она! То правда,
нет*
В моей душе печального укора,
20 И мне печали не дал свет,
Я не тружусь для счастья ... Но
сомненье
Волнует душу; хоть без слез,

Published version:

Друзья мои! Вам всем так щедро
жизнь дана,
Со всей роскошной красотою!
Страстями сильными, любовью
и тоскою
Кипит богатая, прекрасная она.
Вам отданы ее тревоги и волненья,
Вам отданы ее заботы и труды,—
Чтоб вырвать у судьбы борьбы
плоды,
Вы бьетесь с ней до утомленья!
И в утомленьи том есть счастье! В
битве той
Великое сознанье воли скрыто,
И силы той тяжелою борьбой
Как у бойца могучего развиты;
Не жалуйтесь, что труден подвиг
тот;—
Зато велик! Не говорите,
Что жизнь свою вы отдадите
За жизнь без слез и без забот—
За жизнь *мою!* ..
О, разберем без спора,
Достойна ль зависти онаю Конечно,
нет
В моей душе тяжелого укора,
И мне печали не дал свет,
Я не тружусь для счастья ... Но
сомненье
Волнует душу, хоть без слез,

Но в ней рождается вопрос:
Что это—жизнь иль прозябенье?
25 *Где тут деятельность, где тут*
разгул для сил?
Законам мудрости начто меня
учили?
К кругу бездействия, где сердце
заключили!
Их ни один мудрец не применил!..
Что мне любовь, друзья? Вам мир
ее глубок,
30 *Открыт, блестящ и бесконечен,—*
А для меня она—забытый
островок,
Что вопросительным крючком
отмечен
На карте ... Грустно мореход
Глядит на мир затерянный,
в сомненьи,
35 *Что, есть ли он, иль нет? Он божие*
ль творенье
Или мечта людей?.. И прочь идет
По морю синему, безгрозному, под
зноем;
Чуть движется корабль, повисли
паруса,
И дремлют вдалеке средь душного
покоя
40 Бесцветно—бледны небеса...
А это жизнь, друзья? О, эта
мысль ужасна,
Припомнить, сколько в ней забытых
пало сил,
Что светлых, ясных дум задумано
напрасно,
Как разум наконец изныл,
45 Как все, что жило здесь, в груди, в
душе святого,
Что в долгий, смелый путь душой
припасено,
Разбито и поглощено
Волной ничтожества земного!..
О, не завидуйте! Молитесь, чтобы
дал
50 *Господь, пославший эти силы,*
Вновь встать тому, кто под их
ношей пал,
И дотащиться до могилы!

И в ней рождается вопрос:
Что это—жизнь иль прозябенье?
Где деятельность тут, где тут
разгул для сил?
Законам мудрости начто меня
учили?
К кругу бездействия, где сердце
заключили,
Их ни один мудрец не применил?..
Что мне любовь, друзья? Вам мир
так бесконечен,
Открыт, блестящ, хорош, глубок,—
А для меня весь мир—забытый
островок!..
Он знаком вопросительным
отмечен
На карте жизни ... Грустно мореход
Глядит на остров тот затерянный,
в сомненьи,
Что есть ли он, иль нет?..........
. . . .
. . . . .И далее плывет
По морю синему... Вкруг острова
под зноем
Чуть движется корабль, повисли
паруса,
И дремлют высоко, средь душного
покоя,
Бесцветно-бледны небеса...
Вот жизнь моя, друзья! О, эта
мысль ужасна!
Припомним сколько в ней забытых
пало сил,
И светлых, ясных дум задумано
напрасно,
Как разум наконец изныл,
Как все, что жило здесь, в груди, в
душе, святого,
Что в долгий, смелый путь душой
припасено,
Разбито и поглощено,
Волной ничтожества земного!
О! Не завидуйте! Молитесь, чтобы
дал
Господь, пославший к жизни силы,
Вновь силу встать тому, кто с этой
ношей пал,
Не дотащившись до могилы!..

ВЫ УЛЫБАЕТЕСЬ?...
"Отечественные записки," номер 8 (1852)

Archival version:	*Published version:*

—Вы улыбаетесь?.. юаздумье не
      мешает
	—Вы улыбаетесь?.. юаздумье не
	      мешает

Мне видеть: вам за мной угодно
      наблюдать;
	Мне видеть: вам за мной угодно
	      наблюдать.

Вас это гладкое колечко занимает	Вас это гладкое колечко занимает

И то, что сняв его, я им люблю
      играть.
	И то, что, сняв его, я им люблю
	      играть.

5 —Привычка странная играть
      кольцом венчальным!
	—Привычка странная играть
	      кольцом венчальным!

—Взгляните: может быть оно и вас
      займет,
	—Взгляните: может быть оно и вас
	      займет,

*Напомнит вам самим день светлый
      иль печальный...*
	Напомнит вам о дне иль светлом
	      иль печальном...

Вот вырезан внутри семьсот
      тридцатый год
	Вот вырезан внутри семьсот
	      тридцатый год

И имя женское. Та, что его носила,	И имя женское. *Она* кольцо носила,
10 *Преданье говорит, невестой умерла,*	Невестой—и потом невестой умерла,

И я признаюсь вам: ее кольцо мне
      мило...
	И я признаюсь вам: ее кольцо мне
	      мило...

Их дом был барский дом, и в нем она
      жила,
	Их дом был барский дом, и в нем она
	      жила,

*Как птичка, что родом привыкла к
      клетке тесной.*
	Как птичка грустная, привыкши к
	      клетке тесной.

*Отец был строг, угрюм, носил
      кафтан с звездой*
	Отец был строг, угрюм, с холодною
	      душой,

15 И домогался все чего-то,
      неизвестно...
	И домогался все чего-то,
	      неизвестно...

Мать славилась своей роскошной
      красотой,
	Мать славилась своей роскошной
	      красотой,

Своим таинственным влиянием в
      гостиных.
	Своим таинственным влиянием в
	      гостиной.

А дочь... Она как тень передо мной
      стоит...
	А дочь... Она, как тень, передо мной
	      стоит...

Уж вечер. Купидон на мраморном
      камине
	Уж вечер. Купидон на мраморном
	      камине

20 *За стрелкою часовой лукаво
      сторожит.*
	У стрелки часовой лукаво
	      сторожит.

Она у зеркала одна, совсем одета;	Она у зеркала одна, совсем одета;

Веселый, шумный бал давно невесту
      ждет,
	Веселый, шумный бал давно невесту
	      ждет,

И тот, кому она на зависть, толки
света,
И руку детскую и сердце ...
25 "Союз сей, зависти самих богов
достойный",
Воспет пиитами ... назначенный
супруг
Не мог от лавр чужих уснуть ночей
спокойно,
И стан его согнул томительный
недуг.
Напрасных происков, обманутых
желаний,
30 *Но сладко он умел улыбкою*
прикрыть
Пред сильными земли всю злость
своих страданий;
Улыбкой сам умел счастливить и
язвить,
Приветно кланялся новорожденной
славе,
И это делал он уж много-много лет—
35 Но крылась седина под пудрой
величавой,
А дряхлость бледных рук под
кружевом манжет.
Он вздумал полюбить ... И образ
нежный, милый,
При имени любви опять передо мной:

Она ...

40 *Она балкон поспешно*
растворила
И сходит в темный сад, печальный
и пустой.
Дитя! Ей страшны шум листов,
ночные тени,
Ее отчаянный, свободный первый
шаг ...
Но кто-то перед ней склонился на
колени
45 На сбитых осенью, поблекнувших
листах
И ручка белая с ее кольцом
венчальным
На чью-то голову кудрявую легла,
И слезы горькие лились во тьме
печальной

И тот, кому она на зависть, толки
света,
И руку детскую, и сердце отдает.
"Союз сей, зависти самих богов
достойный",
Воспет пиитами ... Но будущий
супруг
От почестей другим не мог уснуть
спокойно,
И стан его согнул томительный
недуг
Напрасных происков, обманутых
желаний,
Хоть сладко он умел улыбкою
прикрыть
Пред сильными земли всю злость
своих страданий;
Улыбкой сам умел счастливить и
язвить,
Приветно кланялся новорожденной
славе,
И это делал он уж много-много лет—
Но крылась седина под пудрой
величавой,
И дряхлость бледных рук под
кружевом манжет.
Он вздумал полюбить ... И образ
нежный, милый,
При имени любви опять передо
мной! ...

... В ту ночь она балкон поспешно
растворила
И сходит в темный сад, печальный
и пустой.
Дитя! ей страшны шум листов,
ночные тени,
Ее отчаянный, свободный первый
шаг ...
Но кто-то перед ней склонился на
колени
На сбитых осенью, поблекнувших
листах ...
И ручка белая с ее кольцом
венчальным
На чью-то голову кудрявую легла,
И слезы горькие лились во тьме
печальной

И непогода их, обвеяв, унесла . . .
50 *То были слезы о блаженстве*
        невозможном,
О горести его, о горести своей,
О том, чтоб не винил он, пылкий и
        тревожный,
Покорность детскую, чтобы простил
        он ей . . .

И, может быть, лишь он один рыдал
        безвестно,
55 Когда она с земли на небо отошла . . .

—Да, это очень жаль и очень
        интересно;
Но сто восьмнадцать лет! Она б
        стара была.

И непогода их, развеяв, унесла . . .
И были слезы те о счастьи
        невозможном,
О горести его, о горести своей,
О том, чтоб не винил *он*, пылкий и
        тревожный,
В неверности ее, чтобы простил
        он ей . . .

И, может быть, лишь он один рыдал
        безвестно,
Когда она с земли на небо отошла . . .

—Да, это очень жаль и очень
        интересно;
Но сто восьмнадцать лет! Она б
        стара была.

БЫВАЛО С СЕСТРАМИ . . .

Archival version:

Бывало с сестрами, веселой и
        шумной толпой
Проходим под вечер один переулок
        глухой,
Как птички, что вьются в лазурной
        небес вышине,
И звонко щебечут, так резво
        смеются оне.
5 *Все—жаркого солнца пурпурный,*
        огнистый закат,
И длинные тени, и отблеск на
        кровлях палат,
И ветлы, что дремлют, покрытые
        пылью седой,
Цветок, что нечаянно взрос на
        сухой мостовой,
Гуляющих пестрый подчас
        презабавный наряд,—
10 *Все подметят, о всем беззаботно*
        они говорят.
На громкое слово, я помню, и часто
        случалось,
В низком домике старом со скрипом
        окно поднималось.

Published version:

Бывало с сестрами, веселой и
        шумной толпой
Проходим под вечер один переулок
        глухой,
Как птички, что вьются в лазурной
        небес вышине,
И звонко щебечут, так резво
        смеются оне.
И жаркого солнца пурпурный,
        огнистый закат,
И длинные тени, и отблеск на
        кровлях палат,
И старые ветлы, покрытые
        пылью седой,
Нечаянно взросший цветок на
        сухой мостовой,
Гуляющих пестрый подчас
        презабавный наряд,—
Они все подметят, и мне обо всем
        говорят.
На громкое слово, я помню,
        нередко случалось—
Вдруг в домике низком со скрипом
        окно поднималось;

Головка—к трепещущей раме
старинной склонясь,
Молодая, но бледная, долго глядела
на нас.
15 *На сердце, и вечно ее сберегутся*
черты,
Яркий взор, томный лик среди
мрачной кругом темноты,
Колечко на бледной руке, две косы
вокруг щек,
И пыльный луч солнца на них, и
гераний, что грустно поблек
Перед ней на окне, и работа . . . Она на
подружек моих
20 Глядит, будто хочет сказать: "Верно
праздник у них! . ."
И может быть труд своих долгих
бессонных ночей
Узнает на беспечной, веселой
подруге моей,
И столько печали в том взоре, и
жалости столько немой
О грустно утраченной юности,
светлой, роскошной, живой,
25 О жизни что дал ей Господь, чтоб
смеяться, и петь, и любить—
Что этого взора мне долго, вовек
не забыть . . .

Головка—к старинной трепещущей
раме склонясь,
Печальная, бледная, долго глядела
на нас.
На сердце, я век сохраню молодые
черты,
Взор яркий и томный, болезненный
вид красоты,
Колечко на бледной руке, две косы
вокруг щек,
Слезу на реснице . . . Гераний так
грустно поблек
У ней на окошке . . . Она на подружек
моих
Глядит, будто хочет сказать: "Верно
праздник у них! . ."
И может быть труд своих долгих
бессонных ночей
Она узнает на беспечной
подруге моей,—
И столько печали в том взоре, и
жалости столько немой
О грустно утраченной юности,
светлой, роскошной, живой,
О жизни, что дал ей Господь, чтоб
смеяться, и петь, и любить . . .
О, этого взора мне долго, вовек
не забыть! . . .

Елизавета КУЛЬМАН
(1808–25)

КОРИННА

(Пиитические опыты Елизаветы Кульман: в трех частях. Второе издание.
Санкт-Петербург: В типографии Императорской Российской Академии,
1839, 66–70).

Уже два раза в Дельфы
Все племена Эллады
На игры собирались;
Два раза рук плесканья
Увенчанным атлетам:
Но дивный песнью Пиндар
На игры не являлся
Хвалить борцов отважных,
Или рождать отважность,
Пленяя сердце пеньем.
Легла седая старость
На темя песнопевца.
Как из главы Зевеса
Премудрая Афина
Изшла во всем сияньи;
Так из главы Пиндара
Рождалися доселе
Творения восторга,
Очарованья полны;
Но днесь певец, незнавший
Соперника в Элладе,
Подобится горевшей
Полвека непрестанно
И вдруг погасшей сопке.
    Когда в стенах Дельфийских
В последний раз дивились
Его чудесным песням
Сыны Эллады славной;
Почтенные игр судьи
Венец ему победный
Согласно присудили
За то, что из присущих

Никто не смел с ним спорить.
С тех пор златой треножник,
На коем он так часто
Пел славу Аполлона,
В святилище остался
Насупротив престола
Для всех веков грядущих
О нем в воспоминанье.

  Когда умолк певец сей
Единственный и дивный;
Молчавшие доселе
К нему из уваженья
Певцы, не столь счастливо
Природой наделенны,
Являть собранью Греков
И с робостью и скромно,
Свои творенья стали;
Довольны, если сонмы,
Пленявшися не вдавне
Пиндоровым манером,
Их удостоят громких
Иль кликов, или плесков;
Но ждать венцов лавровых
Они не дерзали.

  Тогда младая дева,
Такими одаренна
Красой, приятным гласом
И духом стихотворства,
Приходит робким шагом,
С двумя в руках венками,
Блестящими росою,
В храм бога песнопенья
И истукан Омира
И Пиндаров треножник
Венчая, между ими
Колена преклоняет,
И в умиленьи сердца
К божественным вещает :

  О ты, при чьих я песнях
В младенчестве игривом,
Почасту забывая
Моих голубок милых,
На легких, быстрых крыльях
Фантазии младыя
Вслед за тобой стремилась
В мир созданный тобою,
Мир чудный и прекрасный;

Отважно зацеплялась
Я с вечными богами
И морем, и землею
За цепь златую, мощной
Держимою десницей
Блистательного Зевса,
Сидящего средь облак
На темени Олимпа;
Иль по волнам туманным
Седого океана,
В безмолвьи освященным
Ужасною зарею,
Плыла к вратам суровым
Безжалостного Ада!..
И ты, превосходящий
Пиитов современных
Подобно как вершина
Священного Парнасса
Собою превосходит
Соседственные горы!
Скажите вы по правде,
Осуждена ли небом
Нежнейшая из рода
Людского половина
На вечное младенство?
Не жены ли издревле
Над гордыми мужьями
Победу одержали
Торжественную,—в знаньи
Одним мужьям приличном?
Зачем же удалять их
От тех искусств, которы
Из сердца истекают?
Вы, зависти не зная,
Внушите робкой деве
Потребную отважность,
Чтобы великодушной
Своей достигнуть цели!
Не о победе дело,
Лишь—о защите права
Обиженного пола.
        В волнах Патрасских солнце
Вечернее садилось,
И луч, во храм проникший
Через врата просторны,
Случайно озаряет
Грудное изваянье

Хиосского пиита,
В его чертах степенных
Произведя на время
Умильную улыбку.
        "Счастливым предвещаньем
Желаемого мною
Успеха, принимаю,
Омир, сию улыбку!" —
В восторге восклицает
Довольная Коринна.

        Ночь в смутных сновиденьях
Проходит для певицы.
Восточные вершины
От медленныя рдеют
Зари; вдруг раздается
Трубы далеко-звучной
Глас, страшный и приятный,
Начала игр вестник.

        Боязнь и нетерпенье
Волнуют сердце девы;
Она стопою робкой
Приближилася к месту
Честолюбивых прений.

        Уже искусной песнью
Афинянин восхитил
Взыскательных Гелленов...
За ним единоземец
Бессверстного Омира
Победу Аполлона
Над дерзостным Пифоном
С восторгом прославляет.
В словах картинных, смелых,
В чудесном пеньи слышно
Чудовища паденье,
Пронзенного стрелами
Карающего Феба;
И в память сей победы,
При звуках лирных стены
Дельфийски возрастают.

        Певцу внимали сонмы
Ахеян с восхищеньем.

        Но вот, младая дева
Со златострунной лирой
К судьям игор подходит,
И им вручает свиток
Ее родства, отчизны
Прозванья содержащий;

И судии согласно,
Не медля приглашают
На поприще певицу.
    Пленивши предыграньем
Внимавших ей безмолвно
На лире ей подвластной,
Она поет—и голос
Является достойным
Самих сестр Аполлона:
    "У шумного паденья
Кастальского потока
Феб опочил и смотрит
С весельем на Пифона,
На будущие храмы,
На сонмища народов,
На их дары богаты
И велелепны игры.
    Вдруг слышит за собою
Как бы паренье птицы.
Главу оборотивши,
Спешащего он видит
К нему Эрота с луком
Блестящим в нежной длани.
При всяком шаге бога
Звенят в колчане стрелы.
    С презрением надменным
Взирает молчаливо
Феб на дитя Венеры,
Которое то луком,
То золотым колчаном,
Прельщаяся, играет.
    "Не уж ли знаменитый
Ваш Пафос так стал беден
Игрушками другими,
Приличными ребятам,
Что ты, о жалкий малый,
Решился забавляться
Оружием—приличным
Лишь нашим мощным дланям?"
    "Поклонников усердье
Переполняет всеми
Изделиями искусства
Обширны храмы наши;
Но хочется порою
Заняться мне и важным,
Как, например, унизить
Победоносца гордость."—

Сказал и вынимает
Он две стрелы изтуда,
Одну златую острую,
Другую же свинцову:
Одна любовь рождает,
Другая—отвращенье.

Златой стрелою Феба,
Свинцовой, ранил деву
Красы неизреченной,
На берегах пушистых
Отцовского Пенея
Преследующу зверя,
Эрота тяжки стрелы
И вдалеке опасны!

В душе Аполла пламя
Любви нетерпеливой.
Безрадостно он смотрит
Теперь на храм Дельфийский,
Растущий со дня на день,
На сборище народов;
Его влечется сердце
В Темпейскую долину.

Младую зрел он Дафну,
Она ему прелестней
Харит, прелестней самой
Казалася Киприды.
Для Дафны он охотно
Олимп бы весь оставил.

Но боги, как и смертны,
Игралище Эрота.
Увидев Аполлона,
Она его не любит
И, как от зверя, с страхом
Она бежит от Феба,
Который неусыпно
Гоняется за нею

И вопит: "Разве тать я,
Или пастух, презренный
Тобою, дщерью бога?
Узнай, я сын любимый
Прелестныя Латоны
И мощного Зевеса,
И брат Дианы, коей
Ты младость посвящаешь.

Беги потише, Нимфа!
И я свой бег замедлю,
Чтоб ты не повредила

Об острие ног нежных.
Взгляни хоть раз: не нравлюсь;
Властна ты ненавидеть."
      Напрасно. Дафна шибче
Бежала, и достигши
Пенейских вод, вскричала:
"Спасай меня, родитель!
Иль ежели не можешь,
То уничтожь ты прелесть,
Которая причиной
Потери милой дщери."
      Лишь вырвалось желанье
Из уст прелестных девы;
Вдруг сделалась недвижна,
Корою покрываясь.
Проворны ноги в корни,
Прекрасны длани в ветви,
Густые кудри в листье
Мгновенно превратились.
      И Дафна лавром стала.
Аполл, скорбя, вещает:
"Ты Фебовой супругой
Быть, Дафна, не хотела:
Так будь, по крайней мере,
Его любимым древом."—
      Умолкла песнь Коринны.
Предмета оной новость,
Пленительнейший голос,
Или, быть может, смелость
И прелести певицы
Восхитили внимавших.
Едва в своем восторге
Могли они дождаться
От судей приговора;
И все единогласно
Венец победный деве
Младой приговорили.
      Два раза уж глашатай
Провозвестил, по дальним
Толпам народа шумным,
Младой Коринны имя,
Род, ею ставший славным,
И родину певицы:
Внезапно раздается
У входа на арену
Крик общий: "Пиндар! Пиндар!"
И всюду повторилось

По сонму: "Пиндар! Пиндар!"
  Как некий бог, нисшедший
С Олимпа к земнородным,
Он шествует средь шумной
Толпы народов тесной,
С почтением дающей
Путь для него просторный.
Он к судьям игр подходит.
Сии, своим восстаньем
С седалищей судебных,
Являют уваженье
Пииту венценосну;
Он кротко им вешает:
  "Не с тем я здесь, чтоб младших
Певцов лишить награды,
Заслуженной трудами.
Кумир игор недавний—
Пиндар пришел сегодня
Победой наслаждаться
Славнейшею и новой—
Без ненависти видеть
И признавать достойных
Певцов младых, подпору
Отечественной славы.
Кто в будущие годы
Украсит игры ваши
Пленительным напевом
По смерти недалекой
Породы соловьиной,
Во славе устарелой;
Коль в почестях, в наградах,
Певцам меньшим откажем?"
  Судьи венец лавровый
Вручили песнопевцу;
Он, озираясь, ищет
Прелестную Коринну,
Старавшуюся скрыться.
Но взор всех, обращенный
К певице несравненной
Явил ее к Пиндару.
Он, с нежным соучастьем,
Держа в руке подъятой
Венец, дающий славу,
К трепещущей подходит
И кротко ей вещает:
  "Прими венец победы
Из рук моих, Коринна!

И будь отчизны общей
Веселием и славой,
Как некогда был Пиндар."
     Рек—и венец лавровый
В густых кудрях Коринны
Сам дивный укрепляет.
Ланиты юной девы,
Подобные двум розам,
Родившимся под лавром,
Которых блеск природный
Авроры слезы множат,
Пылают от смущенья
Пред тронутым собраньем,
Кропясь струею слезной,
Рожденной умиленьем.

Анна МОРДОВЦЕВА
(1823–85)

СТАРАЯ СКАЗКА
("Отзвуки жизни," 1842–187-. Саратов: Тип. П.С.Феокритова, 1877, 9–13)

"Donnez moi une ame que aime,—
elle comprenda ce que je dis."
Saint Augustin

Она возрастала,
Она расцветала
 В далекой
 Щирокой
 Отчизне степной.
Она научалась,
Она развивалась
 Блестящей,
 Манящей
 Природой родной.
И птичкой порхая,
Жила, распевая
 И звонко,
 И громко,
 У птичек учась.
И будто из рая
Премудрость такая
 Простая,
 Святая
 Ребенку далась.

Благо отчизны—
От синего неба,
Радости жизни—
От светлого Феба;
Груди дыханье
От ветра степей.
Песнь упованья—
Поет соловей.

Люди-то братья,
Их надо любить.
Миру—объятья
И сердце раскрыть
Любовь—молитва,
Молитва—любовь,
Жизнь—это битва,
А смерть-то жизнь вновь.

II.

С этой мудростию малой,
С этим миросозерцаньем
Хорошо жилось на свете
Бледной девочке кудрявой.

Да! в сторонке благодатной
Любо, весело ребенку:
Божий мир весь перед нею
В мире том ей все понятно,

Все доступно, все родное
Сверху донизу: от неба
До дна тинистого пруда.
Мило все ей,—все живое.

Пчел рои и птичек стаи,
Стаи бабочек нарядных
И жуков, и коромыслов:
Все жужжит, звенит, летая!

Вот в траве густой и сочной
Где малютка приютилась,
Жизнь кишит . . . И суетится
Муравей—мужик оброчный.

Вот рогатый жук копает
Попрохладней детям норку,
А чудовище тарантул
Обогреться выползает.

Над высокою травою
Крошки—божии коровки
Чуть порхнут да и присядут
Разноцветною толпою.

Выше там—прозрачной тучкой,
Легкой, серенькой нависли,
Копошатся и кружатся,
И толпятся мошки кучкой.

Пронеслися—слава Богу . . .
Тишь то, Господи, какая!
Извысока, издалека
Коршун делает тревогу.

Вон плывет он властелином
Мощный, гордый хищник ястреб...
Раскудахталися куры
Разлетались по-над тыном!—

Проплыл мимо,—не спустился . . .
Широко раскинув крылья,—
И, облитый ярким светом,
В пустоте остановился.

А над хищником лукавым
Песня чудная звенела:
Жаворонок рвался к Богу—
"Не подаст ли силу правым? . ."

Жарко. Ясно. Зноем пышет.
Солнце стало на зените,
И, проникнутый лучами,
Воздух вод уж не колышет.

И—не всплеска... Ни журчанья . . .
Словно спят, - не дышат волны . . .
Солнце все заворожило:
Тихо . . . знойно . . . жизни полно . . .

III.

Жизнию полно и детское сердце, и так же притихла
Нина-малютка, как травка, как птичка, как волны . . .
Так же проникнута сладостным зноем полудня,
Чувствует—*что-то* в ней просится к небу и к солнцу,
Словно далекая синяя бездна манит обаянием.—
Солнце . . . оно—чародей-искуситель всевластный—
Жарким дыханьем своим разогрел ароматы—и воздух
Ими пропитанный, лился в грудь Нины отравой,
Сладкой отравою неги, любви, Наслаждения, жизни. . . .
Нитью лучи золотые свои протянул царь вселенский
К каждой былинке, цветку,—ко всему, что могло жить и жило.
Жило живее, полнее, страстнее всего—сердце малютки:
Думалось много ей дум, а в груди все какие-то звуки
Ныли, дрожали, звенели, струились,—и к этим-то звукам
Странно-неясным и смутно-понятным прислушавшись,—жадно
Нине хотелось их музыку высказать словом
Иль песнью,—только б им мир отозвался созвучно.

Мир!.. но какой же?.. Вот этот раздольный, роскошный, великий,—
Слишком великий, чтоб песни нескладные слушать,
Слишком счастливый, чтоб грустные думы принять...

———

Помнит к тому же она, что начальное слово, "бе к Богу".
Свет воссиял только словом "да будет!" Без слова
Миру не быть бы, и царствовал вечно хаос. А "да будет"
Ей не звучало и вызвать из груди божественных звуков—
Некому,—некому первого слова сказать—и кого же
Богом возможно признать?..

———

     А великое *что-то*—
В травах простых и цветах и в деревьях и в крошечных злаках—
Тянется просится к солнцуж *ему* свою дань все приносит
Дерево—листик а травка свой цвет и цветок—ароматы
Тронь лучезарного феба—лазурные выси
Воды рисуют чтоб солнце повсюду его находило;
Больше: чтоб солнце и небо у ног своих зрело.
Так-то могуча могучего сила и сила
Общей любви к нему целой природы... О солнце!
Солнце-властитель! Как ты обаятельно жгуче!..

———

Вот и по утру: восток лишь чуть-чуть позлатился—
Воздух дрогнул знобом страсти и рябью подернулись воды,
Птички ему понесли свои лучшие песни.
В выси лазурной они потонули, а звуки лилися.
Небо, и воздух и лес отдаленный, и ближняя роща,
Поле, луга, побережье и сад огласились их песней
Звонкой, звенящей, рассыпчатой, радостной, страстной.
Солнце—не бог ли?.. Ему ли петь стану?.. Ну! Пусть вызывает...
Немо!?—

                              IV.

Как была—в кудрях—дикарка,
Так и стала пред налой.
Жутко, жутко ей и жалко—
Жалко жизни молодой.

Муж нелюб и старше вдвое,
Неприветлив и угрюм.
"Что-ж то, Господи, такое?"—
Вдруг спросил, проснувшись, ум.

То—родительская воля,
Воля Божья, может быть...
А какая будет доля—
Что заранее тужить!

И задумалась . . . И слышит
Пенье птиц и ропот струй,
Ей в лицо так зноем пышет . . .
Вдруг—"Исаия, ликуй!"

Дико вздрогнула дикарка
Дико глянул глаз живой:
Ей почудилось—под аркой,
Жизни детской, ясной, жаркой
Раздалось "За упокой" . . .

А в церкви все возликовало,
Когда дикарка принимала
Публично—первый поцелуй . . .

. . . .

V.

"Душистый садик мой, который я растила.
Ты, старый дом, в котором родилась,
Родная мать, отец, которых я любила,
Ты, солнце южное, к которому рвалась,
Цветущие поля, широкие равнины,—
Прощайте!—Бог судил вдали от вас мне жить;
Вы не увидите счастливой больше Нины . . .
Несчастную—как знать?—придется, может быть",—
Прощаясь с родиной, так думала дикарка,
Полудитя, уже умевшее молчать,
Уже сознавшая свой жребий горький, жалкий,
Уже привыкшее без жалобы страдать.
Вот подали возок. Вот дверца затворилась.
Вот "трогай!" в темноте так страшно отдалось . . .
И—тронулись. Она перекрестилась,
Со всем родным теперь,—с самой собой простилась,—
И сердце пополам в груди разорвалось.
И ни слезы, ни стона . . . Только руки
Под шубой сжаты. Сжаты крепко . . . так
Что и разнять нельзя . . .
            Назад—домой бежит
За степью снежной мысль . . . А в голове звенит
И все внутри и ноет и болит.

VI.

Город большой не по ней,
Давят те груды камней.
Синее небо осталось далеко,
Светлого солнца совсем не видать...
Муж все такой же—грубый, жестокий,

Жизнь с ним—тюрьма . . . И—совсем одинокой—
Что ей осталось?—Терпеть и молчать,
Муки и мысли, и думу скрывать.
. . . .

VII.

Устроились они ни бедно, ни богато,
Их круг составился из мужниных друзей,
И чаще всех ходили к ним два брата—
Избранники небес, носители идей.
Как вечер ясный тих, с серьезными глазами,
Задумчив, добр и честен как Катон,
Душой и телом чист, и лучшими дарами
Так равномерно был брат старший одарен,
Что сразу же его дикарка полюбила
И прозвала *Гекзаметром* его;
И, робкая,—она с ним смело говорила
И, не спуская глаз, смотрела на него.
Другой . . . Тот был *другой*: она его дичилась,
Хоть он моложе был, живее, веселей,
И в уголку, в тени—при нем всегда садилась,
И, молча, слушала . . . И все казалось ей,
Что непременно он над нею насмеется,
И глупым все найдет, что вымолвит она.
Так грустно ей при нем, так сильно сердце бьется . . .
А речь волшебная все в то же сердце льется—
Нежна, блистательна, разумна и сильна.

———————

Хотелось бы все знать, всему бы научиться,
Чтобы уметь ему разумно отвечать,—
И начала она усерднее молиться,
И стала по ночам украдкою читать.—
Вдруг—с неба ль ей сошла какая благодать,—
А что-то с ней престранное творится:
Печалями вся жизнь ее полна,—
А ей все весело, и отчего—не знает,
Порабощенная, забитая,—она
Горда как царь и все чего-то ожидает,
И все ее как будто поднимает
Какая-то чудесная волна
Из звуков, света и тепла.

VIII.

Вот театр. О, как душно, как жарко
От толпы, от духов, от огней...
Оробела,—и скрылась дикарка
В красной литерной ложе своей.

Песня страстная, тихая льется
Словно светлый, кристальный ручей,—
И знакомым в душе отдается
Что поет человек-соловей.

И уносит к далекому югу,
На раздолье широких степей,
Где приветствует розу-подругу
Той же песнью певец-соловей.

. . . .

Плачет чудный смычок . . . Замирая,
Нина слушает жадно: пред ней
Словно дверь отворяется рая,
Словно что-то сбывается с ней.

. . . .

И оркестр. Шум грозы, жажда воли,
Жар молитвы, порывы страстей . . .
И восторг в ней доходит до боли,
И свершается чудное с ней.

. . . .

Диву дается дикарка: ей все незнакомо, а будто
Знает она все равно как родное, и правда:
Звуки те жили в душе, да и зной тот же самый . . .
Вот он, как прежде, до мозга костей проникает . . .
Всем существом ее чуется южное солнце:
Воздух, такой раскаленный, ее обнимает и веет
Ей ароматом далеких полей . . . И ласкает до зноба
Солнечный луч . . . Вот и дрожь по телу, и кровь в ней
Пламенем льется; и страстно, и жарко, и чудно так в сердце;
Жаждет чего-то душа молодая, жаждет и ждет-не дождется . . .

. . . .

А звуки все льются
Широкой волною,
В душе отдаются
Восторгом, тоскою.

Средь звуков тех бурных
Вдруг слово раздалось . . .
То с высей лазурных
Знать солнце сказалось? . .
Мгновенья святого
Душа не забудет
Ведь было то слово:
"Да будет! да будет!"

Под солнечным взглядом
Так сердце забилось . . .

Ведь солнце-то рядом
Тут с ней очутилось.

Молчавшие струны
В душе зазвучали,
И чувства, и думы
Цвели-расцветали;
И песни и звуки
В слова облекались,
Когда его руки
Ее рук касались.

Лазурные очи
Как звезды сияли,
Ей южные ночи
И дни рисовали,
Смотрели любовно,
Добро и коварно . . .
Вот солнце родное,
Вот Феб лучезарный!

IX.

С той поры нет тоски безысходной,
Позабыто раздолье степей:
Ее солнце при ней неотходно
И что вечер—поет соловей.

И душистою, пышною розой
Расцветает сияньем очей
Молодая душа,—и в них небо,
Небо синее видится ей.

Это небо родного милее,—
Им разумное слово далось
Смутным снам . . . и живется полнее,
Чем на родине дальней жилось.

Это солнце и чище, и ярче,
Входит глубже в мысль, душу ея
И ласкает нежнее и жарче,
И сияет средь ночи и дня.

X.

"Карета готова!"—Взор брошен украдкой
И дрогнуло сердце пугливо и сладко:—
Путь долог, дорога ужасно дурна,—
И улицы глухи, и ночь так темна . . .

Выходят. Уселись. Они-ль это, полно,
Чьи речи лилися шумливо как волны:
Чей смех неустанный весельем звучал,
Кого неразлучными свет называл;
Кто так обращался друг с другом свободно
В гостиной ли скучной, в толпе ли народной,
Где часто видали рука их с рукой,
Как брата родного с любимой сестрой?

Что ж тут друг от друга далеко расселись?
Что ж смолкнули речи? что песни не пелись?
Зачем стих веселья смех детски-живой,
И кажется светлым так мрак им ночной.
Что прячутся лица и скрыты глаза? . .
Не спят ли? Путь долог, темны небеса.
О, нет! Не спалось им . . . В груди их таились
Певучие, резвые птички.
Тоскливо дрожали, метались и бились
В безмолвной своей перекличке.

То тот, то другая откроет окно,—
В карете так жарко, хоть ночь холодна . . .
Озябший их кучер уж дремлет давно,—
Чуть движутся кони, дорога дурна.

Вдруг сел он напротив. Вздрогнула она.
Так душно, так темно, нет в небе луны . . .
Окно уж открылось с *одной* стороны.
И воздух вдыхают они из окна.

Откуда-то светом вдруг тьма озарилась . . .
То очи поднялись . . . в очах потонули . . .
На жарких устах их улыбки мелькнули . . .
Ничто не сказалось, а *все* им открылось.

Расселись еще отдаленней они,
Еще непроглядней тьма ночи;
А видят так ясно и лица, и очи,
И мысли, и чувства, и души свои.

Рванулися птички . . . вспорхнулись . . . слетелись . . .
И речь полилася, и песни запелись,
И детски-веселый вновь смех зазвучал,
Когда ряд огней на мосту заблистал.
И рядом они, как сначала, уселись,
Счастливые оба, острят над собой—
Как словно родной брат с любимой сестрой.

С тех пор нет им горя: все радость, все свет,
Живут, меры счастью не зная;

Что слово—то ласка, что взгляд—то привет . . .
Вот точно как ангелы в рае!

XI.

Счастье ненадолго, радость—гость налетный,
И промчалась жизнь та птичкой мимолетной.

Солнце ее скрылось, горе то ж осталось . . .
И никто не видит как она страдает
И что дальше—хуже . . . И Господь лишь знает,
Сколько ей день каждый муки доставалось.
. . . .

И терпела б молча, за себя страдая,
Да детей-малюток больно истязали . . .
Не стерпело сердце,—и как ей сказали,—
Так и поступила, детушек спасая.
. . . .
. . . .

Помогли ей люди вырваться на волю,
Помогли бедняжке взять иную долю.
. . . .
. . . .

XII.

Виноватых оправданье—клевета на правых,
Честный бой ведь невозможен для людей лукавых;
Ну и режут они слабых за углом кинжалом,
И марают они чистых ядовитым жалом . . .
. . . .

Пускай себе! что б кто ни говорил!
Ее жизнь кончена; остался долг суровый.
И молча, как всегда, и в этой жизни новой
Долг стала исполнять она по мере сил.
. . . .

XIII.

Странный дневник у дикарки, странная книга у ней . . .
В книге страница одна, и написано так на странице:
"*Долг* и *идея его*: вот это, и *только* лишь *это*,
Значит *любить*, как *я* понимаю любовь."
Больше ни слова, ни буквы.
                    Пожалуй и правда!
            Жизнь и мысли идут
                Вольною рекой;

Их не остановишь
Силой никакой.
Запрудить плотиной,—
Правда,—не беда . . .
Да сольется с тиной
Чистая вода!—

Так в дневниках не сыщешь правды чистой,
Все с ложью пополам . . . К чему же дневники?
Что вечно—то в душе бессмертной . . . ну, и помни
Свою задачу каждый, что сама природа
Вписала в душу. А быстробежной мысли не уловишь,
И жизни преходящей не опишешь.
Итак, осталось нам перенестись в ту пору,
Подслушать, подсмотреть, что *думала* она.

XIV.

"Вот я и дома. Те же покои,
Только не тот же покой . . .
Меня замарали уже клеветою,
И, Господи, глупой какой!
Как люди-то слепы! . . Как мелки, как жалки,
Да как же и грязны и пошлы порой! . .
Но что до людей мне, когда так же ярки
И мысли, и чувства в душе молодой.
А он не поверит, сам чистый и правый,
Ни злой клевете, ни злобе лукавой! . .
И как моя злая судьба ни горька,
Как я ни несчастна, но я не жалка!
Без счастья, без доли, без света, без злата
Я все-же сильна, и горда, и богата.
Вкруг—милые дети, в душе—долг и он;
Цель жизни ясна мне и путь озарен.

Буду трудиться,
Терпеть, не роптать,
Жарко молиться,
Безмолвно страдать.
И Бог за терпенье
За труд, за страданье,
Услышит моленье,
Пошлет упованье,
Одно упованье
За годы страданья,
За годы терпенья;
Минуту свиданья,
Привета мгновенье."
. . . .

XV.

Бодро выносила горе, труд, мученье,
За одну минуту, за одно мгновенье . . .
. . . .

Лет прошло немало. Привелось опять
Ей в сторонке дальней, хмурой побывать.
И куда девались муки и страданье:
На одну минуту дал Бог *упованье* . . .
. . . .

Только позабыла, бедная, она,
Что принявши чашу, надо пить до дна;
Что когда ей дастся по глубокой вере,
Может вдруг раздастся : Noli me tangere! . .
. . . .

Будет ли минута? . . Будет ли мгновенье? . .
Ну! Христос не принял разве поношенья?
Разве Он не пролил, неповинный, кровь
За свои страданья, слезы, труд, любовь? . .
. . . .

Горемыка жарко Господу молилась:
Видеть ей хотелось: *видеть* ей случилось . . .
. . . .

И в родные степи возвратилась вновь,
Взяв с собой крест новый, старую любовь.

XVI.

Ну! доскажем же быль. Долгих мук не снесла.
Надломились могучие силы:—
Захворала; калекой в постелю слегла—
Так и будет лежать до могилы.
За двенадцать-то лет всех любезных детей
На далеко, навек проводила.
Нет вокруг никого—ни семьи, ни друзей,
Да и *жизнь* уж *свою* схоронила.
Да!—в могиле и жизнь. Одинока, больна,
Горький век свой кончает она,
День и ночь оставаясь средь милых теней
С *вечной памятью*—песнью заветной своей.

Елизавета ШАХОВА
(1822–99)

ПРОГУЛКА У ВЗМОРЬЯ

Стихотворения Елизаветы Шаховой.
Санкт-Петербург: Р(осс.) А(кад.), 1839, 35–37.

Вчера, я в день бурный у взморья мечтала,
И долго в раздумьи глубоком внимала,
Как волны сердились на мертвый гранит,
Что он на их ропот упорно молчит.
Лазурные гневно вкруг камня клубились,
Стеною недвижной его стеснены,
Так внятно, так бурно на волю просились,
Как будто им мало речной ширины.
О волны! я думала, вы ль не свободны?
И мне ваша участь завидна была!
Ужели со мною вы жребием сходны?..
Тут быстро подруга ко мне подошла,
На шумные волны рукой показала,
И что-то над ними держа, мне сказала:

    "Смотри, как с моря глубиной
    Я совершу обряд венчальный,
    Смотри, мой перстень золотой
    Залог ей будет обручальный."
    И... в воду кануло кольцо!..
    Взглянула Нине я в лицо,—
    Но голубое покрывало
    Струясь, черты ее скрывало;
    Она склонилась над водой,
    Заговорила... не со мной:
    "Минувших дней очарованье,
    Исчезни в бурной глубине!
    Не вспоминай былого мне,
    И потопи мое страданье".
    Я поняла ее печаль,
    Ее вдвойне мне стало жаль.
    —Зачем мечтами горе множить?
    Ужели так тебя мог
    Воспоминание растревожить?

—Мой друг! что было, то прошло!
Рассейся, грустью произвольной
Не увеличивай скорбей;
И настоящих бед довольно
Для молодой души твоей!—
Она не слушала, сидела
В плаще закутана своем,
Как тень на камне гробовом;
Я долго на нее смотрела,
И замечталась, говор волн,
И шум работы корабельной,
Вдали, по влаге беспредельной,
Носимый ветром утлый челн,
Мысль о подруге, все манило—
Меня к тоске, к мечте унылой!..

Анна ТУРЧАНИНОВА
(1774–1848)

ПЕСЕНКА ОБ ЛЕОНАРДЕ И БЛОНДИНЕ
из пьесы "Ночеходец, или Лунатик"
("Ипокрена, или утехи любославия" на 1799 год, ч. 4, стр. 273–85.)

Полна луна просияла над дремлющим морем.
Нечто, как духи, шумит меж гробов!
Какой-то там призрак уныло и с горем
К спящему морю проходит меж зыбких цветов.

Блондины воздушная, тонкая тень
Саваном белым, как снег, приодета,
К спящему морю столь томно идешь . . .
О волны! Вы юношу к ней призовите.

Лес зашумел, а там гул отозвался вдали.
Голубосветла Венеры звезда потемнела;
Бледна подъемлется тень, обагренна в крови:
То Леонард появился из недра молчащей пучины.

Блондина прелестна была, Леонард был прекрасен;
Таких прелюбезных цветков никогда не увидит весна!
Сердечные, розовые узы любви
В один бесподобный пучок два цветка съединили.

Уж пролетело в приятных беседах несколько лун;
Уж ближе и ближе мерцала желанная цель;
Уж скоро был должен брачный обет
Сопречь неразрывно любезну чету,

Как вдруг на ретивом ржущем коне
По стогнам Гренады герольд разъежжает;
Зовет он к отважной битве быков
Всех грандов страны той, бояр и рабов.

"Ступай, и награду за доблесть прими!",—
Вещал Леонардов отец нежноюному сыну.
"Блондины любовь наградит лишь того,
Чья крепкая грудь только мужеством дышит".

"Люблю я героя",—Блондина рекла,—
"Но если жених мой средь битвы падет,

Что в жизни тогда мне? Ах! Щутите; нет!
Ах! Кто Леонарда возьмет у меня?"

"Так вой и рыдай ты! Ведь подлая кровь
Мне рыцаря-внука в потомство не даст.
Мне женщина с рабской душой не нужна.
Любовь уж исчезла, исчез твой жених!"

Безмолвна, смятенна, печальна, бледна,
Подобна фиалке увядшей стоит
И голову томно склоняет на грудь:
"Ступай ты на битву, иду я во гроб!"

Едва лишь в приятных и нежных красах
Заря пробудилась на тонких парах,
На быстром коне Леонард уж летит,
Вокруг его челядь теснится, кричит.

Немедля открылись перилы пред ним,
Ржет конь его бодрый, ярится, храпит.
Ристалище трижды уже проскакал;
Как с ревом стремится свирепый боец.

Приветствует рыцарь с размаху мечом,
Боец разъярился, ревет и храпит,
Рогами вдруг рыцаря поднял с коня
И к самой решетке стремит как стрелу.

Вдруг с воплем вторгается юная дева,
В отчаяньи руки простерши, бежит.
"Погиб Леонард мой!"—С ужасным свирепством
Терзает невинную лютый боец.

Кончаясь уж, руку дает жениху,
Когда он со смертью боролся в песке.
"Прости, мой любезный, прости уж навек!
Нас в гробе любовь навсегда съединит."

От страшного сна Леонард пробудился—
Но свет показался ему преужасной пустыней.
Повсюду гнала его сильная горесть,
Доколе печаль погрузилась в безмолвное море.

Коль шум лишь отдастся в молчащем сем море,
Поспешно Блондина выходит из гроба,
Сердечно объемлет тень милу пучины,
На диком брегу, что она обитает . . .

Notes

Introduction

1. For example, D. S. Mirsky argues that Russian poetry of the Golden Age was not Romantic (*History of Russian Literature*, 73). L. G. Leighton describes how Soviet scholars reduced the Russian Romantic Movement to the years 1816–25 for ideological reasons ("Romanticism," in *Handbook of Russian Literature*, ed. Victor Terras, 372). An essay by John Mersereau is assertively titled "Yes, Virginia, There Was a Russian Romantic Movement" (in *The Ardis Anthology of Russian Romanticism*, ed. Christine Rydel (Ann Arbor, Mich.: Ardis, 1984), 511–17).

2. On Russian Romanticism: L. G. Leighton, *Russian Romanticism: Two Essays* (Mouton: The Hague, 1975); Brown, *History of Russian Literature*; Rudolf Neuhauser, *The Romantic Age in Russian Literature: Poetic and Esthetic Norms: An Anthology of Original Texts (1800–1850)* (München: Otto Sagner, 1975); Sigrid McLaughlin, "Russia: Romaniceskij - Romanticeskij - Romantizm," in *'Romantic' and Its Cognates: The European History of a Word*, ed. Hans Eichner (Toronto: University of Toronto Press, 1972), 418–74; Wellek, "Concept of 'Romanticism,'" 147.

3. For example, Marlon Ross writes, "Romanticism is historically a masculine phenomenon" ("Romantic Quest and Conquest," 29).

On the problematic aspects of Romanticism for women, see Gilbert and Gubar, introduction to *Shakespeare's Sisters*, xxi; Diane Long Hoeveler, *Romantic Androgyny: The Woman Within* (University Park: Pennsylvania State University Press, 1979); Homans, *Women Writers and Poetic Identity* 41–103; Susan Levin, *Dorothy Wordsworth and Romanticism* (New Brunswick, N.J.: Rutgers University Press, 1987); Mellor, *Romanticism and Gender*; Mellor, *Romanticism and Feminism*, especially Alan Richardson's "Romanticism and the Colonization of the Feminine," 13–25; Tayler and Luria, "Gender and Genre"; Ross, *Contours of Masculine Desire*; Feldman and Kelley, *Romantic Women Writers*; Wolfson, "Romanticism and Gender," 385–96;. Harriet Kramer Linkin and Stephen C. Behrendt, eds., *Romanticism and Women Poets: Opening the Doors of Reception* (Lexington: University of Kentucky, 1999).

4. Moore, introduction to *Selected Poems*, 1. For similar reasons it would have

been difficult for women writers to evoke what Keats referred to as the "Words-worthian or egotistical sublime" (Preminger and Brogan, *New Princeton Ency-clopedia of Poetry and Poetics*, 1086).

    5. See Carroll, "Politics of 'Originality,'" 136–63.

    6. By gender I refer to the distinction between (biological) sex and (cultural) gender first drawn by anthropologists such as Margaret Mead (e.g., *Sex and Tem-perament*, 1935) and by Simone de Beauvoir (*Le deuxième sexe*, 1949), and which was elaborated by feminist scholars starting in the 1970s. But see the discussion of "sex" and "gender" as yet another binary opposition to be deconstructed in Kathryn Woodward, ed., *Identity and Difference* (London: Sage, 1997), 61.

    7. Although Shakhova's first name appears as "Elizaveta" in most reference books (e.g., N. N. Golitsyn, *Bibliograficheskii slovar' russkikh pisatel'nits* [Sankt-Peterburg: V. S. Balashev, 1889]; Ledkovsky, Rosenthal, and Zirin, *Dictionary of Russian Women Writers*) and also on the title page of her 1839 collection of po-etry (*Stikhotvoreniia Elizavety Shakhovoi*), I use "Elisaveta," as this is the form that appears on the title page of her *Opyt v stikhakh piatnadtsatiletnei devitsy* (1836), *Mirianka i otshel'nitsa* (1849), and at the end of her memoir of Turgenev pub-lished in 1913 ("V nachale zhizni i na poroge vechnosti," *Russkaia starina*, no. 1 [1913], 162–67), as well as in her grandson's edition of her work, *Sobranie sochi-nenii v stikhakh Elisavety Shakhovoi* (1911). Similarly, although Kul'man's first name appears as Elizaveta in most, but not all nineteenth- and twentieth-century biobibliographic sources, I use Elisaveta, the form in which it appears in the 1839 edition of her works and in Karl Grossheinrich's biography of her ("Elisaveta Kul'man i ee stikhotvoreniia,").

    Other poets of this generation include Vera Petrovna Golovina, Sofiia Pe-trovna Golitsyna (1804–89), Varvara Lizogub, Evgeniia Maikova (1803–80), Var-vara Maksheeva, Klavdiia Selekhova (d. 1857), Sara Tolstaia (1821–38), and Eka-terina Timasheva (1798–1881).

    8. All of these noncanonical poets appear in B. Ia. Bukhshtab's anthology, *Po-ety 1840–1850-kh godov*, except for Apollon Maikov, Aleksei Khomiakov, and Aleksei Kol'tsov, the subject of separate Biblioteka poeta collections. (See bibli-ography.) None of them except Maikov, Khomiakov, and Kol'tsov appear in Ter-ras, *Handbook of Russian Literature*. Other noncanonical men poets of this gener-ation included in Bukhshtab's anthology are Nikolai Berg, E. N. Grebenka, I. I. Kreshchev, M. A. Stakhovich, F. A. Koni, N. A. Karatygin, and I. I. Panaev. As in the case of the women poets discussed, I chose the noncanonical men poets on the basis of the quality and quantity of their work.

    9. *Otryvok* can be translated as "excerpt" or "fragment." On the *otryvok iz po-emy* as a genre, see Zhirmunskii, *Bairon i Pushkin*, 318–20; on the aesthetic sig-nificance of the fragment for Romanticism see Greenleaf, *Pushkin and Romantic Fashion*, 21–36.

    10. Unpublished work: a notebook of Bakunina's poetry (mostly unpub-lished) is located in the Bakunin Archive, f. 16, op. 10, PD (see my "Praskov'ia Bakunina and the Poetess's Dilemma," in *Russkie pisatel'nitsy i literaturnyi prot-sess*, ed. M. Sh. Fainshtein [Wilhelmshorst: F. K. Göpfert, 1995], 43–57). A note-book of Gotovtseva's poetry is in the Bartenev Archive, f. 46, op. 2, ed. kh. 426, RGALI; V. R. Zotov wrote that he had a notebook of Khvoshchinskaia's poems,

half of which he never published ("Peterburg v sorokovykh godakh," 558). Two other notebooks of Khvoshchinskaia's largely unpublished poetry are located in f. 541, op. 1, ed. kh. 3 and 5, RGALI.

In a memoir about Mordovtseva written soon after her death, her husband was quoted as saying that most of her work was never published (Gorizontov, "Fel'eton," 1).

In a letter dated October–December 1839, Teplova wrote Mikhail Maksimovich that she had written several prose tales (*povesti v proze*), which apparently have been lost. After Teplova's death, her sister, Serafima, sent a notebook of Teplova's unpublished poetry to M. P. Pogodin, editor of *Moskvitianin*, but no more was heard of it (Vatsuro, "Zhizn' i poeziia Nadezhdy Teplovoi," 33, 37–38).

On Pavlova's missing works, see Munir Sendich, "'Ot Moskvy do Drezdena': Pavlova's Unpublished Memoirs," *Russian Literature Journal* 102 (1975): 57–58.

On Kul'man's lost poetry, see Fainshtein, *Pisatel'nitsy pushkinskoi pory*, 23. Shakhovskaia only published one narrative poem, *Snovidenie* (1833), and two short poems: "K M. N. Z[agoskinu]" (To M. N. Zagoskin) (*Molva*, no. 45 [June 1832]) and "Liudmila" (*Molva*, no. 52 [Apr. 19, 1832]), the latter apparently part of a longer work, perhaps a *povest' v stikhakh*. On Shakhovskaia, who appears to have been one of the prototypes for Zinaida in Turgenev's "Pervaia liubov'" (First love), see N. Chernov, "Povest' I. S. Turgeneva 'Pervaia liubov'' i ee real'nye istochniki," *Voprosy literatury*, no. 9 (1973): 225–41.

11. On the 1863 edition of Pavlova's poetry, see N. I. Gaidenkov, "Primechaniia," in Pavlova, *Polnoe sobranie stikhotvorenii*, 547. On Khvoshchinskaia's objections to having her poetry rewritten, see Zotov "Nadezhda Dmitrievna Khvoshchinskaia," 94–95. On Teplova and Mikhail Maksimovich, see Vatsuro, "Zhizn' i poeziia Nadezhdy Teplovoi," 26. Blagovo discusses the many poems by Zhadovskaia that were omitted or published in incorrect form in the posthumous *Polnoe sobranie sochinenii* (1885–86) that Zhadovskaia's brother hastily assembled, apparently for financial reasons. Zhadovskaia's niece and long-time secretary, Nastas'ia Fedorova, complained that she was not allowed to contribute to it at all (V. A. Blagovo, *Poeziia i lichnost' Iu. V. Zhadovskoi* [Saratov: Izd. Saratovskogo universiteta, 1981], 31–36). See also N. Fedorova, "Vospominanie ob Iu. V. Zhadovskoi," *Istoricheskii vestnik*, 8 (Nov. 1887): 394–407.

12. On Pushkin, see A. S. Pushkin, *Polnoe sobranie sochinenii v desiati tomakh* (Leningrad: Nauka, 1977), 3: 473; E. M. Shneiderman, "E. I. Guber," in *Poety 1840–1850kh godov*, 131–32. On the editorial practices of *Biblioteka dlia chteniia*, see Aronson and Reiser, *Literaturnye kruzhki i salony*, 16.

13. Thick journals included poetry, serialized novels, literary critical essays, and reviews as well as sections on history, science, travel literature, and fashion. Petr Fedotov, best known as a satirical artist, also chose not to publish his poetry because he did not believe that it would pass the censorship. However, he had a successful career as a *samizdat* poet, reading his poems aloud to groups of friends and encouraging them to copy and circulate them. See *Poety 1840–1850kh godov*, 379, 520, and Fedotov's "K moim chitateliam, stikhov moikh razbirateliam" (To my readers, strict examiners of my verse, 1850).

14. But also Khomiakov, who had problems with the censorship because of his Slavophilism; Lermontov, who died at twenty-seven; Del'vig, who died at

thirty-three; Kol'tsov, who died at thirty-three; Mil'keev, who died at thirty-one; and Guber, who died at thirty-two. During their lives Iazykov and Tiutchev each published three books of poetry, Baratynskii six, Fet eight, and Pushkin twenty-six. Maikov published nine books of poetry, including six editions of his poetic works, and Miller three editions of his works.

15. While, of course, no "official" canon of Russian literature exists, one may infer which literary works are considered central from those chosen as topics of literary criticism and research, those appearing on course reading lists, mentioned in literary histories, and included in anthologies.

16. As will be discussed in chapter 3, the themes and genres men Russian Romantics preferred included lyrics about the archetype of the (male-gendered) poet, a return to a (female-gendered) nature, and relationships with submissive women or femmes fatales; *poemy* (narrative poems) about Byronic heroes; and elegies about lost love or deceased heroes with whom they identified. Women poets could not use such themes and genres without transforming them. Joe Andrew, perhaps somewhat reductively, concludes that all of Russian literature between 1820 and 1840 concerned sexual relations between men and women from the male point of view ("her defeat, his victory"), in which women were portrayed as "an impossible collage of conflicting and irreconcilable stereotypes" (*Narrative and Desire in Russian Literature*, 215, 214, 216).

17. Three women (out of a total of fourteen poets) appear in *Poety 1840–1850-kh godov,* and three (out of a total of forty-eight) appear in N. M. Gaidenkov, ed., *Russkie poety XIX veka* (Moskva: Prosveshchenie, 1964). One woman poet appears in Nikolai Bannikov, ed., *Tri veka russkoi poezii* (Moskva: Prosveshchenie, 1968), and one in the two volumes of L. Ia. Ginzberg, ed., *Poety 1820–1830 godov* (Leningrad: Sovetskii pisatel', 1972). No women poets appear at all in A. Krakovskaia and S. Chulkov, eds., *Russkaia poeziia XIX veka* (Moskva: Khudozhestvennaia literatura, 1974); S. M. Petrov, ed., *Istoriia russkoi literatury XIX veka* (Moskva: Prosveshchenie, 1970); Christine Rydel, ed., *Ardis Anthology of Russian Romanticism;* or in William Brown's four-volume *History of Russian Literature of the Romantic Period.*

Russian literary historians have tended to treat women poets separately, unequally, and often condescendingly in such collections as N. K. Bannikov, ed., *Russkie poetessy XIX veka* (Moskva: Sovetskaia Rossiia, 1979); Uchenova, *Tsaritsy muz;* and Fainshtein's study, *Pisatel'nitsy pushkinskoi pory,* works that nonetheless have been very useful in recovering these women's poetry.

18. While I do not use Pierre Bourdieu's entire paradigm, my term "literary social capital" is indebted to his discussion of the "different kinds" and "overall volume of capital understood as the set of actually usable resources and powers—economic capital, cultural capital, and also social capital" (*Distinction*, 114–15). Here I am concerned with the usable resources and powers that determine writers' positions within a hierarchy defined by reception and subsequent reputation. As we shall see, writers' economic and cultural capital plays an important role in determining their literary social capital. See also John Guillory, *Cultural Capital: The Problem of Literary Canon Formation* (Chicago: University of Chicago Press, 1993). This is not to deny that writers' literary reputations and canonical status rise and fall because of literary political factors as well.

19. The phrase "self-appointed successor" is Catriona Kelly's. My thanks to her as well for several thoughts that I used in this discussion of canonicity. Fet, whom I include among the canonical men poets, while not close to Pushkin was friends with Ivan Turgenev and Lev Tolstoy.

20. On Pushkin's low opinion of women poets and women readers, see V. Brio, "Pushkin o vozmozhnosti zhenskoi literatury," *Pushkinskii sbornik* (Ierusalim: Tsentr po izucheniiu slavianskikh iazykov i literatur pri Evreiskom universitete, 1997), 1: 1, 187–200. Brio demonstrates the persistence of such attitudes by suggesting at the end of the article that it is still an open question whether a woman's literature is possible. For Pushkin's unflattering description of the poet Aleksandra Fuks, whom he visited in Kazan', see Bobrov, "A. A. Fuks i kazanskie literatory 30–40kh godov," 495–96.

21. Katerina Clark shows that in the plots of the most prestigious Soviet literary genre, the socialist realist novel—which she compares with male initiation rites and epics—women are either absent or depicted as dangerous temptresses or witches (*The Soviet Novel: History as Ritual* [Chicago: University of Chicago Press, 1981], 182–85). In this atmosphere, not surprisingly, Soviet women writers dissociated themselves from "women's writing" (i.e., writing as women). See Helena Goscilo, "Paradigm Lost? Contemporary Women's Fiction," in *Women Writers in Russian Literature* (Westport, Conn.: Greenwood, 1994), 205–28.

22. Kiselev, "Poetessa i tsar'," 144; N. I. Iakushkin, ed., *Serdtsa chutkogo prozren'em . . . : Povesti i rasskazy russkikh pisatel'nits XIX v.* (Moskva: Sovetskaia Rossiia, 1991), 552.

23. For example, Boris Romanov refers to Rostopchina by her childhood nickname, "Dodo" (introduction to *Stikhotvoreniia, proza, pis'ma*, 13). M. Sh. Fainshtein calls Kul'man, Teplova, Rostopchina, and Pavlova by their first names (*Pisatel'nitsy pushkinskoi pory*, 11, 86, 91, 96, 106, 110, 118).

24. See the bibliography of primary sources used in this study.

25. Elaine Showalter first used the term "gynocritics" in "Towards a Feminist Poetics," 22–41. Patrocinio Schweickart cites and comments on Annette Kolodny's discussion of "interpretive strategies" in "Reading Ourselves," 29.

26. Showalter, "Feminist Criticism in the Wilderness," 15. See also Barbara Heldt: "If this study separates the two canons into male and female . . . one can also envision future criticisms written with a view to an eventual reintegration" (*Terrible Perfection*, 9), and Janel Mueller: "No less than the relational categories of femininity and masculinity, women's writing has historically been undertaken and maintained in dynamic relation to men's writing" ("Feminist Poetics," 216).

27. Throughout this study, the date following a poem's title refers to its first publication, unless an editor has provided a poem's date of composition. It should be noted that many women poets first published their works long after they were written.

28. For the dating of Zhadovskaia's poem, see E. M. Shneiderman, "Primechaniia," in *Poety 1840–1850-kh godov*, 495. All translations are mine unless otherwise noted.

29. See E. N. Kupreianova, "Primechaniia," in Baratynskii, *Polnoe sobranie stikhotvorenii*, 371.

30. In the West, the recovery of Pavlova started with Munir Sendich's dissertation "The Life and Works of Karolina Pavlova" and his subsequent series of articles about her work. Barbara Heldt first put Pavlova into a feminist critical context in the introduction to her translation—the first—of Pavlova's *Dvoinaia zhizn'* (*A Double Life*) in 1979. See also Susanne Fusso and Alexander Lehrman, eds., *Essays on Karolina Pavlova* (Evanston, Ill.: Northwestern University Press, 2001). Soviet editions of Pavlova: *Polnoe sobranie stikhotvorenii*, ed. N. Kovarskii (Leningrad: Sovetskii pisatel' 1939); *Polnoe sobranie stikhotvorenii*, ed. Pavel Gromov; and *Stikhotvoreniia*, ed. E. N. Lebedev (Moskva: Sovetskaia Rossiia, 1985). For Soviet Pavlova criticism, see chapter 6.

In the West Helena Goscilo first translated and introduced Rostopchina's "Chin i den'gi" ("Rank and Money," in *Russian and Polish Women's Fiction*, ed. Helena Goscilo [Knoxville, Tenn.: University of Tennessee Press, 1985], 50–84). Soviet editions of Rostopchina: *E. P. Rostopchina: Stikhotvoreniia, proza, pis'ma* (1986); *Talisman* (1987); and *Schastlivaia zhenshchina*, ed. A. M. Ranchin (Moskva: Izd.-vo Pravda, 1991).

Soviet editions of Zhadovskaia are *Izbrannye stikhotvoreniia* and V. A. Blagovo, *Poeziia i lichnost' Iu. V. Zhadovskoi.*

For Teplova, V. E. Vatsuro, "Zhizn' i poeziia Nadezhdy Teplovoi," 16–43.

More generally, many long-forgotten Russian women writers appear in Nikolaev's multivolume *Russkie pisateli 1800–1917: biograficheskii slovar'.*

In the West, some of the earliest works of recovery were *Russian Literature Triquarterly* 9 (1974); Goscilo, *Russian and Polish Women's Fiction;* Heldt, *Terrible Perfection;* Andrew, *Women in Russian Literature;* Ledkovsky, Rosenthal, and Zirin, *Dictionary of Russian Women Writers;* Kelly, *History of Russian Women's Writing;* Catriona Kelly, ed., *An Anthology of Russian Women's Writing, 1777–1992* (Oxford: Oxford University Press, 1994).

31. Peter Berger and Thomas Luckmann, *The Social Construction of Reality* (New York: Doubleday, 1967). On the sexual, racial, and class politics of canons, see Dale Spender, *Women of Ideas and What Men Have Done to Them* (Boston: Routledge & Kegan Paul, 1982), and her *Mothers of the Novel: One Hundred Good Women Novelists before Jane Austen* (New York: Pandora, 1986); Alice Walker, *In Search of Our Mother's Gardens* (San Diego: Harcourt Brace Jovanovich, 1983); Robert von Hallberg, ed., *Canons* (Chicago: University of Chicago Press, 1983); Jane Tompkins, *Sensational Designs: The Cultural Work of American Fiction 1790–1860* (New York: Oxford University Press, 1991); Catherine Belsey and Jane Moore, eds., *The Feminist Reader: Essays in Gender and the Politics of Literary Criticism* (Houndsmills, Basingstoke, Hampshire: Macmillan Education, 1989); and Berenice Caroll, "The Politics of 'Originality': Women and the Class System of the Intellect," *Journal of Women's History* 2, no. 2 (fall 1990): 136–63.

32. On the definition of the Pushkin pleiad, see Leighton, *Russian Romanticism*, 16, and John Mersereau, "The Nineteenth Century," in *The Cambridge History of Russian Literature*, ed. Charles Moser (New York: Cambridge University Press, 1992), 143. For Lermontov's encyclopedia, see *Lermontovskaia entsiklopediia*, ed. V. A. Manuilov.

Although Soviet scholars generally ignored Fet's unprogressive views on politics, they deplored Pavlova's much less conservative views as a sign of her irrelevance to the history of literature. (See the introductions to the two pre-1980 editions of her works.) No other Soviet scholarship about Pavlova appeared before the 1980s, with the exception of a few mentions of her as a translator (*Russkie pisateli o perevode* [Leningrad: Sovetskii pisatel', 1960], 321, 422; I. S. Alekseeva, "Perevodcheskii stil' Karoliny Pavlovoi," *Vestnik Leningradskogo universiteta,* no. 8 (1981), *Istoriia literaturnogo iazyka,* no. 2, 55–59); and one reference to her as the author of a lyric for Liszt (B. Smirenskii, "Zabytyi romans Lista," *Smena* no. 13 [1957]: 24).

33. For example, John Guillory writes, "Aesthetics and political economy . . . between them divide the world of cultural products into works of art and commodities" (*Cultural Capital,* 337). "When aesthetic artifacts are certified as 'works of art' they become bearers of cultural capital and as such are unequally distributed" (281). "Aesthetic judgement is the recognition of cultural capital" (336).

34. In the field of American literature, where feminist scholars started working earlier than in Russian, the recovery of many nineteenth-century women writers generally has not led to their reevaluation, as Judith Fetterley shows. "Commentary: Nineteenth-Century American Women Writers and the Politics of Recovery," *American Literary History* 6: 3 (fall 1994): 600–611. Fetterley discusses the factors that have prevented the development of the interpretive strategies necessary for such a reevaluation.

35. The following is based on Donovan, "Toward a Women's Poetics," 98–109; and Modleski, *Loving with a Vengeance.* See also Elaine Showalter, "Piecing and Writing," in *The Poetics of Gender,* ed. Nancy Miller (New York: Columbia University Press, 1986), 222–47.

36. Interestingly, Aleksandra Fuks, who lost three daughters and a son, never alludes to their deaths in her poetry, except perhaps obliquely in "Poslanie Dmitriiu Petrovichu Oznobishinu" (Epistle to Dmitrii Petrovich Oznobishin, 1834), which begins "Sredi semeinykh ogorchenii" (Amidst family grief). On the death of Fuks's children, see K.V. Larskii and P. A. Ponomarev, "Karl Fedorovich Fuks i ego vremia," in *Kazanskii literaturnyi sbornik* (Kazan: Tip. M. A. Gladyshevoi, 1878), 499.

37. One also thinks of Poe's theory that the best writing can be read at one sitting and produces one single effect ("unity of effect or impression") ("Twice-Told Tales" [1842], in *Essays and Reviews,* by Edgar Allan Poe [New York: Literary Classics of the United States, 1984], 571).

38. Shari Benstock quoted by Sonia Hofkosh, in "Sexual Politics and Literary History," 136.

39. While during this period both men and women in society were very self-aware, I would distinguish women's self-consciousness under the perpetually sexualizing male gaze—even the self-consciousness of the coquette who exploited that gaze—from the performative self-consciousness of the dandy who freely chose his role (see chapter 4, note 20). On the portrayal of women in Western art as the sexualized object of the male gaze, see Berger et al., *Ways of Seeing,* 45–64. On women and the male gaze in film, see Laura Mulvey, "Visual Pleasure and Narrative Cinema," in *Feminist Film Theory: A Reader,* ed. Sue Thornham (New York: New York University Press, 1999), 58–69. On Teplova, see Rosneck, "Nadezhda Teplova," 1: 121–32.

40. Mellor points out that British women often dismissed their men contemporaries: "Although they read the canonical men Romantic poets with interest and some approval, they often dismissed them as amoral, self-indulgent, or incomprehensible" ("Criticism of Their Own," 31). One thinks of Khvoshchinskaia's judgment of Pushkin: "For me it was always offensive when our criticism began by comparing Pushkin with Byron and then put them on the same level. Here's someone to whom can be attributed all which was attributed to the latter, only still more cheaply, and basely: deliberate atheism (and cowardly sanctimoniousness at the same time), filthy sensuality, etc. You know, after all, how I love him, our master. Please, for a minute, don't argue (I, after all, swear that I recognize him as an 'artist'), not forgetting that they are contemporaries—that Byron could be one of his teachers, compare them now and tell me whether I am not right, if harsh? Here's an exemplar of vanity, vainglory, of a worshiper of success and of a passion for his own success" (Quoted in Semevskii, "N. D. Khvoshchinskaia-Zaionchkovskaia," 11: 100). Khvoshchinskaia's Russian is even more obscure than this translation suggests. I suspect that she had difficulty clearly expressing such heretical views about Pushkin, knowing that they would evoke negative reactions.

41. Belinskii, "Zhertva: Literaturnyi eskiz. Sochinenie g-zhi Monborn [Montborne]," in *Polnoe sobranie sochinenii*, 1: 225. First published in *Molva* 10, nos. 27–30 (1835): 9–20.

42. On the German-based "Romantic irony," see Anne Mellor's *English Romantic Irony* (Cambridge, Mass.: Harvard University Press, 1980), and Maxim D. Shrayer, "Rethinking Romantic Irony: Puškin, Byron, Schlegel and *The Queen of Spades*," *SEEJ* 36, no. 4 (1992): 397–414.

43. Unfortunately, Kulka himself creates, in Hélène Cixous's terms, a "binary hierarchical opposition" (see chapter 2) between male art and female kitsch. Kulka defines kitsch as "anti-art" and genders it as female, with references to "soap operas" (16), "emotionally charged subject matter," "mothers with babies, children in tears, sentimental leanings" (26), "romanticized melodramatic tales written for young Victorian ladies," "supermarket novels," and "cheap romance" (97). All his references to art and artists, however, are male.

Chapter 1. Social Conditions

1. In general the position of women in Russia during the mid-nineteenth century closely resembled that of women in the rest of Europe and the United States, judging by laws and prescriptions, which may not, however, entirely reflect social reality. For a five-country comparison, see my "Mid-nineteenth-century Domestic Ideology in Russia," in *Women in Russian Culture*, ed. Rosalind Marsh (Oxford: Berghahn, 1998), 78–97. Barbara Clements notes that throughout the period "the injunction that women subordinate themselves to men . . . was applied to all women regardless of social rank" ("Introduction: Accommodation, Resistance, Transformation," 3). This is not, however, to ignore the privileges upper-class Russian women enjoyed in relation to women and men of other classes. For a discussion of the similarities and differences between Russian class and gender hierarchies, see my "Karolina Pavlova's 'At the Tea

Table' and the Politics of Class and Gender," *Russian Review* 53 (April 1994): 2, 271–84.

2. Women born serfs never had access to higher education. On the lives of women serfs, see Mary Matossian, "The Peasant Way of Life," in *Russian Peasant Women*, ed. Beatrice Farnsworth and Lynne Viola (New York: Oxford University Press, 1992), 27. However, a few men born serfs—or to landowners and serf women—through upper-class sponsorship obtained the university or institute educations that enabled them to take a place in educated society (e.g., Vasilii Zhukovskii, Nikolai Pavlov, Aleksandr Nikitenko, Aleksei Kol'tsov, Mikhail Pogodin). On the upward mobility possible to men through salons, see William Todd, *Fiction and Society in the Age of Pushkin: Ideology, Institutions and Narrative* (Cambridge, Mass.: Harvard University Press, 1986), 61–63.

3. During the nineteenth century only the well-to-do could enter a Russian monastery or nunnery, since applicants had to supply both an entrance donation and lifetime support for themselves (Brenda Meehan-Waters, "To Save Oneself: Russian Peasant Women and the Development of Women's Religious Communities in Prerevolutionary Russia," in *Russian Peasant Women*, ed. B. Farnsworth and L. Viola, 121–22).

4. Under the 1835 *Svod zakonov*, a sister inherited one-fourteenth of her brother's share of immovable (real) property and one-eighth of her brother's share of movable property (Aleksei Vasil'evich Kunitsyn, *O pravakh nasledovaniia lits zhenskogo pola* [Khar'kov, 1844], 9). See also *Zhenskoe pravo: Svod uzakonenii i postanovlenii otnosiashchikhsia do zhenskogo pola* (Sankt-Peterburg: K. N. Plotnikov, 1873), 180–81. Michelle Marrese, however, writes that in some cases parents (especially mothers) gave daughters a larger share of immovable and movable property than was prescribed by law (*A Woman's Kingdom: Noblewomen and the Control of Property in Russia, 1700–1861* [Ithaca: Cornell University Press, 2002], 148, 153, 155).

5. *Zhenskoe pravo*, 108. The commentary states, "It is the unconditional duty of spouses to live together" (108).

See also Engelstein, *Keys to Happiness*, 32; Wagner, *Marriage, Property and Law*, 65. On marriage law for those of other religions living in Russia, see Engelstein, 28.

On the Church's regulation of marriage, see Freeze, "Bringing Order to the Russian Family," 744. Freeze writes that in the nineteenth century the Russian Orthodox Church "virtually eliminated the legal possibility of terminating a marriage" (711), granting between 1836 and 1860 a yearly average of thirty-three annulments (724) and fifty-eight divorces for the entire Russian empire (733).

On married women's property rights, see also, Stites, *The Women's Liberation Movement in Russia* (Princeton: Princeton University Press, 1978), 7. Michelle Marrese in *A Woman's Kingdom* documents several cases of Russian noblewomen actively managing their own and their husbands' estates. She notes, however, that many noblewomen gave over the management of their estates to a husband or male relative and that an increasingly critical attitude toward women in authority developed from the end of the eighteenth century.

6. On Pavlova, see Pavel Gromov, "Karolina Pavlova," in Pavlova, *Polnoe sobranie stikhotvorenii*, 42–43, and Sendich, "Life and Works of Karolina Pavlova,"

61. On Mordovtseva, see G. P. Murenina, "Vy zhili nedarom," in *Saratovskie druz'ia Chernyshevskogo*, ed. I. V. Porokh (Saratov: Privolzhskoe knizhnoe iz-datel'stvo, 1985), 59; Mordovtseva's autobiographical poema, *Staraia skazka*, in *Otzvuki zhizni*, 17–19, 27; and P. Iudin's less than sympathetic "Mordovtsevy v Saratove," *Istoricheskii vestnik* (March 1907): 931–32. On Khvoshchinskaia, see Polovtsov et al., *Russkii biograficheskii slovar'*, 21: 302.

7. On Rostopchina's poetry, see "Evdokiia Rostopchina," in *Russian and Polish Women's Fiction*, ed. H. Goscilo, 45. As will be discussed in chapter 4, however, Rostopchina could only begin to publish after her marriage.

On Pavlova, see Barbara Heldt, "Karolina Pavlova: The Woman Poet and the Double Life," in *A Double Life*, by Karolina Pavlova, trans. Barbara Heldt (Oakland: Barbary Coast Books, 1986), xi. Also see Pavlova's poem "Pishu ne smelo ia, ne chasto," printed in V. K. Zontikov, "'Pishu ne smelo ia, ne chasto . . .' (Stikhotvorenie Karoliny Pavlovoi)," in *Vstrechi s proshlym*, ed. N. B. Bolkova, no. 4 (Moskva: Sovetskaia Rossiia, 1982), 35–39. Pavlova's seemingly self-deprecating letter of 1854 to I. I. Panaev, which Heldt discusses ("Karolina Pavlova," x), on close reading reveals considerable irony. See Pavlova's gleeful description of it in her letter (Oct. 13, 1854) to Boris Utin. Munir Sendich, "Boris Utin in Pavlova's Poems and Correspondence: Pavlova's Unpublished Letters (17) to Utin," *Russian Language Journal* 28, no. 100 (spring 1974), 80.

For Teplova, see Vatsuro, "Zhizn' i poeziia Nadezhdy Teplovoi," 30, 31, 33.

On Zhadovskaia, see Fedorova, "Vospominaniia ob Iu. V. Zhadovskoi," 402, and Blagovo, *Poeziia i lichnost' Iu. V. Zhadovskoi*, 27, 31, 72. For possible reasons that Zhadovskaia stopped writing, see Blagovo, 62, 63, 64, 70, 73.

For a discussion of Bakunina, the third unmarried poet, who fell silent in the late 1850s, see my "Praskov'ia Bakunina and the Poetess's Dilemma," 43–57.

8. Additional examples of such advantageous marriages are those of N. M. Karamzin (1766–1826), whose first wife, E. I. Protasova (1767–1802), was the sister-in-law of the Freemason A. A. Pleshcheev and sister of the salon hostess A. I. Pleshcheeva (Terras, *Handbook of Russian Literature*, 215). Karamzin's second wife, Ekaterina Andreevna Viazemskaia, A. F. Tiutcheva writes, was the half sister of the prominent poet and critic Petr Viazemskii (*Pri dvore dvukh imperatoro*, 69–70). ["On [Karamzin] byl sviazan tesnoi druzhboi s Zhukovskim, kotoromu vposledstvii bylo porucheno vospitanie naslednika, i s Viazemskim, na vnebrachnoi sestre kotorogo on byl zhenat" (He was connected in close friendship with Zhukovskii, who subsequently was entrusted with the education of the heir to the throne, and with Viazemskii, to whose out-of-wedlock sister he was married)] (quoted in Aronson and Reiser, *Literaturnye kruzhki i salony*, 162). See also I. B. Chizhova, *Khoziaiki literaturnykh salonov Peterburga pervoi poloviny XIX v.* (Sankt-Peterburg: Izd. Serdtse, 1993), 79.

On Tiutchev, see Valerii Briusov, "F. I. Tiutchev: Kritiko-biograficheskii ocherk," in *Polnoe sobranie sochinenii F. I. Tiutcheva* (Sankt-Peterburg: A. F. Marks, 1913), 10–11, 14.

On Fet, see Harry Weber, ed., *Modern Encyclopedia of Russian and Soviet Literature* (Gulf Breeze, Fla: Academic International Press, 1977–89), 7: 195, and P. V. Bykov, "Predislovie," in Tiutchev, *Polnoe sobranie sochinenii*, 3.

On Baratynskii, see M. L. Gofman, "E. A. Boratynskii (Biograficheskii ocherk)," in Baratynskii, *Polnoe sobranie sochinenii*, 1: lxiv. Gofman makes a point of telling us that Engel'gardt was not beautiful, although we never hear about the physical attractiveness of the husbands of women poets.

Pushkin, of course, could make the socially sanctioned decision to turn over the physical responsibility of his children to others. While he helped care for them by writing poetry for which he got paid, this was not an option open to women poets.

9. While the roots of domestic ideology may be traced as far back as the Greeks and the Bible, the Industrial Revolution—which allowed working-class women to gain economic self-sufficiency—inspired an outpouring of the ideology in Europe. For the origins of Russian domestic ideology, its promulgation in the periodic press, and Belinskii's reactions to it (all discussed later), see my "Mid-nineteenth-century Domestic Ideology in Russia." For a recent reconsideration of the ideology of separate spheres see Cathy N. Davidson and Jessamyn Hatcher, eds., *No More Separate Spheres!* (Durham: Duke University Press, 2002).

10. Ross, *Contours of Masculine Desire*, 188–90, 192; Myers, "Learning, Virtue, and the Term 'Bluestocking,'" 285.

11. Ross, *Contours of Masculine Desire*, 188. For George Sand's reception in Russia, see Lesley Herrmann, "George Sand and the Nineteenth-Century Russian Novel: The Quest for a Heroine," (Ph.D. diss., Columbia University, 1979), and V. I. Kondorskaia, "V. G. Belinskii o Zhorzh Sand," in *Uchenye zapiski*, no. 28 (38), ed. G. G. Mel'nichenko (Iaroslavl': Russkii iazyk i literatura, 1958), 141–65. In Russia during the 1830s and early 1840s, a woman who wrote or who showed too much independence was called a *zhorzhsandistka*.

12. "Sovet," quoted in Bannikov, *Russkie poetessy XIX veka*, 9. The poem appears as "Epigramma" in *Polnoe sobranie sochinenii E. A. Boratynskogo*, ed. M. L. Gofman (Sankt-Peterburg: Izd. Razriada iziashchnoi slovesnosti Imperatorskoi Akademii nauk, 1914), 1: 88. For a discussion of the hostility against Russian women writers at this time, see Kelly, *History of Russian Women's Writing*, 34–56.

13. The following discussion is based on Rakhmannyi [N. N. Verevkin], "Zhenshchina pisatel'nitsa," *Biblioteka dlia chteniia* 23, no. 281 (1837); Mar'ia Korsini, "Zhenshchina-pisatel'nitsa," in *Ocherki sovremennoi zhizni* (Sankt-Peterburg, 1848); Peterburgskii turist [Aleksandr Druzhinin], "Zhenshchina-pisatel'nitsa," *Syn otechestva*, no. 1 (April 8, 1856): 7–11.

14. On Druzhinin as "liberator" of women, see B. P. Gorodetskii, ed., *Istoriia russkoi literatury* (Moskva: Akademiia nauk, 1955), 564.

15. "Perepiska sestry s bratom" appeared in *Zvezdochka* 4 (Oct. 1845), 27–48, a children's magazine published by Aleksandra Ishimova. The italics in the citations are the author's.

16. On women's writing as sexual display or prostitution, see Kelly, *History of Russian Women's Writing*, 75, and Catherine Gallagher, "George Eliot and Daniel Deronda: The Prostitute and the Jewish Question," in *Sex, Politics, and Science in the Nineteenth Century Novel*, ed. Ruth Yeazell (Baltimore: Johns Hopkins University Press, 1986), 39–62. I have found only two mid-nineteenth-century Russian stories that concern women writers who are depicted as serious artists;

both are by Aleksandra Zrazhevskaia: "Zhenshchina—poet i avtor (Otryvok iz romana)," *Moskvitianin*, no. 9 (1842): 42–80, and "Devushka-Poet: Otryvok iz romana," *Moskvitianin*, no. 2 (1844): 368–403. In both cases the heroine is doomed.

17. In a short review of Teplova's work the reviewer referred to it seven times as *milyi* (sweet) ("Stikhotvoreniia Nadezhdy Teplovoi," *Severnaia pchela* 175 [1834]: 697–98). In our day, too, prominent U.S. reviewers have praised as "modest" Marianne Moore, Elizabeth Bishop, Louise Bogan, and even Adrienne Rich and Sylvia Plath (Ostriker, *Stealing the Language*, 3–4).

The 1851 journal article is Emil' Montegiu's "O zhenshchinakh poetakh v severnoi Amerike," *Biblioteka dlia chteniia* 108 (1851): 124–33. This article appears to be a translation from the French, an additional example of the importation into Russia of Western attitudes toward women.

18. See Belinskii, "No, never can a woman author either love or be a wife and mother" ("*Zhertva*," in *Polnoe sobranie sochinenii*, 1: 226. Originally published in *Molva* 10 (1835): 27–30).

19. But see Osip Mandelshtam's statement that Mayakovskii is in danger of becoming a poetess (Boym, *Death in Quotation Marks*, 196) and Byron's attacks on Thomas Moore as feminized (Ross, *Contours of Masculine Desire* 28–30).

20. See Clements, "Introduction: Accommodation, Resistance, Transformation," 1–13.

21. For ultrafeminine depictions of women by Rostopchina, see "Sovet zhenshchinam" (Advice to women, 1838), "Kak dolzhny pisat' zhenshchiny" (How women should write, 1840), "Kak liubiat zhenshchiny" (How women love, 1841), and "Russkim zhenshchinam" (To Russian women, 1856). Rostopchina's poetic stance, however, is more complex and interesting than these poems would suggest at first glance, as is discussed in chapter 4.

22. Chernyshevskii, "Stikhotvoreniia grafini Rostopchinoi," 1: 249. I use here and in chapter 4 Louis Pedrotti's ingenious translation of "Ia bal liubliu! Otdaite baly mne!" (I love a party! Give me parties!) See his "Scandal of Countess Rostopčina's Polish-Russian Allegory," 212 n. 1.

23. Bakunina, "Rozhdenie nezabudki," *Maiak* 15 (1841): 29–30; "Groza," *Maiak* 4 (1840): 33.

See also Praskov'ia Bakunina, "Otvet A.V. Zrazhevskoi na pis'mo (Sokrashchenyi kurs knizhnoi zoologii) napechatannoe v pervom nomere Maiaka 1842 g.," *Maiak* 2, no. 3 (1842): 14–17. On Zrazhevskaia, see Polovtsov et al., *Russkii biograficheskii slovar'*, 7: 494–97, and Ledkovsky, Rosenthal, and Zirin, *Dictionary of Russian Women Writers*, 757–58.

24. For attacks on Pavlova and Kul'man, see my "Nineteenth-Century Women Poets: Critical Reception vs. Self-Definition," in *Women Writers in Russian Literature*, ed. Toby Clyman and Diana Greene (Westport, Conn.: Greenwood, 1994), 104–6, 97–99. For a survey of Kul'man's classics-inspired work, see Judith Vowles, "The Inexperienced Muse: Russian Women and Poetry in the First Half of the Nineteenth Century," in *A History of Women's Writing in Russia*, ed. Adele Marie Barker and Jehanne M. Gheith (New York: Cambridge University Press, 2002), 69–71. On Gotovtseva's epistle to Pushkin (which appeared in *Severnye tsvety* [1829] with poems to her by Viazemskii and Pushkin), see "Primechaniia" in *Pushkin*, ed. S. A. Vengerov (Sankt-Peterburg: Brokgauz-

Efron, 1911), 5: ix–x. Viazemskii's letter to Pushkin about Gotovtseva sexualized and trivialized her—perhaps to spare Pushkin's feelings but also, it would appear, as an expression of male bonding against women writers. "Do me the kindness, friend Aleksandr Sergeevich, to put together a little madrigal in response [to Gotovtseva's epistle to Pushkin]. Don't disgrace your pimp. . . . [I]t is fun to indulge a young girl. [Gotovtseva at the time was twenty-nine.] Here are my verses to her, so we can print this Susannah between two old adulterers." On Shakhovskaia, see my "Praskov'ia Bakunina and the Poetess's Dilemma," 50. The complaint about Khvoshchinskaia, probably written by Vladimir Zotov, appears in "Peterburgskii vestnik," *Panteon,* no. 8 (Aug. 1852): 17.

25. Critics imposed the role of poetess on Zhadovskaia; they emphasized her "songs of feminine bondage," ignored her other themes, and treated her experiments with prosody as evidence of her inability to write verses that scanned. See my "Nineteenth-Century Women Poets," 99–101, and Mary Zirin, "Iuliia Zhadovskaia," in Tomei, *Russian Women Writers,* 1: 374. On the contrast between Bakunina's published and unpublished works, see my "Praskov'ia Bakunina and the Poetess's Dilemma."

Rusalki, which I've translated as "water spirits" or "mermaids," in Russian folklore function as fertility spirits. They also were said to be the spirits of seduced and abandoned young women who had drowned themselves. Appearing near bodies of water, they might revenge themselves by drowning or destroying men. On *rusalki* see Linda Ivanits, *Russian Folk Belief* (Armonk, N.Y.: M.E. Sharpe, 1989), 75–81, and Natalie Moyle [Kononenko], "Mermaids (Rusalki) and Russian Beliefs about Women," *New Studies in Russian Language and Literature,* ed. Anna Crone and Catherine Chvany (Columbus: Slavica, 1986), 221–38.

26. For an analysis of this poem and the relationship between Pavlova and Rostopchina, see Taylor, "Autobiographical Poetry or Poetic Autobiography," 33–48.

27. On Shakhovskaia's epic, see my "Praskov'ia Bakunina and the Poetess's Dilemma," 49–50.

28. On the movement of Russian literature from the "gentlemen's" party to the "plebeians" in the 1830s, see Mirsky, *History of Russian Literature,* 96–97. In the following discussion of male Romantic institutions, I am indebted to Todd, *Fiction and Society in the Age of Pushkin,* and Theodore Ziolkowski, *German Romanticism and Its Institutions* (Princeton, N.J.: Princeton University Press, 1990).

29. Walter Ong, quoted in Tayler and Luria, "Gender and Genre," 100. See also David F. Noble, *A World without Women: The Christian Clerical Culture of Western Science* (New York: A. A. Knopf, 1992).

30. Pushkin, for example, who was an indifferent student at Tsarskoe Selo, alluded several times to Ovid and Sappho and wrote elegies, epigrams, an anacreontic ode, and a *vakkhicheskaia pesn'* (Bacchic song). While these women poets did not need knowledge of classical languages to use classical genres, they used them far less frequently and comfortably than did their classically educated contemporaries, as shall be discussed in chapter 3. See also Tayler and Luria, "Gender and Genre," 101–3; Wellek, "Concept of Romanticism in Literary History," 149–50.

31. Mirsky, *History of Russian Literature,* 74. On anacreontic poetry, see J. M.

Ritchie, "The Anacreontic Poets: Gleim, Uz, and Gotz," in *German Men of Letters,* ed. Alex Natan and Brian Keith-Smith (London: Oswald Wolff, 1972), 6: 123–45, and Patricia A. Rosenmeyer, *The Poetics of Imitation: Anacreon and the Anacreontic Tradition* (Cambridge: Cambridge University Press, 1992).

On the importance of the cult of male friendship, Bacchic, and anacreontic poetry for the poets of Pushkin's generation, see Verkhovskii, *Poety pushkinskoi pory,* 32, 56. Pushkin wrote a tribute to Anacreon, "Kobylitsa molodaia" (1828), originally titled "Podrazhanie Anakreonu" (A. S. Pushkin, *Sobranie sochinenii* [Moskva: Khudozhestvennaia literatura, 1974], 2: 571), which will be discussed in chapter 2.

See also K. V. Grossgeinrik [Grossheinrich], "Elisaveta Kul'man i ee stikhotvoreniia," trans. from the German by M. and E. Burnashevy in *Biblioteka dlia chteniia,* 5 (May 1849): 5; Elisaveta Kul'man, "K Anakreonu," in *Piiticheskie opyty: v trekh chastiakh,* 6–8.

. 32. On Kul'man's challenge to classical androcentric traditions, see my "Nineteenth-Century Russian Women Writers," 98–99. Frank Göpfert argues for Kul'man's place in German literary history in "Zwei russische Dichterinnen und ihre Beziehungen zum deutschen Kulturkreis: Elisaveta Kul'man und Sarra Tolstaja," *Die Welt der Slaven* 38, no. 2 (n.s. 17, no. 2) (1993): 227–34.

33. On male literary circles and *al'manahki* (annual literary collections), see Todd, *Fiction and Society in the Age of Pushkin,* 64–65, and Vatsuro, "Zhizn' i poeziia Nadezhdy Teplovoi," 19–21. The impossibility of a woman publishing an annual literary collection at this time is reflected in Vatsuro's bemused description of Teplova's desire to do so: "[A]nd with winning simplemindedness [*s podkupaiushchim prostodushiem*] [Teplova] requested from Maksimovich the addresses of her suggested contributors: Pushkin, Somov, Baratynskii, Khomiakov, Pogodin" (30).

Of the canonical men poets, Pushkin edited *Sovremennik,* Del'vig edited *Severnye tsvety,* Baratynskii was connected with both *Moskovskii vestnik* and the short-lived *Evropeets* (The European). Of the noncanonical men poets, Miller founded his own journal, *Razvlechenie* (Amusement), Guber served as literary critic for *Biblioteka dlia chteniia,* and Maikov was on the editorial board of *Moskvitianin.*

34. On Zhukovskii and Karamzin, see Semenko, *Vasily Zhukovsky,* 17–20. See also A. S. Pushkin, *Polnoe sobranie sochinenii v desiati tomakh* (Leningrad: Nauka, 1977), 3: 473.

Tiutchev: Valerii Briusov, "F. I. Tiutchev: Kritiko-biogaricheskii ocherk," in *Polnoe sobranie sochinenii F. I. Tiutcheva,* ed. P. B. Bykova (Sankt-Peterburg: A. F. Marks, 1913), 13.

Lermontov: Tukalevskii, Introduction to *Polnoe sobranie sochinenii,* xx; Garrard, *Mikhail Lermontov,* 23.

Baratynskii: M. L. Gofman, "E. A. Boratynskii (Biograficheskii ocherk)," in *Polnoe sobranie sochinenii E. A. Boratynskogo* (Sankt-Peterburg: Izd. Razriada iziashchnoi slovesnosti Imp. Akademii nauk: 1914), xlv.

Khomiakov: Khomiakov, *Stikhotvoreniia i dramy,* 563–64.

Del'vig: B.V. Tomashevskii, "A. A. Del'vig," in Del'vig, *Polnoe sobranie stikhotvorenii,* 5; Gofman, "E. A. Boratynskii (Biograficheskii ocherk)," xlviii.

Iazykov: K. K. Bakhmeier, introduction to *Polnoe sobranie stikhotvorenii*, by N. M. Iazykov, 28, 42.

Fet: Tatyana Whittaker, "Fet [Shenshin], Afanasii Afanas'evich," in Weber, *Modern Encyclopedia of Russia and Soviet Literature*, 7: 194, 196; Valerii Briusov, "Predislovie," in *Polnoe sobranie sochinenii F. I. Tiutcheva*, 18.

Kol'tsov: L. Plotkin, "A. V. Kol'tsov," in Kol'tsov, *Stikhotvoreniia*, 13, 17.

Maikov: "Apollon Nikolaevich Maikov," in Nikolaev, *Russkie pisateli 1800–1917*, 3: 454. B. F. Egorov, introduction to *Stikhotvoreniia i dramy*, by A. S. Khomiakov, 10.

35. Viazemskii: "Rostopchina," in Ledkovsky, Rosenthal, and Zirin, *Dictionary of Russian Women Writers*, 540–41; "Gotovtseva," in Nikolaev, *Russkie pisateli 1800–1917*, 1: 659.

On Zhukovskii and Mil'keev, see chapter 7. Zhukovskii, who first met Kol'tsov in Saint Petersburg in 1836, visited Voronezh in 1837. At that time he met twice with Kol'tsov and also urged the local *gimnaziia* teachers to help Kol'tsov to improve his education. See L. Plotkin, "A. V. Kol'tsov," in Kol'tsov, *Stikhotvoreniia*, 12; A. I. Liashchenko, "A.V. Kol'tsov (biograficheskii ocherk)," in Kol'sov, *Polnoe sobranie sochinenii A. V. Kol'tsova*, xxvii–xxviii.

For Belinskii's attitudes toward women, see V. I. Kondorskaia, "V. G. Belinskii o Zhorzh Sand," in *Uchenye zapiski, Russkii iazyk i literatura*, ed. G. G. Mel'nichenko (Iaroslavl', 1958), no. 28 (38), 137–66, and Vishnevskaia, "Tema sotsial'nogo bespraviia zhenshchiny v literaturnom nasledii Belinskogo," 116: 5, 292–96; Belinskii, "Sochineniia Zeneidy R-voi," in *Polnoe sobranie sochinenii*, 7: 654 (first published in *Otechestvennye zapiski* 31, no. 11 (1843): 1–24). Belinskii on Zhadovskaia: "Vzgliad na russkuiu literaturu 1846 goda," *Polnoe sobranie sochinenii*, 10: 35 (first published in *Sovremennik* 1, no. 1, section 3 (1847): 1–56.

36. Teplova, for example, was forced to work through M. A. Maksimovich in order to get a book of poetry published; her frustration and impatience may be seen her in her letters to him (Vatsuro, "Zhizn' i poeziia Nadezhdy Teplovoi"). Similarly, Vladimir Zotov "placed" Khvoshchinskaia's poetry in *Literaturnaia gazeta*, without paying her for it (Semevskii, "N. D. Khvoshchinskaia Zaionchkovskaia," 10: 54).

37. For examples of the kind of laudatory poems written to women at this time, see Gitta Hammarberg, "Flirting with Words: Domestic Albums, 1770–1840," in *Russia, Women, Culture*, ed. Helena Goscilo and Beth Holmgren (Bloomington: Indiana University Press, 1996).

38. Khodasevich writes that Count Vladimir Sollogub allowed no women at his literary evenings but that an exception was made for Rostopchina ("Grafinia E. P. Rostopchina," 43). Compare men's opportunities for professional advancement in salons (note 2) with K. D. Kavelin's memoir of A. P. Elagina's salon, in which he stresses approvingly that the hostesses did not write (in *Literaturnye salony i kruzhki: Pervaia polovina XIX v.*, ed. N. L. Brodskii [Moskva: Akademiia, 1930], 329).

39. The six salon hostesses mentioned (in Brodskii, *Literarynye salony i kruzhki*) are Volkonskaia, Karamzina, Elagina, Pavlova, Rostopchina, and Fuks. Pavlova was able to read her work at salons hosted by Elagina and Volkonskaia.

Chapter 2. Literary Conventions

1. On the friendly epistle, see Taylor, "Friendly Epistle in Russian Poetry." Taylor notes that while they could serve as addressee, "women rarely wrote friendly epistles" (118). She characterizes the genre as "a celebration of poets' symposia, fueled by alcoholic drink" (322), its core consisting of "affirmations of friendship and that 'You are a poet'" (325). As in the case of anacreontic poetry, such male bonding experiences rarely included women. In addition to Batiushkov's "Vakkhanka" (1814–15), already cited in chapter 1, see A. N. Maikov's "Vakkhanka" (1841), Fet's "Vakkhanka" ("Zachem, kak gazel'," 1840) and "Vakkhanka" ("Pod ten'iu sladostnoi poludennogo sada," 1843), and Del'vig's "Videnie" (1819–20), a Bacchic poem with metaphysical overtones.

2. On men Romantic poets as priests, see Gilbert and Gubar, introduction to *Shakespeare's Sisters*, xxi. On the tradition of the poet-prophet in nineteenth-century Russian literature, see Pamela Davidson, "The Moral Dimension of the Prophetic Ideal: Pushkin and His Readers," *Slavic Review* 61, no. 3 (fall 2002): 490–518. Shelley's conclusion to *Defence of Poetry* (1821): "Poets are the unacknowledged legislators of the world."

3. Examples of Russian poets' self-representation as bards include Zhukovskii's famous "Pevets vo stane russkikh voinov" (The singer in the camp of Russian warriors, 1812), Iazykov's "Pesn' barda vo vremia vladychestva tatar v Rossii" (Song of the bard during the time of the Tatar's dominion of Russia, 1823), "Baian k russkomu voinu" (Baian to a Russian warrior, 1824), "Pesn' Baiana" (Baian's song, 1824), Del'vig's "Romans" (Romance, 1824), Davydov's Hussar poems, and Lermontov's "Pesn' barda" (Song of the bard, 1830).

4. On the ballad revival, see A. B. Friedman, *Ballad Revival*, and Katz, *Literary Ballad*.
On the influence of Ossian in Russia, see Iu. D. Levin, *Ossian v russkoi literature konets XVIII-pervaia tret' XIX veka*. (Leningrad: Nauka, 1980), 154, 157, 164, 172, 180, 191. Among the Russian writers who cited Macpherson, Levin lists Karamzin (whose translation of Ossian appeared in 1798), Batiushkov, Kiukhel'beker, Pushkin, and Lermontov.

5. For example, in Tiutchev's "Ne ver', ne ver' poètu, deva!" (Don't trust, don't trust the poet, maiden! 1839) the speaker portrays poets as so sexually powerful ("all-powerful, like the elements") that they suck dry maidens' hearts as a bee does a flower. A similar sexual power disparity can be found in Iazykov's "Poèt" (1831), in which a young woman, hopelessly in love with a poet, cannot sleep at night. He, however, sleeps peacefully. Other examples of the poet's sexual prowess with his muse and others can be found in Pushkin's "Muza" (The muse, 1821), "Vot Muza rezvaia boltun'ia" (Here is the playful, chatterbox muse, 1821), "Solovei i roza," (The nightingale and the rose, 1827), and *Evgenii Onegin* 8, I–VI (1829); Lermontov's "Poèt" (1828), Fet's "Muza" (1854) and "Muze" (1857), Guber's "Krasavitsa" (The beauty, 1838), Maikov's "Svirel'" (The reed-pipe, 1840), and Kol'tsov's "Solovei" (The nightingale, 1841).

6. Most of these women poets must have known Mme. de Staël's novel *Corinne* (1807), which concerns a nineteenth-century namesake of the Greek

poet, also a woman poet of genius, but one for whom there is no place in society. I found only one allusion to the Greek Corinna among these poets, however: Kul'man's depiction of Corinna's victory over Pindar in the poetry contest at Delphi ("Korinna," 1839; see Appendix). Kul'man's knowledge of Greek would have made Corinna's work accessible to her.

7. Evgenii Sviiasov, "Safo i 'zhenskaia poeziia' kontsa XVIII-nachala XX vekov," in *Russkie pisatel'nitsy i literaturnyi protsess v kontse XVIII-pervoi treti XX vv.*, ed. M. Sh. Fainshtein (Wilhelmshorst: Göpfert, 1995), 15–18. Albin Lesky dismisses as myth the story of Sappho's suicide over Phaon (*History of Greek Literature* [London: Methuen, 1966], 140). Only two woman poets in this group refer to Sappho. Kul'man wrote a dramatic monologue depicting Sappho's suicide ("Safo," 1839). Gotovtseva, who did not know Greek but who studied with Iurii Bartenev, the classically educated director of the Kostroma *gimnaziia* (Nikolaev, *Russkie pisateli, 1800–1917*, 1: 166, 659), wrote an imitation of one of Sappho's lyrics that was never published, "Ozhidanie (podrazhanie Safo)," Bartenev Archive, f. 46, op. 2, d. 426, poem no. 28, RGALI.

8. Mikhailov, "Istoriia drevnei slovesnosti," 612. Presumably, this author is Mikhail Larionovich Mikhailov (1829–65), later known as a publicist for women's emancipation (see Stites, *Women's Liberation Movement in Russia*, 38, 41). Although Mikhailov would only have been eighteen at this time, V. A. Viktorovich writes that he was a contributor to *Literaturnaia gazeta* ("Zotov, Vadimir Rafailovich," in *Russkie pisateli*, ed. P. A. Nikolaev, 3: 355).

Although Pushkin in "Safo" (1825) has her declare her love for a young man who, in his first youth, resembles a woman, Sappho was not generally identified as a lesbian until the beginning of the twentieth century. See Taubman, "Women Poets of the Silver Age," 173.

9. Rostopchina's "Ot poeta k tsariam" (From the poet to the tsars, 1856), in which she addresses all tsars in the name of poets.

10. In the Bible God only speaks directly to prophets, never to any woman. While he does communicate through angels with two women—Hagar and Mary—in both cases the messages they receive are not religious truths or commands, but rather the news that they are pregnant (Genesis 21: 17, Luke 1: 26–38). On the significance of God's not talking to women in the Bible, see Homans, *Women Writers and Poetic Identity*, 30.

11. On cross-gendered poems, see Parker and Willhardt, "The Cross-Gendered Poem," 193–210. In Russian literature, see Sarah Pratt, "The Obverse of Self: Gender Shifts in Poems by Tjutcev and Axmatova," in *Russian Literature and Psychoanalysis*, ed. Daniel Rancour-Laferriere (Amsterdam: John Benjamin's Publishing, 1989), 225–44; Anna Gotovtseva, "Videnie," in *Literaturnyi Muzeum na 1827 g.* (Moskva: Tip. S. Selivanovskogo, 1827), 162. Gotovtseva also wrote a much more powerful (but unpublished) religious vision poem, "Probuzhde-nie," reminiscent of Pushkin's "Prorok" (1826) (Bartenev Archive, f.46, op.2, n. 426, poem no. 34, RGALI); Teplova, "Videnie," 1838.

See also Bakunina's poem titled "Videnie" (A vision) in an archival copy (Oleninykh Archive, f. 542, n. 124, RNB) but which is called "Siialo utro ob-novleniem" (The morning shone with a renewal) in the published version, *al'-*

manakh, Utreniaia zaria (S. Pb.: Tip A. Pliushara, 1840), 436. In the poem the spirit
of a dead baby chastises the speaker for her grief. The visionary poetry of
Elisaveta Shakhova, who became a nun, must be considered separately.

Men poets wrote poems titled "Videnie" as well: Del'vig (1814–20); Tiutchev
(1829); Fet (1843); Iazykov (1825); Lermontov (1831); Khomiakov (1840); and Guber (1859).

12. Feldman and Kelley, introduction to *Romantic Women Writers*, 9. Other
poems in which women poets adapt the role of bard or poet-patriot include
Pavlova's "Razgovor v Kremle" (Conversation in the Kremlin, 1854), in which a
Russian explains to an Englishman and a Frenchman Russia's spiritual mission
in the world, and Shakhova's prayer for the health of Nicholas I, "Chuvstvo rossi-
ianki k otsu naroda" (A woman of the Russian Empire's feeling for the father of
the people, 1839). See also Zhadovskaia, "Polnochnaia molitva" (Midnight
prayer, 1858), Kul'man, "Voin i pevets" (The warrior and the singer, 1833), and
Lisitsyna, "K rodine" (For the motherland, 1829).

13. For a discussion of Southey's *Joan of Arc,* see Curran, *Poetic Form and
British Romanticism,* 167–68, and chapter 6 of this volume. On Durova, see Mary
Zirin, translator's introduction, in Nadezhda Durova, *The Cavalry Maiden: Journals of a Russian Officer in the Napoleonic Wars,* trans. Mary Zirin (Bloomington:
Indiana University Press, 1989), ix–xxvii. See also "La Vision" (1825) by the
French poet Delphine Gay (Mme. de Giradin), in which Joan of Arc appears to
the poet and encourages her to proclaim herself "Muse de la patrie." Discussed
in Jean Balde, *Mme de Giradin: Textes choisis et commentes* (Paris: Plon, 1913), 25–
27. See also Anna Mordovtseva, "Slava vam na boi vozstavshim," in *Otzvuki
zhizni 1842–187-,* 3.

14. Bakunina, "Moi chertenok" (1834? see appendix) and "Epilog" (Bakunin
Archive, f. 16, op. 10, n. 5, p. 10 verso, and p. 39 verso, PD); Khvoshchinskaia,
"Uzh vecher; na dvore stuchit moroz ugriumyi," *Literaturnaia gazeta,* no. 49 (Dec.
9, 1848), 778; Teplova, "Videnie" (A vision, 1860), "K geniiu" (To my genius,
1860); Zhadovskaia, "Vozrozhdenie" (Rebirth, 1858); Bakunina, "Poslanie k
drugu E[katerina] L. Sh[akhovskaia]" (1832) (Bakunin Archive, f.15, op. 10, n. 5,
p. 15 verso to 16 verso, PD). In this poem Bakunina contrasts her shy *genii* (who
in other poems is described as a *chertenok* [imp]) with Shakovskaia's more fiery
one.

15. Male muses, *geniia,* also occur occasionally in men's poetry. The speaker
in Del'vig's "Razgovor s geniem" (Conversation with my genius, 1814–17) con-
verses with his genius, who has been sent from heaven to teach him to sing his
dreams. In Khomiakov's "Videnie" (1840) an angel, "a heavenly brother," visits
the speaker-poet in a vision that gives him the ability to write poetry. Other
examples of male muses can be found in Lermontov, "K geniiu" (1829), Mil'-
keev, "Artist-muzykant" (The artist-musician, 1843), and Guber, "Pechal'
vdokhnoveniia" (The sadness of inspiration, 1837).

16. Noncanonical men poets also wrote poems to traditional muses: Guber
("Sud'ba poeta" [The fate of the poet, 1833] and "Krasavitsa" [The beauty, 1845])
and Maikov ("Sny" [Dreams, 1835]).

17. Judith Pascoe, "Mary Robinson and the Literary Marketplace," in *Romantic Women Writers,* ed. Paula Feldman and Theresa Kelley, 260, 262. See Carla

Hesse, "Reading Signatures: Female Authorship and Revolutionary Law in France, 1750–1850," *Eighteenth-Century Studies* 22, no. 3 (spring 1989): 469–87, for a discussion of French women writers' signatures in relation to their legal status and right to the proceeds of their published works. Nancy K. Miller and Joan DeJean discuss women writers' signatures in relation to their anxiety about being reduced to a sexualized body ("The Text's Heroine: A Feminist Critic and Her Fictions," *Diacritics* 12 [summer 1982]: 48–53; Joan DeJean, "Lafayette's Ellipses: The Privileges of Anonymity," *PMLA* 99, no. 5 [1984]: 884–902).

18. On marked and unmarked endings, see Jane Taubman, "Women Poets of the Silver Age," 172–73.

19. Pavlova signed two poems "Novootkrytyi poèt" (A newly discovered poet) (*Polnoe sobranie stikhotvorenii*, 563). Rostopchina used G. E. R. and A.; Mordovtseva variously signed herself B-z, A. B-i, and A. B-ts, and Bakunina signed one poem ("Dva dnia") P. B. (Masanov, *Slovar' psevdonimov;* Smirnov-Sokol'skii, *Russkie literaturnye al'manakhi i sborniki XVIII–XIX vv.*). On Bakunina's use of marked and unmarked signatures, see my "Praskov'ia Bakunina and the Poetess's Dilemma," 48.

20. On Khvoshchinskaia as a prose writer, see chapter 5, note 1.

21. Parker and Willhardt, "The Cross-Gendered Poem," 198. Wayne Booth's discussion of "implied authors" in fiction can be extended to the speakers of poems (*Rhetoric of Fiction*, 151–53).

22. See V. A. Blagovo's extended comparison of the *liricheskie geroini* of Shakhova, Pavlova, Rostopchina, and Zhadovskaia. While he implies that each poem by a man poet can have its own *liricheskii geroi*, when he turns to the women poets his focus shifts to defining the one *liricheskaia geroinia* he attributes to each (*Poeziia i lichnost' Iu. V. Zhadovskoi*, 73–115). Homans discusses the personae, masks, and fictiveness that have been imposed on women but also argues their importance for twentieth-century women poets (*Women Writers and Poetic Identity*, 38–39, 216–17).

23. V. G. Belinskii, "Stikhotvoreniia grafini E. Rostopchinoi," in *Polnoe sobranie sochinenii*, 5: 457–58. First appeared in *Otechestvennye zapiski* 18, no. 9 (1841): 5–8.

24. Kn. Viazemskii, "Otryvok iz pis'ma A. I. G-oi," *Dennitsa* (1830): 122–23 (also in S. D. Sheremetev, ed., *Polnoe sobranie sochinenii Kniazia P. A. Viazemskogo,* [Sankt-Peterburg: M. M. Staiulevich, 1978], 2: 139–40).

25. On Khvoshchinskaia and Pavlova, see chapters 5 and 6. See also Faddei Bulgarin's sarcastic, unsigned review of Aleksandra Fuks's *Stikhotvoreniia* (1834), which appeared in *Severnaia pchela*, no. 194 (Aug. 29, 1834): 773–74: "Don't think, however, that Mrs. Fuks's *Poems* are philosophical; they also are not anthological, nor anacreonic, by no means ideological, nor psychological, and certainly not political" (775) (review is attributed to Bulgarin in Bobrov, "A. A. Fuks i kazanskie literatory 30–40-kh godov," 27).

26. Cross-gendered poems by women include Bakunina's "Dva dnia" (Two days, 1841). Here a male-voiced speaker describes two days—one of "amorous dreams fulfilled," the other of disappointment and despair—that showed him life's inconstancy and the need to rely on God. Gotovtseva's "Odinochestvo" (a translation of Lamartine's "L'Isolement" [1820], [Bartenev Archive, f. 46, op. 2,

n. 426, poem no. 1, RGALI]) is a similar male-voiced meditation on the importance of the eternal. Pavlova wrote three cross-gendered poems: "Strannik" (The
wanderer, 1843), "Vezde i vsegda" (Everywhere and always, 1846), and "Sputnitsa feia" (The fairy traveling companion, 1858). See chapter 6 for discussion of
her use of gender marking in her poetry. Other cross-gendered poems include
Lisitsyna's "Pesn' syna nad mogiloi materi" (A son's song at his mother's grave,
1829), "K nevernoi" (To an unfaithful woman, 1829), "Kozak k tovarishcham"
(A Cossack to his comrades, 1829), and "Byl'" (A true story, 1829); and Fuks's
"Pavel i Virginiia" (Paul et Virginie, 1834) and "Schastlivye druz'ia! primite moi
sovet" (Lucky friends! Take my advice, 1834). Kul'man in *Pamiatnik Berenike*
(Monument to Berenike, 1839) wrote poems in the personae of ten classical men
poets, but with no attempt to hide her gender.

Regarding cross-gendered poems by men poets, see, for example, Pushkin,
an early draft of "Dioneia," in *Polnoe sobranie sochinenii*, 1: 200; 2: 684. It has been
suggested that Tatiana's letter to Onegin could be considered a cross-gendered
poem. However, it is presented through the additional persona of a narrator—
albeit one whom Vladimir Nabokov has described as "a stylized Pushkin"
(translator's introduction to *Eugene Onegin*, 1: 6). On Pushkin's cross-gendered
experiments in prose, "Roslavlev" (the beginning of a novel) and "Otryvok iz
neizdannykh zapisok damy (1811 god)" (Excerpt from unpublished memoirs of
a lady, 1811), which appeared in his *Sovremennik* in 1836, see V. Brio, "Pushkin o
vozmozhnosti zhenskoi literatury," 187–200.

Cross-gendered poems by other men poets include Del'vig's "Russkaia pesnia (I ia vyidu l' na krylechko)" (Russian song [And I will go out on the porch],
1828) and "Russkaia pesnia (Kak za rechen'koi slobodushka stoit)" (Russian
song [As the suburb stands beyond the rivulet], 1828); Fet's "Zerkalo v zerkalo,
s trepetnym lepetom" (Mirror into the mirror with trembling babble, 1842), "Ia
liubliu ego zharko: On tigrom v boiu" (I love him passionately: He is like a tiger
in battle, 1847), "Ne divis', chto ia cherna" (Don't be surprised that I am black,
1847), "Sestra" (Sister, 1857), and "Vsiu noch' gremel ovrag sosednii" (All night
the neighboring ravine roared, 1872); Tiutchev's "Ne govori menia on, kak i
prezhde, liubit" (Don't tell me that he loves me as he formerly did, 1851–52);
Kol'tsov's "Pesn' rusalki" (Song of the rusalka, 1829), "Kol'tso" (The ring, 1830),
"Russkaia pesnia (Ia liubila ego . . .)" (Russian song [I loved him], 1841), and
"Pesnia (Chto on khodit za mnoi . . .)" (Song [Why does he follow me], 1842);
Miller's "Russkaia pesn'" (Russian song, 1872) and "Ionna d'Ark Shilleru" (Joan
of Arc to Schiller, 1849); and Maikov's "Ia b tebia potselovala" (I would kiss you,
1860). On Tiutchev's poem, see Sarah Pratt, "Obverse of Self," 228–234. In contrast to women's cross-gendered poems, in which the speaker is generally the
author's social equal, in men's cross-gendered poems the speaker is generally a
peasant or an "Eastern" woman. On Russian Orientalism, see Greenleaf, *Pushkin
and Romantic Fashion*, especially chapter 3, "The Foreign Fountain: Self as Other
in the Oriental Poem."

Men's translations of female-voiced poems may also be considered a kind
of cross-gendered poem. For example, in Miller's "Plach Iaroslavnyi (iz Slovo
o polku Igoreve)" (Iaroslavna's lament [from *The Lay of Igor's Host*], 1848)
Iaroslavna, Prince Igor's wife, laments on the city walls that her husband has been

wounded in battle. Maikov translated three poems by Sappho ("Zachem venkom iz list'ev lavra" [Why like a wreath from laurel leaves, 1841], "Zvezda bozhestvennoi Kipridy" [Star of divine Venus, 1841], "On iunyi polubog i on— u nog tvoikh!" [He is a young demigod and he is at your feet, 1875]).

27. Bartenev Archive, f. 46, op. 2, n. 426, poems nos.1 and 2, RGALI. "K N. N." appeared in *Moskovskii telegraf*, no. 11 (1826): 115. For "L'Isolement" and Lamartine's commentary on it, see A. de Lamartine *Premieres et nouvelles meditations poétiques*, vol. 1 of *Oeuvres de Lamartine* (Paris: Hachette, 1886), 19–21.

28. Khvoshchinskaia, "Solntse segodnia za tucheiu chernoi takoi zakatilosia," *Otechestvennye zapiski* 83, no. 8 (1852): 317.

29. On implied readers, see W. Daniel Wilson, "Readers in Texts," *PMLA* 96, no. 5 (1981): 848–63.

For a short time at the beginning of the nineteenth century, Nikolai Karamzin led a group of writers who considered upper-class women their ideal readers. See Gitta Hammarberg, "Reading à la Mode: The First Russian Women's Journals," in *Reflections on Russia in the Eighteenth Century*, ed. Joachim Klein, Simon Dixon, and Maarten Fraanje (Köln: Böhlau Verlag, 2001), 218–32, and Judith Vowles, "The 'Feminization' of Russian Literature: Women, Language, and Literature in Eighteenth-Century Russia," in *Women Writers in Russian Literature*, ed. Toby W. Clyman and Diana Greene (Westport: Greenwood Press, 1994), 35–40. By the late 1820s, however, it had become fashionable to denigrate women's minds (see chapter 1) and aesthetic capabilities. See V. Brio for Pushkin's low opinion of women readers ("Pushkin o vozmozhnosti zhenskoi literatury," 187–200). The status of Russian women readers suffered additionally at this time because Russia imported from Europe eighteenth-century "male hostility to the acts of imagination and identification involved in women reading." Women's novel-reading was construed as a sexual act of "adulterous imagination," an idea reflected in Pushkin's comments in *Evgenii Onegin* on the reading habits of Tatiana and her mother. See Andrew Ashfield, introduction to *Romantic Women Poets, 1770–1838*, 1: xii–xiv.

30. On nineteenth-century male and female literatures, see Gilbert and Gubar, *Madwoman in the Attic*; Elaine Showalter, *A Literature of Their Own: British Women Novelists from Brontë to Lessing* (Princeton: Princeton University Press, 1977); Baym, *Women's Fiction*.

On U.S. women's magazines, see Caroline Garnsey, "Ladies' Magazines to 1850: The Beginnings of an Industry," *New York Public Library Bulletin* 58 (1954): 74–88. On editors' expectations, see Isobel Armstrong, "The Gush of the Feminine: How Can We Read Women's Poetry of the Romantic Period?" in *Romantic Women Writers*, ed. Paula Feldman and Theresa Kelley, 15.

Cheryl Walker argues that Emily Dickinson, who rejected the marketplace, was able to transform many of the poetess conventions into great poetry (*Nightingale's Burden*).

31. Pavlova addressed several poems to women. "Da, mnogo bylo nas, mladencheskikh podrug" (Yes, we were many, friends from early childhood, 1839) describes a group of friends whose happiness and freedom as girls contrasts with the burdens they have come to know as adults. Similarly, in "Byla ty s nami nerazluchna" (We were inseparable, 1843) the speaker describes a once

unworldly, inspired woman, who has experienced great suffering in the world. See also "Prochtia stikhotvoreniia molodoi zhenshchiny" (On reading the poetry of a young woman, 1863), about Zhadovskaia's poetry. Other poems addressed to women include Teplova's "K sestre (Kogda nastupit chas zhelannyi)" (To my sister [When the wished for hour arrives], 1860), "K sestre (Mila mne predannost' tvoia)" (To my sister [Your devotion it sweet to me], 1860), and "V pamiat' M. A. L[isitsyn]-oi" (In memory of M. A. Lisitsyna, 1860); Garelina's "Druz'ia moi! ne smeites' nado mnoi" (My friends! Do not laugh at me, 1870), "Ne govorite mne druz'ia" (Do not tell me, friends, 1870), and "I ia, druz'ia moi, ne znala" (And I didn't know, my friends, 1870); Gotovtseva's "K druz'iam" (To my friends, Bartenev Archive, f. 46, n. 426, poem no. 27, RGALI); Lisitsyna's "Golubok: K S. S. T-oi" (The little dove: To S. S. T., 1829), "K nezabvennoi" (To an unforgettable woman, 1829), and "K S. S. T-oi" (To S. S. T, 1829); and Shakhova's "Progulka u vzmor'ia" (A walk by the seashore, 1839).

    32. Khvoshchinskaia's "'Vy ulybaetes'? . . . Razdum'e ne meshaet'" (You are smiling? . . . My pensiveness doesn't prevent) (*Otechestvennye zapiski* 83, no. 8 [1852]: 315–16 [discussed in chapter 5]) similarly closes with a man complacently dismissing a woman's suffering. Other examples include Lisitsyna, "Zavetnaia gora" (The secret mountain, 1829); Zhadovskaia, "Poseshchenie" (The visit, 1858); and Rostopchina, "Nasil'nyi brak" (The forced marriage, 1856).

    Other examples of the silenced male Other include Zhadovskaia, "Ty vsiudu predo mnoi: poveet li vesna" (You are everywhere before me: Whether spring begins to be felt, 1858), and Lisitsyna, "Romans (Vse proshlo, chto serdtsu l'stilo)" (Romance [Everything has passed away that deluded the heart], 1829).

    33. The tradition of gendering nature as female is apparently cross-cultural. See Sherry Ortner's classic essay, "Is Female to Male as Nature Is to Culture?" in *Women, Culture and Society,* ed. Michelle Zimbalist Rosaldo and Louise Lamphere (Stanford, Calif.: Stanford University Press, 1974), 43–66. Also see Maureen Devine, *Woman and Nature: Literary Reconceptualizations* (Metuchen, N.J.: Scarecrow Press, 1972).

    34. See Alan Richardson, "Romanticism and the Colonization of the Feminine," 13–25. Anne Mellor describes attempts by British romantic poets "to reassign the all-creating powers of a nature gendered as feminine to a masculine poetic imagination" in *Romanticism and Gender,* 20. Margaret Homans writes, "The masculine self dominates and internalizes otherness . . . frequently identified as feminine, whether she is nature, the representation of a human woman or some phantom of desire" (*Women Writers and Poetic Identity,* 12). See also Feldman and Kelley, eds., *Romantic Women Writers,* and Susan M. Levin, *Dorothy Wordsworth and Romanticism,* 34, 36.

    35. On *rusalki,* see chapter 1, note 25.

    36. Aleksandr Pushkin, "Tsygany," *Sobranie sochinenii v desiati tomakh* (Moskva: Khudozhestvennaia literatura, 1975), 3: 152. This is not to ignore the questions Pushkin raises about the benefits of freedom versus society but rather to emphasize Pushkin's use of traditionally gendered categories of culture and nature. He did not, after all, write the *poema* about an alienated and possibly criminal Saint Petersburg woman who runs away to the gypsies and murders her fickle lover because she wants freedom only for herself.

37. Michael Wachtel argues that this poem should be understood as a "rejoinder to Pushkin's [ballad] 'Black Shawl'" ("Chernaia shal'," 1820) (*Development of Russian Verse*, 33, 31–34).

38. Other such examples of sexualized nature appear in "Noch' svetla, moroz siiaet" (The night is bright, the frost is radiant, 1847); "V lunnom siianii" (In the lunar radiance, 1885); "Shepot, robkoe dykhan'e" (A whisper, timid breathing, 1850); and "Kakoe schastie: i noch' i my odni!" (What happiness: It's night and we're alone! 1854).

As for nature as female Other in Tiutchev's work, see also Pratt, *Russian Metaphysical Romanticism*. Although Pratt does not discuss gender as a category, she does mention Tiutchev's gendering of nature as female (48), the Romantic paradigm of "metaphysical 'marriage' of man and nature" (41–42), and the image of nature as mother (48). Pratt also cites Tiutchev's "Ot zhizni toi, chto bushevala zdes'" (1871), a poem that ends with the lines, "She [Nature] greets all her children . . . equally, each in turn, with her omnivorous and pacifying abyss" (43, translation Pratt's). One need not be a Freudian or a Jungian to see here the image of the devouring mother.

Noncanonical men poets also gendered nature as female or as a backdrop for sexual encounters. For example, in Maikov's "Vesna" (1880) winter, portrayed as an old, ugly hag, must make way for spring, characterized as a young and attractive woman. In "Pod dozhdem" (1886), the speaker celebrates the storm that created the mood and the occasion for intimacy that resulted in a love affair.

39. For the nightingale as poet, see Pushkin "Solovei i roza" (The nightingale and the rose, 1827) and Kol'tsov, "Solovei" (The nightingale, 1831).

Regarding personifications of nature as male, in Lermontov's "Pan" (1829), Pan, the spirit of the woods, appears to the speaker with a wineglass in one hand and his pipe in the other to teach him how to write poetry. A. P. Maikov in "Pan" (1869) depicts Pan asleep in the woods at noon surrounded by sleeping animals. Other examples of nature personified as male include Fedotov's "Ten' i solntse" (Shadow and sun) and "Pchela i tsvetok" (The bee and the flower, 1849), in which the flower (*tsvetok*, gendered male in Russian) represents an impoverished man artist.

Regarding the moon as *luna* (female gender) in noncanonical men poets (in addition to those by canonical men poets cited in the preceding paragraph), see Mil'keev "Luna" (1843) and "K lune" (1843). Fedotov uses *krasavitsa luna* to ridicule the conventions of Romantic poetry, an indication of how widespread was such a female personification ("K moim chitateliam, stikhov moikh strogim razbirateliam" [To my readers, strict examiners of my verse, 1850]).

For *Mesiats* versus *luna*, see Guber, "Mesiats" (1859). See also Miller's use of both *mesiats* and *luna* in his "Rusalka: Ballada." In the first stanza he uses *mesiats* for the moon when it is simply part of the landscape. In the eleventh stanza he uses *luna* when the moon uncannily disappears behind a cloud "as if on purpose," allowing a *rusalka* (female nature at its most dangerous) to catch and kill a Cossack.

40. The notebook of Gotovtseva's mostly unpublished poems is located in f. 46, op. 2, d. 426 RGALI. Rostopchina's poem appears in *Dnevnik devushki*, 10: iv (219–20). The three examples from Khvoshchinskaia may be found in *Literatur-*

naia gazeta 39 (Sept. 25, 1847): 613; *Moskvitianin* 15 (1853): 110; *Illiustratsiia* (Jan. 2, 1858): 7, respectively.

41. On Bakunina's unpublished poetry, see my "Praskov'ia Bakunina and the Poetess's Dilemma," 43–57. See also Kul'man's "Kopaiskii rybar" (The Kopais fisherman, 1839), in which a storm at sea is personified as a combination of the feminine (*volny*) and the masculine (*vetry*). This androgynous image contrasts with contemporary men poets' depiction of storms as raging females (Iazykov's "Buria" [The storm, 1839], Lermontov's "Groza" [The thunderstorm, 1830], and Fet's "Nyne pervyi my slishali grom" [Now we heard thunder for the first time, 1883]).

42. Johnson, *The Poems of Emily Dickinson*, 3: 1114. In Turgenev's "Poezdka v poles'e" (1857), the forest is presented as similarly uninterested in humanity, but the point of the story appears to be the narrator's epiphany in which he comes to understand the life of nature (*zhizn' prirody*).

43. See Margaret Homans's discussion of the implications of the Garden of Eden myth for women poets in *Women Writers and Poetic Identity*, 29–31.

44. Of course, the men poets who had been classically educated (Pushkin, Del'vig, Fet, Khomiakov, Maikov, etc.) also evoked the worlds of ancient Rome and Greece in their poetry, but usually in Bacchic or anacreontic poetry, i.e., poetic fantasies about a pre-Christian world of sexually available women.

45. Garelina also writes of "merciless fate" in "Tebia kak angela spasen'ia" (You, like an angel of salvation, 1870).

Chapter 3. Gender and Genre

1. For various taxonomies and hierarchies of genre starting with Plato and continuing to the present, see Fowler, *Kinds of Literature*.

2. Fowler, *Kinds of Literature*, 111, 122. It was Aristotle who first wrote of "kinds" of literature in his *Poetics*. Fowler's use of "kind," although logical, has not been adapted by subsequent genre theorists, as can be seen from the quotations that follow. In the following discussion, therefore, I, too, generally use "genre" to refer to kinds of literature.

3. I am thinking of such scholars as Fredric Jameson in *The Political Unconscious: Narrative as a Socially Symbolic Act* (Ithaca, N.Y.: Cornell University Press, 1981) and Anne Cranny-Francis in *Feminist Fiction: Feminist Uses of Generic Fiction*. Gerhart defines ideology as "the lies that keep the powerful in power" (*Genre Choices, Gender Questions*, 190). On ideology, see Terry Eagleton's *Ideology: An Introduction* (New York: Verso, 1991); Jameson, *Political Unconscious*, 106; Gerhart, *Genre Choices, Gender Questions*, 189–90. For ideologies of class and race in relation to Russian literary genres, see my "Gender and Genre in Pavlova's *A Double Life*," *Slavic Review* 54, no. 3 (1995): 567; and "Karolina Pavlova's 'At the Tea Table' and the Politics of Class and Gender," 271–84.

4. In a Russian literary context Michael Wachtel confirms Russ's conclusion when he states, "Pushkin's example alone . . . serves as eloquent testimony that the greatest poets are not necessarily the most radical innovators" (*Development of Russian Verse*, 16). "A poet's attitude to the larger literary tradition is revealed with striking clarity when his [sic] work is placed in the formal and semantic

context established by his predecessors" (241). To which Russ might reply, But what if that "larger literary tradition" is unusable? I have taken the term "gender norm" from Susan Stanford Friedman, "Gender and Genre Anxiety," 203–28.

5. The following discussion has also benefited from scholarship that applies genre theory specifically to Russian poetry: Gasparov, *Metr i smysl'*, and *Ocherk istorii russkogo stikha;* Scherr, *Russian Poetry: Meter, Rhythm, and Rhyme;* Wachtel, *Development of Russian Verse;* and Taylor, "Friendly Epistle in Russian Poetry."

6. Walter J. Ong, *Orality and Literacy: The Technologizing of the Word* (London: Methuen, 1982), 111–15; see also chapter 1 of the present volume, on the influence of Latin and neoclassicism into the nineteenth century; Wilkie, *Romantic Poets and Epic Tradition;* Stuart Curran, *Poetic Form and British Romanticism,* 13. Keats, the son of a livery stable manager and trained as a surgeon, was the one exception.

7. Quoted in Brown, *History of Russian Literature of the Romantic Period,* 2: 64. Brown's translation.

8. N. Siniavskii and M. Tsiavlovskii, eds., *Pushkin v pechati, 1814–1837: Khronologicheskii ukazatel' proizvedenii Pushkina, napechatannykh pri ego zhizni* (Moskva: L. E. Bukhgeim, 1914).

9. Various literary historians have judged other groups of genres most representative of the Romantic era: the ballad, the elegy, and the song (Lauren Leighton, "Romanticism," in *Handbook of Russian Literature,* ed. Victor Terras, 375); the sonnet, the hymn, the ode, the pastoral, the romance, and the epic (Curran, *Poetic Form and British Romanticism);* the elegy, the idyll, and the ballad (K. N. Girgor'ian, ed., *Russkii romantizm* (Leningrad: Nauka, 1978).

10. The *poema* is described as a "verse epic" in Terras, *Handbook of Russian Literature,* 344. On the descent of the ballad from the epic, see note 32.

11. The women Friedman discusses include Elizabeth Barrett Browning, H.D., Mary Tighe, and Diane de Prima. Paula Feldman lists seven eighteenth-century British women who wrote epics (Feldman, introduction to *British Women Poets of the Romantic Era,* xxx n. 4).

In Russia, Zinaida Volkonskaia is the only woman who wrote a work that resembles an epic; her posthumously published *Skazanie ob Olge* (Paris: V. Gasper, 1865), a Walter Scott–like novel, focuses on the marriage and events leading up to the conversion to Christianity of Ol'ga, the legendary figure in the *Primary Chronicles.*

Women did figure as *bogatyry* (epic heroes) and *polianitsy* (Amazons) in a few early *byliny* (Russian folk epics). See Natalie Kononenko, "Women as Performers of Oral Literature: A Reexamination of Epic and Lament," in *Women Writers in Russian Literature,* ed. Toby Clyman and Diana Greene (Westport, Conn.: Greenwood Press, 1994), 19.

12. Stuart Curran writes of Blake's "creation of the artist as epic hero" (*Poetic Form and British Romanticism,* 175), a tendency continued in Wordsworth's *Prelude* and in other Romantic works. Similarly, Susan Friedman discusses lyric poems by Romantic poets that constitute "personal epics" ("Gender and Genre Anxiety," 224 n. 15).

13. Two noteworthy exceptions to male protagonists in epics are Robert Southey's *Joan of Arc* (1796), discussed in chapter 6, and Shelley's *Queen Mab*

(1813), both works described as epics of "visionary and libertarian subversion" (Curran, *Poetic Form*,173). The only epic heroine celebrated in Russia appeared in Ivan Kozlov's *poema, Kniaginia Natalia Dolgorukaia* (1828). Dolgorukaia, who followed her husband into exile and became a nun after his execution, did not challenge gender norms.

14. See Curran, *Poetic Form*, 173; Terras, *Handbook of Russian Literature*, 344–45; and Zhirmunskii, *Bairon i Pushkin*, 239.

15. K. K. Bukhmeier, "N. M. Iazykov," in Iazykov, *Polnoe sobranie stikhotvorenii*, 36.

16. The one exception I have found is Elisaveta Shakhova's "Sila pokaiania (asketicheskaia poema, v trekh chastiakh)" (The force of repentence [an ascetic *poema* in three parts], 1841). Shakova also subtitled her play *Iudif'* (Judith, 1876) "poema po bibleiskomu tekstu, v dramaticheskoi forme v stikhakh, v piati deistviiakh" (A verse epic after the biblical text in dramatic form in verse in five acts).

Discussion of the use of the term "poema" by Pushkin, Lermontov, and Baratynskii follows. For discussion of Iazykov's *poemy*, see K. K. Bukhmeier, "N. N. Iazykov," 37–42. Perhaps because of the prestige of the term "poema," editors often posthumously bestow it on works. My focus here is on poets' own generic subtitles, as will be discussed later.

That Russian literary scholars continued to consider the *poema* both a prestigious and a male-identified genre through much of the twentieth century may be seen from such studies (in which no women writers appear) as Aleksandr Sokolov, *Ocherki po istorii russkoi poemy, XVIII i pervoi poloviny XIX veka* (Moskva: Izd-vo Moskovskogo universiteta, 1955); Leonid Dolgopolov, *Poemy Bloka i russkaia poema kontsa 19-nachala 20 vekov* (Leningrad: Nauka, 1964); Iu. Lebedev, *N. A. Nekrasov i russkaia poema 1840–50 gg.* (Iaroslavl': Verkhne-volzhskoe knizhn. izd-vo, 1971); and A. N. Berezneva, *Russkaia romanticheskaia poema: Lermontov, Nekrasov, Blok* (Saratov: Izd-vo Saratovskogo universiteta, 1976).

17. See Siniavskii and Tsiavlovskii, *Pushkin v pechati. Bakhchisaraiskii fontan* appeared again as *sochinenie* in 1830, and *Kavkazskii plennik* appeared as *sochinenie* in 1829. In general, women do not seem to have written *romanticheskie poemy*, with or without generic titles. Among the authors of the two hundred *poemy* and excerpts from *poemy* that Zhirmunskii surveys, he mentions only four women: Aleksandra Fuks ("Kniazha Khabiba," 1841, and "Osnovanie goroda Kazani," 1836); Z-va ("Vziatie Azova," 1829); Ol'ga Kriukova ("Donets," 1833); and V. Lizogub ("Ziuleika," 1845).

18. E. A. Baratynskii, *Stikhotvoreniia, poemy*, ed. L. G. Frizman (Moskva: Nauka, 1982), 629, 630, 633, 638.

19. The five works Lermontov referred to as *poemy* are *Sashka* (subtitled "Pravstvennaia poema"); an unfinished fragment titled "nachalo poemy"; *Korsar*, subtitled *poema; Angel smerti*, to which he referred in his notebook as a *poema;* and the 1831 version of *Demon*, subtitled *poema*, although in the final 1841 version he changed the subtitle to *vostochnaia povest'*.

Konstantin Aksakov described *Dvoinaia zhizn'* as a *poema* in 1847 (quoted in Sendich, "Life and Works of Karolina Pavlova," 229–31). Aksakov is identified as the author of this anonymous article in Valerii Briusov, "Materialy dlia biografii Karoliny Pavlovoi," in *Sobranie sochinenii,* by Karolina Pavlova (Moskva: K. F. Nekrasov, 1915), xxxi–xxxii.

20. On literary orientalism, see Martha Pike Conant, *The Oriental Tale in England in the Nineteenth Century* (New York: Columbia University Press, 1908); Edward Said, *Orientalism* (New York: Vintage Books, 1979); Joyce Zonana, "The Sultan and the Slave: Feminist Orientalism and the Structure of Jane Eyre," in *Revising the Word and the World,* ed. Veve Clark, Ruth-Ellen Joeres, and Madelon Sprengnether (Chicago: University of Chicago Press, 1993), 165–90.

21. On the *povest' v stikhakh,* see Zhirmunskii, *Bairon i Pushkin,* 237, 238, and Lebedev, *N. A. Nekrasov i russkaia poema 1840–50 gg.,* 3, 18.

22. It is interesting that Fuks subtitled her works *povesti v stikhakh* rather than *poemy,* despite their epic themes (e.g., the founding of a city) and authentic "exotic" details based on Fuks's ethnographic research (see especially chapter 2 of "Kniazhna Khabiba").

23. Other *povesti v stikhakh* by these women poets not discussed here include Lisitsyna's fragment (*otryvok*), "Povest' Ol'gi" (1829), in which, strangely, no character named Ol'ga appears; Shakhovskaia's fragment "Liudmila" (1832); Teplova's "Zhertva liubvi" (A victim of love, 1842); and Shakhova's three other *povesti v stikhakh,* which appeared in her 1839 *Stikhotvoreniia,* "Nevesta (byl')" (The bride [a true story]), "Gusar-Zatvornik (povest')" (The hussar-hermit [a story]), and "Tri zari ili slepets (povest')" (Three dawns, or the blind man).

Several scholars have pointed out that literary periodization, like many other critical categories, must also be reconsidered when we discuss women's writing. For example, Elaine Showalter writes, "Insofar as our concepts of literary periodization are based on men's writing, women's writing must be forcibly assimilated to an irrelevant grid" ("Feminist Criticism in the Wilderness," 33). See also Kelly, *History of Russian Women's Writing,* 23; and Christine Tomei, introduction to *Russian Women Writers,* ed. C. Tomei, 1: xxiii. While most literary historians consider the *poema* to have exhausted itself as a genre by the 1840s (see Terras, *Handbook of Russian Literature,* 234; Zhirmunskii, *Bairon i Pushkin,* 318; Lebedev, *N. A. Nekrasov i russkaia poema,* 4), several of the women's *povesti v stikhakh* discussed here date from as late as the 1870s. In addition, many of these works appeared long after they had been written because of the difficulty women writers experienced in getting published (discussed in the introduction). This is true particularly for the work of Mordovtseva, Garelina, and Pavlova.

24. In the Tatar legend on which the work is based, the unnamed Tatar heroine is already married and does not undergo any ordeal. A contemporary reviewer congratulated Fuks on reworking the "quarrelsome Tatar woman" (*branchivaia Tatarka*) into the "most charming Fatima" (*Osnovanie goroda Kazani*) ("Literaturnaia letopis'," section 6, *Biblioteka dlia chteniia* 22 [Apr. 1837]: 2).

25. *Raut,* ed. N. V. Sushkov (Moskva, 1851), 313.

26. Pavlova, *Polnoe sobranie stikhotvorenii,* 310. Page numbers of subsequent citations to this work will be indicated in parentheses in the text.

27. Khvoshchinskaia, *Derevenskii sluchai: povest' v stikhakh;* see also Khvoshchinskaia's "'Vy ulybaetes'? . . . Razdum'e ne meshaet'" (You are smiling? . . . My pensiveness doesn't prevent me), published as the first of her "Piat' stikhotvorenii," *Otechestvennye zapiski* 83, no.8 (1852): 315–17.

28. Shakhova, "Perst Bozhii" (1839), "Strashnyi krasavets" (1840), and "Izg-nannik" (1840), in *Povesti v stikhakh Elisavety Shakhovoi*. Early examples of the Gothic tale as a woman's genre include Ann Radcliffe's *Mysteries of Udolpho* (1794) and Mary Shelley's *Frankenstein* (1816). On the Gothic as a genre for women's stories, see Frances Restuccia, "Female Gothic Writing: Under Cover to Alice," *Genre* 18 (fall 1986): 245–66; and Tania Modleski, *Loving with a Vengeance*, 59–84.

29. Parts of "Otryvki iz neokonchennogo rasskaza" appeared in the posthumous edition of Zhadovskaia's works, edited by her brother, *Polnoe sobranie sochinenii Iulii Zhadovskoi*, 1: 143–51, but it was never published in full. See Blagovo's discussion in *Poeziia i lichnost' Iu. V. Zhadovskoi*, 17, 35.

30. Zhadovskaia, "Poseshchenie," in *Stikhotvoreniia Iulii Zhadovskoi*, 135–40. On the *svetskaia povest'* as a woman's genre, see my "Gender and Genre in Pavlova's *A Double Life*," 563–77.

31. Mordovtseva, *Otzvuki zhizni*, 10–32.

32. See Brown, *Russian Literature of the Romantic Period*, 1: 199; A. Friedman, *Ballad Revival*, 292–326, 170–71; Katz, *Literary Ballad in Early Nineteenth-Century Russian Literature*, 17. On the relationship of ballads to the epic or heroic *poema*, see A. N. Sokolov, *Ocherki po istorii russkoi poemy XVIII i pervoi poloviny XIX veka*, 10–11.

33. A. Friedman, *Ballad Revival*, 265, discusses the influence of the ballad revival on Wordsworth's *Lyrical Ballads* and the work of Blake, Coleridge, Keats, Scott, and Tennyson.

34. According to V. I. Chernyshev, the first use of the term *ballada* for Russian folk ballads was in 1936; as late as 1902 a group of folk ballads appeared with the description "Nizshie epicheskie" (literally "lowest epics") (introduction to *Russkaia ballada*, v).

35. Zhukovskii wrote, "My chosen genre of poetry is the ballad" (Katz, *Literary Ballad*, 39). Michael Wachtel describes Zhukovsky's influence on the Russian ballad: "Zhukovsky created for the Russian reader a firm association between a poetic form (amphibrachic tetrameter couplets with exclusively masculine rhyme), genre (the ballad), and plot (betrayal and revenge)" (*Development of Russian Verse*, 56). Similar images of women as men's victims or as false and evil occur in Pushkin's ballads. In "Chernaia shal'" (The black shawl, 1820), for example, a man kills his false love after beheading and stomping on the body of the man who was kissing her. In "Zhenikh" (1824–25) Natasha witnesses a brigand murder a young woman and barely escapes the same fate, while in "Voron k voronu letit" (1828) a woman arranges her husband's murder in order to be with her lover. Other such depictions of women occur in Lermontov's ballads, "Nad morem krasavitsa-deva sidit" (Above the sea a beautiful maiden sits, 1829), "Pechatka" (The glove, 1829), "Gost'" (The guest, written in the 1830s), "Trostnik" (The reed, 1832), "Rusalka," (The mermaid, 1832), and "Kuda tak provorno" (Where so quickly, 1832), all discussed by Katz. See also Del'vig's "Romance" ("Prosnisia, rytsar', put' dalek") (Romance [Awaken, knight, the way is far], 1820); Fet's "Zmei" (The dragon, 1847), "Taina" (The secret, 1842), and "Gero i Leandr" (Hero and Leander, 1847); Miller's "Rusalka: Ballada" (1849); and Kol'tsov's "Rytsar' (Ballada)" (The knight [A ballad], 1827).

36. Pavlova wrote poetry in German and French, as well as Russian, and translated poetry from German, French, Polish, and English; Zhadovskaia and Mordovtseva translated Heine; Gotovsteva translated Lamartine; Khvoshchin-skaia knew Latin, Italian, and French; Lisitsyna translated the English aestheti-cian Hugh Blaire; Kul′man knew Greek, Latin, Italian, French, German, English, Spanish, and Portuguese.

37. Discussed in Katz, *Literary Ballad*, 21–23. Although Katz refers to Tur-chaninova as "the obscure poetess" (21), she was a poet who published in sev-eral literary journals, as well as a translator, a philosopher, and the author of at least three books: *Otryvki iz sochinenii (v stikhakh)* (1803), *Natural′naia etika ili za-kony nravstvennosti ot sozertsaniia prirody neposredstvenno proistekaiushchie, perev. s latinskogo, stikhami* (1803), and *Lettres philosophiques de M. Fontaine et de m-lle Tourtchaninoff* (Paris, 1817).

38. It will be noted that the children fare equally badly in the husband's and in the wife's dreams.

39. Preminger and Brogan, *New Princeton Encyclopedia of Poetry and Poetics*, 322–25. On the twentieth-century elegy, see Peter M. Sacks, *The English Elegy: Studies in the Genre from Spenser to Yeats* (Baltimore: Johns Hopkins University Press, 1985); and Zeiger, *Beyond Consolation*.

40. Tomashevskii, *Pushkin*, 1: 119. The Russian scholar Vadim Vatsuro also discusses the elegy as a meditation (see his *Lirika pushkinskoi pory: Elegicheskaia shkola* [Sankt-Peterburg: Nauka, 1994]) as does Lidiia Ginzburg (in *O lirike*, 201).

41. Sacks, *English Elegy*, 3. Monika Greenleaf cites Sacks's work in her *Pushkin and Romantic Fashion*, 91–92.

42. Sacks, *English Elegy*, 8. Sacks's androcentricism can be seen in the two myths he considers central to the elegy, those of Daphne and Apollo and of Sy-rinx and Pan. In both cases a male divinity attempts to rape a nymph who, to save herself, transforms into a laurel tree and a reed, respectively, which the male then mutilates in the name of art. Apollo tears off a branch of the tree to make the laurel wreath, the traditional prize for poets; Pan similarly breaks off the reed, drills holes in it, and turns it into a pipe, a musical instrument. Sacks describes Apollo and Pan as successful mourners, because like the elegist, they create art out of "metamorphized [frustrated] sexual force" (7). Melissa Zeiger notes that Sacks's two myths of "successful" (male) mourning are founded on the "unre-marked consumption of women" (*Beyond Consolation*, 5). Such creation myths, which show the origins of (men's) art in the violated bodies of women, date from classical times. See Maikov's "Muza, boginia Olimpa, vruchila dve zvuchnye fleity" (The muse, an Olympian goddess, entrusted two sonorous flutes, 1841), in which Maikov condenses and rewrites these two myths by having the (female) muse give two flutes to Pan and Apollo. While it remains unclear whether the muse thus tacitly approves the fates of Daphne and Syrinx or displaces them, Pan and Apollo proceed to use the flutes in a musical duel. That these two myths affected women writers is suggested by the fact that one of these poets, Elisaveta Kul′man, in "Korinna" (see appendix), rewrote the Apollo/Daphne myth to show Daphne's defeat of Apollo and a woman poet's triumph over men (see my "Nineteenth-Century Women Poets: Critical Reception vs. Self-Definition," 98–99).

As for Sacks' theory of mourning, it is harder in Russian to make a case for an oedipal struggle between the (male) mourner and a (male) personified death over a (female) object of mourning. While in Germanic languages "death" is gendered as male (e.g., the Erl König, Father Time with his sickle), in Russian *smert'* is a female-gendered noun. See also Karl Guthke, *The Gender of Death: A Cultural History in Art and Literature* (Cambridge: Cambridge University Press, 1999). It is true, however, that the objects of mourning that appear most often in Russian elegies are female-gendered nouns: *liubov'*, *nadezhda*, *mechta*, *iunost'*.

43. The ability to bear a child, at least, was not an unmixed blessing for women, as they could not control pregnancy, which often resulted in death for mother and/or child. Lina Bernstein quotes the unpublished letters of A. P. Elagina (1789–1877), who repeatedly expresses her fear of death in childbirth and also the shame she feels because of her adult son's contemptuous attitude toward her frequent pregnancies ("Private and Public Personas: Negotiating the Mommy Track in the Age of Nicholas I," paper presented at the American Association for the Advancement of Slavic Studies Convention, Seattle, Nov. 1997). See also Lina Bernstein, "Women on the Verge of a New Language: Russian Salon Hostesses in the First Half of the Nineteenth Century," in *Russia, Women, Culture*, ed. Helena Goscilo and Beth Holmgren (Bloomington: Indiana University Press), 209–24.

44. Fet titled the first section of his *Osnovnoe sobranie* "Elegii i dumy." Shakhova, "Elegiia," in *Mirianka i otshel'nitsa*, 19; Teplova, "Elegiia," in *Stikhotvoreniia N. Teplovoi*, 52, 73; Lisitsyna, "Elegiia," in *Stikhi i proza*, 37, 41. On Maikov, see *Izbrannye proizvedeniia*, 789, 798.

45. Regarding the ability to love, the speaker in Del'vig's "Elegiia" ("Kogda dusha, prosilas' ty" [Soul, when you asked], 1821–22) declares that the pain of love has made him stop desiring it. In Del'vig's "Razocharovanie" (Disillusionment, 1824), the speaker, who has renounced love, foresees his death. See also Lermontov, "Elegiia (O! Esli b dni moi tekli)" [O! If my days flowed], 1829); Baratynskii, "Razuverenie (Elegiia)" (Discussion, 1821); Iazykov, "Elegiia (Svoboden ia)" [I am free], 1824).

An example of graphically described sexual pleasure can be found in Iazykov, "Elegiia (Skazhi: Kogda)" (Tell me: When, 1823–25). Both Baratynskii's "Elegiia Podrazhanie Lafaru (Dremala roshcha nad potokom)" (Elegy in imitation of [Charles] La Fave [The grove slumbered over the stream], 1820) and Iazykov's "Proshchai, krasavitsa moia"(Farewell, my beauty, 1825) mention the consolation of future lovers.

46. Pushkin and Del'vig, "Elegiia na smert' Anny L'vovny" (Elegy on the death of Anna L'vovna, 1825); Del'vig, "Na smert' kuchera Agafona" (On the death of the coachman Agafon, 1814–17) and "Na smert' sobachki Aminki" (On the death of the lapdog Aminka, 1814–17).

47. Men's funerary elegies include Baratynskii, "Na smert' Gete" (On the death of Goethe, 1832); Del'vig, "Na smert' Derzhavina" (1819); Fet, "Na smert' A. V. Druzhinina" (1864), "Pamiati V. I. Botkina" (1869), "Pamiati N. Ia. Danilevskogo" (1886); Tiutchev, "29-oe ianvaria 1837" (January 29, 1837, 1837), "Na dreve chelovechestva vysokom" (On the high tree of mankind, 1832 [on

Goethe]); Khomiakov, "Elegiia na smert' V. K(ireevskogo)" (1827), "K V. K[ireev-skomu]" (1827); Guber, "Na smert' Pushkina" (1837); Miller, "Na konchinu F. N. Glinki" (1881); Maikov, "Na smert' Lermontova," "Na smert' M. I. Glinki" (1857); Kol'tsov, "Les (Posviashcheno pamiati A. S. Pushkina)" (The forest [dedicated to the memory of A. S. Pushkin], 1837).

On Teplova's relationship with Lisitsyna, see Vatsuro, "Zhizn' i poeziia Nadezhdy Teplovoi," 18–19. Rostopchina appears also to have written a funerary elegy for Pushkin, "29 ianvaria 1837," that has never been found (see chapter 4, note 31). Stephanie Sandler considers Rostopchina's "Chernovaia kniga Pushkina" (1838) to be a funerary elegy ("The Law, the Body, and the Book: Three Poems on the Death of Pushkin," *Canadian-American Slavic Studies* 23, no. 3 (fall 1989): 298–311).

48. *New Princeton Encyclopedia of Poetry and Poetics*, 324. On genre anxiety, see S. Friedman, "Gender and Genre Anxiety."

49. An unusual poem by a man poet mourning the death of a young girl is Del'vig's "Na smert' . . . (Sel'skaia elegiia)" (On the death of . . . [A village elegy], 1821–22), but unlike any elegy written by the women poets, Del'vig attributes the girl's death to unrequited love for a man.

Among noncanonical poets, poems about the death of young women or children appear more frequently. Mil'keev's "Pokoinitsa" (The deceased woman, 1843) compares to a bride a dead young woman whose friends are gathering flowers for her funeral. On "the wedding of the dead," a Russian folk ritual, see Kononenko, "Women as Performers of Oral Literature," 25, 32 n. 40. A. N. Maikov wrote a cycle of three poems on the death of his daughter ("Docheri" [To my daughter], 1866), and Khomiakov wrote "K detiam" (To my children, 1839) on the death of his two sons. See also Miller, "Na mogile Klavdii M." (At the grave of Klavdia M., 1881).

50. Mirsky, *History of Russian Literature*, 74.

Lidiia Ginzburg traces the *druzheskoe poslanie* (friendly epistle) to Horace, Boileau, and Voltaire, as it combines elegiac and anacreonic motifs, freedom-loving dreams, Voltairian skepticism, satire, and epigram as well as the Horatian tradition of laziness and wisdom (*O lirike*, 198, 23, 40).

On the gendering of the *druzheskoe poslanie*, see also Stephanie Sandler and Judith Vowles, "Beginning to Be a Poet: Baratynsky and Pavlova," in *Russian Subjects: Empire, Nation, and the Culture of the Golden Age*, ed. Monika Greenleaf and Stephen Moeller-Sally (Evanston, Ill.: Northwestern University Press, 1998), 152–63. Aleksandra Fuks's "Poslanie Lize" (1834), rather than asking for consolation from a woman friend, offers it.

51. Sacks, *English Elegy*, 8. On women displacing desires to the afterlife, see Walker, *Nightingale's Burden*, 35, 45. See Carol Gilligan on men's and women's different attitudes toward attachment and separation, *In a Different Voice*, 7–9. Among canonical poets Lermontov wrote two prayers "Molitva" (1837) and "Molitva" ("V minuty zhizni trudnuiu,") (Prayer [In a difficult moment of life], 1839). Iazykov also wrote two such poems ("Molitva," [Prayer, 1825], "Molitva," [1825]), and Baratynskii one, "Molitva" (1842 or 1843). Noncanonical men poets wrote a great deal more than canonical ones on the consolations of religion. See Kol'tsov, "Pered obrazom Spasitelia" (Before an image of the Saviour, 1830);

Khomiakov, "Po prochtenii psalma" (On reading a psalm, 1856); Mil'keev, "Uteshenie" (Consolation, 1843); "Zatvornitsy" (The hermitesses, 1843); Guber, "Molitva" (Prayer, 1839), "Moia molitva" (My prayer, 1859); Miller, "V sviatie dni Khristovi Voskresen'ia" (In the holy days of Christ's resurrection, 1881).

52. I base this discussion of the *prichitanie* on Chistov, introduction to *Prichitaniia*, 5–46. The *prichitanie* is also known as *prichet'*, *vop*, *voi*, *zhal*, *krik*, *plach*, *zaplachka*, *goloshenie*. Chistov writes that in the past *prichitaniia* may also have been performed to mourn other community events such as fires and famines (5). On Russian accentual and metrical verse, see Scherr, *Russian Poetry*. Natalie Kononenko notes the many similarities between the lament and the epic, and argues for their common origin "Women as Performers of Oral Literature," 18–33.

53. Stuart Curran similarly observes that when a Romantic poet "sets out to write a villanelle or an ode, no less than a sonnet, the first question is not one of subject matter but of the logic inherent in the form. . . . The formal structuring principle in large part predetermines ideological orientation. . . . Generic choice has already committed [the poet] to . . . a mode of apprehension. It is an ideological construct and it may be in place, forcing choice, before a word is written or the subject matter is even conceived" (*Poetic Form and British Romanticism*, 10–11).

54. Kiukhel'beker (in the previously mentioned essay "O napravelenii nashei poezii," 1824) attacks the elegy and praises the ode. Pushkin responded by ridiculing Kiukhel'beker in *Evgenii Onegin* (IV, 32, ll.14–33): "Pishite ody, gospoda," etc.

55. Abrams, *Natural Supernaturalism*, 255. For quests ending in union with the feminine other, see Miller, "Sonety" (1872) and Maikov, "Sny" (1855).

56. Perry, "Romanticism," 3–11. In Russia, Viazemskii doubted the existence of a Romantic movement (Brown, *History of Russian Literature of the Romantic Period*, 2: 59).

57. Gerhart Hoffmeister, ed., *European Romanticism: Literary Cross-Currents, Modes, and Models* (Detroit: Wayne State University Press, 1990).

58. Bakunina, "Otryvok iz skazaniia v stikhakh Iulianiia Nikomidiiskaia," in *Sbornik v pol'zu bednykh semeistv Basmannogo otdeleniia na 1849* (Moskva: Tip A. Semena, 1849), 39–42.

In these women's poetry, female desire is depicted in terms of its effects on the woman. In Garelina's "Druz'ia moi! Ne smeites' nado mnoi" (My friends! Don't laugh at me, 1870), for example, the speaker cries, misses her beloved, thinks about him all the time, and loses interest in everything else. In Teplova's "K . . ." (To . . ., 1830) the speaker's spirit is troubled, her breast excited, her heart anguished. See also Gotovtseva "K. P.," *Literaturnyi Muzeum na 1827*, and "31-e dekabria," *Literaturnaia gazeta*, no. 38 (Sept. 18, 1847): 597; Lisitsyna , "K. N. . . . N . . ." (To N . . . N . . . , 1829); Pavlova, "Donna Inezil'ia" (1842); Rostopchina, *Neizvestnyi roman* (An unknown romance, 1856); Teplova, "K. O. F." (To O. F., 1847); Zhadovskaia, "Vzgliad" (A glance, 1885).

Compare with men poets' depiction of male desire. In Iazykov's "Pesnia (Ia zhdu tebia, kogda vechernei mgloiu)" (Song [I wait for you when like an evening mist], 1829) the speaker waits for a woman at dusk to reveal her eyes, mouth, and breast. See also Iazykov's "Elegiia (Zdes' gory s dvukh storon stoiat)" (Elegy [Here mountains stand on both sides], 1839) and "Elegiia (Ty voskhititel'na! Ty pyshno rastsvetaesh')" (Elegy [You are ravishing! You bloom luxuriantly], 1820s), and Fet's "Kak maiskii golubookii" (Like a blue-eyed May, 1842).

Domestic affections: Fuks, for example, in "Vecher na dache" (Evening at the dacha, 1834) describes a scene of marital contentment. Teplova expresses her love for her sister in several poems, for example, "K sestre, v al'bom" (To my sister, for her album, 1838) and "K sestre (Kogda nastanet chas zhelannyi)" (To my sister [When the desired hour comes], 1838). She also movingly describes feelings of loss at the death of a husband and daughter in "Son" (A dream, 1845) and "Na smert' docheri" (On the death of my daughter, 1846). See also Garelina, "Moi vernyi drug i brat" (My faithful friend and brother, 1870) and "K bratu" (To my brother, 1870); Khvoshchinskaia, "Materi" (To my mother), *Syn otechestva*, no. 11 (1842): 1–2, and "Byvalo, s sestrami veseloi i shumnoi tolpoi" (My sisters and I in a cheerful and noisy crowd used to, 1847); Mordovtseva, "Moei materi" (To my mother, 1877); Shakhova, "Materi" (1839); Bakunina, "Poslanie k materi" (An epistle to my mother, 1833).

Female childhood: The speaker in Pavlova's "Sonet" (Sonnet, 1839), for example, encourages a child to enjoy Russian folklore. The speaker-poet concludes that a poet also must keep a child's soul. See also Pavlova's "Da, mnogo nas" (Yes, we were many, 1839), mentioned earlier. Teplova in "Sovet" (Advice, 1837) ironically warns a girl not to continue writing poetry, which she describes as "a dangerous gift for maidens." See also Teplova's "K nei" (To her, 1860) and Lisitsyna's "Pesn'" (Song, 1829).

Motherhood: For example, the speaker in Rostopchina's "Iskushenie" (Temptation, 1839) expresses feelings of tender concern for her two babies (see chapter 4 for discussion). In Mordovsteva's "Kolybel'naia pesnia" (Cradle song, 1877), however, the speaker bitterly warns her child of the disillusionments that await it in life. See also Garelina, "Spi, moi kroshechka beztsennoi" (Sleep my priceless, little one, 1870).

Female old age: Two very contrasting attitudes toward old age can be found in Garelina's "Akh, vy kudri" (Oh, you curls, 1870), in which the speaker regrets her physical losses, and Pavlova's balladlike "Starukha" (The old woman, 1840), in which an old woman puts a young man under a spell with her stories, that is, with her art.

59. Perhaps the most famous such poem is Rostopchina's "Nasil'nyi brak" (The forced marriage, 1845), in which she compared Russia's annexation of Poland to a forced marriage (discussed in chapter 4). Khvoshchinskaia in "'Vy ulybaetes'? . . . Razdum'e ne meshaet'" (You are smiling? My pensiveness doesn't prevent, 1852) (discussed in chapter 5) shows that women's upbringings make it impossible for them even to protest against such marriages. See also Garelina, "Mne zhal' tebia, ty pogibaesh'" (I pity you, you are perishing, 1870) and Zhadovskaia, "Otryvki iz neokonchennogo razskaza" (Excerpts from an unfinished story, 1885).

60. I would extend to most of these women poets Pamela Perkins's observation that in the lyrics of Pavlova and Emily Dickinson there is "a sense of solitude (*uedinenie*), an isolation that could be conceived as enhanced by the fact of

gender" (*Burden of Sufferance*, 26). Modleski comments on the similar isolation and excessive solitude of twentieth-century American housewives (*Loving with a Vengeance*, 89–90, 108, 112).

61. Poems of sitting by an open window at night: Garelina, "Vse v prirode pozabylos'" (Everything in nature has forgotten itself, 1870); Gotovtseva, "Noch'" (Night, 1829); Khvoshchinskaia, "U okna" (By the window, 1850), "Kogda poroi v tumannyi dom" (When sometimes to the dull house, 1846), "Shumit osennyi dozhd', noch' temnaia niskhodit" (The autumn rain whispers, dark night falls, 1848); Lisitsyna, "K mesiatsu" (To the moon, 1829); Zhadovskaia, "V sumerki" (At twilight, 1844–47), "Ia liubliu smotret' (I love to watch, 1844–47), "Vechernie dumy" (Evening meditations, 1847–56), "Noch' . . . vot, v sad tenistyi" (Night . . . there is the shadowy garden, 1847–56); Fuks, "Raz s dushevnoiu toskoiu" (Once with a soulful sadness, 1834).

62. Kol'tsov's "Vopl' stradaniia" (A cry of suffering, 1840), which starts with the word *naprasno*, is a very unusual poem among the work of men poets. Interestingly, in A. N. Maikov's "Ispoved'" (Confession, 1841) the words *druz'ia, naprasno*, and *tshchetno* all appear in the first two lines, but in the service of an anacreontic theme. The speaker confesses to his (men) friends that he loses control of himself when he sees "a smile on the lips of a modest girl."

63. Unbearable isolation, despair, longing for death and transcendence: Khvoshchinskaia in "Druz'ia moi! Vam vsem tak shchedro zhizn' dana" (My friends! To you all so generously life has been given, 1847) (See discussion in chapter 5) describes a woman's feelings of isolation, uselessness, and futility. The speaker compares herself to a remote island away from any trade route, one that a ship would only find by accident. Gotovtseva in "Tuda khochu" (I want to go there, 1827) expresses a desire to transcend the pain of life by going to heaven. See also Khvoshchinskaia "V sumerki" (At twilight, 1857); Gotovtseva "To skorotechnoi, to lenivoi" (Sometimes flowing quickly, sometimes lazily, 1829) and "V toske zadumchivoi kak chasto ia mechtaiu" (In thoughtful melancholy so often I dream, 1829); Mordovtseva, "Byvaiut dni dushevnogo razlada" (There are days of spiritual discord, 1877) and "Byvaiut strashnye, tiazhelye mgnoven'ia!"(There are terrifying, painful moments!, 1877); Teplova, "Russkaia pesnia" (Russian song, 1860), "Zabyt'e" (Oblivion, 1860), and "Pererozhdenie" (Rebirth, 1835); Garelina, "Dushu nevinuiu, dushu blazhenuiu" (My innocent, blessed soul, 1870).

64. Some of the male canonical poets occasionally wrote poems to family members. Pushkin in an early poem ("Sestre," 1814) expressed his loneliness for his sister. Baratynskii thanked his sister for visiting him during a difficult time in "Sestre" (To my sister, 1822). Other such poems include Iazykov, "K bratu" (To my brother, 1822), and Tiutchev, "Brat, stol'ko let soputstvovalshii mne" (Brother, how many years having accompanied me, 1870). The noncanonical men poets, however, wrote many more poems to family members. The first poem in Guber's *Stikhotvoreniia* (1845), serving almost as a dedication, is "Mogila materi" (My mother's grave). Guber also describes his mother in "Tri snovideniia" (Three dreams, 1837). See also Miller, "Sonety" (Sonnets, 1872), about his mother, and "Moei materi" (To my mother, 1872), a translation from the Ger-

man; Khomiakov "V al'bom sestre" (For my sister's album, 1826); Kol'tsov, "Malen'komu bratu" (To my younger brother, 1829) and "Sestre" (To my sister, 1829).

65. See my "Nineteenth-Century Women Poets: Critical Reception vs. Self-Definition," 95–109.

66. Elaine Marks and Isabelle de Courtivron, eds., *New French Feminisms* (Amherst: University of Massachusetts Press, 1980), 16.

67. Alice Rossi, ed., *The Feminist Papers* (New York: Bantam, 1981), 7–15.

68. For the influence of Rousseau and *Emile* in Russia, see Andrew Wachtel, *The Battle for Childhood: The Creation of a Russian Myth* (Stanford, Calif.: Stanford University Press, 1990), 38, 71.

69. See Edward Brown's accounts of how Mikhail Bakunin, Vissarion Belinskii, and Nikolai Stankevich treated Bakunin's sisters, Varvara and Liuba (*Stankevich and His Moscow Circle, 1830–1840* [Stanford, Calif.: Stanford University Press, 1966], 66, 69, 77, 79, 80, 118).

70. "Lyric," in *New Princeton Encyclopedia of Poetry and Poetics*, ed. A. Preminger and T. V. F. Brogan, 721.

Chapter 4. Evdokiia Rostopchina

1. I base my analysis on the following biographical sketches.

Nineteenth century: Berg, "Grafinia Rostopchina v Moskve," 691–708 (reprinted in E. P. Rostopchina, *Schastlivaia zhenshchina* [Moskva: Izd.-vo Pravda, 1991], 391–400); Bykov, "Russkie zhenshchiny-pisatel'nitsy," 238–43; E. S. Nekrasova, "Grafinia E. P. Rostopchina," *Vestnik Evropy* 3 (March–April 1885): 42–81; Dmitrii Mikhailovich Pogodin, "Grafinia E. P. Rostopchina i ee vechera," 401–3; Grafinia L[idiia] A. Rostopchina, "Pravda o moei babushke," *Istoricheskii vestnik*, no. 95 (1904): 50–66, 427–40, 864–81; no. 96 (1904): 47–68; and "Semeinaia khronika (fragmenty)," 404–11; D[mitrii] Sushkov, "K biografii grafini E. P. Rostopchinoi," *Istoricheskii vestnik* 5 (1881): 300–305 (reprinted from an unsigned archival copy in E. P. Rostopchina, *Schastlivaia zhenshchina*, 412–14); S. Sushkov, "Biograficheskii ocherk," 1: iii–xlviii; M. Tsebrikova, "Russkie zhenshchiny pisatel'nitsy," *Nedelia* (May 30, 1876): 13–17, 430–43.

Twentieth century: Afanas'ev, "'Da, zhenskaia dusha,'" 3–18; N. V. Bannikov, "Ot sostavitelia," in his *Russkie poetessy XIX veka*, 5–12, 43–45; Ernst, "Karolina Pavlova i gr. Evdokiia Rastopchina [*sic*]," 5–35; Fainshtein, *Pisatel'nitsy pushkinskoi pory*, 83–104; Irina Filipenko, "Moskovskie literaturnye salony," *Moskovskii zhurnal* 7 (1991): 50–52; Helena Goscilo, "Evdokiia Rostopchina," in *Russian and Polish Women's Fiction*, ed. H. Goscilo, 45; and "Evdokiia Petrovna Rostopchina," in *Dictionary of Russian Women Writers*, ed. M. Ledkovsky, C. Rosenthal, and M. Zirin, 540–44; Khodasevich, "Grafinia E. P. Rostopchina: Ee zhizn' i lirika," 35–53; Kiselev, "Poetessa i tsar'," 144–56; Kiselev-Sergenin, "Taina grafini E. P. Rostopchinoi," *Neva* 9 (1994): 267–84; and "Po staromu sledu (o ballade E. Rostopchinoi 'Nasil'nyi brak')," 137–52; Pedrotti, "Scandal of Countess Rostopčina's Polish-Russian Allegory," 2, 196–214; Ranchin, editor's introduction to *Schastlivaia zhenshchina*, 5–14; Romanov, editor's introduction ["Liricheskii dnevnik

Evdokii Rostopchinoi"] to *Stikhotvoreniia, proza, pis'ma,* 5–27; V. V. Uchenova, "Vy vspomnite menia!" in *Tsaritsy muz,* ed. V.V. Uchenova, 3–14, 418–19; and "Zvuki chistoi dushi," *Molodaia gvardiia* 3 (1989): 185–87.

2. We find the story of Rostopchina's first publication in Afanas'ev, "'Da, zhenskaia dusha,'" 5–6; Bannikov, "Ot sostavitelia," 43; Khodasevich, "Grafinia E. P. Rostopchina," 42–43; D. Sushkov, "K biografii grafini E. P. Rostopchinoi," 303; S. Sushkov, "Biograficheskii ocherk," 1: vi–vii; L. Rostopchina, "Pravda o moei babushke," *Istoricheskii vestnik,* no. 95 (January–March, 1904): 874; Uchenova, "Vy vspomnite menia!" 418; and "Zvuki chistoi dushi," 185.

3. Compare, for example, with Pushkin, who, after finishing his first extended work, *Ruslan i Liudmila,* received a portrait from Zhukovskii with the inscription, "To a victorious pupil from a defeated master" (Dmitry Mirsky, *Pushkin* [New York: E. P. Dutton, 1963], 37).

4. By several accounts it took some time to identify Avdotiia Sushkova (as she was called then) as the poem's author because Viazemskii had "Talisman" printed over the signature "D . . . a"—perhaps for her nickname, Dodo, or because he thought her full name was Dar'ia.

5. Rostopchina subtitled the poem "Ballada i allegoriia" on the manuscript version (Kiselev, "Poetessa i tsar'," 154). On "Nasil'nyi brak," see Kiselev, "Poetessa i tsar'" and "Po staromu sledu"; Pedrotti, "Scandal of Countess Rostopčina's Polish-Russian Allegory," and L. Rostopchina, "Semeinaia khronika (fragmenty)," 407–8.

6. The Gogol story first appeared in Berg, "Grafinia Rostopchina v Moskve," 693–94 (and was reprinted in 1991 in *Schastlivaia zhenshchina;* see note 1). It was repeated in Bykov, "Russkie zhenshchiny-pisatel'nitsy," 239–40; Fainshtein, *Pisatel'nitsy pushkinskoi pory,* 95; Romanov, editor's introduction, 21; and Kiselev, "Poetessa i tsar'" (but not in his "Po staromu sledu"). Nekrasova repeats the story while questioning it ("Grafinia E. P. Rostopchina," 55). Pedrotti argues for it at length in "Scandal of Countess Rostopčina's Polish-Russian Allegory," 208–10. I have not found any reference to "Nasil'nyi brak" in anything written by or about Gogol.

"Nasil'nyi brak" was later published in Herzen's émigré journal *Poliarnaia zvezda* 2 (1856).

7. Similarly, A. Ia. Bulgakov, the Moscow postmaster general at the time, hypothesized in a letter to his son that Rostopchina must have a "Polonophile" lover, presumably because he did not consider it possible for Rostopchina to have any political views of her own (Kiselev, "Po staromu sledu," 137). On *Vybranye mesta* and Gogol's political views, see Henri Troyat, *Gogol* (Paris: Flammarion, 1971), 558, 231.

8. For Rostopchina's cover letter to Bulgarin, see Kiselev, "Poetessa i tsar'," 145.

9. Rostopchina and Pushkin: Romanov, editor's introduction, 10–11; Bannikov, "Ot sostavitelia," 43, 237–38; Afanas'ev, "'Da, zhenskaia dusha,'" 5; Fainshtein, *Pisatel'nitsy pushkinskoi pory,* 87.

Rostopchina and Lermontov: S. Sushkov, "Biograficheskii ocherk," 1: xiv; Berg, "Grafinia Rostopchina v Moskve," 696; *Poety 1840–1850-kh godov,* ed. B. Ia.

Bukhshtab and E. M. Shneiderman, 477 n. 19; Romanov, editor's introduction, 19–20.

Rostopchina as seduced and abandoned: Khodasevich, "Grafinia E. P. Rostopchina," 47–48; Kiselev-Sergenin, "Taina grafini E. P Rostopchinoi," 278. Several of these biographies also denigrate Rostopchina by referring to her childhood nickname, "Dodo" (Pedrotti, "Scandal of Countess Rostopčina's Polish-Russian Allegory," 197; Khodasevich, "Grafinia E. P. Rostopchina," 36, 37, 38, 39; Romanov, editor's introduction, 13; Fainshtein, *Pisatel'nitsy pushkin-soi pory,* 86, 91, 96), not a practice one encounters in biographies of men poets.

Rostopchina bores her guests: Berg, "Grafinia Rostopchina v Moskve," 703; Pogodin, "Grafinia E. P Rostopchina i ee vechera," 401; Aronson and Reiser, *Literaturnye kruzhki i salony,* 288.

10. Pogodin, "Grafinia E. P. Rostopchina i ee vechera," 401; also quoted in Afanas'ev, "'Da, zhenskaia dusha,'" 12.

11. Berg, 696, 700, reprinted in *Schastlivaia zhenshchina,* 391–403. These sexualized physical descriptions have been cited and reprinted for over one hundred years.

12. On Pushkin's relationship with his sister-in-law, see Serene Vitale, *Pushkin's Button* (New York: Farrar, Straus & Giroux, 1999), 68–69, 72, 218, 225. On Tiutchev and Denisieva, see Jesse Zeldin, introduction to *Poems and Political Letters of F. I. Tyutchev* (Knoxville: University of Tennessee, 1973), 6.

13. "[Rostopchin's] instability appeared later. . . . From birth he had manifested irascibility and harshness but had his disposition been restrained by a more skillful hand it might have given his moral character a completely different direction" (L. Rostopchina, "Semeinaia khronika (fragmenty)," 406–7). "Evdokiia Petrovna's marriage was unhappy . . . for many reasons, discussion of which in print I recognize is pointless and indecent" [suspension points in original] (S. Sushkov, "Biograficheskii ocherk," 1: vii:). "[It is known that Rostopchin] was a person with some 'peculiarities,' that he thought little about his wife, dividing most of his time between horse breeding and collecting pictures, and that before 1836 they did not have children" (Khodasevich, "Grafinia E. P. Rostopchina," 39). Kiselev-Sergenin quotes an account claiming that Rostopchin "for a long time kept an actress" ("Taina grafini Rostopchinoi," 277). On Rostopchina's two children by Andrei Karamzin, see Kiselev-Sergenin, "Taina grafini Rostopchinoi," 271; also Goscilo, "Evdokiia Petrovna Rostopchina," in *Dictionary of Russian Women Writers,* 541; I. A. Bitiugova, "Olga Andreevna Golokhastova," in Nikolaev, *Russkie pisateli 1800–1917,* 1: 618–19. Khodasevich implies that her first child, born in 1837, also was not by Rostopchin ("Grafinia E. P. Rostopchina," 41).

14. Kiselev-Sergenin, "Taina grafini Rostopchinoi."

15. For example, Romanov notes that the woman addressee of Rostopchina's book of poetry *Zelenaia kniga* has not been identified (*Stikhotvoreniia, proza, pis'ma,* 410).

16. D. Sushkov, "K biografii grafini E. P. Rostopchinoi"; S. Sushkov, "Biograficheskii ocherk," 1: v–vi.

17. Nekrasova, "Grafinia E. P. Rostopchina," 43–44; Romanov, editor's in-

troduction, 10; N. Alekseeva and Mary Zirin, "Mariia Sushkova," in *Dictionary of Russian Women Writers*, ed. M. Ledkovsky, C. Rosenthal, and M. Zirin, 628–29.

18. Belinskii, "Sochineniia Zeneidy R-voi," in his *Polnoe sobranie sochinenii*, 7: 656. First appeared in *Otechestvennye zapiski* 31, no. 11 (1843): 1–24.

19. S. M. Zagoskin quoted in Filipenko, "Moskovskie literaturnye salony," 52; Khodasevich, "Grafinia E. P. Rostopchina," 40, 44.

20. Pavlova also describes interactions in society as matters of life and death. In her poem "My stranno soshlis'" (We came together strangely, 1854) she compares a salon conversation between two people who have just met to a feud (*raspria*). In her "Za chainym stolom" (At the tea table, 1859) she characterizes the opening conversation between the Princess and Wismer as a "merciless duel" between two "antagonists"—a "seasoned warrior" and "an Amazon"—whose words are compared to "sword thrusts" (Karolina Pavlova, "At the Tea Table," trans. Diana Greene and Mary Zirin, in *Anthology of Russian Women's Writing*, ed. C. Kelley, 37). On the performative aspects of nineteenth-century European society for both men and women, see Rhonda Garelick, *Rising Star: Dandyism, Gender and Performance in the Fin de Siècle* (Princeton, N.J.: Princeton University Press, 1998); Jessica R. Feldman, *Gender on the Divide: The Dandy in Modernist Literature* (Ithaca, N.Y.: Cornell University Press, 1993). On the paradoxes of nineteenth-century women's performance of the female role, see Judith Anne Rosen's dissertation, "Performing Femininity in British Victorian Culture," University of California at Berkeley, 1995.

21. See Vitale's account of Pushkin's appearances at balls, salons, visits, and parties in the months before his duel (*Pushkin's Button*, 218–19, 220, 223).

22. S. Sushkov, "Biograficheskii ocherk," 1: xi–xii; Khodasevich, "Grafinia E. P. Rostopchina," 45.

23. V. F. Odoevskomu, 15-go genvaria [*sic*] 1848, in E. Rostopchina, *Stikhotvoreniia, proza, pis'ma*, 338.

24. L. Rostopchina, "Semeinaia khronika (fragmenty)," 408. On Rostopchina's salon, see Filipenko, "Moskovskie literaturnye salony," and Aronson and Reiser, *Literaturnye kruzhki i salony*, 199–202, 287–89.

25. Quoted in the original French in Khodasevich, "Grafinia E. P. Rostopchina," 45.

26. *Poety 1840–1850-kh godov*, ed. B. Ia. Bukhshtab and E. M. Shneiderman, 474 n. 3. On Rostopchina's translation of Pushkin, see V. Nepomniashchii, "Sud'ba odnogo stikhotvoreniia," *Voprosy literatury* 5 (1984): 144–61.

27. "Vmesto predisloviia," in *Stikhotvoreniia grafini Rostopchinoi*, 2nd. ed. (Sankt-Peterburg: Smirdin, 1856–57), 1: 3–4.

28. Interestingly, the only poem by Rostopchina that Belinskii ever praised unreservedly was "Ravnodushnoi," in which the narrator tells a young and beautiful woman that her intention to take the veil is selfish because God has ordered women to be men's consolation and spiritual salvation. Belinskii wrote, "Yes, *such* thoughts and feelings prove that the talent of Countess Rostopchina can find a wider and more worthy sphere for itself." One wonders if Belinskii would have found the poem as socially significant if the young woman had been depicted as ugly (V. G. Belinskii, "Stikhotvoreniia grafini E. Rostopchinoi," in

his *Polnoe sobranie sochinenii*, 5: 460; italics in original). Judith Vowles writes that "Ravnodushnoi" is directed at Elisaveta Shakhova ("The Inexperienced Muse," 77).

It should be noted that along with Chernyshevskii and Dobroliubov two radical women critics, Ekaterina Nekrasova (1841–1905) and Mar'ia Tsebrikova (1835–1917), also wrote articles attacking Rostopchina. While both women took Rostopchina to task for frivolity and for hostility toward class politics, neither treats Rostopchina with the dismissive contempt of their men colleagues. Tsebrikova even expresses occasional grudging admiration for Rostopchina.

29. Platon Meshcherskii: Khodasevich, "Grafinia E. P. Rostopchina," 39.

Petr Meshcherskii: Romanov, notes to "Neizvestnyi roman," in E. Rostopchina, *Stikhotvoreniia, proza, pis'ma*, 419.

Andrei Karamzin: Kiselev-Sergenin, "Taina grafini E. P. Rostopchinoi," 283. Kiselev-Sergenin congratulates himself on proving that Rostopchina was not the heartless coquette Chernyshevskii claimed she was.

30. Afanas'ev, "'Da, zhenskaia dusha,'" 6; quotation from Pletnev, letter to Ia. K. Grot, December 10, 1840, in E. Rostopchina, *Talisman*, 276.

31. N. A. Dobroliubov, "U pristani," *Sovremennik* 10 (1857), reprinted in N. A. Dobroliubov, *Sobranie sochinenii v trekh tomakh* (Moskva: Gos. izd. khudozhestvennoi literatury, 1950), 1: 423–39.

Rostopchina's political views cannot be easily categorized. Kiselev-Sergenin speculates that Rostopchina denounced the 1848 revolutions in order to get back into the good graces of Nicholas I after the publication of "Nasil'nyi brak" ("Po staromu sledu," 146). Certainly, starting in 1853 Rostopchina wrote a series of patriotic poems embodying the doctrine of Nicholas's regime: *pravoslavie, samoderzhavie, i narodnost'* (orthodoxy, autocracy, nationality). See "Nashim brat'iam: Iugo-vostochnym pravoslavnym" (To our brothers: The southeastern Orthodox, 1853), "Khristianam" (To Christians, 1854), "Otvet nekotorym bezymiannym stikhtotvoreniam" (Answer to some anonymous poetry, 1854), "Na osviashchenie edinovercheskoi tserkvi" (On the sanctifaction of the Edinoverie Church [an Old Believer sect that reached an organizational compromise with the official Orthodox Church], 1854), "Pesnia russkim voinam, ranenym v Sevastopole" (Song for the Russian warriors wounded in Sevastopol, 1855), "Molitva ob opolchennykh" (Prayer about the militia, 1855), "Alekseiu Petrovichu Ermolovu" (1855), "Molitva za sviatuiu Rus'" (Prayer for Holy Russia, 1855), "Russkomu narodu" (For the Russian people, 1855), and "Kuplety" (Couplets, 1856). On official nationality, see Nicholas Riasanovsky, *Nicholas I and Official Nationality in Russia, 1825–1855* (Berkeley: University of California Press, 1969).

In addition, like Baratynskii, Zhukovskii, and other poets of the Golden Age who lived into the 1830s, 1840s, and 1850s, Rostopchina regretted its passing (Mirsky, *History of Russian Literature*, 75) and criticized the views of the *raznochintsy* (nineteenth-century radical intellectuals of nonaristocratic origins) in her poetry and letters. See Baratynskii's "Poslednii poet" (1835) and Rostopchina's "Oda poezii: Anakhronizm" (Ode to poetry: An anachronism, 1852) and "Moim kritikam" (To my critics, 1856); also Rostopchina's letters to A. V. Druzhinin (May 27, 1854, and Oct. 28, 1854) in E. Rostopchina, *Stikhotvoreniia, proza, pis'ma*, 364–65, 368–69.

However, Rostopchina at the end of her life had notices put into two French newspapers in which, while denying that she had written several epigrams against Russian officials attributed to her, she depicted herself as a revolutionary poet. "Completely independent in heart and soul, she can openly express her ideas, even at the risk of displeasing extremely suspicious people. But the pen that inscribed and made famous 'Nasil'nyi brak' (1845) and 'Jan. 29, 1837' (unpublished verses on the death of the poet Pushkin) that pen would never lower itself to lampoons and epigrams" (Kiselev-Sergenin, "Po staromu sledu," 148, cited in Russian translation). And, as we shall see, Rostopchina could not be considered conservative in the views about women she expressed as late as 1854.

32. Khodasevich in "Grafinia E. P. Rostopchina" uses the word *banal'nost'* (banality) to describe Rostopchina seven times. Bykov: "Her generation attributed too great a significance to her poetic activity" ("Russkie zhenshchiny-pisatel'nitsy," 241).

33. As mentioned in the introduction, in the 1960s Rostopchina was considered a forgotten poet. Starting in the 1970s Rostopchina's work appeared in anthologies such as *Poety 1840–50-kh godov* (1972), *Russkie poetessy XIX veka* (1979), *Tsaritsy muz* (1989), *Moskovskaia muza* (1998), and in separate volumes such as *Stikhotvoreniia, proza, pis'ma* (1986), *Talisman* (1989), and *Schastlivaia zhenshchina* (1991).

Mikhail Fainshtein uncomfortably echoes N. A. Dobroliubov in stating that the characters in Rostopchina's novel *U pristani* "somehow lack moral qualities" (*Pisatelnitsy pushkinskoi pory,* 100). In general, though, Soviet criticism ignored the details of Rostopchina's sexual life, as it did those of all public and historical figures.

Rostopchina as a patriot: Romanov, editor's introduction, 12; Afanas'ev, "'Da, zhenskaia dusha,'" 15. The first of a selection of her unknown poems, which appeared in *Molodaia gvardiia* in 1989 ("Zvuki chistoi dushi," 3: 185–87), was her patriotic ode "Na pamiatnik Susanilu."

Rostopchina as protestor against society: Romanov, editor's introduction, 11, 16, 19; Afanas'ev, "'Da, zhenskaia dusha,'" 11.

34. K. Pavlova, *Double Life.* For recent Pavlova criticism, see chapter 6.

35. Aksakov, *Ivan Sergeevich Aksakov v ego pis'makh* (Moskva: M. G. Volchaninov, 1888), 1: 307.

36. Nikolai Chernyshevskii, "Novye knigi," *Sovremennik* 56, section 4 (1856): 11.

37. Romanov, editor's introduction, 5–27. "It is possible to follow Rostopchina's whole life in her verse as in a diary" (Khodasevich, "Grafinia E. P. Rostopchina," 39). "Whatever Rostopchina wrote about, she first and foremost wrote about herself" (Romanov, editor's introduction, 22). Sergei Ernst in a 1916 article ("Karolina Pavlova i gr. Evdokiia Rastopchina," 22) wrote that "all the volumes of Countess Rostopchina's poetry function as if they were her diary—a repository of everything its owner felt and experienced, great and small, good and bad," a characterization Pedrotti approvingly paraphrased in 1986 ("Scandal of Countess Rostopčina's Polish-Russian Allegory," 211). Nekrasova ("Grafinia E. P. Rostopchina," 44–45) uses Rostopchina's novel, *Schastlivaia zhen-*

shchina, as a source of biographical information, and Romanov (editor's introduction, 22) discusses Rostopchina's novel in verse, *Dnevnik devuskhi*, exclusively as autobiography. Similarly, in a review of Rostopchina's 1856 poetry collection, "Stikhotvoreniia grafini Rostopchinoi," Chernyshevskii assumed that all of Rostopchina's poems had the same speaker, who was Rostopchina herself. Chernyshevskii called this speaker Rostopchina's "lyric I" and proceeded to lambaste it for immorality.

38. "It is well known that with Pushkin the authorial 'bio' and the lyric 'I' of his heroes are often very close, almost merging" (Yuri Druzhnikov, *Contemporary Russian Myths*, 153).

39. Khodasevich, "Grafinia E. P. Rostopchina," 45; Pedrotti, "Scandal of Countess Rostopčina's Polish-Russian Allegory," 211–12; Uchenova, *Tsaritsy muz*, 5–6; and Romanov, editor's introduction, 17.

40. On women's defensive use of the "modesty topos," see introduction and Mellor, *Romanticism and Gender*, 8.

41. Belinskii, "Stikhotvoreniia grafini E. Rostopchinoi, "*Polnoe sobranie sochinenii*, 5: 459; Ernst, "Karolina Pavlova i gr. Evdokiia Rastopchina," 32; Ranchin, editor's introduction, 5 n. 2. See also Bernice Carroll's "The Politics of Originality: Women and the Class System of the Intellect," in which she argues that "original" is a political term used to create "lines of inheritance for control of rewards" for powerful men, rewards that are denied to women, among others (147).

42. Nekrasova, "Grafinia E. P. Rostopchina," 51; Aronson and Reiser, *Literaturnye kruzhki i salony*, 287.

43. Sandler, introduction to *Rereading Russian Poetry*, 5. Rostopchina invariably used *poèt*, never *poetessa*, for her female personas. See her "Poslednii tsvetok" (1835), "Iskushenie" (1839), "Pesn' vozvrata" (1847), and *Dnevnik devushki* 6: iii.

44. We find Rostopchina referred to as a "*poèt*" in reviews by Pletnev, Aksakov, Kireevskii (*Polnoe sobranie sochinenii* [Moskva: V. tip. Bakhmeteva, 1861 [reprint, Ann Arbor: Ardis, 1983], 1: 118); Druzhinin, Bykov, Berg, and Belinskii ("Stikhotvoreniia grafini E. Rostopchinoi," in *Polnoe sobranie sochinenii*, 4: 456) although, as we have seen, they discuss her work in gendered and condescending terms. Later nineteenth-century writers (Chernyshevskii, Ernst, and Rostopchina's brother Sergei Sushkov) refer to her as a *poetessa*, as do all twentieth-century accounts of Rostopchina that I have read (Khodasevich, Ranchin, Romanov, Afanas'ev, Kiselev, and Fainshtein). Fainshtein unconsciously illustrates the change from calling Rostopchina a *poèt* to a *poetessa*. He writes, "Pletnev . . . wrote about the talent of the *poetessa*, 'She is without doubt the first *poèt* now of Russia'" (*Pisatel'nitsy pushkinskoi pory*, 92; italics mine). Rostopchina appears to have been demoted still further from *poèt*; she recently appeared on a Russian newspaper's daily birthday list identified as *literator* (man/woman of letters), a term generally not associated with poets ("Odinnadtsataia polosa: Dni rozhdeniia," *Moskovskii komsomolets*, Jan. 4, 1999, 643Kb, Universal Database of Russian Newspapers, July 20, 2000).

45. Ivan Aksakov, "Stikhotvoreniia grafini E. P. Rastopchina [sic]," in his *Ivan Sergeevich Aksakov v ego pismakh*, 1: 309, 310–12.

46. *Rastianutyi:* Ranchin, editor's introduction, 9; Bannikov, *Russkie poetessy XIX veka,* 44. *Zatianuty:* Romanov, editor's introduction, 24. Her brother Sergei Sushkov (1: xxvi) deplores the "slishkom obil'nom kolichestve eia pozdnieishikh proizvedenii" (the too abundant quantity of her late works). Ernst, in "Karolina Pavlova i gr. Evdokiia Rastopchina," uses the word *slishkom* (too much) at least five times in relation to Rostopchina.

47. Rostopchina's popularity because of women: Khodasevich, "Grafinia E. P. Rostopchina," 46: "Readers, especially women, were carried away with admiration"; Bykov, "Russkie zhenshchiny-pisatel'nitsy," 240: "She had particularly warm admirers among women"; Druzhinin, "Stikhotvoreniia grafini Rostopchinoi," 7: 157: "Countess Rostopchina has the most passionate worshippers among women"; S. Sushkov, "Biograficheskii ocherk," 1: ix: "All Russian intelligent society was carried away by admiration [for her verses], in particular, the representatives of its beautiful half"; Romanov, editor's introduction, 16: "Her verse was widely read and copied (especially by ladies)." An example of the charge that her work lacked universality can be found in Ernst, "Karolina Pavlova i gr. Evdokiia Rastopchina," 34.

48. Kline, "Baratynsky," in *Handbook of Russian Literature,* ed. Victor Terras, 39, 40.

49. Kermode, *Forms of Attention,* 72, 74, 76, 90. This is not to ignore the fact that the reputations of canonical writers can suffer periods of eclipse, as did Pushkin's at the end of his life and immediately following his death.

50. For example, Rostopchina's daughter suggests that Belinskii, Russia's most influential critic, only started attacking Rostopchina's work because she would not receive him in her salon (L. A. Rostopchina, "Pravda o moei babushke," 95: 868.

Also very influential was the condescending introduction of Rostopchina's brother Sergei Sushkov to the 1890 edition of her works, which he edited. Sushkov was a political conservative, an officer in the Caucuses, and later in Paris editor of the Russian Orthodox *L'Union chrétienne* ("Biograficheskii ocherk," ix, xliv). During Rostopchina's lifetime he tried to prevent her from publishing her "Doch' Don Zhuana" (Don Juan's daughter) because he considered it indecent. See A. F. Koni, "Iz portfeli starogo zhurnalista," *Russkii arkhiv* 3, no. 257 (1909). In his introduction Sushkov criticized Rostopchina's writing style, attributed her literary success to her looks and to the fact that she was a woman, and claimed she wrote "Nasil'nyi brak" "under the influence of false and stupid gossip she heard abroad" (x, xvi). In general, it is worth comparing this edition of Rostopchina's work with the 1856–57 edition that Rostopchina herself oversaw. There are significant differences.

On the inhospitableness of Soviet ideology and socialist realist criticism to women's experience, see the introduction. Also Norma Noonan, "Marxism and Feminism in the USSR: Irreconcilable Differences?" *Women and Politics* 8, no. 1 (1988): 31–49; Helena Goscilo, "Paradigm Lost? Contemporary Women's Fiction," 205–28.

51. See chapter 1 for the development in the first third of the nineteenth century of the image of the poetess along with domestic ideology.

52. Among the several studies and anthologies of American and British po-

etesses are Walker, *Nightingale's Burden;* Ostriker, *Stealing the Language;* Walker, *American Women Poets of the Nineteenth Century;* Feldman, *British Women Poets of the Romantic Era;* Ashfield, *Romantic Women Poets 1770–1838;* Linkin and Behrendt, *Romanticism and Women Poets.*

It should be remembered that socioeconomic conditions for women differed in Russia, the United States, and Britain. So, for example, in the United States a middle-class woman could earn "significant amounts of money by publishing poetry" in magazines for a new "semi-educated class" of women (Walker, *American Women Poets,* xxii; Walker, *Nightingale's Burden,* 36). Walker estimates that in the United States in the mid-nineteenth century five hundred women worked as writers, editors, and contributors to such journals, a circumstance that affected the quantity and quality of poetry written (*Nightingale's Burden,* 74). Such was not the case in Russia.

53. Susan Wolfson, "Felicia Hemans and the Revolving Doors of Reception," in *Romanticism and Women Poets,* 214.

54. E. Rostopchina, "Iz portfel'ia starogo zhurnalista," 257–58. Domestic ideology portrayed women as both morally superior to men and obliged to be submissive to them ("the angel in the house"). Some women in the United States and elsewhere attempted to use this contradiction to empower women. See my "Mid-nineteenth-Century Domestic Ideology in Russia," 88.

55. *Ocherki bol'shogo sveta* (1839); *Stikhotvoreniia* (1841); *Neliudimka* (1850); *Schastlivaia zhenshchina* (1852); *U pristani* (1857); *Polnoe sobranie stikhotvorenii* (1856–57).

56. Belinskii obliquely refers to "Iskushenie" in "Sochineniia Zeneidy R-voi" when he writes, "All [Rostopchina's] thoughts and feelings seem to whirl to the music of Strauss," an allusion to the lines "With their invincible playfulness / The waltzes of Laner and Strauss captivate the beautiful women" (*Polnoe sobranie sochinenii,* 7: 656). See Bykov, "Russkie zhenshchiny-pisatel'nitsy," 242; Ernst, "Karolina Pavlova i gr. Evdokiia Rastopchina," 28; Chernyshevskii, "Stikhotvoreniia grafini Rostopchinoi," 2; Nekrasova, "Grafinia E. P. Rostopchina," 46; Tsebrikova, "Russkiia zhenshchiny pisatel'nitsy," 437. Afanas'ev suggests that Rostopchina was not serious when she wrote the poem ("'Da, zhenskaia dusha,'" 11).

More than 130 years later it was still considered shocking to question women's primary vocation as mother. See Dorothy Dinnerstein, *The Mermaid and the Minotaur: Sexual Arrangements and Human Malaise* (New York: Harper & Row, 1976).

57. E.g., Afanas'ev, "'Da, zhenskaia dusha,'" 9.

58. Osgood quoted in Walker, *American Women Poets of the Nineteenth Century,* 133. Similarly, the U.S. editor and poet Sarah Hale wrote, "The path of poetry, like every other path in life, is to the tread of woman exceedingly circumscribed. She may not revel in the luxuriance of fancies, images and thoughts, or indulge in the license of choosing themes at will, like the lords of creation" (quoted in Ostriker, *Stealing the Language,* 30).

59. Among the few scholars to credit Rostopchina with irony are Stephanie Sandler ("Law, the Body, and the Book," 36) and Catriona Kelly (*History of Russian Women's Writing,* 46).

60. *Dnevnik devuskhi* first appeared serialized in *Moskvitianin,* starting with the March 1850 issue, as *Poeziia i proza zhizni: Dnevnik devushki: Roman v stikhakh,* with the note "pisano 1839–41, ispravleno 1845" (written in 1839–41, revised 1845). N. A. Dobroliubov, *"U pristani,"* in *Sobranie sochinenii* (Moskva: Gos. izd. khud. lit., 1962), 2: 71; Bannikov, *Russkie poetessy XIX veka,* 44; Romanov, editor's introduction, 9, 22. Excerpts appear in *Schastlivaia zhenshchina* (Moskva: Izd. Pravda, 1991).

61. See Dale Spender's discussion of sexual harassment in the intellectual realm (*Women of Ideas and What Men Have Done to Them,* 22–24).

Chapter 5. Nadezhda Khvoshchinskaia

1. On Khvoshchinskaia, see Hoogenboom, Hilde, and Arja Rosenholm, *Ia zhivu ot pochty do pochty: Iz perepiski N.D. Khvoshchinskoi* (Wilhelmhorst: Verlag F. K. Gopfort, 2001); and Hoogenboom, Hilde, and and Arja Rosenholm, eds. *The Sisters Khvoshchinskoi* (Amsterdam: Rodopi, forthcoming). On Khvoshchinskaia as a prose writer, see L. A. Chizhikov, *Nadezhda Dmitrievna Khvoshchinskaia-Zaionchkovskaia (V. Krestovskii-psevdonim) 20 maia, 1825–1889 iiun' 8: Bibliografiche-skie o nei materialy* (Odessa: Tsentral'naia tipografiia S. Rozenshtraukha i N. Lemberga, 1914); Jehanne Gheith, *Finding the Middle Ground: Krestovskii, Tur, and the Power of Ambivalence in Nineteenth-Century Russian Women's Prose* (Evanston, Ill.: Northwestern University Press, 2003); Ledkovsky, Rosenthal, and Zirin, *Dictionary of Russian Women Writers,* 286–88; K. D. Muratova, ed., *Istoriia russkoi litera-tury XIX veka: Bibliograficheskii ukazatel'* (Moskva: Izd. Akademi Nauk SSSR, 1962), 381–83; Arja Rosenholm, "Writing the Self: Creativity and the Female Author: Nadezhda Dmitrievna Khvoshchinskaya (1824–89)," in *Gender Restructuring in Russian Studies,* ed. Marianne Liljestrom, Eila Mantysaari, and Arja Rosenholm (Tampere, Finland: University of Tampere, 1993), 193–208; Karen Rosneck, intro-duction to Nadezhda Khvoshchinskaya, *The Boarding-School Girl* (Evanston, Ill.: Northwestern University Press, 2000), ix–xxx; Karla Thomas Solomon, "Na-dezhda Khvoshchinskaia," in *Russian Women Writers,* ed. Christine Tomei, 1: 261–67; Mary Zirin, "Women's Prose Fiction in the Age of Realism," in *Women Writers in Russian Literature,* ed. Toby W. Clyman and Diana Greene, 86–88.

At most, these works mention in passing that Khvoshchinskaia started her literary career by writing poetry. One exception is A. P. Mogilianskii, who writes that Khvoshchinskaia has been underrated as a poet and refers to "nalichie u nee nezauradnogo poeticheskogo darovaniia" (the presence in her of an excep-tional poetic gift) ("N. D. i S. D. Khvoshchinskie," 234–35). He does not, how-ever, discuss any of Khvoshchinskaia's poetry. Besides writing poetry and prose, Khvoshchinskaia wrote criticism in *Otechestvennye zapiski* under the name Porechnikov and in *Russkie vedomosti* under various initials.

2. Biographical information is based on A. [G.] Karrik, "Iz vospominanii o N. D. Khvoshchinskoi-Zaionchkovskoi," *Zhenskoe delo,* nos. 9, 11, 12 (1899); P. Khvoshchinskaia, "Nadezhda Khvoshchinskaia," 1: i–xviii; Ledkovsky, Ro-senthal, and Zirin, *Dictionary of Russian Women Writers,* 286–91; Semevskii, "N. D. Khvoshchinskaia-Zaionchkovskaia"; Tsebrikova, "Ocherk zhizni N. D. Khvoshchinskoi-Zaionchkovskoi."

Khvoshchinskaia's year of birth appears as 1825 in several nineteenth-century sources: N. N. Golitsyn, *Bibliograficheskii slovar' russkikh pisatel'nits*, 262; D. D. Iazykov, *Obzor zhizni i trudov russkikh pisatelei i pisatel'nits* (Moskva: Universitetskaia tipografiia, 1905), 9: 25; Semevskii, "N. D. Khvoshchinskaia-Zaionchkovskaia"; Tsebrikova, "Ocherk zhizni N. D. Khvoshchinskoi-Zaionchkovskoi," in *Russkii biografifcheskii slovar'* (Moskva and Sankt-Peterburg: Imp. Russkoe Istoricheskoe obshchestvo, 1896–1918), 21: 301–3; and even in Muratova, *Istoriia russkoi literatury XIX veka: Ukazatel'*, 381. It appears as 1824, however, in the most authoritative and most recent sources: the biographical essay by Khvoshchinskaia's sister Praskov'ia, "Nadezhda Khvoshchinskaia," and in the memoir of a close friend, A. G. Karrik, "Iz vospominanii," as well as in *Istoriia russkoi literatury*, vol. 9, part. 2, 234; *Kratkaia literaturnaia entsiklopediia* (Moskva: Sovetskaia Entsiklopediia, 1962–75); Ledkovsky, Rosenthal, and Zirin, *Dictionary of Russian Women Writers*, 286; and Tomei, *Russian Women Writers*, 1: 261. Aleksandr Potapov mentions documents indicating that Khvoshchinskaia was born in 1822 (*Neizrechennyi svet: Deviat' vekov Riazani: Literatura* (Riazan': Novoe vremia, 1996), 52.

3. One uncle paid for Sof'ia Khvoshchinskaia's education at the Moscow Ekaterininskii institut. Other relatives in Saint Petersburg introduced Khvoshchinskaia into literary circles when she first visited there in 1852. One of Dmitrii Kesarevich's brothers helped him to get reinstated in the civil service.

4. Khvoshchinskaia is quoted as writing of her family's financial problems: "In this way I was led very early to know life in all its details and poverty, and people in all their relations and injustices. Our father, while loving and taking care of us, didn't keep his troubles from us and didn't let us grow up ignorant of life's difficulties" (Semevskii, "N. D. Khvoshchinskaia-Zaionchkovskaia," 10: 50).

5. P. Khvoshchinskaia, "Nadezhda Khvoshchinskaia," viii. This is not to idealize Dmitrii Kesarevich. One gathers from Praskov'ia Khvoshchinskaia's memoir that he was a hypersensitive, choleric, and irritable person: "Nervous and impatient, he was constantly getting irritated. His old friend . . . was afraid of our father's irascible disposition. . . . The governor tried to calm father down" (vii); "[N. D.] used to have heated arguments with father" (viii); "This made a terrible, frightening impression on Father, very suspicious by nature" (vii); "Father was so agitated by the account of everything he had lived through, that he felt faint" (ii). Senkovskii writes that in 1888, the year before she died, Khvoshchinskaia started writing a story about a young woman exploited by her father ("N. D. Khvoshchinskaia-Zaionchkovskaia," *Russkaia mysl'* 12 [1890]: 142).

6. The inscription is cited in Semevskii, "N. D. Khvoshchinskaia-Zaionchkovskaia," 10: 53. Khvoshchinskaia wrote, "Ia pisala mnogo stikhov; eto nravilos' osobenno moemu ottsu" (I wrote many poems; this particularly pleased my father) (quoted in Semevskii, ibid. The notebook is now located in f. 541, ed. 3, no. 1, RGALI).

7. Semevskii, "N. D. Khvoshchinskaia-Zaionchkovskaia," 10: 58. P. Khvoshchinskaia, "Nadezhda Khvoshchinskaia," ii, and Tsebrikova, "Ocherk zhizni," 7–8, also discuss relatives' and neighbors' disapproval of Khvoshchinskaia's writing.

8. Accounts of Khvoshchinskaia's depressions appear in P. Khvoshchinskaia, Semevskii, and Tsebrikova.

9. Tsebrikova recounts that A. A. Kraevskii, editor of *Otechestvennye zapiski*, consistently underpaid Khvoshchinskaia for her work or did not pay her at all; she also describes the abusiveness of Khvoshchinskaia's husband. Praskov'ia Khvoshchinskaia depicts Khvoshchinskaia's goddaughter, Sonia, and Vera Aleksandrovna Moskaleva, with whom Khvoshchinskaia lived at the end of her life, as unworthy of her sister. Praskov'ia Khvoshchinskaia, however, appears to have been jealous of Sonia and was angry at Moskaleva, who, she claimed, alienated Khvoshchinskaia from her family. In any case, Khvoshchinskaia in the course of her life managed to free herself from Zotov's abusive tutelage, from her husband, and from life in Riazan'. For Khvoshchinskaia's feelings about Riazan', see Semevskii, "N. D. Khvoshchinskaia-Zaionchkovskaia," 12: 126–27, and Semevskii, "N. D. Khvoshchinskaia-Zaionchkovskaia," *Russkaia starina* (Feb. 1891): 462.

10. For discussion of the gynosocial world of nineteenth-century American women, see Caroll Smith-Rosenberg, *Disorderly Conduct: Visions of Gender in Victorian America* (New York: Oxford University Press, 1985). For comparison with the Brontës, see Ol'ga Demidova, "Khvoshchinskaia, Sofiia Dmitrievna," in Ledkovsky, Rosenthal, and Zirin, *Dictionary of Russian Women Writers*, 289.

11. Karrik in "Iz vospominanii o N. D. Khvoshchinskoi" describes the group of young women that formed around the Khvoshchinskaia sisters in Riazan'.

12. Vinitskaia, "Vospominaniia o N. D. Khvoshchinskoi," 155. On the writers Aleksandra Aleksandrovna Vinitskaia and Mar'ia Tsebrikova, see Ledkovsky, Rosenthal, and Zirin, *Dictionary of Russian Women Writers*, 714–15, 659–62.

13. For a concise explanation of essentialist versus socially constructed theories of gender, see Jagose, *Queer Theory*, 8–9. The following discussion, which documents changes in the definition of femininity between the late nineteenth and the early twenty-first century, supports the socially constructed position.

14. Petr Boborykin, editor of *Biblioteka dlia chteniia* 1863–65, quoted in Semevskii, "N. D. Khvoshchinskaia-Zaionchkovskaia," 10: 76–77.

15. We find similar (and generally negative) sex-appeal ratings in memoirs and biographies of Karolina Pavlova (see chapter 6, note 14), Anna Mordovtseva, and Evdokiia Rostopchina.

Ivan Gorizontov, who tutored Mordovtseva's daughter, described the poet in the following way: "A[nna] N[ikanorovna] did not at all conform to that standard by which I measured the female sex; she little resembled a 'lady' or even a woman: her hair cut short, dressed in some kind of dressing gown, loud, distinct, and firm in speech, with bold, sweeping gestures, with a face sharply defined by large features, she reminded me more of a man than a 'lady'" ("Fel'eton: Vospominanie ob Anne Nikanorovne Mordovtsevoi," 1). Of course, even if a woman poet was considered to have sex appeal, that did not protect her from ridicule, as we have seen in Rostopchina's case.

16. "Net, ia ne nazovu," no. 179 in Khvoshchinskaia's notebook, first published in *Otechestvennye zapiski*, no. 8 (1852), also in *Panteon*, no. 8 (1852), and in

Sbornik luchshikh proizvedenii russkoi poezii, ed. Nikolai Shcherbina (Sankt-Peterburg: E. Prats, 1858), 400. Regarding critical interpretation, see Tsebrikova, "Ocherk zhizni," 4; A. Karrik, "Iz Vospominaniia o N. D. Khvoshchinskoi-Zaionchkovskoi," 12: 82; N. V. Gerbel', *Russkie poety v biografiakh i obraztsakh* (Sankt-Peterburg: Tip. Imperatorskaia Akademii Nauk, 1879), 583; and *Poety 1840–1850-kh godov*, 266–67. "Net, ia ne nazovu obmanom" is also cited as one of Khvoshchinskaia's three best poems in the *Russkii biograficheskii slovar'*.

17. Regarding her cigar smoking, see Tsebrikova, "Ocherk zhizni," 8; Semevskii, "N. D. Khvoshchinskaia-Zaionchkovskaia," 10: 55; P. Khvoshchinskaia, "Nadezhda Khvoshchinskaia," ix; Karrik, 4. As recently as 1999 Khvoshchinskaia was described as having "masculine habits" (Tomei, *Russian Women Writers*, 262; Semevskii, "N. D. Khvoshchinskaia-Zaionchkovskaia," 12: 142; Tsebrikova, "Ocherk zhizni," 39).

18. Belinskii, "Sochineniia Zeneidy R-voi," in his *Polnoe sobranie sochinenii*, 7: 654. First published in *Otechestvennye zapiski* 31, no. 1, section 5 (1843): 1–24. Men critics continued to use such sexual metaphors to denigrate women's achievements well into the twentieth century. One also thinks of Osip Mandel'shtam's comment, cited in English by Svetlana Boym: "Adalis and Marina Tsvetaeva are prophetesses, and so is Sophia Parnok. Their prophecy is like domestic needlework." Boym points out, "In this cultural paradigm women can excel only in *textiles*, but not in *texts*" (*Death in Quotation Marks*, 193, 195, author's italics).

Similarly, Mary Ellmann quotes several contemporary men writers who compare "the female mind" to a uterus, a kitchen, or a temple, "an enclosed space in which what other and (as we always say) *seminal* minds have provided is stored away or tended or worshipped"; a "domestic container of some sort, a recipe file or Thermos jug . . . always as an empty object in which others put things" (*Thinking about Women*, 13–15, author's italics).

19. Semevskii, "N. D. Khvoshchinskaia-Zaionchkovskaia," 10: 134. Semevskii calls Khvoshchinskaia cowardly (10: 55), expresses disapproval at the fact that she was thirteen years older than her husband (11: 83), and dismisses many of her literary critical views (11: 110).

20. Smith-Rosenberg, "Female World of Love and Ritual: Relations between Women in Nineteenth-Century America," 1–29; and Jonathan Ned Katz, *The Invention of Heterosexuality* (New York: Dutton, 1995), 50–51.

21. On the nineteenth-century belief that "good women had no sex drive," see Faderman, *Surpassing the Love of Men*, 156, 149–77.

22. D. D. Iazykov, *Obzor zhizni i trudov pokoinykh russkikh pisatelei* (Sankt-Peterburg: Tip. A. S. Suborina, 1885–1916); Masanov, *Slovar' psevdonimov.*

23. Karrik, "Iz vospominanii," 39; Zotov, "Nadezhda Dmitrievna Khvoshchinskaia," 96–97.

24. On domestic ideology in Russia, see my "Mid-nineteenth-Century Domestic Ideology in Russia," 78–97.

25. Tsebrikova, "Ocherk zhizni," 9–10; Semevskii, "N. D. Khvoshchinskaia-Zaionchkovskaia," 10: 58, 59 n. 3, 63, 65, 96.

26. Anne Mellor in referring to the "modesty topos" (see introduction) sug-

gests that at least some women writers treated socially prescribed modesty as a literary convention (*Romanticism and Gender*, 8). Some, however, took the injunction against women's writing much more seriously, as I argue in chapter 1.

27. On Khvoshchinskaia's "modesty," see, for example, Bykov, *Siluety dalekogo proshlogo*, 184. Praskov'ia Khvoshchinskaia wrote that her sister opposed all *posmertnaia glasnost'* (posthumous publicity, xiii) and claims to have written a biographical essay about her (which appeared anonymously as the introduction to an edition of Khvoshchinskaia's collected works) only to defend the reputation of her family.

28. For various commentaries on Dickinson's rejection of fame in this poem, see Joseph Duchac, *The Poems of Emily Dickinson: An Annotated Guide to Commentary Published in English 1890–1977* (Boston: G. K. Hall, 1979), 277–79, and Ostriker, *Stealing the Language*, 40–41.

29. Tsebrikova writes of Khvoshchinskaia's refusal to allow obituaries of Sof'ia ("Ocherk zhizni," 12). On Khvoshchinskaia's anger at Zotov, see Bykov, *Siluety dalekogo proshlogo*, 185, 186. Tsibrikova discusses Khvoshchinskaia's use of male pseudonyms for her literary criticism in order not be identified ("Ocherk zhizni," 28–29).

30. Charlotte Rosenthal and Mary Zirin write that while Russian women felt free to publish under their own names during the Golden Age, when lyrical poetry, a "feminine" genre, dominated, "during the period of Russian realism (roughly 1850 to 1880) women . . . increasingly resorted to masculine or neuter-gendered pseudonyms in order to get a fair hearing for their portrayals of contemporary society" ("Russia," 111).

31. Mogilianskii, "N. D. i S. D. Khvoshchinskaia," 234. Also mentioned in A. Chechneva, "Soratnitsa velikikh: Nadezhda Dmitrievna Khvoshchinskaia," in *Gordost' zemli Riazanskoi* (Moskva: Moskovskii Rabochii, 1973), 238. My thanks to Romy Taylor for bringing the poem to my attention. It is also possible that even earlier poems by Khvoshchinskaia appeared in *Illustratsiia*, as she sent at least one poem to this journal under the pseudonym Dans L'espace according to her sister, Praskov'ia ("Nadezhda Khvoshchinskaia," 8). Thanks to Karen Rosneck for this suggestion.

32. Rosenthal, Ledkovsky, and Zirin, eds., *Dictionary of Russian Women Writers*, 287; *Russkie pisateli, 1800–1917: Biograficheskii slovar'* (Moskva: Izd-vo "Sovetskaia Entsiklopediia," 1989–), 3: 355.

33. On the Petrashevskii circle and its "satellite groups," see Joseph Frank, *Dostoevsky: The Seeds of Revolt, 1821–1849* (Princeton, N.J.: Princeton University Press, 1976), 273, 241–91.

34. A. G. Dement'eva, A. V. Zapadov, and M. S. Cherepakhov, eds., *Russkaia periodicheskaia pechat' 1702–1894: Spravochnik* (Moskva: Gosudarstvennoe izd-vo politicheskoi literatury, 1959), 362.

35. Semevskii, "N. D. Khvoshchinskaia-Zaionchkovskaia," 10: 54, and Tsebrikova, "Ocherk zhizni," 7, state that Khvoshchinskaia was not paid for her poetry.

In 1890, a year after Khvoshchinskaia's death, Zotov wrote: "I have more than 120 poems by N. D., written by her in the course of the first twelve years of her literary career (1846–57). Of these I placed in various periodical publications fewer than half. In entrusting her verses to me she always wished to see them collected in a book. Now such a book, comprised of her best pieces, would fill out the literary profile of a sympathetic authoress [*pisatel'nitsa*]" ("Peterburg v sorokovykh godakh," 558).

36. Zotov also wrote about Khvoshchinskaia in his memoir "Peterburg v sorokovykh godov," *Istovicheskii vestnik* 5 (May 1890): 296–300, and in "Peter-burgskii vestnik literatury," *Panteon* 8 (August 1852): 13–21. Even when Zotov claims to be quoting from Khvoshchinskaia's letters, one hesitates to accept his citations as accurate. As late as 1890 he was still rewriting her poems, as can be seen by comparing three that he published for the first time that year (*Istorich-eskii vestnik,* no. 6, 556–57) with their autograph versions. Those poems all con-cern the 1848 revolutions: "Sredi bor'by i razrushen'ia," no. 190 in the notebook; "Tri slova!" no. 195 in the notebook; and "Opiat' temno v dali," no. 191 in the notebook.

37. F. 541, ed. 3, no. 1, RGALI. It would appear that the larger notebook is the one discussed in Anna Chechneva, "'Gore tselogo mira volnuet mne dushu . . .': Tetrad'. I tselaia zhizn'," in *Literaturnaia Riazan'* (Moskva: Moskovskii Rabochii, 1990), 275–79, an article that describes and cites from it without identifying its location. It is possible, however, that additional autograph notebooks (e.g., the notebooks that Khvoshchinskaia sent Zotov) are extant.

38. Blotting-books (notebooks composed of blotting paper for writing letters, etc. away from a desk), although perhaps an obscure artifact today, were taken for granted in nineteenth-century Europe and America, as reflected in the liter-ature of the time. For example, in Victor Hugo's *Les Misérables,* in the chapter titled "Buvard, Bavard" (IV: 15: 1), Cosette's blotting-book, left open in front of a mirror, shows Jean Valjean the contents of the note she has just written to Mar-ius. My thanks to Nancy Burstein for drawing my attention to this example. In Sarah Orne Jewett's *The Country of the Pointed Firs* (1896) the narrator writes, "I reached for my hat, and taking blotting-book under my arm . . . walked out past the fragrant green garden and up the dusty road" (New York: Dover, 1994), 5.

39. On Zotov's 1890 memoir see note 36. Zotov, "Peterburg v sorokovykh godakh," 558, and "Nadezhda Dmitrievna Khvoshchinskaia," 94.

In the discussion that follows, I identify each poem from Khvoshchinskaia's notebook by the number that appears above it. (For convenience, I have changed these Roman numerals to Arabic.) Although Khvoshchinskaia also numbered the poems (in Arabic numerals) in the notebook's table of contents, she appears accidentally to have skipped several titles, starting with no. 99. Thus, the num-ber of the poem in the table of contents does not always correspond to its more reliable number in the notebook itself. Here and elsewhere I assume that Khvoshchinskaia sent Zotov her poems in the same form in which they appear in the notebooks.

40. For example, Brenda Hillman discusses the "intellectual and physical excitement" created by Dickinson's "quirkish punctuation" and criticizes the "pre-1955 bowdlerized punctuation, all the 'correct' periods and commas" (preface to *Emily Dickinson, Poems,* vii, xi). See also Brita Lindberg-Seyersted,

Emily Dickinson's Punctuation (Oslo: American Institute, University of Oslo, 1976), 1–5, for a summary of scholarship on the importance of punctuation in the work of Dickinson and others.

41. It is possible that Zotov excised some of these eighteen lines because of fear of censorship, but several of the censored lines pose no possible threat to church or state.

42. Charles Ruud, *Fighting Words: Imperial Censorship and the Russian Press* (Toronto: University of Toronto Press, 1982), 79, 83–90. On the history of censorship in Russia, see also Sidney Monas, *The Third Section: Police and Society in Russia under Nicholas I* (Cambridge, Mass.: Harvard University Press, 1961); Mariana Tax Choldin, *A Fence around the Empire: Russian Censorship of Western Ideas under the Tsars* (Durham, N.C.: Duke University Press, 1985); Nicholas Riasanovsky, *Nicholas I and Official Nationality* (Berkeley: University of California Press, 1969).

43. "Peterburgskii vestnik" *Panteon*, no. 8 (Aug. 1852): 15. Although this article is unsigned, I attribute it to Zotov, who directed the *Khronika* (chronicle of events) section of *Panteon* from 1852 to 1856 (Nikolaev, *Russkie pisateli*, 3: 354). It might be objected that Zotov cannot be the author of this article because the author writes that he does not know Khvoshchinskaia personally (15), while by 1852 Zotov had been corresponding with Khvoshchinskaia for some years. However, at the time the article was written Zotov was planning a trip to Riazan', where he would meet Khvoshchinskaia face to face for the first time. In this context I believe he might very well have written that he did not know Khvoshchinskaia personally. The trip took place in the summer of 1852 (Semevskii, "N. D. Khvoshchinskaia-Zaionchkovskaia," 59). In this article Zotov also further changed several other poems.

44. On frame narratives, see Charles Isenberg, *Telling Silence: Russian Frame Narratives of Renunciation* (Evanston, Ill.: Northwestern University Press), 1993.

45. Praskov'ia Khvoshchinskaia ("Nadezhda Khvoshchinskaia," vi) recounts that her sister was deeply affected by the revolutions of 1848, about which Khvoshchinskaia wrote several poems. See note 36.

46. Gerbel', *Khrestomatiia dlia vsekh*, 581. Gerbel' subsequently revised and republished this anthology several times (1879, 1880, 1888) under the title *Russkie poety v biografiiakh i obraztsakh*, without changing the section on Khvoshchinskaia. Khvoshchinskaia dryly commented on Gerbel's introduction (in which he also stated that she wrote too much prose and that only three of her *povesti* [tales] were good): "His article is rather strange (it is even surprising that a writer to whom her biographer relates in such a way could end up in the 'Anthology')" (Bykov, *Siluety dalekogo proshlogo*, 186).

47. Bibliographies of Khvoshchinskaia's poetry: N. N. Golitsyn, *Bibliograficheskii slovar' russkikh pisatel'nits*, 262; D. D. Iazykov, *Obzor zhizni i trudov russkikh pisatelei i pisatel'nits*, 9: 25–30; S. I. Ponomarev, "Nashi pisatel'nitsy," *Sbornik Otdeleniia Russkogo Iazyka i Slovestnosti* 52, no. 7 (1891): 60–71.

48. This is not to suggest that Khvoshchinskaia had an easy time with other journal editors. Tsebrikova ("Ocherk zhizni," 9) and Semevskii ("N. D. Khvoshchinskaia-Zaionchkovskaia," 10: 63–64) detail A. A. Kraevskii's dishonest financial dealings with Khvoshchinskaia and her sister Sof'ia.

49. Zotov, "Peterburg v sorokovykh godakh," 296. Zotov quotes Khvo-shchinskaia as having written, "I can only sing, because there is no feeling that would not awaken feelings in my soul. But to scrutinize, analyze, and describe, I don't know if I can, if I will ever be in a condition [*sostoianie*] to do that."

50. On the shift in popularity from poetry to prose in Russia starting in the 1830s, see Mirsky, *History of Russian Literature*, 126. See also Khvoshchinskaia's translation from the French, "Proshchanie s poeziei," *Literaturnaia gazeta*, no. 45 (Nov. 11, 1848): 709–10, and Rostopchina's poem expressing similar feelings, "Oda poezii (Anakhronizm)" (1852), which starts "Tebe razvenchannoi bogine / Tebe poklon moi i privet" (To you, dethroned goddess / To you my respects and my greeting).

51. "Zametki i razmyshleniia novogo poeta po povodu russkoi zhurnalistiki avg. 1852," 105–6. Nekrasov is identified as "Novyi poet" in I. F. Masanov, *Slovar' psevdonimov russkikh pisatelei*, 2: 274.

52. "Bibliografiia," *Sovremennik* 43, no. 1 (Jan. 1854): 10. Nekrasov is identified as the author of this anonymous review in Vladimir Emmanuilovich Bograd, *Zhurnal "Sovremnnik," 1847–1866: Ukazatel' soderzhaniia* (Moskva: Gos. Izd-vo khudozhestvenoi literatury, 1959), 235.

53. Thomas H. Johnson, *Emily Dickinson: An Interpretive Biography* (Cambridge, Mass.: Belknap Press of Harvard University Press, 1955), 120.

54. Johnson, *Emily Dickinson*, 56, 112–44, especially 117–20.

Chapter 6. Karolina Pavlova

1. For recent Pavlova scholarship, see Fusso and Lehrman, *Essays on Karolina Pavlova*. Anthologies that omit Pavlova (and, for the most part, all women poets) include Verkhovskii, *Poety pushkinskoi pory;* Bannikov, *Tri veka russkoi poezii;* Petrov, *Istoriia russkoi literatury XIX veka;* L. Ia. Ginzberg, ed., *Poety 1820–1830 godov*, 2 vols. (Leningrad: Sovetskii pisatel', 1972); E. Vinokurov, ed., *Russkaia poeziia XIX veka* (Moskva: Khudozhestvennaia literatura, 1974); Anoshkina and L. D. Gromova, eds., *Istoriia russkoi literatury XIX veka: 40–60 gody* (Moskva: Izdatel'stvo Moskovskogo Universiteta, 1998).

2. *Das Nordlicht* (Dresden: In der Arnoldischen Buchhandlung, 1833); *Les Preludes* (Paris: Typographie de Firmin Didot Frères, 1839); *Dvoinaia zhizn'* (Moskva: Tip. Got'e i Monigetti, 1848); *Razgovor v Kremle* (Sankt-Peterburg: V tip. Iakova Geia, 1854); *Stikhotvoreniia* (Moskva: Tip. Stepanovoi, 1863).

Since her death, the following works have appeared: *Sobranie sochinenii*, ed. Valerii Briusov; *Polnoe sobranie stikhotvorenii*, ed. N. Kovarskii; *Polnoe sobranie stikhotvorenii*, ed. Pavel Gromov; *Stikhotvoreniia*, ed. E. N. Lebedev (Moskva: Sovetskaia Rossiia, 1985).

3. It is not necessary here to give a complete biographical account of Pavlova's life, as several are now available. See B. Rapgof, *Karolina Pavlova: Materialy dlia izucheniia zhizni i tvorchestva* (Petrograd: Izdatel'stvo Tirema, 1916); Sendich, "Life and Works of Karolina Pavlova"; Pavel Gromov, "Karolina Pavlova," in *Polnoe sobranie stikhotvorenii*, by Karolina Pavlova, 5–72; and my "Karolina Pavlova," in *Russian Women Writers*, ed. Christine Tomei, 1: 313–21.

Pavlova as a curiosity: Konstantin Khranevich, "Mitskevich i Karolina Ianish," *Istoricheskii vestnik* 67 (1897): 1080–86; N. Ashukin, "Karolina Pavlova," *Put'*, no. 1 (1914): 29–37; Ernst, "Karolina Pavlova i gr. Evdokiia Rastopchina [*sic*]," 5–35; V. Fridkin, "Al'bomy Karoliny Pavlovoi," *Nauka i zhizn'*, no. 12 (1987): 140–48.

4. On Pavlova's missing works, see Munir Sendich, "'Ot Moskvy do Drezdena': Pavlova's Unpublished Memoirs," 57–58.

5. See chapter 5, note 50 on the decline of poetry in Russia in the 1830s.

6. On the Beautiful Lady versus the *neznakomka*, see my "Images of Women in Fedor Sologub," *Proceedings of the Kentucky Foreign Language Conference, Slavic Section* 4, no. 1 (1986): 90–103.

7. On the importance of early-nineteenth-century salons in the production of Russian literature, see Todd, *Fiction and Society in the Age of Pushkin*; Bernstein "Women on the Verge of a New Language," 209–24; Bernstein, "Avdot'ia Petrovna Elagina and Her Contributions to Russian Letters," *SEEJ* 40 (1996): 2, 215–35; Bernstein, "Private and Public Personas: Negotiating the Mommy Track in the Age of Nicholas I"; Hammarberg, "Flirting with Words," 297–320; N. L. Brodskii, *Literaturnye salony i kruzhki*, 326–31; and Aronson and Reiser, *Literaturnye kruzhki i salony*.

8. Nikolai Vasil'evich Berg, cited in Valerii Briusov, "K. K. Pavlova," *Ezhemesiachnye sochineniia* 12 (1903): 282. Panaev's comment appears in "Peterburgskie novosti," *Sovremennikt* 48 (1854): 135. Dmitrii Grigorovich, Ivan Panaev, and Aleksandr Nikitenko's ridicule of Pavlova is noted in Sendich, "Life and Works of Karolina Pavlova," 51–52.

9. See Evgenii Bobrov, "A. A. Fuks i kazanskie literatury 30–40kh godov," 6: 481–509 and 7: 5–35.

10. Material on Elagina's salon based on Bernstein, "Avdot'ia Petrovna Elagina" and "Private and Public Personas"; Aronson and Reiser, *Literaturnye kruzhki*, 158–61, 277–78; and Brodskii, *Literaturnye salony*, 326–31. On Zhukovskii and Elagina, see Bernstein, "Avdot'ia Petrovna Elagina and Her Contribution to Russian Letters," 218 ff.; Carl von Zedlitz, "Biograficheskii ocherk," in *Sobranie sochinenii Zhukovskogo* (Sankt-peterburg: Izdanie knigoprodavtsa I. I. Glazunova, 1878), 1: xxiv; and Aronson and Reiser, *Literaturnye kruzhki*, 159. On Karamzin's second wife, see chapter 1, note 8. On Elagina's influence in literary circles, see Bernstein, "Private and Public Personas," 13.

11. Information on Pavlova based on Rapgof, *Karolina Pavlova;* Sendich, "Life and Works of Karolina Pavlova," 2–38; and Karolina Pavlova, "Moi vospominaniia," *Russkii arkhiv*, no. 3 (1875): 232. Interestingly, Claire Clairmont, Mary Shelley's half-sister and the mother of Byron's child Allegra, who worked as a governess, companion, and language tutor in Moscow from 1825–27, mentions in her diary that she gave Pavlova English lessons (*Literaturnoe nasledstvo*, no. 91 [Moskva: Nauka, 1982], 312. See also *The Journals of Claire Clairmont*, ed. Marion Kingston Stocking (Cambridge, Mass.: Harvard University Press, 1968), 374–97, in which Clairmont records five visits to Pavlova and her father, Karl Jaenisch.

12. Pavlova, *Polnoe sobranie stikhotvorenii*, 232. Subsequent citations from this edition are indicated in the text by page numbers in parentheses.

13. Those who ridiculed Pavlova's knowledge of languages include Iazykov in a letter to his brothers in 1832 (quoted in Sendich, "Life and Works of Karolina

Pavlova," 33); Avdot'ia Panaeva in her memoirs, *Vospominaniia* (Moskva: Khu-dozhestvennaia literatura, 1972), 136; and Rostopchina in a poem that made fun of Pavlova's exchange of open letters with Panaev in "Peterburgskie novosti," 135. (On Pavlova's letter to Panaev, see also chapter 1, note 7.)

> И читала с поэмой чухонской
> Свой санскритской с нее ж перевод,
> [. . . . .]
> (По-китайски, не то по-японски
> Эта дама стихи издает)

⤳

> (And she read from a Finnish *poema* with her Sanskrit translation
> This lady publishes verses in Chinese or in Japanese)
> (*Stikhotvoreniia, proza, pis'ma*, 372)

Pavlova's husband attempted to turn Pavlova's German background against her when he expressed what Briusov describes as "hypocritical" concern to his friends about the "German" education Pavlova was giving their son ("K. K. Pavlova," 286).

14. The historian Petr Bartenev (1829–1912) wrote in his obituary of Pavlova: "Nature did not endow her with physical beauty, although it did generously provide her with abilities, in particular for languages" ("Karolina Pavlova," 119). The Symbolist poet and future editor of a two-volume edition of Pavlova's works, Valerii Briusov, wrote, "Karolina was not beautiful. But in these [early] years she could have been attractive in her youth and freshness" ("K. K. Pavlova," 275). The writer and journalist Aleksandr Herzen (1812–70) wrote of Pavlova that he "did not like her voice, and . . . her physical appearance was not quite to her credit"; the writer Dmitrii Grigorevich described Pavlova as "a bony lady of tall stature, with a face reminiscent of an energetic man rather than a woman"; the censor and memoirist Aleksandr Nikitenko (1804–77) described her as "offensive with her 'jabbering and obtrusiveness'" (Herzen, Grigorovich, and Nikitenko in Sendich, "Life and Works of Karolina Pavlova," 45, 51, 52, respectively; I have modified Sendich's translations).

15. Writers in love with Pavlova: Sendich, "Life and Works of Karolina Pavlova," 23, 30. Briusov writes, "I. Kireevskii's rapture about Karolina's verses gave cause to suspect him of a tender feeling for the already not so young female writer." Kireevskii's "rapture" consisted of the comment that he found in Pavlova's German poetry qualities increasingly rare in Russian women's poetry: originality and strength of imagination. Kireevskii also expressed the wish that Pavlova would try writing poetry in Russian as well as in French and German (Ivan Kireev, "O russkikh pisatel'nitsakh (pis'mo k Anne Petrovne Zontaga)" [Zontag was Elagina's sister], originally appeared in the *al'manakh Podarok Bednym*, 1834. Also in *Polnoe sobranie sochinenii Ivana Vasil'evicha Kireevskogo* (Moskva: Tip. P. Bakhmetev, 1961; reprint Ann Arbor, Mich.: Ardis, 1983), 123.

16. Elagina, in a letter to her husband (Sept. 6, 1826), mentions that Jaenisch had visited her three times in a few days (Bernstein, "Avdot'ia Petrovna Elagina," 225, 226). See also Sendich, "Life and Works of Karolina Pavlova," 29.

17. On Volkonskaia and Alexander I, see Bayara Aroutunova, *Lives in Letters: Princess Zinaida Volkonskaya and Her Correspondence* (Columbus, Ohio: Slavica, 1994), 92–132.

18. Articles on Pavlova and Mickiewicz: Józef Tretiak, "Karolina Jaenisch," in *Szkice literackie*, vol. 1 (W. Krakowie: Spółka Wydawnicza Polska, 1896); Konstantin Khranevich, "Mitskevich i Karolina Ianish," *Istoricheskii vestnik* 67 (1897): 1080–86; Waclaw Lednicki, "Wiersze Karoliny Pawlow (Jaenisch) do Mickiewicz," *Przyjaciele Moskale* 8 (1933): 243–59; Jan Orlowski, "Mickiewicz w poezji Karoliny Jaenisch-Pawlowej," *Przeglad-Humanistyczyn* 20, no. 8 (1976): 67–75; Munir Sendich, "Karolina Jaenisch (Pavlova) and Adam Mickiewicz," *Polish Review* 14, no. 3 (1969): 68–78; David Brodsky, "Karolina Pavlova and Adam Mickiewicz: Biographical and Literary Relations," unpublished bibliography, 1999.

19. For a list of Pavlova's translations, see *Polnoe sobranie stikhotvorenii* (1964), 581–99. Letter to Pushkin cited (in Russian) in Sendich, "Life and Works of Karolina Pavlova," 115 n. 84. Sendich contrasts the very positive reviews Pavlova received for her translations with the absence of reviews or negative reviews of her poetry ("Life and Works of Karolina Pavlova," 221–51). In 1839 Belinskii enthusiastically praised Pavlova's translations into French and Russian ("Russkie zhurnaly," *Moskovskii Nabliudatel'* 2, no. 4, section 4 (1839): 100–38, reprinted in his *Polnoe sobranie sochinenii*, 3: 191). One year later in 1840, however, in a letter to the critic Vasilii Botkin (1811–69) Belinskii blamed Konstantin Aksakov for unduly influencing him in favor of Pavlova's work. "Konstantin Aksakov told us stories about the divine translations of K. K. Pavlova, and we began to howl [*razvopoliis'*]. . . . Wonderful verse, wonderful translations, only I don't have the strength to read them" (cited [in Russian] in Sendich, "Life and Works of Karolina Pavlova," 223). Belinskii in his 1843 article "Sochinenie Zeneidy R-oi" (reprinted in *Polnoe sobranie sochinenii*, 7: 655) again praised Pavlova's ability as a translator but criticized her taste, especially in translating works by Iazykov and Khomiakov (two Slavophiles with whom Belinskii, a Westernizer, had ideological differences). Belinskii's (and Panaev's) subsequent hostility both to Pavlova's poetry and to Pavlova herself may be inferred from the following passage from M. P. Pogodin's memoirs: "Miss Pavlova, Panaev recounts, one time with her characteristic glibness completely overcame Granovskii for a couple of weeks. She read him all her *poemy* and poems, and Granovskii, attracted by Pavlova's rhetoric, began to praise her verse excessively [*ne v meru voskhvaliat' eia stikhi*]. His friends made fun of him, especially Belinskii. That attraction didn't last long" (*Zhizn' i trudy M. P. Pogodina*, 12: 276, quoted in Briusov, "K. K. Pavlova," 283.).

20. On Pavlova and A. K. Tolstoy, see Munir Sendich, "Twelve Unpublished Letters of Karolina Pavlova to Aleksei Tolstoy," *Russian Literature Triquarterly* 9 (1974): 541–58. On Pavlova's pension from Elena Pavlovna, whose salon Pavlova had attended in 1854, see Sendich, "Life and Works of Karolina Pavlova," 69, 79. On Elena Pavlovna, wife of Nicholas's younger brother Mikhail, see I. E. Andreevskii, ed., *Entsiklopedicheskii slovar'*, 11a : 600–601; and Bruce Lincoln, *In the Vanguard of Reform: Russia's Enlightened Bureaucrats* (Dekalb, Ill.: Northern Illinois University Press, 1990), 148–62.

21. Attendees at Pavlova's salon: Munir Sendich, "Moscow Literary Salons: Thursdays at Karolina Pavlova's," *Die Welt der Slaven* 17, no. 2 (1972): 341–57. Although Ogarev edited *Russkaia potaennaia literatura*, Herzen published it (see *Russkie pisateli*, 2: 355). For Pavlova's publications in *al'manakhi*, see Smirnov-Sokol'skii, *Russkie literaturnye al'manakhi i sborniki XVIII–XIX vv.*, 201, 220–21, 231, 240, 243, 246–47, 248.

22. Shashkova, "Epokha Belinskogo," 79–80. For an account of the historic gendering of "genius" as male, see Battersby, *Gender and Genius*.

23. See Barbara Heldt, "Karolina Pavlova: The Woman Poet and the Double Life," in *Double Life*, by K. Pavlova, iv–vi. The governor of Moscow had his own accounts to settle with Pavlov, whom he suspected of writing an unflattering epigram about him. He therefore took the occasion of Pavlova's father's complaint to search Pavlov's library. For attacks on Pavlova after Pavlov's arrest, see Briusov, "K. K. Pavlova," 286, and Sendich, "Life and Works of Karolina Pavlova," 63–64.

24. See Saltykov-Shchedrin's review of Pavlova's collected poetry, in which he calls her a representative of "butterfly [i.e., frivolous, art for art's sake] poetry" ("Stikhotvoreniia K. Pavlovoi," *Sovremennik*, no. 6, pt. 2 [1863]: 311–16). We have seen that Rostopchina's literary reputation also diminished at this time. On Pavlova's interest in political issues, see my "Karolina Pavlova," in *Russian Women Writers*, 319–20.

25. Biographical sketch: Briusov, "K. K. Pavlova," 273. The Briusov collected works: Karolina Pavlova, *Sobranie sochinenii*.

On I. M. Briusova (Ionna Matveevna Frunt), see Ionna Briusova, "Materialy k biografii Valeriia Briusov," in Valerii Briusov, *Izbrannye stikhi*, ed. Igor Postupalkii (Moskva: Akademiia, 1933), 125–28; Ernst, "Karolina Pavlova i gr. Evdokiia Rostopchina," 8–9, 11; Rapgof, *Karolina Pavlova*, 44.

On the critical reaction to Briusov's edition of Pavlova's works, see A. I. Belitskii, "Novoe izdanie sochinenii K. K. Pavlovoi," *Izvestiia otdeleniia russkogo iazyka i slovesnosti Rossiiskoi Akademii Nauk* 22 (1918), 201–20. Sendich surveys the Symbolists' revival of Pavlova and the scholarship inspired by Briusov's edition of her works ("Life and Works of Karolina Pavlova," 244–50).

26. Liubov' Gurevich (publisher of *Severnyi vestnik*, which brought Symbolism to Russia) wrote that her journal first introduced these European authors ("Istoriia Severnogo vestnika," in *Russkaia literatura XX veka [1890–1910]*, ed. S. A. Vengerov [Moskva: "Mir," 1914], 1: 248–49).

27. Pavlova attracted the attention of the Symbolists not only because of her relationships with Golden Age poets but also because she mentored Fet, whom they also rediscovered. On Pavlova and Fet, see Irina Reshetilova, "Kniaginia russkogo stikha," in *Chistye prudy: Al'manakh* (Moskva: Moskovskii rabochii, 1989), 695.

28. Kovarskii, introduction to *Polnoe sobranie stikhotvorenii*, by Karolina Pavlova, vi, xxv–xxvl. Sendich, like other Pavlova scholars before him, disputes the characterization of Pavlova as a Slavophile or "unprogressive" ("Life and Works of Karolina Pavlova," 56 n. 55).

29. Sendich on Tschižewskij: "Boris Utin in Pavlova's Poems and Corre-

spondence: Pavlova's Unpublished Letters (17) to Utin," *Russian Language Journal* 28, no. 100 (spring 1974): 63.

30. German works on Pavlova by German Slavists include D. Čyževs'kyj [Tschižewskij] and D. Gerhardt, "Deutsche Puškin-Übersetzungen von Karolina Pavlova," *Germanoslavica* 5, no. 1–2 (1937): 32–52; Barbara Lettman-Sadony, *Karolina Karlovna Pavlova: Eine Dichterin russischdeutscher Wechselseitigkeit* (Munich: O. Sagner, 1971); Frank Göpfert, ed. *Das deutsche Werk Karolina Karolovna Pavlovas: Textsammlung der ersten deutschen Gesamtausgabe* (Wilhelmshorst: F. K. Göpfert, 1994).

31. Letter to me from Zoya Yurieff, July 1999. Sendich, "Life and Works of Karolina Pavlova," iv.

32. Heldt, "Karolina Pavlova: The Woman Poet and the Double Life." See also her *Terrible Perfection,* 111–15, and Fusso and Lehrman, *Essays on Karolina Pavlova. The Modern Language Association International Bibliography* [online database, cited March 12, 2002] lists twenty-one Western articles and dissertations about Pavlova since 1963.

Russian scholarship: Alekseeva, "Perevodcheskii stil' Karoliny Pavlovoi (k voprosu ob individual'nykh perevodchikh stiliakh)," *Vestnik Leningradskogo universiteta,* no. 8 (1981): 55–59, and *Istoriia iazyka literatury,* no. 2, 55–59; V. K. Zontikov, "'Pishu ne smelo ia, ne chasto . . .' (Stikhotvoreniie Karoliny Pavlovoi)," 35–39; E. N. Lebedov, "Poznan'ia rokova chasha (Lirika Karoliny Pavlovoi), in *Stikhotvorenie,* by Karolina Pavlova (Moskva: Sovetskaia Rossiia, 1985), 5–38; Fridkin, "Al'bomy Karoliny Pavlovoi," 140–48; Irina Reshetlova, "Kniaginia russkogo stikha," *Chistye prudy: Al'manakh* (Moskva: Moskovskii rabochii, 1989), 674–713. In addition, for the first time since Briusov's 1915 edition, Pavlova's "Za chainym stolom" was republished in *Serdtsa chutkogo prozren'em . . . : Povesti i rasskazy russkikh pisatel'nits XIX v.* ed. N. I. Iakushin (Moskva: Sovetskaia Rossiia, 1991), 294–333.

33. It is also possible that Pavlova saw her Jewish protagonist as an Oriental "Other" and therefore capable of murder. See the discussion of literary orientalism and the *poema* in chapter 3.

34. On Pavlova's modification of genres in *Dvoinaia zhizn'* and "Za chainym stolom," see my "Gender and Genre in Pavlova's *A Double Life*," 563–77, and "Karolina Pavlova's 'At the Tea Table' and the Politics of Class and Gender," 271–84.

35. In addition to the articles listed in note 34, see my "Karolina Pavlova's 'Tri dushi': The Transfiguration of Biography," *Proceedings of the Kentucky Foreign Language Conference, 1984* (Lexington, Kentucky: Department of Russian and Eastern Studies, 1984), 15–24.

36. On Volkonskaia's opera, see Aroutunova, *Lives in Letters,* 23.

37. On Romantic values, see Christine Rydel, "Lyric Poetry: Introduction," in *Ardis Anthology of Russian Romanticism,* 21.

38. For example, the bibliography *Ukazatel' literatury zhenskogo voprosa na russkom iazyke,* which appeared in *Severnyi Vestnik* 7 (1887), lists six articles about Joan of Arc that appeared in Russian journals between 1842 and 1882 (p. 15). In the United States, Emily Dickinson wrote a poem about Joan of Arc ("A Mien to Move a Queen," 1861), discussed in relation to Southey's play by Elizabeth

Phillips in *Emily Dickinson: Personae and Performance* (University Park: Pennsylvania State University Press, 1988), 171–72. For an interesting survey of nineteenth- and twentieth-century interpretations of Joan of Arc, see Joan Acocella, "Burned Again," *The New Yorker,* Nov. 15, 1999, 98–106.

Although Christine de Pizan's contemporary depiction of Joan of Arc ("Le Ditié de Jeanne d'Arc," dated 1429, the year before Joan's death) also portrayed her positively, Joan's achievements had a very different meaning for de Pizan than for the Romantics. De Pizan celebrates Joan for defeating the English and for enabling Charles VII to be crowned but also expresses the hope that Joan will crush the Hussites, reunite the church after the schism, and lead a crusade for the recapture of the Holy Land (*The Writings of Christine de Pizan,* ed. Charity Cannon Willard [New York: Persea, 1994], 348–63).

Another very popular woman warrior of the time was Nadezhda Durova (1783–1866), who, dressed as a man, fought against Napoleon and later became a writer. Pushkin published Durova's memoirs in his *Sovremennik.* On Durova, see Mary Zirin, "Nadezhda Durova, Russia's 'Cavalry Maiden,'" in *The Cavalry Maiden,* by Nadezhda Durova, trans. Mary Zirin (Bloomington: Indiana University Press, 1989), ix–xxxvii.

39. William Shakespeare, *The First Part of King Henry VI,* ed. Michael Hattaway (Cambridge: Cambridge University Press, 1990), 93, 94, 129, 130, 159, 167, 174; Voltaire, *La Pucelle: Poème en vingt-un chants avec les notes par Voltaire* (Paris: Pierre Didot, 1801).

40. Southey, *Joan of Arc,* 1: 18. See Stuart Curran's discussion of Southey's *Joan of Arc,* which he describes as "anti-war and anti-imperialistic" (*Poetic Form and British Romanticism,* 167–68).

41. On the influence of Shakespeare's depiction of Joan on Schiller, see Heffner, preface to *Die Jungfrau von Orleans,* xiii. It is hard to believe that Schiller would not also have known Southey's epic, given its popularity at the time. (Southey, *Poetical Works,* 1: 19–20, describes the epic's reception.) Heffner writes that Schiller's play is based on Kant's idea that a moral act is one in which duty and inclination collide (preface, xvii–xxi). In the play Joan, therefore, must be shown to "fall" by experiencing sexual desire in order to triumph over this inclination and achieve moral freedom.

42. In Voltaire's mock epic, Saint Denis, patron saint of France and Joan's protector, allows Joan almost to be seduced by her donkey because he feels that she is becoming too self-sufficient:

> Denis volut que son Jeanne, qu'il aime,
> Connut enfin ce q'on est par soi-même,
> Et qu'une femme en tout occasion
> Pour se conduire a besoin d'un patron.
> (canto 20, 240)

> ❧

> (Denis wanted his Joan, whom he loves,
> To know finally what she is by herself,

> And that a woman on all occasions
> In order to behave herself needs a master.)

Southey's depiction:

> Then the Maid
> Rode through the thickest battle; fast they fell,
> Pierced by her forceful spear [. . .]
> [. . .]
> [. . .] Where she turns
> The foe trembles and dies. [. . .]
> (X: lines 330–32, 336–37)

Maikov presents a similar image of Joan of Arc as Valkyrie or banshee in his "Zhanna d'Ark" (1887).

43. For example, Petr Bartenev writes, "K. K. Pavlova's best work, of course, was the novel in prose and verse called *A Double Life*" ("K. K. Pavlova," 122).

44. Tschižewskij, *On Romanticism in Slavic Literature*, 30–42.

45. Romy Taylor ingeniously argues that "Pavlova meant for Cecilia's dream visitor to be identified as Christ" ("Pavlova's *Dvojnaia zhizn'*," 45). I do not, however, find this hypothesis entirely convincing. While the visitor reconnects Cecilia with her spiritual nature—culminating in the epiphany she experiences at the end of chapter 8—he is surrounded with a romantic and sardonic aura and reappears in very different, often secular, but recognizable forms in other Pavlova works. In addition, Cecilia describes her first dream as concerning a man who had died the day before (240), a man who had been characterized as "no longer young but very attractive, malicious but intelligent" (233).

46. Excerpts from *Kadril'* had appeared earlier, the first as early as 1844 in *Moskvitianin*, but the work did not appear in full until 1859. For internal evidence linking "Za chainym stolom" with the 1840s, see my "Karolina Pavlova's 'At the Tea Table.'"

In the discussions of *polozhenie zhenshchiny* of the 1840s, writers such as Pavlova, Elena Gan, Mar'ia Zhukova, Avdotiia Panaeva, and Prince Vladimir Odoevskii denounced the educational and intellectual constraints women in society experienced, as well as the pressure on them to find a "good match," that is, a rich husband, at any emotional cost. The woman question, in contrast, focused on issues of women's education and self-determination. Leading theorists were Nikolai Pirogov, Dmitrii Pisarev, Nikolai Dobroliubov, and M. L. Mihailov. (On Mikhailov, see chapter 2, note 8.) On the various women's movements in Russia, see Stites, *Women's Liberation Movement in Russia*. Stites notes, "One feature of the period . . . was that the propagation of women's emancipation was done almost exclusively by men" (48).

47. Religion operates in *Kadril'* as a background factor only: Nadina prays in vain to escape marrying Andrei Il'ich, yet Providence seems to operate in having the marriage turn out well. Liza survives years of her aunt's abuse through a connection with nature. Having developed a strong sense of ethics and of herself, she is able to see women's longing for Romantic heroes as a form of idolatry (351). Ol'ga compares the ordeal of her first ball to Gethsemane:

Ia gor'kii kubok ves'
Do kapli vypila.

⌒⊗⌒

(I drank the entire bitter cup
To the dregs.)

(340)

The countess also prays in vain that Vadim will survive the duel, and we are told she has spent many nights crying in front of the icon. That icon, reflected in a mirror, is the last image of the poem, perhaps a reminder of more enduring values than those of society. The issue here for Pavlova, however, is not religious but ethical—women's ability to be, in Suzanne Fusso's words, "moral agents" ("Pavlova's *Quadrille*," 124).

48. On frame narratives, see Charles Isenburg, *Telling Silence: Russian Frame Narratives of Renunciation* (Evanston, Ill.: Northwestern University Press, 1993).

49. Pavlova's recurring cruel but loving male figure is reminiscent of the Gothic hero, whom Tania Modleski traces in women's writing from Charlotte Brontë (Mr. Rochester in *Jane Eyre*) to contemporary Harlequin Romances. Modleski attributes the popularity of such texts, which depict "the transformation of brutal (or indeed, murderous) men into tender lovers," to "the insistent denial of the reality of male hostility towards women," and the need for readers to "constantly return to the same text (to texts which are virtually the same) in order to be reconvinced" (*Loving with a Vengeance*, 111).

50. See Fusso, "Pavlova's *Quadrille*," 125–26, on the similarity between the countess's depiction of Vadim and the narrator's depiction of a stern, disapproving Pushkin.

51. Karolina Pavlova, "Za chainym stolom," *Russkii vestnik* 24, no. 2 (Dec. 1859): 799. I cite this version of the text, which presumably Pavlova approved, rather than Briusov's edition in *Sobranie sochinenii*, 2: 335–412, or the late-Soviet edition (which left out one of the work's two epigraphs) in *Serdtsa chutkogo prozren'em.*, ed. N. I. Iakushin, 294–333. Perhaps Pavlova, of German descent and living in Dresden in 1859, identified with both countesses; in Russian the word for countess is the German-derived word *grafinia*. For Russian women's unequal inheritance rights, to which the countess alludes, see chapter 1, note 4.

52. Pavlova, "Za chainym stolom," 797, 839–40. Rostopchina, too, at the end of *Dnevnik devushki* equates marriage with death. The novel ends with the heroine, Zinaida, seriously ill. The narrator tells us that it does not matter whether Zinaida dies physically of the illness or dies morally by recovering and marrying the man to whom she is engaged but whom she does not love.

53. De Laurentis, *Alice Doesn't*, 155. See also Rachel Blau Du Plessis, *Writing beyond the Ending* (Bloomington: Indiana University Press, 1985).

Chapter 7. In Conclusion

1. In addition to the collections of poetry listed in the bibliography (many of which include useful biographical and critical material about the authors), I have

based this discussion of noncanonical men poets on the following sources: I. E. Andreevskii, ed., *Entsiklopedicheskii slovar'*; Ia. D. Leshchinskii, *Pavel Andreev Fedotov: Khudozhnik i poet* (Leningrad: Iskkusstvo, 1946) (regarding Fedotov); Mirsky, *History of Russian Literature*; Nikolaev, *Russkie pisateli 1800–1917*; Terras, *Handbook of Russian Literature*; Mark Azadovskii, *Neizvestnyi poet-sibiriaka: E. Mil'keev* (Chita: Izd. Istoriko-literaturnogo kruzhka pri Gos. Institut narodnogo obrazovaniia, 1922) (regarding Mil'keev).

2. Belinskii did champion Kol'tsov. He also reviewed some of Maikov's works favorably but considered him narrow and best suited to writing anthological poetry.

3. Regarding aristocratic backgrounds, the only partial exception is Fet, who was raised as an aristocrat until age fourteen, when he was declared illegitimate. Fet, however, during his ultimately successful fight to have his noble status restored, attended Moscow University for six years, traveled abroad, was friends with Turgenev, Goncharov, and Lev Tolstoy and in the course of his lifetime published six editions of his poetry. See Richard F. Gustafson, *The Imagination of Spring: The Poetry of Afanasy Fet* (New Haven, Conn.: Yale University Press, 1966), 3–10, 247–49, and Whittaker, "Fet [Shenshin], Afanasii Afanas'evich," 7: 193–202.

Debreczeny notes that the "special élite institutions" of the Lyceum at Tsarskoe Selo and the Cadet Corps "counted more than the university" (*Social Functions of Literature*, 103). This was not the case for Fedotov. Although he attended the Cadet Corps he soon left military life with a very reduced pension to become an artist who satirized the upper class and documented social inequities.

4. The women generally lived longer. Pavlova, Bakunina, Gotovtseva, and Shakhova died in the their seventies or eighties; Garelina, Mordovtseva, and Khvoshchinskaia in their sixties; Zhadovskaia, Fuks, and Rostopchina in their forties; Shakhovskaia, Teplova, and probably Lisitsyna (see Vatsuro, "Zhizn' i poeziia Nadezhdy Teplovoi," 18–19, 21) in their thirties; and Kul'man at seventeen. As mentioned in the introduction, most of these women came from various strata of the aristocracy and were comfortably off. The exceptions were Kul'man, who lived and died in poverty; Mariia Lisitsyna, the daughter of an actor; Teplova, who came from a merchant background; and Khvoshchinskaia, who struggled with poverty for most of her life.

5. Nicholas I rewarded Maikov for one poetry collection with 1,000 rubles and a leave to travel abroad. On the occasion of the fiftieth anniversary of the beginning of his literary career Maikov saw his pension raised from 1,750 to 3,500 rubles, and received a promotion to the rank of *tainyi sovetnik* (confidential advisor).

For Maikov's critics: Mirsky, *History of Russian Literature*, 231; *Entsiklopedicheskii slovar'*, ed. I. E. Andreevskii (Sankt-Peterburg: F.A. Brokgaaz, I. A. E., 1890–1907), 35: 371 (the article is signed by the influential religious philosopher and poet Vladimir Solov'ev).

6. This is not to suggest that the canonical poets wrote no such poems. Several wrote prayers. For example, in Baratynskii's "Molitva" (1842 or 1844) the

speaker asks for the strength to accept God's severe (*strogii*) heaven. Lermontov in "Molitva" (1839) describes the relief a prayer can give in a difficult moment. See also Lermontov, "Molitva" (1829), "Molitva" (1837); Iazykov, "Molitva" (1825), "Molitva" (1835). On poems to family members, see Wolfson, "Romanticism and Gender," 385–96. Poems about children: Lermontov, "Rebenka milogo rozhden'e" (1839), "Rebenku" (1840); Fet, "Rebenku" (1886). A child features in Pushkin's "Brozhu li ia vdol' ulits shumnykh" (1829). However, in the work of canonical poets such poems do not constitute a major theme, while they do in many of the noncanonical men and women poets.

7. Conventional female muses are absent in Miller, Fedotov, Mil'keev, and Khomiakov. Some of the canonical men, like the women, describe a "genii" rather than a muse. Guber addresses his "groznyi genii" (threatening genius) in "Pechal' vdokhnoveniia" (1837), although he also describes a more conventional, but idealized, Beatrice-like figure with maternal overtones in "Sud'ba poeta" (1833). Mil'keev describes a male, diabolical muse in "Artist-muzykant" (1843), a poem in which Mark Azadovskii finds autobiographical features (*Neizvestnyi poet-sibiriak: E. Mil'keev*, 17). Some of the canonical men poets also wrote poems to their *genii*: Del'vig, "Razgovor s geniem" (1814–17), Lermontov, "K geniiu" (1829), Iazykov, "Genii" (1825). However, they wrote many more to conventional female muses, as discussed in chapter 2.

8. Christine Battersby notes that there is a difference between men writing "like" a woman (i.e., incorporating traditionally "feminine" traits, such as intuition and sensitivity), and women writing "as" a woman. "It is *women* who have been excluded from culture," she adds, "not the feminine" (*Gender and Genius*, 137–38, italics in original).

9. Cited in Moi, *Sexual/Textual Politics*, 163–64.

10. Cited, for example, in Liashchenko, "A. V. Kol'tsov (biograficheskii ocherk)," xix, and V. P. Anikin, "Slovo o Kol'tsove," in *Sochineniia*, by Aleksei Kol'tsov, 5.

11. Evgenii Mil'keev, "Pis'mo V. A. Zhukovskomu," *Stikhotvorenie* (Moskva: Gubernskaia tip., 1843), xiii.

12. For information on Kol'tsov's relationship with Belinskii and his reception among radical critics, see L. Plotkin, "A. V. Kol'tsov," in *Stikhotvoreniia*, by A. V. Kol'tsov, 17–21.

Postrevolutionary editions sanitized Kol'tsov's life. For example, before the revolution it had been noted that Kol'tsov pressured the aristocratic writers who befriended him to use their influence to help him win lawsuits connected with his cattle business. After the revolution such behavior was attributed only to Kol'tsov's father. Compare Liashchenko, "A. V. Kol'tsov [biograficheskii ocherk]," xxv, with Anikin, "Slovo o Kol'tsove," 8. Before the revolution there had been discussions about Belinskii's possible damaging influence on Kol'tsov's art. After the revolution such discussion ceased (see Plotkin, "A. V. Kol'tsov," 21–22). In spite of the enthusiasm expressed by Belinskii and Soviet scholars, however, Kol'tsov is not considered canonical, largely because of his lack of an upper-class education. As mentioned previously, he had less than one and a half years of formal schooling.

Bibliography

Primary Sources

Poems referred to in this study can be found in the following print and archival collections, with the exception of those (cited in chapter notes) that appeared only in the periodic press.

GENERAL
Khrestomatiia dlia vsekh: Russkie poety v biografiiakh i obraztsakh. Edited by Nikolai Gerbel'. Sanktpeterburg: Tip. Imperatorskaia Akademii nauk, 1873.
Poety 1840–1850-kh godov. Edited by B. Ia. Bukhshtab and E. M. Shneiderman. Leningrad: Sovetskii pisatel', 1972.
Russkie poetessy XIX veka. Edited by N. V. Banikov. Moskva: Sovetskaia Rossiia, 1979.

PRASKOV'IA BAKUNINA
Notebook of poems. F. 15 [Bakuniny], op. 10, n. 5. Pushkinskii dom.

EVGENII BARATYNSKII
Polnoe sobranie sochenii. Edited by M. L. Gofman. Petrograd: Izdanie Razriada iziashchnoi slovesnosti Imperatorskoi Akademii nauk, 1914–15.
Polnoe sobranie stikhotvorenii. Edited by E. N. Kupreianova. Leningrad: Sovetskii pisatel', 1957.
Stikhotvoreniia, poemy. Edited by L. G. Frizman. Moskva: Nauka, 1982.

ANTON DEL'VIG
Polnoe sobranie stikhotvorenii. Edited by B. V. Tomashevskii. Leningrad: Sovetskii pisatel, 1959.

PAVEL FEDOTOV
Pavel Andreevich Fedotov: Khudozhnik i poet. Leningrad: Iskusstvo, 1946.

AFANASII FET
Polnoe sobranie stikhotvorenii. Edited by B. Ia. Bukhshtab. Leningrad: Sovetskii
    pisatel', 1959.
Stikhotvoreniia i poemy. Edited by B. Ia. Bukhshtab. Leningrad: Sovetskii pisatel',
    1986.

ALEKSANDRA FUKS
Stikhotvoreniia. Kazan': V universitetskoi tip., 1834.
Osnovanie goroda Kazani: Povest' v stikhakh. Kazan: V universitetskoi tip., 1836.
Kniazhna Khabiba: Povest' v stikhakh. Kazan': V universitetskoi tip., 1841.

LIUBOV' GARELINA (PSEUD. NADEZHDA LIBINA)
Sochineniia L. G. ch. 1–2. 2 vols. Vol. 1, *Dramaticheskie sochinenii;* vol. 2,
    Stikhotvoreniia Nadezhdy Libinoi. Moskva: V tip. Bakhmeteva, 1870.

ANNA GOTOVTSEVA
Notebook of poems. F. 46 [Bartenev], op. 2., d. 426. RGALI.

EDUARD GUBER
Sochineniia. Edited by A. G. Tikhmenev. Sankt-Peterburg: A. Smirdin, 1859–60.

NIKOLAI IAZYKOV
Polnoe sobranie stikhotvorenii. Edited by K. K. Bukhmeier. Moskva: Sovetskii pisa-
    tel', 1964.

A. S. KHOMIAKOV
Stikhotvoreniia i dramy. Edited by B. F. Egorov. Leningrad: Sovetskii pisatel', 1969.

ALEKSEI KOL'TSOV
Polnoe sobranie sochinenii. Edited by A. I. Liashchenko. Sankt-Peterburg: Razvri-
    ada iziashchnoi slovestnosti Imperatorskoi Akademii nauk, 1909.
Stikhotvoreniia. Edited by L. Plotkin. Biblioteka poeta, malaia seriia. Leningrad:
    Sovetskii pisatel', 1953.
Sochineniia. Edited by T. N. Bedniakova and V. P. Anikin. Moskva: Izdatel'stvo
    "Pravda," 1984.

NADEZHDA KHVOSHCHINSKAIA
Notebook of poetry. F. 541, op. 1, ed. kh. 3. RGALI.
Album buvard. F. 541, op. 1, ed. kh. 5. RGALI.
Derevenskii sluchai: Povest' v stikhakh. Sankt-Peterburg: Tip. E. Veimara, 1853.

ELISAVETA KUL'MAN
Piiticheskie opyty Elisavety Kul'man: V trekh chastakh. 2nd ed. Sankt-Peterburg: V
    tip. Imperatorskoi Rossiiskoi Akademii, 1839.

MIKHAIL LERMONTOV
Polnoe sobranie sochinenii. Edited by B. M. Eikhenbaum. Moskva: OGIZ, 1948.
Sobranie sochinenii v chetyrekh tomakh. Edited by V. Arkhipov. Moskva: Iz-datel'stvo "Pravda," 1969.
Polnoe sobranie stikhotvorenii v dvukh tomakh. Edited by D. E. Maksimov and E. E. Naidich. Leningrad: Sovetskii pisatel', 1989.

MARIIA LISITSYNA
Stikhi i proza M. Lisitsynoi, 1826–1829. Moskva: V tip. Reshetnikova, 1829.

A. N. MAIKOV
Izbrannye proizvedeniia. Edited by F. Ia. Prima and L. S. Geiro. Leningrad: Sovet-skii pisatel', 1977.

EVGENII MIL'KEEV
Stikhotvoreniia. Moskva: V gubernanskoi tip., 1843.

FEDOR MILLER
Stikhotvoreniia F. Millera, 1841–1848. Moskva: V Politseiskii tip., 1849.
Stikhotvoreniia. 2d ed., corrected and supplemented. 2 vols. Moskva: Tip. Kat-kova, 1860.
Stikhotvoreniia F. B. Millera. 3d ed. Moskva: Tip. F. B. Millera, 1872–81.

ANNA MORDOVTSEVA (PSEUD. A. B-Z)
Otzvuki zhizni, 1842–187-. Saratov: Tip. P. S. Feokritova, 1877.

KAROLINA PAVLOVA
Stikotvreneiia. Moskva: Tipograffia L. I. Stepanovoi, 1863.
Sobranie sochinenii. Edited by Valerii Briusov. Moskva: Izdatel'stvo K. F. Nekrasova, 1915.
Polnoe sobranie stikhotvorenie. Edited by N. Kovarskii. Leningrad: Sovetskii pisa-tel', 1939.
Polnoe sobranie stikhotvorenii. Edited by Pavel Gromov. Moskva: Sovetskii pisa-tel', 1964.
Stikhotvoreniia. Edited by E. N. Lebedev. Moskva: Sovetskaia Rossiia, 1985.
"Za chainym stolom." In *Serdtsa chutkogo prozren'em. . . : Povesti i rasskazy russkikh pisatel'nits XIX v.* Edited by N. I. Iakushin. Moskva: Sovetskaia Rossiia, 1991.

ALEKSANDR PUSHKIN
Polnoe sobranie sochinenii. Edited by V. D. Bonch-Bruevich et al. Moskva: Izd. Akademii nauk, 1937.

EVDOKIIA ROSTOPCHINA
Stikhotvoreniia Grafinii Rostopchinoi. 2nd ed. Sankt-Peterburg: A. Smirdin, 1857.
Dnevnik devushki. Sankt-Peterburg: V. Golovin, 1866.
Sochineniia grafini E. P. Rostopchinoi. Sankt-Peterburg: Tip. I. N. Skorokhodova, 1890.

Stikhotvoreniia, proza, pis'ma. Edited by Boris Romanov. Moskva: Sovetskaia
   Rossiia, 1986.
Talisman. Edited by Viktor Afanas'ev. Moskva: Moskovskii Rabochii, 1987.
Schastlivaia zhenshchina. Edited by A. M. Ranchin. Moskva: Izd.-vo Pravda, 1991.

ELISAVETA SHAKHOVA
Stikhotvoreniia Elizavety Shakhovoi. Sankt-Peterburg: R[oss.] A[kad.], 1839.
Mirianka i otshel'nitsa: Stikhotvoreniia Elisavety Shakhovoi v dvukh chastiakh. Sankt-
   Peterburg: Tip. K. Vingebera, 1849.
Povesti v stikhakh Elisavety Shakhovoi. Sankt-Peterburg: Tip. K. Vingebera, 1842.
Sobranie sochinenii v stikhakh Elisavety Shakhovoi. Published by the author's grand-
   son. Sankt-Peterburg: Ekaterinskaia tip., 1911.

EKATERINA SHAKHOVSKAIA
Snovidenie: Fantasmagoriia. Moskva: V tip. Lazarevykh, 1833.

NADEZHDA TEPLOVA
Stikhotvoreniia N. Teplovoi. 2nd ed., enlarged. Moskva: V tip. Lazarevykh Insti-
   tuta Vostochnykh iazykov, 1838.
Stikhotvoreniia Nadezhdy Teplovoi (Teriukhinoi). 3rd ed., supplemented. Moskva:
   V tip. Katkova, 1860.

F. I. TIUTCHEV
Polnoe sobranie sochinenii. Edited by P. V. Bykov. Sankt-Peterburg: Marks, 1913.
Polnoe sobranie stikhotvorenii v dvukh tomakh. Edited by Georgii Chulkov and
   D. D. Blagoi. Moskva: Terra, 1994.

IULIIA ZHADOVSKAIA
Stikhotvoreniia Iulii Zhadovskoi. Sankt-Peterburg: Tip. E. Pratsa, 1858.
Polnoe sobranie sochinenii. Posthumous ed. Sankt-Peterburg: Izd. P. V.
   Zhadovskogo, 1885.
Sochineniia. Posthumous ed. of poetry and correspondence. Sankt-Peterburg:
   Tip. S. Sobrodeva, 1886.
Izbrannye stikhotvoreniia. Edited by L. Losev. Iaroslavl': Iaroslavskoe knizhnoe
   izd., 1958.

Works Cited

Abrams, M. H. *Natural Supernaturalism.* New York: W. W. Norton, 1971.
Afanas'ev, Viktor. "'Da, zhenskaia dusha dolzhna v teni svetit'sia . . .' : Evdokiia
   Petrovna Rostopchina, 1811–1858: literaturnyi portret." In *Talisman,* by
   Evdokiia Rostopchina, edited by Viktor Afanas'ev. Moskva: Moskovskii
   Rabochii, 1987.
Aksakov, Ivan Sergeevich. *Ivan Sergeevich Aksakov v ego pismakh.* Moskva: M. G.
   Volchaninov, 1888.
Andrew, Joe. *Narrative and Desire in Russian Literature, 1822–1849: The Feminine
   and the Masculine.* New York: St. Martin's Press, 1993.

Aronson, M., and S. Reiser. *Literaturnye kruzhki i salony.* Leningrad: Priboi, 1929.

Ashfield, Andrew, ed. *Romantic Women Poets, 1770–1838.* Manchester: Manchester University Press, 1997.

Azadovskii, Mark. *Neizvestnyi poet-sibiriaka: E. Mil'keev.* Chita: Izd. Istoriko-literaturnogo kruzhka pri Gos. Institut narodnogo obrazovaniia, 1922.

Bannikov, N. V. "Ot sostavitelia." In *Russkie poetessy XIX veka.* Moskva: Sovetskaia Rossiia, 1979.

Barracano Schmidt, Dolores. "The Great American Bitch." *College English* 32 (1971): 900–905.

Bartenev, Petr. "K. K. Pavlova." *Russkii arkhiv,* no. 1 (1894): 119–23.

Battersby, Christine. *Gender and Genius: Towards a Feminist Aesthetics.* London: Women's Press Limited, 1989.

Baym, Nina. *Women's Fiction: A Guide to Novels by and about Women in America, 1820–1970.* Ithaca, N.Y.: Cornell University Press, 1978.

Belinskii, V. G. *Polnoe sobranie sochinenii.* Moskva: Izd. Akademii nauk SSSR, 1953.

Berg, N. V. "Grafinia Rostopchina v Moskve: Otryvok iz vospominanii." *Istoricheskii vestnik* 3 (1893): 691–708.

Berger, John, et. al. *Ways of Seeing.* London: British Broadcasting Corporation, 1972.

Bernstein, Lina. "Avdot'ia Petrovna Elagina and Her Contribution to Russian Letters." *SEEJ* 40, no. 2 (1996): 215–35.

———. "Private and Public Personas: Negotiating the Mommy Track in the Age of Nicholas I." Unpublished paper.

———. "Women on the Verge of a New Language: Russian Salon Hostesses in the First Half of the Nineteenth Century." In *Russia, Women, Culture,* edited by Helena Goscilo and Beth Holmgren. Bloomington: Indiana University Press, 1996.

Bianchi, Martha Dickinson, ed. *Life and Letters of Emily Dickinson.* New York: Biblio & Tannen, 1971.

Blagovo, V. A. *Poeziia i lichnost' Iu. V. Zhadovskoi.* Saratov: Izd. Saratovskogo universiteta, 1981.

Bobrov, Evgenii. "A. A. Fuks i kazanskie literatory 30–40kh godov." *Russkaia starina,* no. 6 (1904): 481–509; no. 7 (1904): 5–35.

Booth, Wayne. *The Rhetoric of Fiction.* Chicago: University of Chicago Press, 1961.

Bourdieu, Pierre. *Distinction : A Social Critique of the Judgement of Taste.* Translated by Richard Nice. Cambridge, Mass: Harvard University Press, 1998.

Boym, Svetlana. *Death in Quotation Marks: Cultural Myths of the Modern Poet.* Cambridge, Mass.: Harvard University Press, 1991.

Briusov, Valerii. "K. K. Pavlova." *Ezhemesiachnye sochineniia,* no. 12 (1903): 273–90.

Brodskii, N. L., ed. *Literaturnye salony i kruzhki: Pervaia polovina XIX v.* Moskva: Akademiia, 1930.

Brown, William. *A History of Russian Literature of the Romantic Period.* Ann Arbor: Ardis, 1986.

Bukhmeier, K. K. Introduction to *Polnoe sobranie stikhotvorenii,* by N. M. Iazykov. Moskva: Sovetskii pisatel', 1964.

Bulgarin, Faddei. "Stikhotvoreniia Aleksandry Fuks." *Severnaia pchela*, no. 194 (1834): 773–75.

Bykov, Petr. "Russkie zhenshchiny-pisatel'nitsy: Grafinia E. P. Rostopchina." *Drevniaia i Novaia Rossiia* 2, no. 5 (1878): 238–43.

———. *Siluety dalekogo proshlogo*. Moskva: Zemlia i Fabrika, 1930.

Carroll, Berenice A. "The Politics of Originality: Women and the Class System of the Intellect." *Journal of Women's History* 2, no. 2 (1990): 136–63.

Chernyshev, V. I. Introduction to *Russkaia ballada*, edited by V. I. Chernyshev. Leningrad: Sovetskii pisatel', 1936.

Chernyshevskii, Nikolai. "Stikhotvoreniia grafini Rostopchinoi." *Sovremennik* 56 (1856): section 4: 3–18.

Chistov, K. V. Introduction to *Prichitaniia*, edited by K. V. Chistov. Leningrad: Sovetskii pisatel', 1960.

Chizhikov, L. A. *Nadezhda Dmitrievna Khvoshchinskaia-Zaionchkovskaia (V. Krestovskii-psevdonim): Bibliograficheskie o nei materialy*. Odessa: Tsentral'naia tipografiia S. Rozenshtraukha i N. Lemberga, 1914.

Cixous, Helene. "Sorties: Out and Out: Attacks/Ways Out/Forays." In *The Feminist Reader: Essays in Gender and the Politics of Literary Criticism*, edited by Catherine Belsey and Jane Moore. Cambridge, Mass: Blackwell, 1991.

Clements, Barbara. "Introduction: Accommodation, Resistance, Transformation." In *Russia's Women: Accommodation, Resistance, Transformation*, edited by Barbara Engel, Barbara Clements, and Christine Worobec. Berkeley: University of California Press, 1991.

Cott, Nancy. *The Bonds of Womanhood: "Woman's Sphere" in New England, 1780–1835*. New Haven, Conn.: Yale University Press, 1977.

Cranny-Francis, Ann. *Feminist Fiction: Feminist Uses of Generic Fiction*. New York: St. Martin's Press, 1990.

Curran, Stuart. *Poetic Form and British Romanticism*. New York: Oxford University Press, 1986.

De Lauretis, Teresa. *Alice Doesn't: Feminism, Semiotics, Cinema*. Bloomington: Indiana University Press, 1984.

Debreczeny, Paul. *Social Functions of Literature: Alexander Pushkin and Russian Culture*. Stanford, Calif.: Stanford University Press, 1997.

Demen'eva, A. G., A. V. Zapadov, and M. S. Cherepakhov, eds. *Russkaia periodicheskaia pechat', 1702–1895: Spravochnik*. Moskva: Gosudarstvennoe izv-do politicheskoi literatury, 1959.

DeShazer, Mary. *Inspiring Women: Reimagining the Muse*. New York: Pergamon Press, 1986.

Donovan, Josephine. "Toward a Women's Poetics." In *Feminist Issues in Literary Scholarship*, edited by Shari Benstock. Bloomington: Indiana University Press, 1987.

Drabble, Margaret, ed. *Oxford Companion to English Literature*. Oxford: Oxford University Press, 1985.

Druzhinin, A. V. "Stikhotvoreniia grafini E. P. Rostopchinoi." In *Sobranie sochinenii*, 7: 150–60. Sankt-Peterburg: Tip. Imp. Akademiia nauk, 1865–67.

Druzhnikov, Yuri. *Contemporary Russian Myths: A Skeptical View of the Literary Past*. Lewiston, N.Y.: Edwin Mellen Press, 1999.

DuPlessis, Rachel Blau. "'Corpses of Poesy': Some Modern Poets and Some Gender Ideologies of Lyric." In *Feminist Measures: Soundings in Poetry and Theory,* edited by Lynn Keller and Cristanne Miller. Ann Arbor: University of Michigan Press, 1994.

Egorov, B. F. Introduction to *Stikhotvoreniia i dramy,* by A. S. Khomiakov, edited by B. F. Egorov. Leningrad: Sovetskii pisatel', 1969.

Ellmann, Mary. *Thinking about Women.* New York: Harcourt Brace Jovanovich, 1968.

Engelstein, Laura. *The Keys to Happiness: Sex and the Search for Modernity in Fin-de-Siecle Russia.* Ithaca, N.Y.: Cornell University Press, 1992.

Ernst, Sergei. "Karolina Pavlova i gr. Evdokiia Rastopchina [sic]." *Russkii bibliofil,* no. 6 (1916): 5–35.

Faderman, Lillian. *Surpassing the Love of Men: Romantic Friendship and Love between Women from the Renaissance to the Present.* New York: William Morrow, 1981.

Fainshtein, M. Sh. *Pisatel'nitsy pushkinskoi pory.* Leningrad: Nauka, 1989.

Fedorova, N[astas'ia]. "Vospominanie ob Iu. V. Zhadovskoi." *Istoricheskii vestnik* 8 (Nov. 1887): 394–407.

Feldman, Paula. Introduction to *British Women Poets of the Romantic Era: An Anthology,* edited by Paula Feldman. Baltimore: Johns Hopkins University Press, 1997.

Feldman, Paula, and Theresa Kelley. Introduction to *Romantic Women Writers: Voices and Countervoices,* edited by Paula Feldman and Theresa Kelley. Hanover, N.H.: University Press of New England, 1995.

Fetterley, Judith. Introduction to *Provisions: A Reader from Nineteenth-Century American Women,* edited by Judith Fetterley. Bloomington: Indiana University Press, 1985.

Filipenko, Irina. "Moskovskie literaturnye salony." *Moskovskii zhurnal* 7 (1991): 50–52.

Foucault, Michel. *The History of Sexuality.* Translated by Robert Hurley. New York: Vintage, 1990.

Fowler, Alastair. *Kinds of Literature: An Introduction to the Theory of Genres and Modes.* Cambridge, Mass: Harvard University Press, 1982.

Freeze, Gregory. "Bringing Order to the Russian Family: Marriage and Divorce in Imperial Russia, 1760–1860." *Journal of Modern History* 62 (1990): 709–46.

Fridkin, V. "Al'bomy Karoliny Pavlovoi." *Nauka i zhizn'* 12 (1987): 140–48.

Friedman, Albert B. *The Ballad Revival: Studies in the Influence of Popular on Sophisticated Poetry.* Chicago: University of Chicago Press, 1961.

Friedman, Susan. "Gender and Genre Anxiety: Elizabeth Barrett Browning and H.D. as Epic Poets." *Tulsa Studies in Women's Literature* 5, no. 2 (1986): 203–28.

———. "Craving Stories: Narrator and Lyricism in Critical Theory and Women's Long Poems." In *Feminist Measures: Soundings in Poetry and Theory,* edited by Lynn Keller and Cristanne Miller, 15–42. Ann Arbor: University of Michigan Press, 1994.

Fusso, Susanne. "Pavlova's *Quadrille:* The Feminine Variant of (the End of) Romanticism." In *Essays on Karolina Pavlova,* edited by Susanne Fusso and Alexander Lehman. Evanston, Ill: Northwestern University Press, 2001.

Garrard, John. *Mikhail Lermontov.* Boston: Twayne, 1982.

Gasparov, M. L. *Metr i smysl: Ob odnom iz mekhanizmov kul'turnoi pamiati.* Moskva: Rossiiskii Gosudarstvennyi Gumanitarnyi Universitet, 1999.

———. *Ocherk istorii russkogo stikha.* Moskva: Fortuna Limited, 2000.

Gerhart, Mary. *Genre Choices, Gender Questions.* Norman: University of Oklahoma Press, 1992.

Gilbert, Sandra. "Female Female Impersonator: Millay and the Theater of Personality." In *Critical Essays on Edna St. Vincent Millay,* edited by William B. Thesing. New York: G. K. Hall, 1993.

Gilbert, Sandra, and Susan Gubar. Introduction to *Shakespeare's Sisters: Feminist Essays on Women Poets,* edited by Sandra Gilbert and Susan Gubar. Bloomington: Indiana University Press, 1979.

———. *The Madwoman in the Attic.* New Haven: Yale University Press, 1986.

Gilligan, Carol. *In A Different Voice.* Cambridge: Harvard University Press, 1982.

Ginzburg, Lidiia. *O lirike.* Leningrad: Sovetskii pisatel', 1974.

Gorizontov, Ivan. "Fel'eton: Vospominanie ob Anne Nikanorovne Mordovstevoi." *Saratovskii listok,* January 18, 1886, 1.

Goscilo, Helena. "Evdokiia Petrovna Rostopchina." In *Dictionary of Russian Women Writers,* edited by Marina Ledkovsky, Charlotte Rosenthal, and Mary Zirin. Westport, Conn.: Greenwood, 1994.

Greenberg, David. *The Construction of Homosexuality.* Chicago: Chicago University Press, 1988.

Greene, Diana. "Domestic Ideology in Mid Nineteenth-Century Russia." In *Women in Russian Culture,* edited by Rosalind Marsh. Oxford: Berghahn, 1998.

———. "Gender and Genre in Pavlova's *A Double Life.*" *Slavic Review* 54, no. 3 (1995): 563–77.

———. "Karolina Pavlova's 'At the Tea Table' and the Politics of Class and Gender." *Russian Review* 53 (April 1994): 2, 271–84.

———. "Karolina Pavlova's 'Tri duski': The Transfiguration of Biography." In *Proceedings of the Kentucky Foreign Language Conference, 1984.* Lexington: Department of Russian and Eastern Studies, 1984.

———. "Nineteenth-Century Women Poets: Critical Reception vs. Self-Definition." In *Women Writers in Russian Literature,* edited by Toby W. Clyman and Diana Greene. Westport, Conn.: Greenwood, 1994.

———. "Praskov'ia Bakunina and the Poetess's Dilemma." In *Russkie pisatel'nitsy i literaturnyi protsess,* edited by M. Sh. Fainshtein. Wilhelmshorst: F. K. Gopfert, 1995.

Greenleaf, Monika. *Pushkin and Romantic Fashion: Fragment, Elegy, Orient, Irony.* Stanford, Calif.: Stanford University Press, 1994.

Grigor'ian, K. N. "Ul'traromanticheskii rod poezii (iz istorii russkoi elegii)." In *Russkii romantizm,* edited by K. N. Grigor'ian. Leningrad: Nauka, 1978.

Grossgeinrikh [Grossheinrich], Karl. "Elisaveta Kul'man i ee stikhotvoreniia." *Biblioteka dlia chteniia,* nos. 4, 5, 6, 8 (1849).

Guillory, John. *Cultural Capital: The Problem of Literary Canon Formation.* Chicago: University of Chicago Press, 1993.

Hammarberg, Gitta. "Flirting with Words: Domestic Albums, 1770–1840." In

Russia, Women, Culture, edited by Helena Goscilo and Beth Holmgren. Bloomington: Indiana University Press, 1996.

Harmon, William, and C. Hugh Holman, eds. *A Handbook to Literature.* 7th ed. Upper Saddle River, N.J.: Prentice Hall, 1996.

Heffner, Roe-Merrill S. Preface to *Die Jungfrau von Orleans: Eines romantische Tragödie,* by Friedrich Schiller. New York: Henry Holt, [1927].

Heldt, Barbara. "Karolina Pavlova: The Woman Poet and the Double Life." In *Karolina Pavlova, A Double Life,* translated by Barbara Heldt. Oakland: Barbary Coast Books, 1986.

———. *Terrible Perfection: Women and Russian Literature.* Bloomington: University of Indiana Press, 1987.

Hillman, Brenda. Preface to *Emily Dickinson: Poems,* edited by Brenda Hillman. Boston: Shambhala, 1995.

Hofkosh, Sonia. "Sexual Politics and Literary History: William Hazlitt's Keswick Escapade and Sarah Hazlitt's Journal." In *At the Limits of Romanticism,* edited by Mary A. Favret and Nicola J. Watson. Bloomington: Indiana University Press, 1993.

Homans, Margaret. *Women Writers and Poetic Identity: Dorothy Wordsworth, Emily Brontë, and Emily Dickinson.* Princeton, N.J.: Princeton University Press, 1980.

Horney, Karen. *Feminine Psychology.* New York: Norton, 1967.

Iakuskin, N. I., ed. *Serdtsa chutkogo prozren'em . . . : Povesti i rasskazy russkikh pisatel'nits XIX v.* Moskva: Sovetskaia Rossiia, 1991.

Iezuitova, R. V. "Ballada v epokhu romantizma." In *Russkii romantizm,* edited by K. N. Grigor'ian. Leningrad: Nauka, 1978.

Jagose, Annamarie. *Queer Theory: An Introduction.* New York: New York University Press, 1996.

Jameson, Fredric. *The Political Unconscious: Narrative as a Socially Symbolic Act.* Ithaca: Cornell University Press, 1981.

Jewett, Sarah Orne. *In the Country of the Pointed Firs.* New York: Dover, 1994.

Johnson, Thomas H., ed. *The Poems of Emily Dickinson, Including Variant Readings Critically Compared with All Known Manuscripts.* Cambridge, Mass.: Belknap Press of Harvard University Press, 1955.

Karrik, A. G. "Iz vospominanii o N. D. Khvoshchinskoi-Zaionchkovskoi." *Zhenskoe delo,* no. 9 (1899): 3–19; no. 11 (1899): 36–53; no. 12 (1899): 59–83.

Katz, Michael R. *The Literary Ballad in Early Nineteenth-Century Russian Literature.* New York: Oxford University Press, 1976.

Keller, Lynn, and Cristanne Miller, ed. *Feminist Measures: Soundings in Poetry and Theory.* Ann Arbor: University of Michigan Press, 1994.

Kelly, Catriona. *A History of Russian Women's Writing.* Oxford: Clarendon Press, 1994.

———. "Reluctant Sibyls: Gender and Intertextuality in the Work of Adelaida Gertsyk and Vera Merkureva." In *Rereading Russian Poetry,* edited by Stephanie Sandler. New Haven, Conn.: Yale University Press, 1999.

Kermode, Frank. *Forms of Attention.* Chicago: University of Chicago Press, 1985.

Khodasevich, Vladislav. "Grafinia E. P. Rostopchina: Ee zhizn' i lirika." *Russkaia mysl',* no. 11 (1916): 35–53.

Khvoshchinskaia, Praskov'ia. "Nadezhda Khvoshchinskaia." In *Sobranie sochi-nenii V. Krestovskogo (Psevdonim)*. Sankt-Peterburg: Izdanie A. S. Surovina, 1892.

Kiselev, V. "Poetessa i tsar'." *Russkaia literatura*, no. 1 (1965): 144–56.

Kiselev-Sergenin, V. S. "Po staromu sledu (o ballade E. Rostopchinoi 'Nasil'nyi brak')." *Russkaia literatura*, no. 3 (1995): 137–52.

———. "Taina grafini E. P. Rostopchinoi." *Neva* 9 (1994): 267–84.

Kiukhel'beker, Vil'gel'm. "Dnevnik Vil'g. Karl. Kiukhel'bekera." *Russkaia starina*, no. 2 (1884): 351–52.

Kononenko, Natalie. "Women as Performers of Oral Literature: A Re-examination of Epic and Lament." In *Women Writers in Russian Literature*, edited by Toby W. Clyman and Diana Greene. Westport, Conn.: Greenwood Press, 1994.

Kulka, Tomas. *Kitsch and Art*. University Park.: Pennsylvania State University Press, 1996.

Lauter, Paul. *Canons and Contexts*. New York: Oxford University Press, 1991.

Ledkovsky, Marina, Charlotte Rosenthal, and Mary Zirin, eds. *Dictionary of Russian Women Writers*. Westport, Conn.: Greenwood Press, 1994.

Liashchenko, A. I. "A. V. Kol'tsov (biograficheskii ocherk)." In *Polnoe sobranie sochinenii A. V. Kol'tsova*, xvii–xxxiv. Sankt-Peterburg: Razriada iziashchnoi slovesnost' Imperatorskoi Akademii nauk, 1909.

Likhacheva, E. *Materialy dlia istorii zhenskogo obrazovaniia v Rossii (1086–1856)*. Sankt-Peterburg: M. M. Stasiulevich, 1899.

Linkin, Harriet Kramer, and Stephen C. Behrendt, ed. *Romanticism and Women Poets: Opening the Doors of Reception*. Lexington: University Press of Kentucky, 1999.

Manuilov, V. A., ed. *Lermontovskaia entsiklopediia*. Moskva: Sovetskaia entsiklopediia, 1981.

Marrese, Michelle. *A Woman's Kingdom: Noblewomen and the Control of Property in Russia, 1700–1861*. Ithaca: Cornell University Press, 2002.

Masanov, I. F. *Slovar' pseudonimov russkikh pisatelei, uchenykh i obshchestvennykh deiatelei*. Moskva: Izd. Vsesoiuznoi Knizhnoi Palaty, 1960.

Mellor, Anne. *Romanticism and Gender*. New York: Routledge, 1993.

———. "A Criticism of Their Own: Romantic Women Literary Critics." In *Questioning Romanticism*, edited by John Beer. Baltimore: Johns Hopkins University Press, 1995.

———, ed. *Romanticism and Feminism*. Bloomington: Indiana University Press, 1998.

Mersereau, John. "Yes, Virginia, There Was a Russian Romantic Movement." In *The Ardis Anthology of Russian Romanticism*, edited by Christine Rydel. Ann Arbor.: Ardis, 1984.

Mikhailov, M. "Istoriia drevnei slovesnosti: Safo i Lezbosskie getery." *Literaturnaia gazeta*, Sept. 25 1847, 610–12.

Mirsky, D. S. *A History of Russian Literature from Its Beginnings to 1900*. New York: Vintage Books, 1958.

Modleski, Tania. *Loving with a Vengeance: Mass-Produced Fantasies for Women*. New York: Routledge, 1984.

Mogilianskii, A. P. "N. D. i S. D. Khvoshchinskie." In *Istoriia russkoi literatury*, vol. 9, bk. 2, 228–37. Moskva: Izd.-vo Akademii nauk SSSR, 1956.

Moi, Toril. *Sexual/Textual Politics*. London: Routledge, 1988.

Montegiu, Emil'. "O zhenshchinakh poetakh v severnoi Amerike." *Biblioteka dlia chteniia*, no. 108 (1851): 124–33.

Moore, Christopher. Introduction to *Selected Poems*, edited by Lord Byron. New York: Gramercy Books, 1994.

Mueller, Janel. "The Feminist Poetics of Aemilia Lanyer's 'Salve Deus Rex Judaeorum.'" In *Feminist Measures: Soundings in Poetry and Theory*, edited by Lynn Keller and Cristanne Miller. Ann Arbor: University of Michigan Press, 1994.

Myers, Sylvia. "Learning, Virtue, and the Term 'Bluestocking.'" *Studies in Eighteenth Century Culture* 15 (1986): 279–88.

Nabokov, Vladimir. Translator's foreword to *A Hero of Our Time*, by Mikhail Lermontov. Garden City, N.Y.: Doubleday, 1958.

———. Translator's introduction to *Eugene Onegin: A Novel in Verse*, by Aleksandr Pushkin. London: Routledge & Kegan Paul, 1964.

[Nekrasov, N. A.]. "Zametki i razmyshleniia novogo poeta po povodu russkoi zhurnalistiki, avg. 1852." *Sovremennik* 35, no. 9 (1852): 105–7.

Nekrasova, E. S. "Grafinia E. P. Rostopchina." *Vestnik Evropy* 3 (March–April 1885): 42–81.

Nikolaev, P. A., ed. *Russkie pisateli, 1800–1917: Biograficheskii slovar'*. Moskva: Sovetskaia entsiklopediia, 1989–.

Nikolai, Gerbel', ed. *Khrestomatiia dlia vsekh: Russkie poety v biografiiakh i obraztsakh*. Sankt-Peterburg: Tip. Imperatorskaia Akademii nauk, 1873.

"Odinnadtsataia polosa: Dni rozhdeniia" *Moskovskii komsomolets*. Universal Database of Russian Newspapers, Jan. 4, 1999 [cited July 20, 2000].

Olsen, Tillie. *Silences*. New York: Delacorte Press, 1978.

Ong, Walter J. *Orality and Literacy: The Technologizing of the Word*. London: Methuen, 1982.

Ostriker, Alicia. *Stealing the Language: The Emergence of Women's Poetry in America*. Boston: Beacon Press, 1986.

Ozerov, L. A. Introduction to *Stikhotvoreniia*, by Afanasii Afanas'evich Fet, edited by L. A. Ozerov. Moskva: Izd-vo "Khodozhestvennaia literatura, 1970.

Panaev, Ivan. "Peterburgskie novosti." *Sovremennik* 48 (1854): 130–38.

Parker, Alan Michael, and Mark Wilhardt, eds. *The Cross-Gendered Poem*. New York: Routledge, 1996.

Pasco, Judith. "Mary Robinson and the Literary Marketplace." In *Romantic Women Writers: Voices and Countervoices*, edited by Paula Feldman and Theresa Kelley. Hanover, N.H.: University Press of New England, 1995.

Pedrotti, Louis. "The Scandal of Countess Rostopčina's Polish-Russian Allegory." *SEEJ* 30, no. 2 (1986): 196–214.

Perkins, Pamela. *The Burden of Sufferance: Women Poets of Russia*. New York: Garland, 1993.

Perry, Seamus. "Romanticism: The Brief History of a Concept." In *A Companion to Romanticism*, edited by Duncan Wu. Oxford: Blackwell, 1998.

Pogodin, Dmitrii Mikhailovich. "Grafinia E. P. Rostopchina i ee vechera." In

Schastlivaia zhenshchina, by Evdokiia Rostopchina, 401. Moskva: Izd.-vo Pravda, 1991.

Polovtsov, A. A., et al., eds. *Russkii biograficheskii slovar'*. Sankt-Peterburg: Izdanie Imperatorskogo russkogo istoricheskogo obshchestva, 1896–1918.

Pratt, Annis. *Archetypal Patterns in Women's Fiction*. Bloomington: Indiana University Press, 1981.

Pratt, Sarah. "The Obverse of Self: Gender Shifts in Poems by Tjutcev and Axmatova." In *Russian Literature and Psychoanalysis*, edited by Daniel Rancour-Laferriere. Amsterdam: John Benjamin's Publishing, 1989.

———. *Russian Metaphysical Romanticism: The Poetry of Tiutchev and Boratynskii*. Stanford, Calif.: Stanford University Press, 1984.

Preminger, Alex, ed. *Princeton Encyclopedia of Poetry and Poetics*. Princeton, N.J.: Princeton University Press, 1974.

Preminger, Alex, and T. V. F. Brogan, eds. *New Princeton Encyclopedia of Poetry and Poetics*. Princeton, N.J.: Princeton University Press, 1993.

Ranchin, A. M. Editor's introduction to *Schastlivaia zhenshchina*, by E. P. Rostopchina. Moskva: Izd.-vo Pravda, 1991.

Rapgof, B. *Karolina Pavlova: Materialy dlia izucheniia zhizni i tvorchestva*. Petrograd: Izdatel'stvo Trirema, 1916.

Reichert, John. "More than Kin and Less than Kind: The Limits of Genre Theory." In *Theories of Literary Genre*, edited by Joseph Strelka. University Park: Penn State University Press, 1978.

Romanov, Boris. Introduction to *Stikhotvoreniia, proza, pis'ma*, by Evdokiia Rostopchina. Moskva: Sovetskaia Rossiia, 1986.

Rosenthal, Charlotte, and Mary Zirin. "Russia." In *Bloomsbury Guide to Women's Literature*, edited by Claire Buck, 109–18. New York: Prentice Hall, 1992.

Rosneck, Karen. "Nadezhda Teplova." In *Russian Women Writers*, edited by Christine Tomei. New York: Garland, 1999.

Ross, Marlon. "Romantic Quest and Conquest: Troping Masculine Power in the Crisis of Poetic Identity." In *Romanticism and Feminism*, edited by Anne Mellor. Bloomington: Indiana University Press, 1988.

———. *The Contours of Masculine Desire: Romanticism and the Rise of Women's Poetry*. New York: Oxford University Press, 1989.

Rostopchina, Evdokiia. "Iz portfel'ia starogo zhurnalista." [Letter to A. F. Koni, May 10, 1854] *Russkii arkhiv*, no. 3 (1909): 257–58.

———. *Stikhotvoreniia, proza, pis'ma*. Moskva: Sovetskaia Rossiia, 1986.

———. *Talisman*. Edited by Victor Afanas'ev. Moskva: Moskovskii Rabochii, 1987.

Rostopchina, Lidiia A. "Pravda o moei babushke." *Istoricheskii vestnik* 95/96 (1904).

———. "Semeinaia khronika (fragmenty)." In *Schastlivaia zhenshchina*, by Evdokiia Rostopchina, edited by A. M. Ranchin. Moskva: Iz. Pravda, 1991.

Rousseau, Jean-Jacques. *Emile, or On Education*. Translated by Allan Bloom. New York: Basic Books, 1979.

Russ, Joana. "What Can a Heroine Do? or Why Women Can't Write." In *Images of Women in Fiction: Feminist Perspectives*, edited by Susan Cornillion, 3–20. Bowling Green, Ohio.: Bowling Green University Popular Press, 1972.

Rydel, Christine, ed. *Ardis Anthology of Russian Romanticism*. Ann Arbor: Ardis, 1984.

Sacks, Peter M. *The English Elegy: Studies in the Genre from Spenser to Yeats*. Baltimore: Johns Hopkins University Press, 1985.

Sandler, Stephanie. Introduction to *Rereading Russian Poetry*. New Haven, Conn.: Yale University Press, 1999.

Scherr, Barry P. *Russian Poetry: Meter, Rhythm, and Rhyme*. Berkeley: University of California Press, 1986.

Schweickart, Patrocinio. "Reading Ourselves: Toward a Feminist Theory of Reading." In *Gender and Reading*, edited by Elizabeth Flynn and Patrocinio Schweickart. Baltimore: Johns Hopkins University Press, 1986.

Semenko, Irina M. *Vasily Zhukovsky*. Boston: Twayne, 1976.

Semevskii, V. "N. D. Khvoshchinskaia-Zaionchkovskaia." *Russkaia mysl'*, no. 10 (1890): 49–89; no. 11 (1890): 83–110; no. 12 (1890): 124–48.

Sendich, Munir. "The Life and Works of Karolina Pavlova." Ph.D. diss., New York University, 1968.

Shakespeare, William. *The First Part of King Henry VI*. Edited by Michael Hattaway. Cambridge: Cambridge University Press, 1990.

Shakhova, Elisaveta. "V nachale zhizni i na poroge vechnosti." *Russkaia starina*, no. 1 (1913): 162–67.

Shashkova, S. "Epokha Belinskogo." *Delo*, no. 3 (1877): 57–94; no. 4 (1877): 7–34.

Shevyrev, Stepan. "Stikhotvoreniia grafini E. Rostopchinoi." *Mokvitianin*, no. 7 (1841): 171–82.

Showalter, Elaine. "Towards a Feminist Poetics." In *Women Writing and Writing about Women*, edited by Mary Jacobus. London: Croom Helm, 1979.

———. "Feminist Criticism in the Wilderness." In *Writing and Sexual Difference*, edited by Elizabeth Abel. Chicago: University of Chicago Press, 1982.

Siniavskii, N., and M. Tsiavlovskii, eds. *Pushkin v pechati, 1814–1837: Khronologicheskii ukazatel' proizvedenii Pushkina, napechatannykh pri ego zhizni*. Moskva: L. E. Bukhgeim, 1914.

Skabichevskii, A. *Sochineniia*. Sankt-Peterburg: Tip. Vysochaishe utverzhdennago Tovarishchestva "Obshchestvannaia Pol'za," 1895.

Smirnov-Sokol'skii, Nikolai. *Russkie literaturnye al'manakhi i sborniki XVIII-XIX vv.* Moskva: Izdatel'stvo "Kniga," 1965.

Smith-Rosenberg, Caroll. "The Female World of Love and Ritual: Relations between Women in Nineteenth-Century America." *Signs: Journal of Women in Culture and Society*, no. 1 (1975): 1–29.

Sokolov, Aleksandr. *Ocherki po istorii russkoi poemy, XVIII i pervoi poloviny XIX veka*. Moskva: Izd-vo Moskovskogo universiteta, 1955.

Southey, Robert. *The Poetical Works of Robert Southey*. Boston: Houghton, Osgood & Company, 1880.

"Stikhotvoreniia Nadezhdy Teplovoi." *Severnaia pchela*, no. 175 (1834): 697–98.

Stites, Richard. *The Women's Liberation Movement in Russia*. Princeton, N.J.: Princeton University Press, 1978.

Sushkov, Dmitrii. "K biografii grafini E. P. Rostopchinoi." *Istoricheskii vestnik* 5 (1881): 300–305.

Sushkov, Sergei. "Biograficheskii ocherk." In *Sochineniia grafini E. P. Rostopchinoi.* Sankt-Peterburg: Tip. I. N. Skorokhodova, 1890.

Taubman, Jane. "Women Poets of the Silver Age." In *Women Writers in Russian Literature,* edited by Toby Clyman and Diana Greene. Westport, Conn.: Greenwood, 1994.

Tayler, Irene, and Gina Luria. "Gender and Genre: Women in British Romantic Literature." In *What Manner of Woman: Essays on English and American Life and Literature,* edited by Marlene Springer. New York: New York University Press, 1977.

Taylor, Romy. "Autobiographical Poetry or Poetic Autobiography: K. Pavlova's 1847 Invective Epistle 'We Are Contemporaries, Countess.'" In *Models of Self: Russian Women's Autobiographical Texts,* edited by Arja Rosenholm, Marianne Liljestrom, and Irina Savkina. Helsinki: Kimimora Publications, 2000.

———. "The Friendly Epistle in Russian Poetry: A History of the Genre." Ph.D. diss., University of Southern California, 2001.

———. "Pavlova's *Dvojnaia zhizn':* An Icon Turns the Plot." In *Essays on Karolina Pavlova,* edited by Susanne Fusso and Alexander Lehman. Evanston, Ill.: Northwestern University Press, 2001.

Terras, Victor, ed. *Handbook of Russian Literature.* New Haven, Conn.: Yale University Press, 1985.

Tiutcheva, A. F. *Pri dvore dvukh imperatorov.* Moskva: M. i S. Sabashnikovykh, 1928.

Tomashevskii, Boris. *Pushkin.* Moskva: Izd. Akademii Nauk SSSR, 1956.

Tomei, Christine, ed. *Russian Women Writers.* New York: Garland, 1999.

Tschiževskij, Dmitrij. *On Romanticism in Slavic Literature.* 's-Gravenhage: Mouton, 1957.

Tsebrikova, Mar'ia. "Ocherk zhizni N. D. Khvoshchinskoi-Zaionchkovskoi." *Mir Bozhii,* no. 12 (1897): 3–40.

Tukalevskii, Vl. Introduction to *Polnoe sobranie sochinenii,* by Mikhail Iur'evich Lermontov. Moskva: OGUZ, 1948.

Uchenova, V. V., ed. *Tsaritsy muz: Russkie poetessy XIX-nachala XIX veka.* Moskva: Sovremennik, 1989.

Vatsuro, Vadim. *Lirika pushkinskoi pory: Elegicheskaia shkola.* Sankt-Peterburg: Nauka, 1994.

———. "Zhizn' i poeziia Nadezhdy Teplovoi." *Pamiatniki kul'tury: Novoe otkrytiia* (1989): 16–43.

Vengarov, S. A., ed. *Pushkin.* Sankt-Peterburg: Brokgauz-Efron, 1911.

Verkhovskii, Iu. N. *Poety pushkinskoi pory.* Moskva: Izd. M. i S. Sabashinkovykh, 1919.

Vinitskaia, A. A. "Vospominaniia o N. D. Khvochshinskoi." *Istoricheskii vestnik,* no. 1 (1890): 146–55.

Vishnevskaia, G. A. "Tema sotsial'nogo bespraviia zhenshchiny v literaturnom nasledii Belinskogo." In *Uchenye zapiski Kazanskogo gosudarstvennogo universiteta,* edited by M. T. Nuzhin. Kazan: Kazanskii gosudarstvennyi universitet, 1956.

Vitale, Serene. *Pushkin's Button.* New York: Farrar, Straus & Giroux, 1999.

Voltaire. *La Pucelle: Poème en vingt-un chants avec les notes par Voltaire*. Paris: Pierre Didot, 1801.

Vowles, Judith. "The Inexperienced Muse: Russian Women and Poetry in the First Half of the Nineteenth Century." In *A History of Women's Writing in Russia*, edited by Adele Marie Barker and Jehanne M. Gheith. New York: Cambridge University Press, 2002.

Wachtel, Michael. *The Development of Russian Verse: Meter and Meaning*. Cambridge: Cambridge University Press, 1998.

Wagner, William. *Marriage, Property, and Law in Late Imperial Russia*. Oxford: Clarendon Press, 1994.

Walker, Cheryl. *The Nightingale's Burden: Women Poets and American Culture before 1900*. Bloomington: Indiana University Press, 1982.

———. Introduction to *American Women Poets of the Nineteenth Century: An Anthology*, edited by Cheryl Walker. New Brunswick, N.J.: Rutgers University Press, 1992.

Wellek, Rene. "The Concept of 'Romanticism' in Literary History (The Unity of European Romanticism)." *Comparative Literature* 1, no. 1 (1949): 147–72.

Welter, Barbara. *Dimity Convictions*. Athens: Ohio University Press, 1976.

Wilkie, Brian. *Romantic Poets and Epic Tradition*. Madison: University of Wisconsin Press, 1965.

Whittaker, Tatyana. "Fet [Shenshin], Afanasii Afanas'evich." In *Modern Encyclopedia of Russia and Soviet Literature*, edited by Harry Weber. Gulf Breeze, Fla: Academic International Press, 1977.

Wolfson, Susan J. "Romanticism and Gender." In *A Companion to Romanticism*, edited by Duncan Wu. Oxford: Blackwell, 1998.

Zeiger, Melissa F. *Beyond Consolation: Death, Sexuality, and the Changing Shapes of Elegy*. Ithaca, N.Y.: Cornell University Press, 1997.

Zhirmunskii, V. M. *Bairon i Pushkin: Pushkin i zapadnye literatury*. Leningrad: Nauka, 1978.

[Zotov, V. R.] "Peterburgskii vestnik." *Panteon*, no. 8 (1852): 13–22.

Zotov, V. R. "Nadezhda Dmitrievna Khvoshchinskaia (iz vospominanii starogo zhurnalista)." *Istoricheskii vestnik* 38, no. 10 (1889): 93–108.

———. "Peterburg v sorokovykh godakh." *Istoricheskii vestnik*, no. 6 (1890): 556–59.

Index

accommodation and resistance: non-canonical men poets, 172; women poets, 28–30
Aesopian language, 19. *See also* censorship
Akhmatova, Anna: "Kogda ia noch'iu zhudu ee prikhoda," 43
Aleksandra Fedorovna, Empress, 94, 95, 100
Alexander I, 141
Alexander II, 94
ambivalence, 18–19, 110. *See also* interpretive strategies
Anacreon, 31; and Kul'man, 32, 42; and Pushkin, 50
anacreontic odes, 31–32, 38
antimuses, 42, 67, 164. *See also* muses, male
Apollo, 43, 44, 247n. 42
archetypes, Romantic, 83
Aristotle, 16, 57, 242n. 2

Bacchic songs. *See vakkhicheskie pesni*
Bakunina, Praskov'ia, 4, 5; depiction of nature, 52–53; depiction of women, 28–29; male muse, 42, 236n. 14; pseudonym, 45; and Zrazhevskaia, 29. Works: "Ballada," 29, 181; "Dva dnia," 237n. 26; "Moi chertenok," 42, 179–80; "Poslanie k drugu," 236n. 14; "Prolog," 25, 182–87;

"Siialo utro obnovlen'em," 18, 78, 235n. 11
ballad, 70–74; and epic, 70, 71; and gender norms, 71–72, 246n. 35; revival, 59, 70–71
Baratynsky, Evgenii, 4; and Del'vig, 34; Elagina, 140; marriage and career, 23; and Pavlova, 11, 67–68; and Zhukovsky, 34. Works: "Epigramma," 24–25; "Kladbishche," 11; "Nalozhnitsa," 11; "Osen'," 10; "Poslednii poet," 38; "Sovet," 24–25; "Tsyganka," 11. *See also* Pavlova, *Kadril'*
bards, 39, 41, 71, 236n. 12
Batiushkov, Konstanin: "Vakkhanka," 32–33
Belinsky, Vissarion: and Batiushkov, 32; and domestic ideology, 24; and Kol'tsov, 34, 170, 173, 279n. 12; and Lermontov, 34; and Mil'keev, 173; and Pavlova, 142, 272n. 19; and Pushkin, 34; and Rostopchina, 45, 93, 97, 101, 256n. 28, 260n. 50; and Tepolov, 17, 85; and women's genius, 18; and women's writing, 35; and Zhadovskaia, 35
Belle dame sans merci, 73, 83
Berg, Nikolai: and Pavlova, 139; and Rostopchina, 90
Biblioteka dlia chteniia, 6, 33, 141, 170
Biblioteka poeta series, 9, 137, 168, 170

binary hierarchical oppositions, 49, 54
blotting-books, 123, 267n. 38
Boileau, Nicholas: *Art poétique*, 59
Botkin, Mariia, 23
Botkin, Vasilii, 23
Botmer, Emilia-Eleonor, 23
Briusov, Valerii: and Pavlova, 141,
    144, 145
Browning, Elizabeth Barrett: *Aurora
    Leigh*, 110
Bulgarin, Faddei, 89
bylina (folk epic), 243n. 11
Byron, George Gordon, 59, 62, 63,
    230n. 19. Works: "The Corsair,"
    63, 73; *Eastern Tales*, 62, 148; "The
    Giaour," 4

canonical poets: common social fac-
    tors, 168, 169; and eternal rele-
    vance, 104–5
canonical status: and gender in Rus-
    sian Romanticism, 8; and schol-
    arly resources, 13
canon of Russian literature, 7, 167,
    173–74, 222n. 15
canons: challenges to, 11–14; expan-
    sions of, 12
Catherine II, 23
censorship: and Guber, 6; and
    Khvoshchinskaia, 122, 126, 132;
    and Russian writers, 19, 132;
    sexual-political, 132
censorship terror, 126
Chernyshevky, Nikolai, 100
civil service, and Russian men poets, 31
Clairmont, Claire: and Pavlova,
    270n. 11
classicism: and androcentrism, 31–33;
    in Russia, 59
class-neutral aesthetic standards, 172
Corinna, 39, 235n. 6. See also Kul'-
    man, "Korinna"
cross-gendered poems, 41, 46, 147,
    237n. 26

Daszkiewicz, Cyprian, 141
Davidson, Lucretia Maria, 155, 156

death: depiction of in women's po-
    etry, 15, 17, 77; and grammatical
    gender, 247–48. *See also* elegy;
    mourning and gender
death or marriage ending, 166
Decembrist Rebellion and poetry, 62,
    95, 97, 106
Del'vig, Anton, 4; and Baratynsky, 34;
    marriage and career, 23; and
    Pushkin, 34; *Severnye tsvety*, 34.
    Works: "Dscher' khladna l'da!,"
    50; "Luna," 50; "Razgovor s ge-
    niem," 236n. 15
Denis'eva, Elena, 23, 91
descriptions of physical appearance
    of Russian women poets:
    Khvoshchinskaia, 116; Mordovt-
    seva, 264n. 15; Pavlova, 141,
    271n. 14; Rostopchina, 90–91
Dickinson, Emily, 45, 124, 136,
    274n. 38. Works: "Apparently
    with no surprise," 54; "I'm No-
    body!," 18, 119
Dido-and-Aeneas convention, 61
divorce, Russia, 22
Dobroliubov, Nikolai, 110
domestic ideology, 23–27, 119, 229n. 9
Dostoevsky, Fedor, 119, 121
dramatic monologues, 47
Dresden, 142, 143
druzheskoe poslanie (friendly epistle,
    verse epistle), 5, 38, 234n. 1
Druzhinin, Aleksandr: "Zhenshchina-
    pisatel'nitsa," 25–26
duels, 31, 161, 165
Dumas, Alexandre, 95
duplicity, 18, 110. *See also* interpretive
    strategies
Durova, Nadezhda, 41, 275n. 38

Elagina, Avdot'ia, 139–40, 141,
    248n. 43; and Zhukovsky, 140
elegy, 74–81; funerary, 77, 248n. 47;
    gender norms, 75, 79, 81; and
    mourning, 75–76. *See also prichi-
    tanie*
Engel'gardt, Anstasiia, 23

epic, 57, 60–62; gender norms, 60–61. *See also bylina; geroicheskaia epopeia; poema*
epic hero, 61, 243n. 13
Evropeets, 140
excerpts from a narrative poem. *See otryvki iz poemy*
exclusions of women from male institutions, 30–37

Fedorovna, Nastas'ia, 22, 221n. 11
Fedotov, Pavel, 4, 168, 169, 171–72, 221n. 13; and Krylov, 170. Works: "K moim chitaleliam," 172, 241n. 39; "Svatovstvo maiora," 172
female female impersonation, 19, 110. *See also* interpretive strategies
femininity, construction of, 115–16
Fet, Afanasii, 4, 13, 278n. 3; marriage and career, 23; and Pavlova, 273n. 27; and Turgenev, 34. Works: "Eshche vesny dushistoi nega," 51; "Glub' nebes opiat' iasna," 51; "Kak maiskii golubookii zefir," 51; "Na smert' Miti Botkina," 77
folk epic. *See bylina*
folk genres, 59, 60. *See also* ballad; *bylina; prichitanie*
formalist virtues, 12, 20
frame narratives, 129, 131, 161
Freud, Sigmund, 75, 76
friendly epistle. *See druzheskoe poslanie*
Fuks, Aleksandra, 4, 5, 225n. 36. Works: "Grecheskaia skazka," 17; *Knizhna Khabiba,* 66; *Osnovanie goroda Kazani,* 66, 245n. 24; "Razgovor s muzoiu," 43
funeral laments, 79. *See also prichitanie*

Garelina, Liubov', 4, 5, 45; reception, 81. Works: "Bezumnaia," 48; "Mama! Chto ty vse zvdykhaesh'?," 73; "Molisia obo mne," 55

Gay, Delphine (Mme, de Giradin), 110, 155, 156, 236n. 13
gender, 220n. 6
gender ideology, 86, 90, 96
gender-neutral aesthetic standards, 19–20, 86–87, 167
gender norms, 83, 112–14; and genre, 58. *See also* ballad; elegy; epic; *romanticheskaia poema*
generic subtitles, 63–64, 67, 68
generic titles, 60, 76
genius, 17–18; as muse, 42, 236n. 15
genre, 57–58; and class, 58; and gender, 57–87, 148–49; neoclassical, 59; and race, 58; Russian Romantic, 59–60. *See also* ballad; elegy; epic; gender norms; *romanticheskaia poema*
genre anxiety, 61, 63, 66–67, 72, 77
Gerbel', Nikolai, 130–31
geroicheskaia epopeia (heroic verse epic), 61–62
God, 27, 38, 41, 54–55; in Bakunina, 18, 237n. 26; in Khvoshchinskaia, 126; in Pavlova, 154, 156, 158, 159, 163–64; in Rostopchina, 256n. 28; in Southey, 150–51; and women in the Bible, 235n. 10
Goethe, Johann Wolfgang von, 141, 170
Gogol', Nikolai, 89–90
Golden Age of Russian literature, 5, 13, 14, 173–74; eclipse of, and end of poetry, 135, 138, 257n. 31, 269n. 50
gothic tale, 69, 246n. 28
Gotovtseva, Anna, 4, 5, 34; and Bartenev, 235n. 7; and depictions of nature, 52; marriage and career, 22; and Pushkin, 29, 230n. 24; reception, 29; sexualization, 231n. 24; signature, 45; and Viazemsky, 35, 45, 231n. 24. Works: "A. S. P.," 18; "K N. N.," 46; "Odinochestvo," 46, 237n. 26
Gouges, Olympe de, 86
government-run boarding schools. *See instituty*

Gray, Thomas: "Elegy Written in a Country Churchyard," 74, 75
Grech, Nikolai, 89
green world fantasy, 69
Grigorovich, Dmitrii, 139
Grossheinrich, Karl, 32
Guber, Eduard, 4, 169; and Pushkin, 170. Works: "Ia po komnatu khochu," 49
gynocritics, 9

heroic verse epic. *See geroicheskaia epopeia*
Homer, 39, 71
Homeric question, 71
homosexuality, invention of, 118
Hugo, Victor: *Préface de Cromwell*, 59

Iazykov, Nikolai, 4, 140, 141. Works: "Bessonitsa," 50–51; "Poèt," 234n. 5
ideology, 242n. 3; and genre, 58. *See also* gender ideology
imagination in Romanticism, 3, 4
implied reader, 47, 48, 49, 239n. 31. *See also* lyrics, implied reader
inheritance and gender in Russia, 21, 227n. 4
institutions, Russian, male, 30–37
instituty (government-run boarding schools), 21, 23
interpretive strategies, 9, 13, 14, 18–19; for noncanonical poets, 172; for Rostopchina, 109–10
intertextuality in women's poetry, 110
irony, 19, 108, 130; in Fedotov, 172; in Khvoshchinskaia, 130; in Pavlova, 19, 157; in Rostopchina, 108, 110; in Teplova, 19. *See also* interpretive strategies

Jaenisch, Karl, 140, 141
Joan of Arc, 66; literary depiction in Dickinson, 274n. 38; in Pavlova, 152–55; in Russia, 274n. 38; in Schiller, 151; in Shakespeare, 150–51; in Southey, 150–51,
276n. 42; in Voltaire, 150, 151, 275n. 42

Karamzin, Andrei, 92, 96, 100
Karamzin, Nikolai, 74, 239n. 29; and Zhukovsky, 34
Kheraskov, Mikhail, 60–61, 62
Khomiakov, Aleksei, 4, 168, 169, 170, 172; and Decembrists, 35; and Elagina, 140; and Iazykov, 140; and Zhukovsky, 34
Khvoshchinskaia, Iuliia Vikent'eva (née Drobysheva-Rubets), 112–13
Khvoshchinskaia, Nadezhda, 4, 5, 6, 16, 112–36; cosmology, 134; depictions of nature, 52; descriptions of her physical appearance, 116; financial constraints, 113, 114, 134–35; and gender norms, 112–19; Gerbel's editing, 130–31; knowledge of Latin, 113; literary debut, 120–21; literary reputation, 112, 134–35, 137; literary social capital, 143; marriage and career, 22, 115, 118; and Nekrasov, 135; and punctuation, 124; on Pushkin, 226n. 40; reception, 29, 39, 115, 120, 135–36; and Revolutions of 1848, 129, 133, 267n. 36; self-representation, 45, 119–20, 133, 266n. 29; themes, 133; turn to prose, 112, 114, 121, 122, 134–35; Zotov's editing, 129–30. Works: "Blednaia deva: Videnie: Ballada," 73; "Byvalo s setrami," 124, 125–29, 133, 134, 192–93; *Derevenskii sluchai*, 68; "Druz'ia!," 124, 125–26, 133, 188–89; *Dzhulio*, 18, 134; "Ia ne tebe otdam," 124, 133; "Klad-bishche," 11, 132, 133, 134; "Net, ia ne nazovu obmanom," 117; "O daite men pole," 123, 124, 134; "Solntse segodnia za tucheiu," 47; "Uzhasno skorbnykh dnei," 124, 133, 134; "Uzh vecher," 133, 134; "Vy ulybaetes'," 68, 129–31, 133, 135, 190–92. *See also* Zotov

Khvoshchinskaia, Praskov'ia, 113, 118
Khvoshchinskaia, Sof'ia, 113, 114,
    115, 116, 118, 120
Khvoshchinsky, Dmitrii Kesarevich,
    112, 113–14, 263n. 5
kinds of literature, 57, 242n. 2
Kireevsky, Ivan, 140, 141
Kireevsky, Petr, 140
Kiukhel'beker, 74; and Kul'man, 28
Kol'tsov, Aleksei, 4, 169, 171, 172–73;
    and Belinsky, 34, 170, 279n. 12;
    literary reputation, 173; and
    Zhukovsky, 35, 233n. 35
Korsini, Mar'ia: "Zhenshchina-
    pisatel'nitsa," 25
Krestovsky, V., 45, 112, 118. *See also*
    Khvoshchinskaia
kruzhki (literary circles), 30, 34, 36, 139
Krylov, Ivan, 170
Kul'man, Elisaveta, 4, 5, 220n. 71; and
    Anacreon, 32, 42; and classicism,
    32, 33; and male muse, 42. Works:
    "K Anakreon," 18, 42; "Korinna,"
    44, 194–202, 235n. 6; "Safo," 47

Lamartine, Alphonse Marie de, 46,
    59, 237n. 26
lament. *See prichitanie*
languages, Russian poets' knowl-
    edge of: European, 247n. 36;
    Khvoshchinskaia, 113; Kul'man,
    31, 33; Latin, 31–32; Pavlova, 40,
    41; Rostopchina, 93
legal separations, Russia, 21–22
Lermontov, Mikhail, 4, 13; and the *po-
    ema*, 64, 244n. 19; and Ros-
    topchina, 90, 101; and
    Zhukovsky, 34. Works: "Klad-
    bishche," 11; "Morskaia
    tsarevna," 50
lesbianism, invention of, 118
Leucas, promontory of, 39
Libina, Nadezhda, 45. *See also* Gare-
    lina
Lisitsyna, Mariia, 4, 5, 30; depiction
    of nature, 52; and signature, 45;
    and Teplova, 30, 77

literary circles. *See kruzhki*
literary gatekeepers, 7, 12, 37, 85, 139,
    167
literary orientalism, 65
literary reputation, 167; factors deter-
    mining, 137–40, 168. *See also*
    Khvoshchinskaia; Kol'tsov; liter-
    ary social capital; Mil'keev;
    Pavlova; Rostopchina
literary social capital, 7, 37, 222n. 18;
    and canonicity, 168, 169; and
    gender, 8, 138–40; and
    Khvoshchinskaia, 143; and
    Pavlova, 140–43
literary standards, 12, 14–15, 172;
    gender-neutral, 19–20
literature, men's and women's, 47
Literaturnaia gazeta, 39, 114, 120, 121,
    128
Lomonosov, Mikhailo, 59
lyceums, influence on Russian men
    poets, 31
lyrics, 5, 20, 81–85; implied reader, 48

Macpherson, James: Ossian poems,
    39, 59
Maikov, Apollon, 4, 35, 169, 170; and
    Pletnev, 34–35
Maksimovich, Mikhail, 6, 34; and
    Dennitsa, 34; and Teplova, 6, 22,
    35, 36, 233n. 36
male gaze, 16, 91, 96, 225n. 39
male privilege, 168, 170
Mandel'shtam, Osip, 230n. 19,
    265n. 18
marked feminine endings (Russian),
    27, 45; Khvoshchinskaia, 120;
    Pavlova, 147
marriage law, Russian, 21–22, 227n. 5
married women's property rights, 22
mentors: for canonical poets, 168;
    and gender, 34–35, 36, 122; and
    Khvoshchinskaia, 121–22; for
    noncanonical poets, 170, 173
Mickiewicz, Adam, 141, 142
Mikhailov, Mikhail Larionovich, 39,
    235n. 8

military life, influence on Russian
     men poets, 31
Mil'keev, Evgenii, 4, 169, 171, 172–3;
     and Belinsky, 173; literary repu-
     tation, 173; and Pavlova, 173; and
     Zhukovsky, 35, 170, 171, 173
Miller, Fedor, 4, 169, 170. Works:
     "Rusalka: Ballada," 241n. 39
Milton, John: *Paradise Lost,* 19, 93
modesty: Byron, 101; Khvoshchin-
     skaia, 119; and men writers, 101;
     Pushkin, 101; topos, 10
Mordovtsev, Daniil, 22
Mordovtseva, Anna, 4, 5, 221n. 10;
     descriptions of physical appear-
     ance, 264n. 15; marriage and ca-
     reer, 22–23; and militarism, 42,
     73; and pseudonyms, 45. Works:
     "Ballada," 73; "Opiat' vsia v
     chernom," 43; *Staraia skazka,* 43,
     70, 203–14; "Vzglianula na sad
     ia," 53, 80
Moskaleva, Vera Aleksandrovna, 115,
     117
Moskovitianin, 33, 67, 173
Moskovskii vestnik, 33
mourning and gender, 75–76, 77
muses: absence of, 44; androgynous,
     43; Apollo, 43, 44; Diana, 44; in
     elegies, 75; female, 43, 44; male,
     42, 44, 236n. 15; in noncanonical
     men's poetry, 279n. 7; in Roman-
     ticism, 3, 37. *See also* antimuses
myth in Romanticism, 3, 4

Nadezhdin, Nikolai Ivanovich, 33
narrative pleasure, 35, 15–16
nature, 49–54; as female, 49–51, 52,
     240n. 33, 241n. 38; as male,
     241n. 39; in noncanonical men's
     poetry, 241n. 38; and Romanti-
     cism, 3, 4, 37; in women's poetry,
     51–54
Nekrasov, Nikolai, 135
neoclassicism, 59
Nicholas I, 126, 133; and Ros-
     topchina, 89, 94, 257n. 31

Nikitenko, Aleksander: and Maikov,
     35; and Pavlova, 139; and *Sovre-
     mennik,* 33
noncanonical men poets, 4, 167–74;
     interpretive strategies, 172; and
     muses, 279n. 7; poetical prac-
     tices, 170–72; prayers, 249n. 51;
     social conditions, 169–70; and
     women poets, 170

ode, 82
Odoevsky, Vladimir: and Ros-
     topchina, 94
Osgood, Frances Sargent, 109
Ossian poems, 39, 59
Other: Eastern, 65, 274n. 33; female,
     16, 27, 49, 68; male, 83, 240n. 32;
     provincial, 171, 172
otryvki iz poemy (excerpts from a nar-
     rative poem), 5, 64, 220n. 9

Panaev, Ivan: and Pavlova, 139,
     228n. 7, 270n. 13
Parny, Evariste Désiré de Forges, 33
Paskhalov, Nikandr, 22
Pavlov, Nikolai, 8–9, 22, 137, 139; ar-
     rest, 143; marriage, 22, 142
Pavlova, Karolina (née Jaenisch), 4, 5, 6,
     137–66; and Aksakov, 272n. 19;
     and Baratynsky, 11, 67–68, 144, 146;
     and Belinsky, 142, 272n. 19; and
     Berg, 139; and Clairmont, 270n. 11;
     cross gender poems, 147; and
     Daszkiewicz, 141; depictions of
     nature in, 53; depictions of society,
     256n. 20; descriptions of her phys-
     ical appearance, 141, 271n. 14; and
     the extraordinary woman, 155,
     156, 158, 161, 166; and Fet,
     273n. 27; and genre, 66–67, 148–
     49; and Goethe, 141; and Grig-
     orovich, 139; and implied reader,
     48, 147–48, 239n. 31; and Ivan
     Kireevsky, 271n. 15; languages,
     140, 141; literary reputation, 8–9,
     12, 137, 145; literary social capital,
     140–43, 144; and male muse, 42,

164; marriage and career, 22; and Mickiewicz, 48, 141–42, 144; and Mil'keev, 173; narrator of, 147, 157, 161; and Nikitenko, 139; and Panaev, 139; as poetess, 9; and *polozhenie zhenshchiny*, 138, 149–66; and Pushkin, 67, 141, 160, 164; reception, 29, 139, 144, 273n. 24; recovery, 98, 144–45, 145–46, 224n. 30; and Rostopchina, 29–30, 270n. 13; salon, 139, 142–43, 144; and Schiller, 41; self-representation, 146–47; and A. K. Tolstoy, 142; as translator, 41, 142, 145, 273n. 29. Works: "Doch' zhida," 47, 73, 148; *Dvoinaia zhizn'*, 17, 19, 48, 53, 140–41, 147, 148, 149, 156–58, 161, 276n. 45; "E. A. Baratynskomu, 67–68, 146; "Fantasmagoria," 147; "Jeanne d' Arc," 149–55; *Kadril'*, 11, 93, 66–68, 158–64, 276n. 47; *Les préludes*, 142; "My sovremennitsy, grafinia," 29–30; "Na 10 noiabria 1840," 48; "Nebo bleshchet biriuzoiu," 53; *Das Nordlicht*, 142; *Ogon'*, 73, 149; "Razgovor v Kremle," 49, 236n. 12; "Sonet," 145, 147; "Starukha," 73, 148–49; "10 noiabria 1840," 48; "Tri dushi," 54, 155–56; "Za chainym stolom," 164–66

pen as penis, 117

"Perepiska sestry s bratom," 26

periodization of literature, 13, 245n. 23

personae, 45–46, 47, 81

Pfeffel, Ernestine, 23

Pletnev, Petr: and Maikov, 34–35; and Mil'keev, 173; and Pushkin, 34; and Rostopchina, 97; and *Sovremennik*, 33

poema (verse epic), 60–66; evolution of, 61–63; gender norms, 62–63, 64–65, 244n. 16; prestige, 62, 63–64; *romanticheskaia poema*, 62–66. *See also bylina*

poet, 27, 37, 82, 133, 155; as epic hero, 243n. 12; and sexual prowess, 234n. 5

poetess (*poetessa*), 26–30, 138; role, 39–40, 47, 48, 105–6. *See also* Pavlova; Rostopchina

Pogodin, Mikhail, 33

Poland, annexation, 89, 90, 106

polozhenie zhenshchiny (women's position in society), 158, 276n. 46; in Pavlova, 149–66. *See also zhenskii vopros*

povesti v stikhakh (verse tales), 65–70, 245n. 23

prayers: men poets, 249n. 51, 278n. 6; women poets, 170

pre-Christian worlds in poetry, 54, 242n. 44

prichitanie (lament), 79–81, 250n. 52

prophets, poets as, 38, 41

pseudonyms, 44–45, 119

Pushkin, Aleksandr, 4, 8, 100, 142; and Anacreon, 50; as antimuse, 42, 164; attitudes toward women, 8, 24; and Byron, 62, 226n. 40; and classicism, 65, 231n. 30; cross-gendered poems, 34, 46; and Durova, 41; and Guber, 170; initiation into literature, 34, 254n. 3; marriage and career, 23, 91; and *romanticheskaia poema*, 62, 63; and Rostopchina, 90, 97, 106, 108–9; Tat'iana, 65, 159; and Viazemsky, 230n. 24; and Volkonskaia, 141; and Zhukovsky, 34, 254n. 3. Works: *Bakhchisaraiskii fontan*, 62, 63, 148; "Besy," 48; and *Dnevnik devushki* (Rostopchina), 16, 106, 110; *Evgenii Onegin*, 4, 16, 24, 63, 101; "K moriu," 11; "Kamennyi gost'," 4; "Kobilitsa molodaia," 50; *Mednyi vsadnik*, 62; "Net, ia ne dorozhu miatezhnym naslazhden'em," 103; "Osen'," 50; *Pikovaia dama*, 160; "Prorok," 38, 153; "Rusalka," 49–50; *Tsygany*, 50, 62, 63, 65, 240n. 36

Pushkin pleiad, 13, 34, 144

quest in Romantic poetry, 82, 83

radical critics, 96, 97, 121, 144, 173

Raich, Semen, 33

Rakhmannyi. *See* Verevkin

reception: of noncanonical men poets, 172–73; of Russian women poets, 85, 167; of Russian women writers, 24–27. *See also* Garelina; Gotovtseva; Khvoshchinskaia; Pavlova; Rostopchina

recovery of Russian women writers, 12. *See also* Pavlova

Revolutions of 1848: and Khvoshchinskaia, 129, 133; and Rostopchina, 257n. 31

Romantic aesthetic and gender, 15, 17

romantic friendships, 118

romanticheskaia poema (Romantic *poema*), 62–66; gender norms, 62–63, 64–65

Romanticism, 3, 4, 82, 83; and gender, 5, 37, 47; as a male institution, 3–4, 7, 37, 56, 85–86; in Russia, 3, 219n. 1

Romantic literary conventions, 38–56

Romantic lyric, 81–85

Romantic *poema. See romanticheskaia poema*

Romantic themes and gender, 82–84

Rostopchin, Andrei, 91–92, 94, 255n. 13

Rostopchin, Fedor Vasilevich, 91

Rostopchina, Evdokiia, 4, 5, 29, 41, 88–111; and Aleksandra Fedorovna, Empress, 94, 95; and Alexander II, 94; and Belinsky, 45, 93, 97, 101, 256n. 28, 260n. 50; and Chernyshevsky, 100; childhood, 92; and Decembrists, 95, 97, 106; descriptions of her physical appearance, 90–91; and Dumas, 95; education, 93; and Gogol', 89; initiation into literature, 88; and Andrei Karamzin, 92, 96, 100; languages, 93; and Lermontov, 90, 101; literary reputation, 8, 12, 91, 96–105; marriage and career, 22; and

Nicholas I, 89, 94, 257n. 31; and Odoevsky, 94; and personae, 45–46; and Pletnev, 97; as poet, 259n. 44; as poetess, 91, 102–3, 105–9, 259n. 44; in her poetry, 108–9, 249n. 47; political views, 96, 97, 257n. 31; and pseudonyms, 45; and Pushkin, 90, 97, 106, 108–9; reception, 96–97, 99–100, 256n. 28; salon, 90, 94, 95; and Sollogub, 233n. 38; and Viazemsky, 35; views on women, 106; and Zhukovsky, 108–9. Works: "Baiu-baiu," 98, 107; "Chernovaia kniga Pushkina," 108–9; *Dnevnik devushki*, 16, 52, 101, 110, 261n. 60; "Iskushenie," 98, 107–8; "Kak dolzhny pisat' zheshchiny," 40, 97–98; "Kak liubat zhenshchiny," 47; "Moia igrushka," 98, 101; "Nasil'nyi brak," 89–90, 94, 95, 97, 106; "Negodovanie," 98, 106; "Neizvestnyi roman," 55, 100, 107; "Ot poeta k tsariam," 106; "Poslednii tsvetok," 98, 101; "Ravnodushnoi," 256n. 28; "Talisman," 88; "Tsirk 19-ogo veka," 93; "Vmesto predisloviia," 95–96

Rostopchina, Lidiia, 89, 92

Rousseau, Jean-Jacques: education of women, 86

rusalka (water spirit), 231n. 25; in Bakunina, 29, 181; in Kol'tsov, 238n. 26; in Miller, 238n. 39; in Pushkin, 49–50; in Zhadovskaia, 52

salons, 30, 139–40; Elagina, 139–40, 141; Fuks, 139; and gender, 35–36, 138–39, 233n. 38; hostesses, 35, 36; Pavlova, 139, 142–44; Rostopchina, 139; Volkonskaia, 141

Saltykova, Sof'ia, 23

Sand, George, 24, 30

Sappho, 38, 39, 112, 235nn. 7, 8

Schiller, Friedrich: and Pavlova, 41; and Zhukovsky, 41. Works: *Die Jungfrau von Orleans*, 41, 149, 151
self-representation, poets: men, 38–39; women, 39–49, 146. *See also* Khvoshchinskaia
Selo Anna, 92
Senkovsky, Osip, 6, 33
Severnaia pchela (The Northern Bee), 89
sexual display, women's writing as, 26, 85, 138, 119, 139
Shakespeare, William: *First Part of Henry VI*, 151
Shakhova, Elisaveta, 4, 5, 43, 68–69, 220n. 7. Works: "Dva sna: Ballada," 73; "Fantaziia," 43; "Izgnannik," 69; "K zhenshchinam poetam," 40; "Perst Bozhii," 69; "Progulka u vzmor'ia," 11, 215–16; "Strashnyi krasavets," 69; "Vdokhnovenie," 43
Shakhovskaia, Ekaterina, 4, 5; reception, 29. Works: *Snovidenie*, 29, 30, 31, 41
signatures, 44–45, 120
silences, 6–7
Skabichevsky, Aleksandr, 27–28
Slavophilism, 49, 140, 168, 173
social capital. *See* literary social capital
society. *See svet*
society tale. *See svetskaia povest'*
Sollogub, Vladimir, 233n. 38
Southey, Robert: and Zhukovsky, 72. Works: *Joan of Arc*, 41, 150–51, 276n. 42
Sovremennik, 33, 34, 135, 170
Staël, Mme de: *Corinne*, 234n. 6
subgenres, 57–58. *See also* genre
sublime, 18, 153, 155, 220n. 4
Sushkov, Nikoai, 67, 93
Sushkov, Sergei: political views, 260n. 50; on Andrei Rostopchin, 92; on Rostopchina, 89, 91, 97, 100, 102
Sushkova, Mariia Vasil'evna, 93

svet (society), 93–94
svetskaia povest' (society tale) 69–70, 156
symbol in Romanticism, 3, 4
Syn otechestva, 121

Tannenberg, Evgeniia, 22, 143
Teleskop, 33
Teplova, Nadezhda, 4, 5, 6, 16, 34; and Belinsky, 17, 85; depictions of nature, 52; and implied reader, 48; and Lisitsyna, 30, 77; and Maksimovich, 6, 22, 35, 233n. 36; marriage and career, 22; reception, 230n. 17. Works: "Na smert' docheri," 80; "Son," 78; "Sovet," 19, 40; "V pamiat' M. A. L-oi," 77
themes in Russian Romantic women's poetry: death of a child, 77, 225n. 36; domestic affections, 251n. 58; family members, 17, 252n. 64; female childhood, 251n. 58; female desire, 250n. 58; female old age, 251n. 58; forced marriages, 68, 84, 133, 152, 251n. 59; isolation, 16, 77, 84; motherhood, 251n. 58; open window, 252n. 61; religion, 16–17, 41, 78–79, 170; transcendence, 16, 252n. 63
"Thick" journals. *See tolstye zhurnaly*
Tiutchev, Fedor, 4, 34; depiction of nature, 53; marriage and career, 23; reputation, 13; and Zhukovsky, 34. Works: "Ne ver' ne ver'," 234n. 5
Tolstoy, A. K., 142
tolstye zhurnaly ("Thick" journals), 24, 112, 143, 221n. 13
translation and gender, 142
travel and Romantic poetry, 36–37
Tsvetaeva, Marina, 27
Turchianinova, Anna, 247n. 37. Works: "Pesenka ob Leonarde i Blondine," 72, 217–18
Turgenev, Ivan: and Fet, 34

universality and gender, 103
university: influence on Russian men
    poets, 33–34; Moscow, 33–34;
    Saint Petersburg, 33–34. *See also*
    mentors

vakkhicheskie pesni (Bacchic songs),
    32–33, 38, 234n. 1
Verevkin, N. N.: "Zhenshchina
    pisatel'nitsa," 25
verse epic. *See poema*
verse epistle. *See druzheskoe poslanie*
verse tales. *See povesti v stikhakh*
Viazemsky, Petr: and Gotovtseva, 35,
    45, 230n. 24; on personae, 45;
    and Pushkin, 230n. 24; on the
    Romantic Movement in Russia,
    59–60; and Rostopchina, 35, 88,
    94, 97, 101
Volkonskaia, Zinaida, 149; and
    Alexander I, 141; salon, 141
Voltaire: *La Pucelle*, 151, 275n. 42

water spirit. *See rusalka*
woman question. *See zhenskii vopros*
women readers, Russian, 239n. 29
women, social conditions: Europe,
    15–17, 86; Russia, 15–17, 21–37
women's position in society. *See
    polozhenie zhenshchiny*
women's sphere, 16, 26–30, 47
Woolf, Virginia, 16
Wordsworth, William, 44, 59, 220n. 4.
    Works: *The Prelude*, 45
writing as a woman, 45, 147, 279n. 8

Zaionchkovsky, Ivan, 22, 115, 118,
    119
Zhadovskaia, Iuliia, 4, 5, 16, 29; and
    Belinsky, 35; depiction of

women, 28; marriage and career,
    22; and personae, 46; reception,
    27–28, 231n. 25. Works: "Kto
    mne rodnia?," 41; "Nikto ne vi-
    novat," 55; "Otryvki iz
    neokonchennogo rasskaza," 69;
    "P[erevleskomu]," 10–11; "Pose-
    shchenie," 69; "Rusalka," 52;
    "Sovet," 53; "Ty menia poz-
    abudesh' ne skoro," 46; "Ty
    skoro menia pozabudesh'," 46;
    "Videnie proroka Ieziekiila," 41
zhenskii vopros (woman question), 8,
    158, 276n. 46. *See also polozhenie
    zhenshchiny*
Zhukovsky, Vasilii: and the ballad,
    71–72, 246n. 35; and Baratynsky,
    34; as bard, 71; and Elegina, 140;
    and the elegy, 74–75; and Nikolai
    Karamzin, 34; and Khomiakov,
    34; and Kol'tsov, 35, 233n. 35;
    and Lermontov, 34; and Mil'-
    keev, 35, 170, 171, 173; and
    Pushkin, 34; and Rostopchina,
    108–9; and Schiller, 41; and
    Southey, 72; and Tiutchev, 34;
    and Zrazhevskaia, 35. Works:
    "Adel'stan," 71; "Ballada v ko-
    toroi opisyvaetsia kak odna
    starushka," 72, 73; "Liudmila,"
    71
Zotov, Vladimir, 116, 121, 123, 135; as
    Khvoshchinskaia's mentor, 39,
    121–22; and *Literaturnaia gazeta*,
    114, 120; rewrites Khvoshchin-
    skaia's poetry, 6, 122–30, 132–33,
    135, 136
Zrazhevskaia, Aleksandra, 29,
    230n. 16; and Zhukovsky, 35
Zvezdochka, 141, 229n. 15